"Sex education is life learning. As our world has evolved so have the topics and approaches to sex education. *Sex Education Research: A Look Between the Sheets* is a timely discussion on these topics. Researchers and practitioners are delving into topics that sexuality educators and other professionals either address or avoid each day in their work. Whether a researcher, educator, or any other sexuality professional, this book provides an opportunity to hear from subject matter experts and the curious, on topics including pleasure, pornography, consent, social media, college health and more. Like the sexuality profession, this book includes a range of perspectives in research topics and current issues; many of which are not discussed in other texts."

Tanya M. Bass, PhD, MS, MEd, CHES®, CSE; *Founder, North Carolina Sexual Health Conference, Raleigh, NC*

"As a recent MPH graduate, *Sex Education: A Look Between the Sheets* is exactly what I needed. The chapters contain important and useful knowledge for those in the field of sexuality as well as those like me trying to find their way in. The chapters are written in more of a narrative than research form, which makes it easier for newcomers like myself to be able to read and understand. The wisdom shared in these chapters makes me feel excited to join this prestigious community of sexuality educators."

Kayla I. Henry, MPH, CHES®

"Having consulted some of the original "sourcebooks" of classic sexuality research studies during his college years, and as present editor of the *American Journal of Sexuality Education (AJSE)*, Taverner intuitively understands the value of strong scientific data behind meaningful theory and practice in sexology. This tenet has not always been front and center in the field of sexuality education, and this book takes a giant step in rectifying that fact. The talented editor of this book has brought together 24 significant research studies that were originally published in *AJSE*, asking the researchers to write about their work in a jargon-free essay format, emphasizing the stories behind their studies and explaining in clear language the value of their work. There are no complex statistical analyses or adventures in obscure phrasing to be navigated, leaving instead eminently readable and informative essays that will be of value to professionals and laypersons alike.

The range of topics covered by the studies in the book is impressively comprehensive. There are chapters on communication with LGBTQ youth, attitudes toward circumcision, sexual consent and sexual pleasure, sexuality education for children with disabilities, promotion of sexual health, explorations of the content and audiences of pornography, prevention of child sexual abuse, and several other timely issues. Interestingly, with the more conversational tone taken by the authors of these papers, there are often emotionally touching aspects of their work that show through more easily than is typical when the content is embedded in the stark technicalities of research. This makes for a refreshing and moving exploration of work that is, at its center, focused on one of the most intimate and personal parts of the human experience.

I can't help but think that editors of all professional journals in the social sciences might be able to learn from the writing approach used to explain research in this book. For me, reading journal papers has always been a labor of love and necessity, but it sometimes feels like an onerous task to sort through the thickets of strained verbiage and technical detail to find the nuggets of knowledge and practical application I really am looking for. Perhaps good, clear expository writing could win out in all our professional communications, with the mechanics of methodology and statistical analysis being explained in appendices of various sorts for those who want to study them in detail.

This is a book that belongs in the libraries of all sexuality educators and educators-in-training. It could also teach all of us who read and write for professional journals some worthwhile lessons about the expression of the essential message."

Gary F. Kelly, *Professor Emeritus of Psychology, Clarkson University; Co-Author,* The New Sexuality

"In his wonderful introduction to *Sex Education Research: A Look Between the Sheets,* Bill Taverner tells us his editorial vision: to inspire an eminently readable, jargon-free, and *enjoyable* collection of previously published research rewritten in a personalized essay format. That he succeeded far beyond even his own hopes and expectations was proven by own experience: once I started reading, I could not put it down. And, neither will you!"

Deborah M. Roffman, MS, CSE, CFLE; *Human Sexuality Educator; Consultant; Author, most recently of* The Science of Babies

"*Sex Education Research* is a treasure trove. The volume distills two dozen recently published sexuality research studies into easy-to-read stories. The reader is easily able to glean the study's key findings, reasons why those findings are important to our field, and implications for future research. Intervention designers, practitioners, researchers, and students of sexuality alike will find much in this rich thought-provoking volume to inform their work and inspire innovation."

Lori A. Rolleri Insignares, MSW, MPH; *President, Lori Rolleri Consulting*

SEX EDUCATION RESEARCH

Curated by the chief editor of the *American Journal of Sexuality Education*, this book presents engaging and accessible chapters that capture current and essential research findings from leaders in the sexuality education field.

William J. Taverner brings together an impressive array of contributors to help sexuality professionals remain up-to-date on the most relevant issues in sex education today. Covering a spectrum of hot sexuality education topics, including abstinence, gender, innovative programs, pleasure, the politics of sexuality education, porn literacy, sexual orientation, and more, each chapter describes key findings on a particular topic, their significance, their practical application, and how these new developments have arrived. The book includes chapters that address individuals across all age ranges, from children to older adults, as well as sexuality education and training programs for specialized professions, such as nurses and school-based health occupations. Practical and clear, this book identifies priorities and trends in the field, addresses marginalized audiences and overlooked topics, and hopes to encourage important discussions to come.

Sex Education Research: A Look Between the Sheets provides a wide range of occupations and academic disciplines with a foundation of research essential to their work, such as public health professionals and students of human sexuality, gender studies, biology, psychology, sociology, as well as community educators, school nurses and health teachers, and administrative leaders affiliated with sexuality education programs at community-based organizations.

William J. Taverner, **MA**, **CSE**, an award-winning sexuality education leader, is the chief editor of the *American Journal of Sexuality Education* and founder and president of the Sex Ed Lecture Series.

SEX EDUCATION RESEARCH

A Look Between the Sheets

William J. Taverner
Editor

Routledge
Taylor & Francis Group
NEW YORK AND LONDON

First published 2023
by Routledge
605 Third Avenue, New York, NY 10158

and by Routledge
4 Park Square, Milton Park, Abingdon, Oxon, OX14 4RN

Routledge is an imprint of the Taylor & Francis Group, an informa business

ISBN: 978-1-032-01205-6 (hbk)
ISBN: 978-1-032-03928-2 (pbk)
ISBN: 978-1-003-18978-7 (ebk)

DOI: 10.4324/9781003189787

Typeset in Bembo
by Apex CoVantage, LLC

CONTENTS

FOREWORD

Eva S. Goldfarb and Lisa D. Lieberman

High-quality sex education is vital to sexual health and overall well-being. When taught by well-trained teachers in grades K-12, with support from parents and the community, age- and developmentally-appropriate sex education provides critically important knowledge, skills, and attitudes that enable young people to achieve and maintain sexual health into adulthood and throughout their lives. Good sex education empowers learners to have healthy relationships, make well-informed decisions about their sexual health, seek out reliable, accurate information about sex and sexuality, appreciate and love themselves for who they are, and treat others—especially those who are marginalized—with dignity and respect. Rigorous, well-designed research can evaluate the outcomes of different approaches to sex education and determine what works best, for whom, and under what circumstances.

In a study published in *The Journal of Adolescent Health*, we conducted a systematic literature review of 30 years of peer reviewed research on the outcomes of sex education.[1] To run a computerized search that would lead us to the widest possible range of studies, we developed, in consultation with other sex education experts, an extensive set of keywords based on the first edition of the *National Sexuality Education Standards*.[2] We examined qualitative and quantitative studies evaluating school-based, K-12 educational approaches within sex education and/or across the curriculum. We searched US and international literature for the 30-year period since 1990. We chose 1990 as our starting date, as that year represents a fundamental shift ushering in a new era in the field of sex education, with the publication of the first *SIECUS Guidelines for Comprehensive Sexuality Education Kindergarten through 12th Grade*,[3] in essence, the precursor to the *National Sex Education Standards*.[4]

We specifically sought to explore the literature for school-based sex education outcomes beyond pregnancy and disease prevention, as those outcomes already dominate the sex education research. From an original list of over 8,000 articles, we reported on the 80 papers that met our study's criteria.

What the research shows is compelling. In short, comprehensive sex education, scaffolded across grades, embedded in supportive school environments and implemented across subject areas, can improve sexual, social, and emotional health, as well as safety and academic outcomes for all young people. Specifically, approaches that address a broad definition of sexual health and take affirming, inclusive, positive approaches to human sexuality have been found to decrease homophobic bullying and harassment, improve life skills (effective communication, empathy, managing feelings, positive self-image, respect for others, and sense of self-control and safety), increase media literacy, increase prevention of child sex abuse, increase prevention of dating and interpersonal violence, and promote healthy relationships. In particular, the study demonstrated the importance of the early grades in laying the foundation for the more challenging and complex concepts typically addressed in the middle and high school grades.

The literature on sex abuse prevention efforts in early grades shows strong evidence that young children can develop self-protective knowledge, intentions, and skills without increasing anxiety. While there are only limited examples of sexuality-related content in the K-5 curriculum outside of child abuse prevention, the data strongly indicate that, when they are taught, such topics are developmentally appropriate and produce positive outcomes while providing a foundation for future learning. Not only are younger children able to discuss sexuality-related issues, but the early grades may, in fact, be the best time to introduce topics related to gender equality, gender identity and expression, sexual orientation, and social justice related to the LGBTQ+ community—before patriarchal, heteronormative and cisnormative values and assumptions become more deeply ingrained and less mutable.

Notably, we found that many of the positive outcomes and promising approaches that worked toward creating affirming, inclusive school environments occurred not only in traditional health or sex education classes but also in art, English, mathematics, music, physical education, and social studies. Interestingly, many of the efforts relied on literature to explore the themes of social justice and oppression in relation to sexuality. In particular, the vast majority of successful approaches to gender norms and LGBTQ+ topics in the elementary grades used literature as the entry point for learning and discussion, most with the goal of increasing appreciation for, and acceptance of, gender and sexual diversity.

The fact that topics falling within sex education can be addressed successfully across the curriculum is encouraging and offers much-needed flexibility to schools, both in terms of available time and finding talented, willing teachers to tackle difficult and important topics. It also provides an opportunity to explore sexuality-related issues in different contexts and by applying a variety of lenses. Affirming, inclusive, positive school environments—across the curriculum—improve safety and learning for all students and have an especially strong positive impact on sexually marginalized youth.

Since the publication of our work, new research and commentary have supported the concepts we addressed in our review. *Sex Education Research: A Look Between the Sheets* addresses a wide range of sex education approaches in schools and other settings that can improve knowledge, attitudes, and behaviors, leading to better relationships and other outcomes for all learners. Presenting overviews of recent articles published in the *American Journal of Sexuality Education* (*AJSE*), William J. Taverner takes on the challenging but vitally needed task of "translating" current research and thinking among professionals in the field for practitioners to apply to their work.

Limited to publications in *AJSE* over the past two years, this timely volume covers a wide range of topics and provides support for broad-based sex education beyond the birds and the bees. It amplifies our conclusion that sex education needs to be conceptualized with a more expansive framework—beyond the middle and high school health education classroom, beyond a narrow focus solely on pregnancy and sexually transmitted infections (STI) prevention, and with a goal of enhancing people's sexual health and well-being throughout life. It also makes the case that sex education efforts need to address the specific needs of their target audiences. Rather than a "one size fits all" model, taken together, the chapters in this book suggest greater effectiveness by using an intersectional approach that considers the various ways that ability, age, ethnicity, experiences, family relationships, gender, race, sexual orientation, support systems, and other factors affect people's sexuality and learning. In other words, sex education works best when it meets people where they are.

This book reinforces the idea that when seeking to understand the "research" on effective sex education, it helps to cast a wide net. The "gold standard" of research, that is, what are known as randomized controlled trials, will always have their place in measuring outcomes, especially in evaluating pregnancy and STI prevention efforts. But they are limited in the type of data that can be collected and the concepts that can be measured, particularly on controversial or sensitive topics or on outcomes that are not easily quantified. By considering a wider range and different types of research, such as case studies, literature reviews, and qualitative studies, as exemplified both in our systematic review and in the chapters here, researchers are better able to measure, and the field better understands, the wide-ranging outcomes of high-quality sex education.

AJSE publishes large and small research and evaluation studies, case studies, as well as broader "thought" pieces. Likewise, this volume includes chapters that explore and measure particular outcomes of programs, chapters that provide general guidance about various types of approaches (e.g., media, parent, or school-based approaches), and chapters that focus on topics where there is very limited research (e.g., attitudes and knowledge about circumcision among high school boys). As well, this volume extends the boundaries of sex education beyond the classroom to include community-based campaigns, health services, policies, and school environments. It considers the requisite support structures needed for sex education to be effective, making the case for improving teachers' understanding of what works; the need for parents to recognize and embrace their essential roles, and understanding how their assumptions and challenges may be keeping them from strong positive communication; and reflecting on how media, including pornography, contribute to broader sexuality attitudes and beliefs and the need for sex education to address this head-on. Thus, in exploring a range of commentaries, literature reviews, and studies, this book offers a unique lens that is part researcher, part sex educator, and part "imaginer." In short, it expands understanding of what sex education can be for those who advocate for sexual health, teach, or write policy but don't necessarily subscribe to academic journals.

Sex education continues to evolve, along with scientific and social progress. From its inception, the field has been hampered by the homogeneity of its scientists (mostly white, cisgender men), its educators (mostly white, cisgender women), and its focus (heteronormative). While there is a long way to go before the diversity of sex education professionals mirrors society at large, we continue to make progress through proactive efforts to elevate historically underrepresented and marginalized voices, and the field as a whole continues to get stronger and more effective as a result. The chapters in this book reflect this movement in our field. The authors represent a wide range of backgrounds and experiences and write about diverse groups of learners. For example, there are chapters addressing the sex education needs of bisexual Latino men, first-generation college students, LGBTQ+ young people and adults, nightlife aficionados, parents and caregivers, people with intellectual and developmental disabilities, and young children. As well, they focus on communities from across the United States to England, Slovenia, and Sweden.

Consistent with this diversity, Taverner's collection of essays and reports ultimately makes some vitally compelling arguments. First, sex education needs to include and consider key issues and topics that are not often discussed in schools and/or in much of the research, such as elevating the importance of pleasure as a legitimate goal of and motivation for sex, and critically analyzing media portrayals of sexuality, including pornography. Second, sex education needs to be focused on primary prevention, addressing young people early, to help set a foundation for learning throughout life. Third, sex education absolutely must take an intersectional approach to improving sexual health. Finally, we must prioritize welcoming, inclusive environments in which all types of learners can ask questions, learn valuable information pertinent to their specific experiences and identities, and develop the skills that will help them live safe, fulfilling lives.

Eva S. Goldfarb and Lisa D. Lieberman

References

1. Goldfarb, E.S., Lieberman, L.D. (2021). Three decades of research: The case for comprehensive sex education. *Journal of Adolescent Health,* 68(1): 13–27 https://doi.org/10.1016/j.jadohealth.2020.07.036
2. Future of Sex Education Initiative (2012). National sexuality education standards: Core content and skills, K-12 [A special publication of the *Journal of School Health*], American School Health Association, Bethesda, MD (2012).
3. Sexuality Information and Education Council of the United States (1991). *Guidelines for comprehensive sexuality education: Kindergarten-12th grade.* Washington, DC: Sexuality Information and Education Council of the United States.
4. Future of Sex Education Initiative (2020). *National sex education standards: Core content and skills, K-12* (2nd ed). American School Health Association.

INTRODUCTION

William J. Taverner

The first sex education research article I ever read was in a cage. I was an undergraduate student at the State University of New York at Albany in the late 1980s, enrolled in a research methods course in the psychology department. The professor was teaching us to use the Social Science Citation Index (SSCI), a resource for locating journal articles that informed the article being examined as well as subsequent articles that cited the article. Volumes of the SSCI could fill the entire length of library walls, several shelves deep. Scholars and students pored through their thick volumes to inform their literature searches. It was my geeky dream to someday return to the university library and look up myself in one of the volumes. That dream would never come to fruition. When I returned to the Albany campus three decades later, the books were no longer there, having long since become defunct in the age of Google Scholar and a modern-day electronic incarnation of the SSCI.

But back to the cage, I had recently discovered that sexology was an actual *profession*. This was an astonishing realization for a young man who went to an all-boys Catholic high school and learned very little about sex. I fell in love with the idea of studying sexuality as *my* future profession, and while there was no major in this discipline at the University at Albany, I created my own ad hoc major with whatever psychology and sociology courses I could find that touched on sexuality, however peripherally. When courses did not overtly examine sexuality, I tailored my assignments in this direction. So when the professor asked us to look up a research article on the SSCI assignment, I selected one from the *Journal of Sex Research*.

The SSCI stacks directed me to a card catalog, which, in turn, pointed me to the library basement and a locked cage that contained all the reading material that was too scandalous to be grouped with the uncaged reading material. A librarian guarded the cage, and I had to prove I had legitimate business there. Once

DOI: 10.4324/9781003189787-1

I cleared the entry gate, I found the *Journal of Sex Research* article I sought, which was kept on a shelf near the complete collection of *Playboy*. I started reading the article and had to stop because it was too difficult to follow. I started reading again and then stopped again. This went on and on. My young brain could not understand all the technical research jargon. I wonder if my old brain could understand it today.

The experience in the cage taught me a few lessons. First, it was a stark reminder of the American shame and stigma surrounding sexuality that cannot be escaped even when examined academically. The librarian's decision to group the *Journal of Sex Research* in a locked cage with *Playboy* also revealed not only an implicit erotophobia but also a lack of understanding of sexuality research as a serious, challenging discipline. I also learned that there was a need to have sexual information made more accessible for readers unfamiliar with analyses of variance, cluster analyses, mixed-methods studies, *t*-tests, and a litany of terms that establish a wall between entry-level readers and their ability to grasp essential developments.

Early in my career, I came upon two excellent books that would influence this one. I read *Readings in Sexology* by Mary A. Watson[1] in graduate school and later I read *Sources: Notable Selections in Human Sexuality* by Gary F. Kelly,[2] who was also the editor of the *Journal of Sex Education and Therapy*.[3] These books included essays by some giants, like Shere Hite, Alfred Kinsey's team, William Masters and Virginia Johnson, and more contemporary authors. I loved these books because they introduced me to sex research without burdening me with scientific jargon that was hard to comprehend. I would get enough of that in my research methods courses; when reading about sex research, I wanted to know the key findings in plain language.

I have not seen books like that in many years, so I thought I would create and edit this one. I have served as editor or co-editor of the *American Journal of Sexuality Education* since its first issue in 2005. Since then, I have administered more than a thousand manuscripts. Manuscripts go through peer review—three or more experts who give critical feedback and recommend whether or not the manuscript should be accepted for publication. About half of the manuscripts are rejected, and the others are "provisionally accepted," meaning they continue through the review process toward ultimate publication as long as they address the provisions outlined by reviewers. Some of my own submissions have been provisionally accepted, and some have been rejected! (The editor goes through blind review too! An editorial advisory board member administers the editor's submissions.)

In envisioning this book, I looked at the body of research published in the *American Journal of Sexuality Education* during the previous two years and invited authors to submit a chapter. I explained that I wanted to know about their research in essay format. I asked them to tell a story about what they researched, what they found, why it is important, and what might be done in the future to build on their work. I told them that I did not want to read about "*n*=" this or "standard deviance" that. In editing, I removed percentage decimals for easier reading. (Do you really need to know that 42.8% will read this introduction and 57.2% will not? Or will 43% and 57% suffice?) I changed the usual APA style of citations—which inserts author and year directly into the narrative—to a style of endnotes that is less intrusive to the flow of the chapters.[4] And I fell in love with what the authors had to say. They reflected thoughtfully on their research and its implications; they were free to express their passion for their scholarly work, whereas research articles must be written in a dispassionate third-person voice. Occasionally, they insisted on including some research terms, which was fine, as long as they also gave an elementary explanation to the reader. If this approach is disappointing to you, by all means, read their original studies in the *American Journal of Sexuality Education!*

This book includes 24 chapters that address a spectrum of sexuality education topics. It loosely follows the ages of audiences taught chronologically, starting with how parents and caregivers might create better environments for their children's sexual learning, to programs for middle school students and high school students, to college campuses and young adults, and concluding with chapters on training teachers. Occasionally, the age organization was disrupted by thematic content, such as grouping the chapters discussing intellectual and developmental disabilities together and the chapters on pornography and sex education, regardless of the age of the learners. This book addresses common trends in sexuality education today, notably the "sex ed for all" campaign that seeks to create inclusive learning for everyone. Thus, there are several chapters on historically marginalized communities, such as those who are LGBTQ+ and people with disabilities. Consent, pleasure, and technology make frequent appearances, topics that reflect newer developments and priorities in sex education. I hope you will appreciate the authentic voices of the 70 contributing authors as much as their scholarship.

Sexuality education research is a fluid, evolving science. In the time it took to develop this book, dozens of even newer research articles have been published in the *American Journal of Sexuality Education*, and dozens more are in various stages of publication, from provisionally accepted to published online. The body of available sex education research grows exponentially when factoring in the *Journal of Adolescent Health, Sex Education*, and other academic journals addressing sex education. Further, the American sociopolitical landscape has changed rapidly since I first started editing this book. Work began during the Trump administration, which was not supportive of sex education. Early in his presidency, Mr. Trump pulled the plug on federal funding for teen pregnancy prevention programs. More recently, "don't say gay" laws were introduced by several states, forbidding educators to acknowledge or teach about gender identity and sexual orientation. And in the days this book is moving to press, Americans learned of the United States Supreme Court's intentions to scrap *Roe v. Wade*, the landmark ruling that legalized abortion. Undoubtedly, lots more will have changed by the time this book is in your hands, so I suggest it be read as a snapshot-in-time of contemporary research in an ever-changing landscape.

There are some people I would like to thank. In March 2020, I started the Sex Ed Lecture Series (www.SexEdLectures.org), a weekly program featuring sex education researchers and other scholars. I have had the good fortune to learn from more than 150 speakers since the program started and to have connected with thousands of fellow sexuality educators who tune in every week. I am grateful for Sex Ed Lecture Series interns Abigail Fussell, Kayla I. Henry, Stefanie LoBue, and Amado Pacheco. They helped by keeping files organized, reviewing revisions, and suggesting the chapter order. I want to thank Heather Evans and Upasruti Biswas at Routledge, supportive guides in this endeavor. Thanks to Eva S. Goldfarb and Lisa D. Lieberman for writing the Foreword. Their research detailing the impact of sex ed over the past 30 years[5] has been a game-changer for everyone studying and advocating for comprehensive sexuality education. I also want to thank some of my closest friends and colleagues who have supported me with my personal and professional growth during the past few years, including Jeffrey Anthony, Tanya Bass, Christopher Black, Maggi Boyer, Matt Carara, Ron Colonna, Rob and Toni Courtney, Nancy Daley-Moore, Ali Glaser, Laci Green, Diane Holschuh, Paul Joannides, Jason Merin, Wayne Pawlowski, Mary Jo Podgurski, Sameera Qureshi, Karen Rayne, Art Robinson, Deborah Roffman, Lori Rolleri Insignares, Bob Selverstone, Sherrie Vavrichek, Marybeth Vinci, Beverly Whipple, my brother Joe, my sister Karen, my parents Bill[6] and Joan, and my wife, Denise. Of course, I wish to thank my children (who are no longer children), Christopher and Robert. That I love them more than anything would be reason enough for the shout-out, but they are also on-call, helping me with copyediting and responding to my texts when I ask, "Is this a thing?" when I encounter something new in young adult culture. I am indebted to the 70 contributing authors for sharing their expertise, insights, and, in many cases, their life's work!

Whenever I work on something collaborative, such as this book with so many contributing authors, I remember my mentor Robert T. ("Bob") Francoeur. Bob was the editor of the *International Encyclopedia of Sexuality*[7] and the author or editor of dozens of other books, including some that we edited together.[8] Bob's talent for finding and convening a broad spectrum of experts was one I admire and emulate. This kind of collaboration feels like playing Tom Sawyer—sitting back and relaxing on a hot summer day while everyone else does the hard work. My name may appear on the cover of this book, but I am like Tom, and the 24 chapters that follow are the magnificently painted fence of the contributing authors. Enjoy the adventure!

References

1. Watson, M.A. (1991). *Readings in sexology*. Kendall/Hunt.
2. Kelly, G.F. (1998). *Sources: Notable selections in human sexuality*. McGraw-Hill/Dushkin.
3. The *Journal of Sex Education and Therapy* went out print after 2001 and was relaunched four years later as the *American Journal of Sexuality Education*.

4. The style of endnotes in this book is called Vancouver. Each citation is numbered, and subsequent uses of the same citation repeat the same number. This is different from the Chicago style in which a citation gets a new number every time a citation is warranted.
5. Goldfarb, E.S., & Lieberman, L.D. (2020). Three decades of research: The case for comprehensive sex education. *Journal of Adolescent Health, 68*(1), 13–27.
6. Yes, we have the same name. Occasionally, a reporter writing about sex education will reach him instead of me, and that is always an interesting conversation.
7. Francoeur, R.T., & Noonan, R. (2004). *The international encyclopedia of sexuality*. Continuum. Note: the Kinsey Institute has generously made the entire encyclopedia available online for free at https://kinseyinstitute.org/collections/archival/ccies.php.
8. See, for example, the sixth and seventh editions of *Taking sides: Clashing views in human sexuality* published in 1998 and 2000 by McGraw-Hill/Dushkin.

1

CAREGIVERS AS SEXUAL HEALTH EDUCATORS

Aryn A. Benoit and Scott T. Ronis

Introduction: The Current State of Sexuality Education

School-based sexual health education approaches in North America vary greatly depending on state and provincial regulations and individual school district standards.[1] Despite public health guidelines to inform the provision of sexual health education (e.g., National Sexuality Education Standards, Sex Information and Education Council of Canada), educators often receive little support in developing and delivering a comprehensive and inclusive curriculum. As a result, youth and parents often perceive school-based sexual health education as insufficient.[1–3] Indeed, many youths describe school-based sexual health education experiences as generally negative and uncomfortable and refer to curricula as heterosexist and gendered (e.g., men are sexual initiators, women are sexual consent gatekeepers).[3] Moreover, given an inherent power dynamic in teacher-student relationships, youth often describe the sexual health education they receive from teachers as uncomfortable, noting that they would prefer to receive such education from other individuals and sources.[3]

Schools are not the only source from which adolescents receive sexual health education.[4] Indeed, the media, including the Internet, literature, music, television, and video games, provide continuous sources of information.[5,6] Unfortunately, because the media often present a broad range of sexual behaviors, the messages children receive are not necessarily age appropriate or reflective of specific family or cultural values. As such, greater exposure to these media-driven sexual messages is linked generally with younger youth engagement in sexual behaviors and the adoption of sexually permissive attitudes, which may then result in unwanted sexual health outcomes (e.g., unwanted teen pregnancy).[6–8]

DOI: 10.4324/9781003189787-2

Given potential drawbacks associated with teacher-delivered or media-driven sexual health education for adolescents, parents—and caregivers more broadly[9]—may be in a better position to offer carefully curated and informative sexual health education to their children.

"Let's Talk about Sex": Parent Delivery of Sexual Health Education

Through frequent communication, parents are in an ideal position to shape their children's sexual behaviors, beliefs, and values. Effective sexual communication between parents and children is linked with healthy sexual development, delayed onset of sexual activity, and reductions in risky sexual behaviors.[10] Despite parents' and children's desire to communicate with each other about sex,[11] many parents do not initiate these conversations due to low comfort, poor communication skills, or a lack of necessary knowledge.[12,13] It is, therefore, worthwhile to provide parents with information and skills to help them develop expertise and comfort in talking with their children about sex. For this chapter, the term "sex" is used to capture an array of sexually intimate behaviors, including but not limited to anal sex, fondling, oral sex, and vaginal-penile intercourse.

When Should Sexual Health Conversations be Initiated?

Parents often wonder when to begin educating their children about sex, sexuality, and sexual health or when to do so in a way that has the most positive impact. Although the average age of initial sexual intercourse is 16 years,[14] empirical research and anecdotal recommendations suggest that parents should begin educating their children about sex and sexual development well before they reach adolescence. Furthermore, although there is limited empirical research examining the ideal age by which parents should introduce various sexual topics to their children, research indicates that early and ongoing comprehensive education is predictive of better outcomes for youth, including in areas of attitudes toward social justice, healthy relationships, and sexual health.[15] In fact, the earlier children receive education regarding various sexual health topics, the more likely they are to delay sexual initiation (i.e., any acknowledged attempt to establish sexual contact) and engage in fewer risky sexual behaviors.[14] Parents can begin introducing sexual health education topics based on developmental appropriateness and perceived readiness instead of waiting until children reach adolescence. Anecdotal evidence and recommendations regarding general ages by which certain sexual topics are introduced to children can help serve as a developmental guide, keeping in mind that there are valid reasons for exceptions to rules of thumb.

Birth to Two Years

Early sexual health education generally focuses on biological attributes. Parents can begin educating their children about sexual health by using proper terminology for genitalia (e.g., vulva, penis). By encouraging anatomically correct terms, children will develop language that can help them communicate about their sexual health. Furthermore, parents should understand that personal exploration is developmentally appropriate, and they should avoid embarrassing or shaming their children, who may be beginning to explore their bodies.

Three to Five Years

In general, 3- to 5-year-old children are developmentally ready to learn about personal boundaries and the boundaries of others, like appropriate and inappropriate touching. Because children at this age often begin to engage in touch-based play like tickling, parents can talk to them about the difference between wanted and unwanted touch and instill a sense of agency over their bodies. Children should learn that they must seek permission to touch others' bodies and that others need permission to touch theirs, regardless of whether the individual is a family member, friend, or stranger. It may also be beneficial at this age to teach children personal refusal statements (e.g., "Stop, I don't like that"), reaffirming that they have the right to say yes or no about how their body is touched. Overall, this information creates a foundation for children's later understandings of consent.

Children in this age group often become more intentional in exploring their genitals.[16] Therefore, parents should continue to use correct terminology to describe genitalia and have age-appropriate conversations with their children about the normal, but private, nature of masturbation and necessary personal hygiene. Children may also begin asking where babies come from and how they get out at this age. Parents can begin conversations with their children about women's primary reproductive organ, the uterus, and the average duration of fetal growth (i.e., nine months) and the modes of delivery, including vaginal births and Cesarian sections.

Six to Eight Years

In addition to the ongoing conversations about appropriate and positive touch of self and others and biological aspects of sexual health, topics related to healthy and harmful relationships, such as bullying or teasing, and sexual abuse should be discussed more explicitly. For instance, children should learn that no one should touch them without their permission. At approximately age 6, children begin to wonder how babies are made. Therefore, children may be introduced to the mechanics of sexual behaviors in a developmentally appropriate way, including conversations regarding reproductive anatomy (e.g., testicles, ovaries) and reproductive cells (e.g., sperm, egg). Discussions pertaining to sex can act as a segue to talk about topics related to families, love, and relationships. Although most children will not have begun to demonstrate pubertal growth, it is worthwhile to use this time to highlight the changes that are taking, or will take, place in their bodies as they mature and to describe human sexual responses.

Nine Years and Older

Puberty begins, on average, between the ages of 11 and 14 years; however, parents should start to talk about anticipated bodily changes before they occur to reduce possible anxiety and embarrassment and foster a sense of autonomy. Once children reach puberty (i.e., menarche and spermarche), parents should discuss sexual topics in more detail, including birth control, dating, sexual intercourse and other sexual behaviors, sexually transmitted infections (STIs), and teen pregnancy. More nuanced sexual topics, including gender identity, healthy relationships, intimacy and pleasure, pornography, sexual consent and assault, sexual identity, and sexualization, should also be reinforced during this developmental period, if not earlier. Throughout adolescence, sexual violence and consent should be talked about frequently to ensure possible social shifts and developing knowledge are reflected. A recent study found that emerging adults wished their parents began having these sensitive sexual conversations by 12 to 13 years of age rather than wait until they were older (e.g., approximately 15 to 16 years old).[10] By initiating conversations about sex and sexual health in early childhood, parents create an open and trusting foundation to establish conversations started by children or parents about more difficult sexual topics as children develop, thus setting the stage for safer adolescent sexual behavior.

What Do Children Need to Know?

Many parents struggle to determine which information is most important to share with their children. When adolescents were asked what sexual topics were addressed by their parents, the majority noted that while dating and STIs were often discussed, parents typically avoided more explicit topics like the mechanics of sexual intercourse and other sexual behaviors.[17] Additional research has shown that during sexuality education conversations, parents tend to focus on the negative outcomes of sex, like STIs, rather than the positive outcomes, like intimacy.[11,18] Furthermore, although sexuality education often does and should cover biological aspects of sexual health like puberty and pregnancy, children should also be educated about the social and emotional aspects of sexual health, including but not limited to sexual orientation and sexual consent. In the following section, suggested sexual topics will be outlined; however, in reality, the topics that parents choose to discuss with their children will depend on personal beliefs, preferences, and values.

Biological Determinants of Sexual Health

First, it is important for children to know about anatomy, birth control, pregnancy, reproduction, and STIs. Sexual health education often focuses on negative sexual health outcomes that can result from failure to use protection during sex (e.g., contracting STIs, unwanted pregnancy).[11] However, research shows that focusing on the positive outcomes of using protection may increase safer sex behaviors among adolescents.[19] Regarding pregnancy and birth control, all youths, regardless of sexual identity or gender expression, should be equally informed about the different methods available for protecting against unwanted pregnancy and understand that contraception is a shared responsibility among sexual partners. Relatedly, youths should have a shared understanding of pregnancy, including the responsibility of raising a child and options for dealing with an unwanted or unplanned pregnancy. Furthermore, adolescents should be familiar with common STIs, associated symptoms, ways of transmission, and options for protecting against STIs. They should also understand that if STI symptoms occur, it is important to talk to a trusting adult or contact a healthcare provider to receive appropriate and efficient treatment. Lastly, adolescents should understand that methods for protecting against pregnancy (e.g., birth control pill) are necessarily not synonymous with methods for protecting against STIs (e.g., condoms).

Social and Emotional Aspects of Sexual Health

Children should have a basic understanding that people's emotional and physical attraction to others is diverse. Accordingly, parents can describe various and fluid sexual orientations and gender identities to their children. In line with these topics, children should be introduced to social topics like heterosexism and homophobia. There is a preponderance of anecdotal evidence suggesting that parents should teach their children about relationships and intimacy, specifically highlighting the characteristics of healthy and unhealthy relationships (e.g., mutual respect, warning signs of dating violence). Likewise, children should have a comprehensive understanding of sexual assault, sexual consent, and technology safety (e.g., risks of 'sexting'). Finally, parents should express the importance of sexual communication and pleasure in romantic relationships during the teenage years.

What Communication Strategies Are Most Effective?

Given that parents are known to be one of the most influential sexual health educators for their children, they must adopt communication skills that will support them in effectively educating their children about sex. Hence, the primary reason why we conducted a study on observed parent-child sexual health communication was to identify key aspects of positive communication.

Parent-Child Comfort

Parents often avoid discussing sexual topics with their children because they perceive these conversations as uncomfortable.[20] Parental discomfort often results from feelings of embarrassment or a lack of self-efficacy in communicating about sexual topics.[21] The level of comfort during these conversations has been identified as one of the key factors that influence the delivery of effective sexuality education.[22] When parents present a high degree of comfort around sexual communication, they talk about sexual topics in greater depth, thus resulting in more positive sexual health outcomes for their children.[23] Furthermore, when parents are perceived as comfortable, their children are less likely to avoid conversations about sex and more likely to start sexual communication with them.[11,24]

We recently completed an observational study on sexual health communication between mothers and their adolescent (12 to 17 years old) children in a naturalistic laboratory setting (i.e., set up as a living room).[25] The observational approach involved an unrevealed differences task in which mothers and children individually completed a measure about key topics relevant in families, including decision-making, degree of emotional closeness, disciplinary strategies, and sexual communication in particular. Family members were asked to rank order their preferred responses and then were given the same measure to discuss and complete together as a family. The task was video recorded and then coded for observed closeness, comfort, and warmth. In addition, self-report measures assessing perceived frequency and content of sexual health conversations outside of the laboratory setting were completed by mothers and adolescents. Using an actor-partner interdependence model to account for the naturally interdependent relationship between mothers and children, this study showed that higher levels of maternal and adolescent comfort during sexual health conversations were associated with higher reported rates of parent-child sexual communication. Higher maternal comfort was conveyed through an open and relaxed body posture and a willingness to discuss sexual topics in detail. Closer physical proximity also demonstrated parental warmth and emotional closeness, which fostered higher comfort levels and a greater number of subsequent conversations.[24] In general, emotional closeness between parent and child is predictive of more parent-child comfort during sexual health conversations. To cultivate this emotional closeness in general, parents can attempt to engage in more frequent non-sexual health-related conversations, which will also help promote more effective sexual communication.[26]

Parents who approach conversations about sex in a serious yet compassionate manner are often perceived by their children as more comfortable (e.g., emphasizing the importance of such conversations for ensuring their child's safety and well-being).[25] Parents should directly initiate sexual conversations and use clear, understandable language, demonstrating greater comfort with sexual topics. Conversely, passive initiation of sexual conversations and vague, non-specific language demonstrate discomfort, thus discouraging children from talking to their parents about sex or asking questions and seeking clarification.[25] Indeed, research has shown that adolescents prefer when conversations about sex are direct and honest.[27] Lastly, it is important that parents give their children opportunities to ask questions and share their own beliefs and opinions about sexual topics. Doing so promotes openness and honesty, which helps children feel more respected by their parents, thus facilitating increased comfort and communication.

The Use of Humor

Humor can be used to enhance and detract from engaging in productive discussions about sexual topics. For instance, parents can use humor, particularly at the beginning of conversations, to alleviate anxiety or create a more comfortable atmosphere.[25,28] Moreover, humor can increase children's interest in learning about sex, increase their memory of sexual information, and generally reduce feelings of tension.[27] Conversely, humor can detract from conversations about sex when parents avoid certain topics.[25] It can make children feel awkward and embarrassed, especially when the child's sexuality becomes the source of parental humor (e.g., teasing a child about having a "crush"). Moreover, humor can increase the likelihood of misunderstandings. For instance, one study examining the use of humor in an online sexuality education forum found that some viewers could not differentiate between humor and facts.[29] Overall, if parents choose to use humor in conversations about sex, they will have to read their child's body language and verbal cues to determine whether it is negatively affecting their child's level of comfort. Furthermore, parents should clarify when they make a joke to ensure they are not confusing their child's understanding of sexual topics.

Everyday Opportunities

Parent-child sexual health education has been considered historically as a one-time event in which the parent attempts to bestow their knowledge and values about sex on their child. Perhaps unsurprisingly, these conversations are assumed to be awkward and typically do not provide sufficient sexual education. Although limited research has examined the specific timing of effective sexuality education communication, parents should ideally respond to cues on behalf of their children to initiate conversations about sex. Sexuality education should not be a one-time, superficial conversation. Rather, parents should recognize natural, everyday opportunities to educate their children about sexual topics. These everyday opportunities act as conversation starters and are often referred to as "teachable moments." For example, if there is a pregnancy in the family, it could be used as an opportunity to initiate a discussion about how babies are made. As another example, if a parent notices a child pull back from a hug from a relative, this can serve as an opportunity to talk about wanted and unwanted touch and how to best respond. Teachable moments can also be used to discuss values and beliefs about sexuality with your child in a non-confrontational way. For instance, social issues concerning sexuality and sexualization (e.g., stigma toward sex and gender minorities, sexual assault) can be discussed as these topics come up in advertisements, movies, music, the news, and television shows. Rather than attempting to cover all sexual topics in one conversation, parents should take advantage of these everyday teachable moments when they occur. This approach to sexual health education will help promote a more comprehensive sexuality education for their children.[25]

Parent-Child Gender

The gender of parent and child is another factor to consider when engaging in sexuality education conversations. Compared to fathers, mothers generally play a greater role in communicating with their children about sexuality.[21,30] However, in our observational study noted previously, we found that adolescent daughters were more comfortable talking to their mothers about sexuality than were adolescent sons.[24] Compared to daughters, sons generally report fewer conversations about sexuality with both parents.[16] Overall, this research suggests that parent-child gender may play an important role in sexual health education for children. For instance, sons may be more comfortable having sexual conversations with key male role models. In addition, it may be necessary for parents to make more of a conscious effort to ensure their sons also receive comprehensive sexual health education. When possible, gender-matching between parent and child may be an effective way to increase comfort during sexuality education conversations. If gender-matching is not possible because of non-traditional family structures (e.g., non-heterosexual or cisgender parents, single parent homes), effective communication can still ensue, so long as parents attempt to create a comfortable atmosphere facilitated by emotional closeness, honesty, and openness. Despite the potential for increased comfort resulting from gender-matching, it is still important to encourage children to engage in sexual health conversations with people across all genders and orientations to experience increased comfort and confidence in communicating about these topics, regardless of others' identities.

Resources to Help Guide Conversations About Sex

Even when parents have sufficient knowledge of age-appropriate sexual health education topics and communication skills that can increase comfort during these conversations, it can still be difficult to start such conversations. Fortunately, there are many great resources that help parents introduce and guide these conversations with children of all ages. Here are some valuable resources that can support sexual health education conversations between parents and their children of all ages, genders, and orientations.

Websites and Online Resources

For Parents

Various websites provide parents with information and helpful resources for guiding sexual health education conversations. For example, www.ashasexualhealth.org/parents, www.plannedparenthood.org/learn/parents, www.sexpositivefamilies.com, and www.teachingsexualhealth.ca are excellent, user-friendly websites that offer parents resources to guide the topic that should be included in sexual health conversations. These websites also provide resources to help parents prepare for and begin conversations about sexuality, including recommended communication strategies for talking about sexual health. Additionally, www.parentcenterhub.org/sexed is an educative website that specifically addresses sexuality for young people with disabilities.

For Children

Some children may be interested in engaging in additional self-guided sexuality education. In these instances, parents can provide their children with websites that contain age-appropriate sexual health education directed toward kids. For example, www.amaze.org provides children approximately 10 to 13 years old with fun, animated videos covering various biological and social-emotional sexual health topics. Relatedly, Amaze Junior www.amaze.org/jr provides age-appropriate sexual education resources and videos for children aged 4 to 9. Websites such as www.goaskalice.columbia.edu, www.safeteens.org, www.scarleteen.com, and www.sexetc.org are tailored to teenagers approximately 14 to 18 years old. They are designed to answer questions teens may have about various sexual health topics and provide guidance for dealing with sexual health concerns.

Educational Books

For Parents

There are countless sexual health education books directed toward parents. For instance, *Talk to Me First: Everything You Need to Know to Become Your Kids' Go-to Person About Sex*[31] and *The New Speaking of Sex: What Your Children Need to Know and When They Need to Know It*[32] are excellent resources that provide parents with knowledge on various sexual topics across all stages of child and adolescent development. These books touch on emotional, intellectual, physical, and spiritual aspects of sexual health, and there are suggestions about how to talk to children at different stages in development. For very specific and updated information about anatomy, developing healthy relationships, safer sex practices, sexuality, and other key topics, *A Modern Approach to the Birds and the Bees: A Comprehensive Guide to Talking About Sexuality*[33] is a great resource. For parents of teens, the book *For Goodness Sex: Changing the Way We Talk to Teens About Sexuality, Values, and Health*[34] provides parents with the tools needed to provide their children with a progressive and realistic sexual health education. Specifically, this book focuses on body image, healthy sexuality, and values. Although these books are highlighted, others can be used to support parents in their quest to educate their children about sex. For a more comprehensive list of sexual health education books for parents, visit *www.parentbooks.ca/Sexuality.html*

For Children

There are numerous educational books available for children and adolescents who wish to read about sex on their own. *Sex Is a Funny Word: A Book About Bodies, Feelings, and You*[35] is a comic book directed toward children aged 8 to 10 years. This book provides information about gender, physical development, and sexuality and represents different ethnicities, gender identities, and sexual orientations. Although this book is directed toward children, it can also encourage further conversations between parents and children. *S.E.X., Second Edition: The All-You-Need-To-Know Sexuality Guide to Get You Through Your Teens and Twenties*[36] is an excellent resource directed toward children aged 13 and older. This book covers numerous sexual health topics, including consent, contraceptives, relationships, safer sex, self-image, sexual and gender identity, and sexual assault and abuse. This book includes simple language and takes a no-shame approach to provide accurate and comprehensive information. For a more comprehensive list of sexual health education books directed toward children, adolescents, and young adults, visit www.parents.com/kids/health/best-sex-education-books-for-kids-by-age.

References

1. See, for example Action Canada. (2020). *The state of sex-ed in Canada*. www.action-canadashr.org/.
2. Planned Parenthood. (2021). *What's the state of sex education in the U.S.?* www.planned-parenthood.org/.
3. Pound, P., Langford, R., & Campbell, R. (2016). What do young people think about their school-based sex and relationship education? A qualitative synthesis of young people's views and experiences. *British Medical Journal, 6*(9), 1–14.
4. Somers, C.L., & Surmann, A.T. (2005). Sources and timing of sex education: Relations with American adolescent sexual attitudes and behavior. *Educational Review, 57*(1), 37–54.
5. Harris, A.L. (2011). Media and technology in adolescent sexual education and safety. *Journal of Obstetric, Gynecologic, & Neonatal Nursing, 40*(2), 235–242. doi:10.1111/j.1552-6909.2011.01218.x

6. L'Engle, K.L., Brown, J., & Kenneavy, K. (2006). The mass media are an important context for adolescents' sexual behavior. *Journal of Adolescent Health, 38*, 186–192. doi:10.1016/j.jadohealth.2005.03.020
7. Braun-Courville, D., & Rojas, M. (2009). Exposure to sexually explicit websites and adolescent sexual attitudes and behaviors. *Journal of Adolescent Health, 45*, 156–162. doi:10.1016/j.jadohealth.2008.12.004
8. Martino, S., Collins, R., Elliott, M., Strachman, A., Kanouse, D., & Berry, S. (2006). Exposure to degrading versus nondegrading music lyrics and sexual behavior among youth. *Pediatrics, 118*, 430–441. doi:10.1542/peds.2006-0131.
9. Use of the term parent(s) is intended to include all primary caregivers.
10. Grossman, J.M., Tracy, A.J., Charmaraman, L., Ceder, I., & Erkut, S. (2014). Protective effects of middle school comprehensive sex education with family involvement. *Journal of School Health, 84*, 739–747. doi:10.1111/josh.12199.
11. Pariera, K.L., & Brody, E. (2018). "Talk more about it": Emerging adults' attitudes about how and when parents should talk about sex. *Sexuality Research and Social Policy, 15*, 219–229. doi:10.1007/s13178-017-0314-9
12. Jerman, P., & Constantine, N.A. (2010). Demographic and psychological predictors of parent—adolescent communication about sex: A representative statewide analysis. *Journal of Youth and Adolescence, 39*, 1164–1174. doi:10.1007/s10964-010-9546-1
13. Lefkowitz, E.S., & Stoppa, T.M. (2006). Positive sexual communication and socialization in the parent—adolescent context. *New Directions for Child and Adolescent Development, 12*, 39–55. doi:10.1002/cd.161.
14. Ronis, S.T., & O'Sullivan, L.F. (2011). A longitudinal analysis of predictors of male and female adolescents' transitions to intimate sexual behavior. *Journal of Adolescent Health, 49*, 321–323. doi:10.1016/j.jadohealth.2010.12.010
15. Goldfarb, E.S., & Lieberman, L.D. (2021). Three decades of research: The case for comprehensive sex education. *Journal of Adolescent Health, 68*, 13–27. doi:10.1016/j.jadohealth.2020.07.036
16. Friedrich, W.N., Fisher, J., Broughton, D., Houston, M., & Shafran, C.R. (1998). Normative sexual behavior in children: A contemporary sample. *Pediatrics, 101*(4), E9.
17. Sneed, C.D. (2008). Parent-adolescent communication about sex: The impact of content and comfort on adolescent sexual behavior. *Journal of HIV/AIDS Prevention in Children and Youth, 9*, 70–83. doi:10.1080/10698370802126477
18. Evans, R., Widman, L., Kamke, K., & Stewart, J.L. (2020). Gender differences in parents' communication with their adolescent children about sexual risk and sex-positive topics. *The Journal of Sex Research, 57*(2), 177–188. doi:10.1080/00224499.2019.1661345
19. Whiting, W., Pharr, J.R., Buttner, M.P., & Lough, N.L. (2019). Behavioral interventions to increase condom use among college students in the United States: A systemic review. *Health Education and Behavior, 46*(5), 877–888. doi:10.1177/1090198119853008
20. Ballard, S.M., & Gross, K.H. (2009). Exploring parental perspectives on parent-child sexual communication. *American Journal of Sexuality Education, 4*(1), 40–57. doi:10.1080/15546120902733141
21. Malacane, M., & Beckmeyer, J.J. (2016). A review of parent-based barriers to parent-adolescent communication about sex and sexuality: Implications for sex and family educators. *American Journal of Sexuality Education, 11*(1), 27–40. doi:10.1080/15546128.2016.1146187
22. Guzman, B.L., Schlehofer-Sutton, M.M., Villanueva, C.M., Stritto, M.E.D., Casad, B.J., & Feria, A. (2003). Let's talk about sex: How comfortable discussions about sex impact teen sexual behavior. *Journal of Health Communication, 8*(6), 583–598. doi:10.1080/716100416
23. Ashcraft, A.M., & Murray, P.J. (2017). Talking to parents about adolescent sexuality. *Pediatric Clinics of North America, 64*(2), 305–320. doi:10.1016/j.pcl.2016.11.002

24. Grossman, J.M., Sarwar, P.F., Richer, A.M., & Erkut, S. (2017). We talked about sex." "No, we didn't": Exploring adolescent and parent agreement about sexuality communication. *American Journal of Sexuality Education, 12*(4), 343–357. doi:10.1080/15546128.2017.1372829
25. Malcom, K.E., & Ronis, S.T. (2021). Observed comfort in sexual communication between mothers and adolescents. *American Journal of Sexuality Education, 16*(1), 107–123. doi:10.1080/15546128.2020.1838376
26. Nielsen, S.K., Latty, C.R., & Angera, J.J. (2013). Factors that contribute to fathers being perceived as good or poor sexuality educators for their daughters. *Fathering, 11*(1), 52–70. doi:10.3149/fth.1101.52
27. Peterson, S.H. (2007). The importance of fathers: Contextualizing sexual risk taking in "low-risk" African American adolescent girls. *Journal of Human Behavior in the Social Environment, 15,* 329–346. doi:10.1300/J137v13n03_05
28. Vogel, M.R. (1995). Is humor a useful teaching tool in human sexuality education? Perspectives of sixth-grade students. *Dissertations available from ProQuest*. AAI9543153.
29. Campo, S., Askelson, N.M., Spies, E.L., & Losch, M. (2010). Caution, the use of humor may lead to confusion: Evaluation of a video podcast of the mid-west teen sex show. *American Journal of Sexuality Education, 5*(3), 201–216. doi:10.1080/15546128.2010.503857
30. Widman, L., Choukas-Bradley, S., Noar, S.M., Nesi, J., & Garrett, K. (2016). Parent-adolescent sexual communication and adolescent safer sex behavior: A meta-analysis. *JAMA Pediatrics, 170*(1), 52–61. doi:10.1001/jamapediatrics.2015.2731
31. Roffman, D. (2012). *Talk to me first: Everything you need to know to become your kids' "go-to" person about sex*. Da Capo Press.
32. Hickling, M. (2005). *The new speaking of sex: What your children need to know and when they need to know it*. Wood Lake Books.
33. Pickering, R. (2020). *A modern approach to the birds and the bees: A parent's comprehensive guide to talking about sexuality*. Mango Publishing.
34. Vernacchio, A. (2014). *For goodness sex: Changing the way we talk to teens about sexuality, values, and health*. HarperCollins.
35. Silverberg, C. (2015). *Sex is a funny word: A book about bodies, feelings, and you*. Seven Stories Press.
36. Corinna, H. (2016). *SEX second edition: The all-you-need-to-know sexuality guide to get you through your teens and twenties*. Da Capo Lifelong Books.

2

SEX, BLOOD, AND REDEFINING "WOMANHOOD"

Intervening Early Intimate Health Messages

Jacqueline N. Gunning, Angela Cooke-Jackson and Valerie Rubinsky

> Our [sexual education] teacher, a 50-year-old male, told us: "So that about wraps it up, and there is only one thing left for me to say: Boys, let's all be glad we were not born as women." Then all the boys in our class erupted in laughter, pointing fingers at us and laughing hysterically. I never talked to any of the other girls about it, but I for one felt absolutely horrible and miserable in that moment. I still think about that moment from time to time. Maybe this is why I occasionally hate being female and wish I'd been born male.
>
> (Participant 45)[1]

As exhibited by this participant's recollection, young women[2] are socialized with messages about their reproductive and sexual health that have lasting implications on how they view their bodies, health, and sense of self. These messages from influential individuals in their lives *stick*—whether from teachers, family members, friends, medical practitioners, or others; these messages are *memorable*, meaning when asked, they are easily recalled and often point to a change in behavior, thought, or view. With this understanding, we embarked on a research study that sought to understand just what messages young women receive about their reproductive and sexual health and the impact those messages have. If we know what messages are considered *helpful*, and contrastingly those deemed *harmful*, sexual health educators and researchers will be more equipped to create curricula that benefit, empower, and leave a lasting, positive impact on adolescents and young adults.

Utilizing two theoretical frameworks that center interpersonal communication as an agent for change—the theory of memorable messages[3] and holistic communicology of sexuality[4]—we published our findings in an *American Journal of Sexuality Education* article titled "Negotiating Shame, Sex, Abstinence, and

DOI: 10.4324/9781003189787-3

Period Sex: Women's Shift From Harmful Memorable Messages About Reproductive and Sexual Health."[1] This research study identified *harmful* memorable messages young women receive about their intimate health, alongside *desired* messages they wish they had received instead. This juxtaposition of memorable messages allowed us to identify early messages that young women deem helpful and informative to their development of a healthy perception of body, self, and health. We use the term *intimate health* to refer to female sexual and reproductive health, aligning with our research lab, Intimate Communication Lab, and recent anthology of scholarly writings surrounding this topic, *Communicating Intimate Health*. The term *intimate* health acknowledges that personal health is relational and political—we rarely experience our health only as a cognitive or embodied experience; thus, it becomes a communicative issue, too. Discussing sexual and reproductive health is vulnerable and intimate—even in relationships that we may not characterize as such—thus, we choose to use this term.

In this chapter, we extend our article by delving deeper into these desired messages, asking how socializing individuals (e.g., teachers, family members, friends) can design comprehensive, inclusive, and helpful intimate health education and disrupt harmful messages and narratives for and about female bodies. We hope that whispered giggles, unhelpful commentary, and simplified anatomical discussions shaded by shame and embarrassment become sexual education experiences of the past. There is much to dream and create regarding the future of sexual education: introductions to the monthly female reproductive cycle, courses on the myriad of pleasuring experiences that can be defined as "sex," alternative and sustainable menstrual and contraceptive management options, among others. Centering the call "I wish," we ask young women to be our guides in disrupting antiquated and confining constructs of "womanhood" and designing sexual education for all.

"Fertile Myrtle," "Aunt Flo," and Other Secrets: Early Intimate Health Messaging

> "Don't have sex. If you have sex, you're going to get pregnant and we're going to kick you out." This was the sex talk from my parents . . . it was effective to the point that I didn't have vaginal sex until I was 19 but did everything else under the sun . . . that, while [these activities] wouldn't result in pregnancy, could result in STIs. . . .
>
> (Participant 102)[1]

For many individuals, the first health messages they receive are from their parents or guardians, healthcare providers, educators, friends, or school-based sexual education programs. These memorable messages are communicated verbally and impact the development of their health behaviors, perceptions of their bodies, and formation of their identity. Exploring intimate health socialization through memorable messages allows us to "identify both the repetitive or impactful narratives that inform women's understanding of their intimate health, but also aid in identifying where other messages may challenge, disrupt, or intervene in harmful or inadequate ones."[3] In asking young women what messages they wish they had received, we can identify opportunities to disrupt and intervene health messages that are, at best, not helpful and, at worst, harmful.

When reflecting upon memorable messages about reproductive and sexual health, participants recalled many shaded by shame and expectations of silence. These messages left them feeling confused, unsupported, and afraid to ask questions, perceiving conversations about their intimate health as "taboo."[1] In our study, participants identified five themes that characterized the memorable negative messages they received about their reproductive and sexual health, including (1) feelings of shame and silence in sexual education; (2) conversations about period sex; (3) conversations about safe sex; (4) social expectations surrounding abortion; and (5) social expectations surrounding childbearing, with resulting fears of infertility. We will briefly discuss these themes before delving into opportunities to disrupt and intervene in messages deemed harmful or unhelpful.

First, like these participant reflections exhibit, many of the messages received prompt *feelings of shame and silence in sexual education*, failing to provide realistic, readily applicable, and "sex-positive" health information. As school sexual education programs are typically introduced during pre-pubescence, participants recalled desiring more respect, maturity, and sex-positivity from educators leading these conversations.[1] Outdated sexual education curricula that equate "sex" to vaginal intercourse overlook other forms of sexual intimacy that can place individuals at risk for sexually transmitted infections and diseases. Messaging that focuses on intercourse as the sole form of sexual intimacy also privileges heteronormative relationships and able bodies, further ostracizing individuals who resonate with alternative sexual activities.[5] Research specifically on early LGBTQ+ sexual health messaging found that people of diverse genders desire messages prioritizing positivity, pleasure, and dialogue and affirming the spectrum of gender and sexual identities.[3] Participants discussed religious, purity-based, abstinence-only sexual education. Those with religious backgrounds cited an increase in shame surrounding how they viewed their bodies and engagement in unsafe non-penetrative sexual health practices. This is known from more than a decade of purity messages in familial communication.[6,7]

Memorable early conversations about sex often included *specific messages about period sex and safe sex practices*. The specificity of messages about period sex was particularly interesting and unexpected, as the questions posed did not mention sexual intercourse during menstruation. Previous research focusing on ideal early messages about menstruation found similarly desired messages about sex and sexuality, including normalizing conversations, a comprehensive introduction to menstrual management options, and challenging the gendered notion that menstruation signals "becoming a woman."[8] The intersection of menstruation and sexuality heightens these societal messages and expectations, offering a unique opportunity for individuals to disrupt shame-based beliefs and feelings at once. Many participants credit partners for helping them heal negative perceptions of their bodies related to menstruation and sex by engaging in conversations about period sex.[1,9]

Additionally, participants noted the importance of prioritizing conversations about safe sex practices. These conversations encouraged individuals to fully educate themselves before engaging in sexual activities, including preparing protective methods to prevent sexually transmitted infections and pregnancy and ensuring their comfort, consent, and safety. The most effective messages were those that gave agency—encouraging education, research, and self-reflection related to individual preferences and desires—and prioritized intimacy with a respectful and safe partner. These messages teach young women that sexual intimacy is their choice, to be engaged in however they want and with whomever they want, but that safety and a depth of thought should be given before engaging.

Finally, participants spoke of *larger societal reproductive health messages surrounding abortion and childbearing expectations*, which prompted fears of infertility. These permeating societal messages show how deeply intertwined childbearing is to ideas of "womanhood," with assigned female individuals socialized with this expectation. These messages often evoked fear, which in turn affected individual sexuality—the fear of pregnancy and/or a moral, religious, or access-based inability to get an abortion impeded women's sexual agency, dictating their choice of birth control or engagement in sexual activities. Messages that equate being female with an expectation of childbearing ostracize individuals who may not want children or cannot have children and prompt gender dysphoria for individuals who were assigned but do not identify as female. Women are socialized with messages about fertility and childbearing that do not discuss the possibility of infertility or an inability to conceive naturally, sowing fear and sadness in those who lived their whole lives expecting to have children only to learn that they are unable to. This particular message and fear of infertility has shown up across research studies, in our study about sexual health messaging,[1] messaging about emerging adulthood autoimmune disease,[10] and memorable messages about infertility,[11] highlighting a need for more and earlier dialogue surrounding the experience of infertility.

These permeating interpersonal and societal messages surrounding reproductive and sexual health give insight into the socializing influences that assigned female individuals navigate alongside discovering individual identity, sexuality, and healthy behaviors.

Putting the "Talk" Back in "Sex Talk": Moments of Disruption and Positive Change

In light of these message themes and permeating societal narratives surrounding female bodies, there is a clear call for a shift in perception, treatment, and education. Considering this, we asked participants to identify moments that helped disrupt, change, or evolve negative perceptions they may have held about their reproductive and sexual health. Our intent was simple: Who better to give insight into shaping the future of sexual education than women who have evolved, developed, and educated themselves and one another beyond what their upbringing provided? This retrospective lens provides a rich wisdom and insight that can only be garnered from lived experience. Through retrospective sense-making, individuals form meanings, values, beliefs, and coping mechanisms and make sense of their health and lived experiences.[12] In the context of sexual health conversations, this development of individual values and beliefs surrounding sexual and reproductive health decisions is important to individual well-being and identity formation.[12]

As a result, our research study identified four salient influences for their development of positive understandings of reproductive and sexual health: (1) open, honest dialogue; (2) further, self-directed education; (3) accepting and taking ownership of their bodies and symptom management; and (4) the evolution of gender identity and redefining "womanhood." We will explain these themes and discuss opportunities for educational integration and curriculum development in turn.

The melodic words of Salt-N-Pepa's 1990 hit "Let's Talk About Sex" are still sung today, crooning "let's talk about sex, baby. Let's talk about you and me. Let's talk about all the good things and the bad things in between. Let's talk about sex!" Yet conversations about sex are still treated as "taboo": topics to be whispered at teenage sleepovers or articulated quickly in coded language—"the birds and bees," "Aunt Flo," "Fertile Myrtle . . ." the list goes on. Even though research has shown that conversations about sexual health and safety are predictive of lower levels of sexual risk-taking,[13] American society still struggles with interpersonal conversations about sex. This must change if we want our young people to be knowledgeable about their bodies, sexuality, consent, and safety. If conversations about sexuality are treated as taboo, shameful, to be kept secret or silent, generations to come will continue to treat these topics the same way.

Participants noted a reduction in shame surrounding their bodies when they began to engage in *open, honest dialogue* about their reproductive and sexual health. These open, honest conversations were had with friends, family members, intimate partners, and influential others, as well as larger societal conversations surrounding women's bodies and gendered expectations. Such discussions created a safe space for individuals to explore their preferences, including contraceptive and menstrual management options, and expressions of sexuality and intimacy. Conversations that encouraged acceptance of developing and changing bodies and prioritized finding menstrual and contraceptive management options that suited each individual were critical to disrupting feelings of shame, stigma and concealing behaviors.

These conversations often sparked *further, self-directed education* surrounding topics of sex, reproductive health, fertility, and menstruation, serving as a catalyst for their improved perceptions of their bodies, health, and sense of self. Sources of independent research and information included websites, books, and social media, as well as asking questions of family, friends, and medical practitioners.

Some individuals noted that this newfound agency and autonomy of their bodies and health decisions sparked a career shift, prompting them to transition into medical and sexual health–related career paths. By providing tailored resources and further readings for young adults, we can offer avenues for exploration and continued questioning on topics that may not be prioritized in early sexual education courses.

A catalyst for individuals' positive shift in perceptions of health and identity was when they *accepted and took ownership of their bodies and symptom management*. This often stemmed from individuals educating themselves about the inner workings of their bodies and finding contraceptive and reproductive management options that worked best for them. Becoming invested and autonomous in their health decisions increased self-worth, body positivity, and agency over their bodies and health. Examples include exploring what menstrual and contraceptive management options work best for their bodies,[14] seeking competent and compassionate medical care, and normalizing bodily functions.

Finally, *the evolution of gender identity and redefining* "womanhood" significantly impacted individuals' transition away from harmful societal messages about female reproductive and sexual health. This disruption often came from conversations with friends, challenging traditional gender roles and expectations of femininity, and further self-education. Some participants noted a shift of contraceptive responsibility from the individual who can get pregnant to both intimate partners. Gender non-conforming and trans individuals found that differentiating menstruation as separate from "womanhood" helped with dysphoria and challenged antiquated definitions and expectations of gender.[15]

These moments of disruption and catalysts for a change in perception are essential when developing sexual health curriculum for young individuals. By knowing what moments are most impactful in developing a healthy sense of self, body, and health behaviors, researchers and educators are more equipped to provide lasting, positive sexual and reproductive health messages and practices across ages and stages of life.

Dreaming and Designing Ideal Reproductive and Intimate Health Messages

Memorable messages play a key role in young adults' identity development, autonomy over their bodies, and health decisions. As noted in this study, many of these messages come from sexual education programs, friends, family members, and influential others, showing that memorable message research can aid in the development of comprehensive, thoughtful sexual education in schools. Understandings and perceptions of reproductive and sexual health are malleable; women in this study identified harmful messages that they received and the influences that helped them challenge those unhelpful notions and develop healthier understandings of their sexual and reproductive health. With comprehensive understanding, space for conversation and questioning, and community support, individuals can heal early wounds that impede positive views of intimacy, sexuality, and their health. In this chapter, we considered a holistic communicological approach[4] to sex education. A holistic communicology of sexuality emphasizes that the experience of sex and sexual health is relational and grounded in communication.

A holistic communicological approach to sexual education invites all community members to be a part of this development. Friends, peers, school programs, and influential socializing others all serve different roles in an individual's growth, from first messages and conversations to later developed understandings and questioning. As young women explore sexuality and gender across their lives, they are more apt to shed messaging and deeply held beliefs that no longer serve them. By identifying the catalysts for a shift in perception formed by prior messaging, we can effectively integrate these influences into school-based sexual education courses and individual educational materials so that future generations have less to unlearn and challenge. It is the interest of memorable messages research and sexual education courses to equip youth with comprehensive sexual and reproductive health information early, thoroughly, and thoughtfully so that they may explore their sexuality in safe, syntonic ways from the start.

From the findings of our study, we offer a few practical suggestions for sexual health educators. First, ongoing, comprehensive dialogue surrounding reproductive and sexual health is integral to the development of positive understandings of reproductive health and sexuality. This includes access to resources, additional educational materials, and critical, interpersonal conversations as they develop facets of their sexual health. A deep understanding of the female reproductive system and inner workings is important for developing bodily autonomy and agency over health decisions, including contraceptive and menstrual management choices.[14] Regarding contraceptive management and pregnancy prevention, it is important to teach the various phases of the female reproductive cycle to those born with a body that can become pregnant. This includes educating on signs of ovulation and menstruation so that they are equipped to prevent or promote pregnancy on a biological level, as well as utilizing hormonal or non-hormonal contraceptive options. It would behoove sexual health educators to include discussions on less-discussed women's health issues, including infertility, endometriosis,[16] pelvic, vaginal, vulvar, or other overlapping chronic pain conditions, signs of infection, and other reproductive health concerns to monitor. Early conversations about managing vaginal health aid in reducing the stigma surrounding women's health issues and affirming that pelvic and vaginal pain should be believed and treated.[17,18]

Additionally, women desire education on the variety of menstrual management options available, from traditional tampons and pads to alternative methods, including menstrual cups, discs, and reusable period pads and underwear. Many participants expressed notable ease in menstrual management once they found alternative methods that worked for them. For instance, many participants cited preferences for a menstrual cup, which puts individuals in physical contact with their menstrual blood. Because menstrual blood changes in consistency and color throughout the menstrual cycle, using methods like a cup can teach individuals how to look for signs that their discharge may be "off." As women are more susceptible to normalizing pain and having their symptoms dismissed by medical providers,[9,17] it is important for early education to prioritize curricula that teach them to know and understand their unique bodies, so they may learn what is their "normal," what is not, and when to seek medical care.

As it relates to inclusive sexuality education, educators must ensure that lessons on sexuality extend beyond heteronormative understandings of sex, offering sexual health resources that encompass all that sex and intimacy can be, regardless of gender or sexual anatomy. These resources should center consent, pleasure, and agency as non-negotiables in sexual activities and intimate partnership. By socializing individuals with strong understandings of consent and pleasure from an early age, we begin to dismantle the societal systems that perpetuate and tolerate harm and abuse in intimate partnerships.

Finally, these conversations should continue beyond adolescent and young adult development into life, evolving with individual needs and desires and coming from a variety of formal and informal sources. Positive reproductive and sexual health information is key to women's overall health and well-being. No educational program or source is perfect; instead of striving for perfection, we should prioritize curiosity, questioning, consent, and comfort. Research has come far in identifying what is helpful for young adults' sexual development; there are endless books, online sources, podcasts, articles, among others, that educate on all topics of sexual intimacy and reproductive health. Our job is to provide comprehensive education and guide young people toward resources and information that apply their individual needs and desires. Sexual education is not one-size-fits-all, so we must stop treating it as such. In doing so, we will more effectively educate our young people, foster agency and autonomy, and create memorable messages that normalize all bodies, desires, and needs.

References

1. Gunning, J., Cooke-Jackson, A., & Rubinsky, V. (2019). Negotiating shame, silence, abstinence, and period sex: Women's shift from harmful memorable messages about reproductive and sexual health. *American Journal of Sexuality Education, 15*, 111–137. http://doi.org/10.1080/15546128.2019.1669511
2. In favor of consistency and brevity, we will use the term *women* when referring to the participant population of this study, however, these findings include young, assigned-female-at-birth (AFAB) individuals who may identify as male or non-binary. Though the majority of our sample represented cisgender female individuals, we received responses from individuals who were born female but hold a different gender identity. We point readers to chapters within this volume focus on LGBTQ+ individuals for further reading.

3. Cooke-Jackson, A., & Rubinsky, V. (2021). Theory of memorable messages: Theorizing message disruption. In A. Cooke-Jackson, & V. Rubinsky (Eds.), *Communicating intimate health* (pp. 89–98). Lexington Books.
4. Manning, J. (2014). Communication and healthy sexual practices: Toward a holistic communicology of sexuality. In M. E. Heaves (Ed.), *Applications in health communication* (pp. 263–286). Kendall-Hunt.
5. Kattari, S.K. (2015). "Getting it": Identity and sexual communication for sexual and gender minorities with physical disabilities. *Sexuality & Culture, 19*(4), 882–899. www.doi.org/10.1007/s12119–015–9298-x
6. Manning, J. (2021). Intimate conversations about sex and sexuality: Lessons learned from studying purity pledges. In A. Cooke-Jackson, & V. Rubinsky (Eds.), *Communicating intimate health* (pp. 51–62). Lexington Books.
7. Manning, J. (2015). Paradoxes of (im)purity: Affirming heteronormativity and queering heterosexuality in family discourses of purity pledges. *Women's Studies in Communication, 38*(1), 1–19. https://doi.org/10.1080/07491409.2014.954687
8. Rubinsky, V., Gunning, J., & Cooke-Jackson, A. (2018). "I thought I was dying": (Un)Supportive communication surrounding early menstruation experiences. *Health Communication, 35*, 242–252. http://doi.org/10.1080/10410236.2018.1548337
9. Rubinsky, V., McMahon, T., Cooke-Jackson, A., & Gunning, J. N. (2021). "Just put a towel down": Approaching conversations about period sex with an intimate partner. *Sexuality & Culture*, 1–17. https://doi.org/10.1007/s12119-021-09821-0
10. Gunning, J. (2021). Wisdom narratives: Communicated sense-making in emerging adulthood autoimmune disease. *Communication Studies Theses, Dissertations, and Student Research, 53*. https://digitalcommons.unl.edu/commstuddiss/53
11. Voorhees, H., Koenig Kellas, J., Palmer-Wackerly, A., Gunning, J., Marsh, J., & Baker, J. (2021). Memorable messages of support during the infertility experience. Paper presentation at the virtual 71st *Annual international communication association conference.*
12. Koenig Kellas, J. (2018). Communicated narrative sense-making theory: Linking storytelling and wellbeing. In Braithwaite, D.O., Suter, E.A., & Floyd, K. (Ed.), *Engaging theories in family communication* (2nd ed, pp. 63–74). Routledge.
13. Holman, A., & Koenig Kellas, J. (2018). "Say something instead of nothing": Adolescents' perceptions of memorable conversations about sex-related topics with their parents. *Communication Monographs, 85*(3), 357–379. http://doi.org/10.1080/03637751.2018.1426870
14. Hudak, N. & Gunning, J. (2021) A dialogic forum on feminist implications of birth control discourse. In A. Cooke-Jackson, & V. Rubinsky (Eds.), *Communicating intimate health* (pp. 263–287). Lexington Books.
15. Rubinsky, V., & Cooke-Jackson, A. (2017). "Where is the love?" Expanding and theorizing with LGBTQ memorable messages of sex and sexuality. *Health Communication, 32*(12), 1472–1480. https://doi.org/10.1080/10410236.2016.1230809
16. Norman, A. (2018). *Ask me about my uterus: A quest to make doctors believe in women's pain*. Bold Type Books.
17. Hintz, E.A. (2022). "It's all in your head": A meta-synthesis of qualitative research about disenfranchising talk experienced by female patients with chronic overlapping pain conditions. *Health Communication*, 1–15. https://doi.org/https://www.tandfonline.com/loi/hhth20
18. Scott, K.D., Hintz, E.A., & Harris, T.M. (2020). "Having pain is normal": How talk about chronic pelvic and genital pain reflects messages from menarche. *Health Communication*. https://doi.org/10.1080/10410236.2020.1837464

3

FIGHTING OPPRESSIVE MASCULINITY AT HOME

Sex Talks with Gay, Bisexual, and Queer Sons

Dalmacio D. Flores, Eliza C. Magland, Kate Hennessy, Isabel Martinez, Frances Anjelique Agudo, and Sarah Abboud

> My mom would watch the Hispanic version of TV court shows and every once in a while, there would be a case where there would be a gay man. And my aunt didn't really understand it. My mom said, "It's like two men that want to be together. . . . They decide which one's going to be the woman, and he dresses up like the woman. And he does what the woman is supposed to do in the relationship."
>
> —Ramos (18 years old, Latino, gay)

Recent societal acceptance of lesbian, gay, bisexual, transgender, and queer (LGBTQ) identities has been accompanied by a younger age of coming out; however, this phase is also accompanied by a heteronormative regulation of sexual and gender identities. Starting at a young age, children are socialized into heteronormativity, "the mundane, everyday ways that heterosexuality is privileged and taken for granted."[1] Heterosexuality and a binary understanding of gender (man/woman; masculinity/femininity) are often assumed and rewarded in family, marriage, religion, and educational systems.[2,3] These beliefs of what is normal and what is not marginalize LGBTQ youth and negatively impact their sexual, physical, social, and mental health.[4–7] In particular, gay, bisexual, and queer (GBQ) adolescent males are forced into traditional notions of masculinity (e.g., strong, emotionless, controlling) that perpetuate bullying and discrimination against those who do not conform to these standards.

GBQ adolescent males make up a disproportionate number of new HIV infections. In 2018, among all 13- to 24-year-olds in the United States, GBQ adolescent males accounted for 92% of new HIV diagnoses and 21% of new HIV diagnoses among all GBQ male age groups in the United States.[8] Within this

DOI: 10.4324/9781003189787-4

population of GBQ adolescent males, Black and Latino individuals are disproportionately affected by HIV diagnoses.[9] Research shows that GBQ adolescent males are more likely to engage in sexual risk behaviors such as condomless intercourse, early debut, and forced sex than their heterosexual counterparts.[10]

Traditional assumptions of gender norms and heterosexuality are learned very early in childhood.[1] This early learning process provides parents with multiple teaching opportunities for a comprehensive and inclusive approach to communicating about sex. Parent-child sex communication (PCSC) is one such factor that may be integral in preventing sexually transmitted infections (STI) in young GBQ males. The following sections will focus on the various structures that impact PCSC.

PCSC and Its Promise to Address Disparities

Four decades of research on PCSC has identified multiple mechanisms that positively impact adolescent sexual health outcomes. When effective, discussions at home about sex can improve condom use, the ability to resist pressure to have sex, HIV/STI conversations before sex, and the access to reproductive and sexual health services.[11,12] While research into PCSC has been extensive, minimal attention has extended to GBQ males. Since GBQ males are at the highest risk of HIV infection, more focus needs to be placed on the parental role in sons' sex education.[13]

Data Source

We conducted one-on-one interviews with a diverse group of 30 GBQ males, 15 to 20 years old, in North Carolina in 2016. From these 90-minute interviews, we identified commonalities evident across their stories. This chapter organizes the findings according to how factors external to the family directly or indirectly affect discussions about sex in the home. While "sex talks" as traditionally defined are conversations between a parent and a child, we will describe how multiple factors outside the home and external to the parent and child establish and reinforce rigid standards of masculinity.

A Bioecological Framework

The pervasiveness of traditional notions of masculinity and the promising role that PCSC can play to address this issue may be viewed through the lens of a bioecological framework.[14] According to this model, human development occurs through dynamic interactions between the child and the multiple environments the child occupies, including the family, community, and larger world. Each of these systems acts upon the other to drive forward the social and emotional growth of the young human. These environments are systems that extend outward from and encircle the child—starting with the microsystem, consisting of the family and peers; followed by the mesosystem of the church and school; then the exosystem, which includes media, politics, and current events; and finally, the

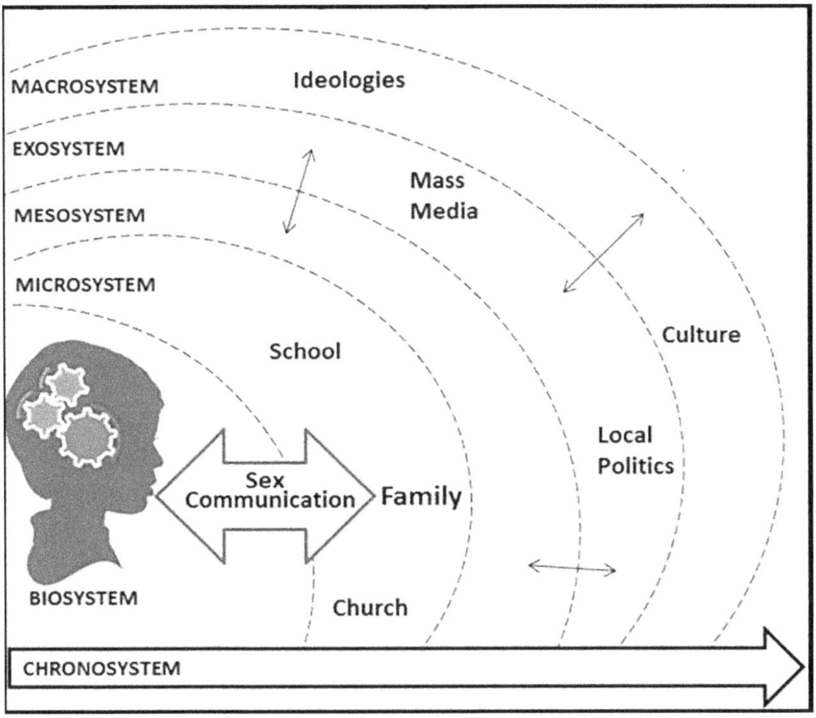

FIGURE 3.1 Parent-child sex communication as depicted within the bioecological framework.

macrosystem, or the broader cultural and ideological context in which the child exists (Figure 3.1).

Sexually diverse adolescents develop within the same ecological systems as heterosexual youth. However, unlike heterosexual youth, their attractions and sexuality are less likely to be represented and affirmed by their environment.[14–16] GBQ males both succeed and face unique challenges as they mature in heteronormative environments.[17] As family, school, and religion have been shown to act as positive and negative influencers of LGBTQ well-being, examining PCSC within the bioecological framework can help us better understand whether and how these systems perpetuate heteronormative beliefs and rigid, traditional masculinity within this group of youth.[18]

Siblings and Peers

Peers and siblings play an integral role within the microsystem of developing youth. Research on heterosexual youth shows that siblings act as confidants and mentors,[19] provide support, and facilitate more frequent family discussions about safe sex.[20] LGBTQ youth identify peers as valued support, despite the harmful impact of bullying that many LGBTQ youth experience.[21] Negative peer experiences are associated with poor health and school outcomes;[21,22] however, friendship and community support contribute to improved self-esteem, feelings of acceptance, and disclosure of sexual orientation.[23,24]

Our research found that peers and siblings provided both support and acceptance to GBQ youth. Participants frequently stated that they came out to siblings or peers before disclosing to parents. These early coming-out experiences served as opportunities where GBQ sons could practice disclosure and determine the best ways of sharing this important information with parents. Siblings, in particular, were sometimes a resource or go-between while parents were becoming accustomed to their son's newly revealed sexual orientation. For example, one son remembered the multiple ways his brother was an ally after he came out:

> I told my brother a couple months prior. He's a really good ally . . . [After disclosure] he called my dad and yelled at him for not reacting better in the beginning. I think it helped that he called and yelled at him for a while.

While participants recalled these positive sibling influences, they also described their siblings' non-affirming roles. GBQ sons were sometimes included in sex conversations geared toward their heterosexual siblings. These talks reinforced heterosexual norms that left participants wondering how the information applied to them. One brother remembered thinking:

> I don't know if this all applies to me, but I was not going to bring that up! In my mind, "This conversation is geared maybe more toward my sister," because they didn't bring up at all other sexualities.

Participants also shared how their parents used their siblings to emphasize traditional notions of masculinity. One son recalled his mother's response to his attempts at playing with his sister's toys:

> I would try to play with my sister because she would have these Barbies and My Little Ponies. I wanted one so badly but I couldn't have one. . . . I would [also] act just like my sister around the house or be dancing around and my mom would just get really upset about that. She'd say, "No. Be more like your brother."

In addition, peers were a main source of sex information for GBQ sons. Peers were approached when participants felt too awkward or unable to bring up sex topics with parents and provided both initial and continued sex education. The following anecdote illustrates the role peers play in sexual socialization:

> I remember being in 5th grade and just knowing that one of my friends was dating one of my other friends. . . . And then I just remember someone

> saying, "Oh, they were having S-E-X." We were even afraid to say the word. That's when it first came up, and that's when I asked "Oh, what is that?" because I didn't know. And then my friends basically described it as when a guy and a girl are in a relationship and they use their private parts to get closer together.

Heteronormative Sex Education and PCSC

In the last four decades, while there has been widespread implementation of school-based sex education programs, only 11 states in the United States mandate instruction to be inclusive of sexual orientation or gender identity.[25] The percentage of schools that provide curricula on HIV, STI, or pregnancy prevention information relevant to LGBTQ youth ranges from 11.0% to 56% across states.[26] Comprehensive curricula use inclusive language and terminology, identify safe spaces at school, prohibit harassment based on sexual orientation or gender identity, encourage staff to attend professional development on inclusive and safe environment, and facilitate access to LGBTQ-inclusive social, psychological, and healthcare services.[26] The National School Climate Survey reported that in 2019, only 8% of LGBTQ students reported that their health classes provided inclusive sex education.[27]

The significant lack of LGBTQ-inclusive sex education at schools is accompanied by heteronormative school climates that create hostile environments for LGBTQ youth. Thus, while the school system may be crucial in the healthy sexual socialization education of heterosexual youth, the same cannot be said for LGBTQ youth. Compounding this problem is relinquishing the responsibility for sex education by many parents to the school. As one of our participants shared:

> I think they figured, "OK, the school's doing it, so I don't need to." And they confirmed that recently because at a baby shower game when they asked all parents questions, like "At what age did you have the sex talk?" And my parents were like "Never. The school does it for you."

Half of the participants recalled attending sex education classes around fifth grade in our study. They reported these classes impacted PCSC in several ways. Some participants stated that the required consent forms triggered their parents to broach the sex talk. These conversations included alternative perspectives from the mostly abstinence-based school model, such as sharing their thoughts regarding specific topics. For the participants who did not have any pre-sex education discussions or follow-up, this implied parental confidence in what the school system was teaching. One GBQ male recalled:

> After Sex Ed, I told him [father] what we did in school that day, and he basically told me "Oh, yeah, just don't do it because someone's going to get pregnant or you're going to get a disease and you're going to ruin your life." That was the extent of the conversation.

Religion

Based on our interviews, religion deterred sex communication due to tenets that tout homophobia and promote religious ideologies, justifying rejection and mistreatment of LGBTQ individuals.[28] LGBTQ adolescents raised in religious homes that uphold these tenets learn early in life to hide same-sex attractions in order to conform to religious expectations.[29] Not only do these learned expectations affect the outward behavior of LGBTQ youth, but these assumptions of straightness can also instill and perpetuate negative feelings about an individual's own LGBTQ identity, resulting in internalized homophobia[30] and identity conflict.[31] These various structures of oppression within some religions can prevent LGBTQ adolescents from asking parents their emergent questions regarding health and sexuality.

In our study, one-third of the participants reported that religion impacted sex communication at home. According to these participants, their parents' level of religiosity dictated the content of discussions about sex and their parents' attitudes about same-sex attraction. We found that parents who were active in church most often discussed abstinence from premarital sex. One participant with religious parents reported that any discussion about the exploration of sexuality was steeped in shame, which the participant said continued to affect him years later. A Latino participant reported being bullied outside of the home. Because of religious silence around sexuality within his home, he recalled praying to God to change his voice since he said, "Maybe if my voice was different it [bullying] would all go away."

Our participants whose parents were not religious reported more frequent and easier conversations about sex than those who grew up in religious homes. From an early age, sons who asked and received information about LGBTQ topics were from non-religious households. At 4 and 8 years old, two participants whose parents were not religious could seek information from their parents about who and what gay people were. Conversely, participants from more religious families, mostly Hispanic/Latino and Black households, did not ask their parents LGBTQ-related questions even if the participants had questions or already knew that they had same-sex attractions. These GBQ sons from religious households avoided PCSC as they did not want to draw any potential attention to their same-sex curiosities or attractions.

New Media and Mobile Technology

Among the ecological influences of family sex communication, media through mobile technology appears to be the most salient. Access to online resources by GBQ males puts these youth in charge of their own learning to explore their sexualities without parental supervision.[32,33] Since traditional venues like school-based sex education often do not include LGBTQ topics,[34] and most topics covered by parents are limited to abstinence, HIV/STI prevention, and birth control, GBQ adolescent males report looking to the Internet to find answers to their sexuality-specific questions.[35]

Television provided the actual word for their emerging identities and feelings for most participants. While a few of our participants reported that they asked their parents what "gay" meant, most participants understood the topic was taboo and explored their questions themselves. The ability to find information without parental assistance established early self-reliance for these GBQ youth. Participants recalled a number of Google queries—"How do gay people have sex?" "Am I gay?" "What's it like being gay?" "What does gay mean?"—and other online searches including "define gay" and "same-sex attraction." Additionally, more than half of our participants shared how inadvertent exposure to sexually explicit media during online searches became early sources of sex information. A 15-year-old queer participant recalled:

> I Googled and I looked up sex and I'm expecting like, "Ah, sex is the name for where babies come from." . . . So then I got all these gigantic porn sites—they advertise so aggressively that I think it was a little bit much for my little eight year old mind. . . . And so that I think is probably the most educational moment.

While research shows that GBQ adolescent males report a preference for sex education that is detailed and specific, given the plethora of misinformation online and its potential to normalize risky behaviors, GBQ youth must be able to access reliable sex information.[35] Therefore, rather than viewing the Internet as competition for GBQ sons' attention, parents can be assisted in teaching sons how to become discerning consumers of online information and develop media literacy.[36] Parents can guide sons in developing this competency by finding correct information online and regulating and negotiating safe internet use as they explore their GBQ identities.

Aside from face-to-face conversations, many participants disclosed their sexual orientation to parents through text or online messaging, emails, tweets, and Tumblr postings. Distinct nonverbal cues may be missed when parents and GBQ sons communicate online and through text messaging compared to face-to-face interactions. Further research is needed to explore the impact of sexuality and sex conversations orchestrated through technology.

Politics/Current Events

Current events, politics, and the media were noteworthy triggers of sex communication in the homes of our participants. As youth, they were aware of changing laws and debates regarding marriage equality and the Defense of Marriage Act's overturning in 2015. We found that these powerful events spurred youth to consider their sexuality and prompt family discussion more seriously. Some participants reported using these events to initiate sex conversations and educate or even counter their parents on LGBTQ issues. Others used their parents' reactions to media to determine whether they felt safe bringing up LGBTQ topics that were important to them, including disclosing their sexual orientation.

Political events had an additional effect on PCSC in one military family. This son described having previously had a supportive relationship with his father and frequent, open communication about sex. However, the father's multiple deployments to the Middle East and subsequent post traumatic stress disorder effectively removed that support, both physically and emotionally. In this way, foreign policy played an unanticipated role in this adolescent's sexual development and his father's ability to communicate with him. After each succeeding deployment:

> He [father] just didn't give robust answers. It probably had to do with him coming back from Afghanistan. He had trouble with that. [My relationship issues with my then-boyfriend] bothered me, but I just didn't talk to him [father] about it.

Traditional Definition of Gender and Masculinity

From early ages, participants were aware of "masculine ways of acting" and had experienced interactions with parents emphasizing societal standards for boy behavior. In addition, many participants reported receiving negative messages about people with same-sex attractions and their behaviors. These early communications informed sons of the gendered roles they would be expected to fulfill as they grew.

Sex communication was also impacted by fathers' ideas regarding traditional masculinity and emotion. In our study, at least two of the sons remembered that their fathers viewed sex conversations with their sons as feminine because it warranted the verbalization of parental affection. A 15-year-old queer participant recalls the response his father gave when his mom observed their child displaying effeminate characteristics: "Well, no. That's my son. That's my strong man. He's not gay."

Other early communication from parents led to expectations of traditional masculine standards, which reinforced expectations of future gendered roles. Numerous participants expressed that their mothers would fret over which girls they might take to prom or the wife they were supposed to marry. A 20-year-old Caucasian gay man shared:

> She's always told me, "Oh, when you get married you need to find a wife that's this,". . . . Not just sticking to the whole 'You're Going to Marry a Woman,' but also sticking to the gender norms of what the woman and the man are supposed to be following. "The man is the one that's the breadwinner. He's the one that works. And then the wife stays at home. She takes care of the kids."

These parents' expectations affected their ability to respond to their son's disclosure as GBQ. We found that even in the more accepting families, the shock in the disclosure and confirmation of the child's sexuality hindered the parent's initial ability to communicate acceptance or express concern for their sons' future. According to one 18-year-old, Black, bisexual participant, his mother's ability to converse with him changed after he came out as bisexual:

> She won't call me and talk to me about my relationships anymore. She won't say "Oh, do you have a girlfriend?" or "Do you have a boyfriend?" . . . She'll just call me and ask me how my day went, ask me what I did with my weekend, and stuff like that.

Significance of Findings

The results of this study finally allow us to piece together the multiple ways oppressive standards of masculinity permeate the ecological settings that GBQ youth and their parents navigate. We have illustrated how societal norms facilitate and inhibit the sexual socialization of this underserved population. We have also articulated how family discussions are affected by multiple intersecting ecological layers and have suggested ways parents can create a more welcoming home environment.

Sex educators are in unique positions to augment the information this youth group is craving but not receiving from parents and teachers. They may craft programming that answers GBQ males' emergent questions in ways that are being ignored at home, in school, or within the larger society. Further, they can access the traditional spaces where youth receive sexual socialization and advocate for the inclusion of GBQ males' concerns. As a professional group, sex educators can begin to make homes and schools more inclusive by teaching adults to be mindful of LGBTQ youths' unique developmental needs. This book provides a wellspring of how sex education can be innovative and inclusive. PCSC is one illustration of the multiple ways sex educators can break down the barriers to and enhance inclusive, free-flowing family discussions about sexuality.

As sex educators take on this challenge, they must balance the task of correcting parents' heteronormative assumptions without undermining or alienating parents. As the expert on their child, the parent can be supported in their desire to hold family sex conversations and encouraged to incorporate the inclusive sex information from the educator into their own expertise. Sex educators can acknowledge parents' good intentions while helping them question their held traditional beliefs. Respecting family connection while helping parents recognize blind spots in their view may reduce parental defensiveness, leading to dismissing all the valuable, inclusive information the sex educator is attempting to provide.

While a major change in thinking is unlikely to happen overnight, the goal of sex educators can be to increase parental awareness of toxic masculinity and comfort in addressing this topic with their sons. Sex educators can help parents define and identify heteronormativity and gender stereotypes in their environment and then seize opportunities to call out these stereotypes in the presence of their sons. Finally, parents can be taught to accept and address their mistakes, regardless of the length of time since they occurred. When parents realize they have missed a teaching opportunity or participated in an episode of harmful gender stereotyping, they can return to these incidents with their children as it is never too late to make a correction. Sex educators play a valuable role in supporting parents as they navigate this process.

Future Directions

This preliminary work highlights unique family communication attributes from cisgender male youth who identify as GBQ. Future work must focus on collecting parallel data from parents of GBQ males. Discordant reports about family-based sexuality discussions are well established,[13] and gathering parents' recollections and suggestions for inclusive PCSC is the next logical step to formulating interventions. An urgent further action for sex educators would involve utilizing this data for GBQ-inclusive family programming. Additionally, future research should be extended to families with youth who identify as lesbian, bisexual, or queer females and their sex discussions with parents. Similarly, research involving families with transgender or nonbinary youth with cisgender parents is crucial as these families have unique concerns that may have commonalities or differences to those experienced by LGBQ cisgender youth.

References

1. Myers, K., & Raymond, L. (2010). Elementary school girls and heteronormativity. *Gender & Society, 24*, 167–188.
2. Herz, M., & Johansson, T. (2015). The normativity of the concept of heteronormativity. *Journal of Homosexuality, 62*(8), 1009–1020.
3. Ward, J. (2009). The reaches of heteronormativity: An introduction. *Gender & Society, 23*, 433–439.
4. Bauermeister, J., Connochie, D., Jadwin-Cakmak, L., & Meanley, S. (2017). Gender policing during childhood and the psychological well-being of young adult sexual minority men in the United States. *American Journal of Men's Health, 11*(3), 693–701.
5. Hall, J., & LaFrance, B. (2012). 'That's gay': Sexual prejudice, gender identity, norms, and homophobic communication. *Communication Quarterly, 60*(1), 35–58.
6. Russell, S., & Fish, J. (2016). Mental health in lesbian, gay, bisexual, and transgender (LGBT) youth. *Annual Review of Clinical Psychology, 12*(1), 465–487.
7. Wilkinson, L., & Pearson, J. (2009). School culture and the well-being of same-sex-attracted youth. *Gender & Society, 23*, 542–568.
8. Centers for Disease Control and Prevention. (2020, April). *HIV and Youth*. www.cdc.gov/hiv/group/age/youth/index.html
9. Centers for Disease Control and Prevention. (2018). *HIV surveillance report, 2018 (Updated)* (vol. 31). www.cdc.gov/hiv/pdf/library/reports/surveillance/cdc-hiv-surveillance-report-2018-updated-vol-31.pdf

10. Centers for Disease Control and Prevention. (2019). *Youth risk behavior survey: Data summary & trend reports 2009–2019*. www.cdc.gov/hiv/pdf/library/reports/surveillance/cdc-hiv-surveillance-report-2018-updated-vol-31.pdf
11. Sutton, M., Lasswell, S., Lanier, Y., & Miller, K. (2014). Impact of parent-child communication interventions on sex behaviors and cognitive outcomes for Black/African-American and Hispanic/Latino Youth: A systematic review, 1988–2012. *Journal of Adolescent Health, 54*(4), 369–384.
12. Widman, L., Choukas-Bradley, S., Noar, S., Nesi, J., & Garrett, K. (2016). Parent-adolescent sexual communication and adolescent safer sex behavior. *JAMA Pediatrics, 170*(1), 52.
13. Flores, D., & Barroso, J. (2017). 21st century parent—child sex communication in the United States: A process review. *The Journal of Sex Research, 54*(4–5), 532–548.
14. Bronfenbrenner, U., & Morris, P.A. (2006). The bioecological model of human development. In R.M. Lerner (Eds.), *Handbook of child psychology* (pp. 793–828). John Wiley & Sons
15. Hobaica, S., Schofield, K., & Kwon, P. (2019). "Here's your anatomy . . . Good luck": Transgender individuals in cisnormative sex education. *American Journal of Sexuality Education, 14*(3), 358–387.
16. Rubinsky, V., & Cooke-Jackson, A. (2021). "It would be nice to know I'm allowed to exist": Designing ideal familial adolescent messages for LGBTQ women's sexual health. *American Journal of Sexuality Education*, 1–19.
17. Rodgers, S.M. (2017). Transitional age lesbian, gay, bisexual, transgender, and questioning youth: issues of diversity, integrated identities, and mental health. *Child and Adolescent Psychiatric Clinics, 26*(2), 297–309.
18. Higa, D., Hoppe, M., Lindhorst, T., Mincer, S., Beadnell, B., Morrison, D., Wells, E.A., Avry, T., & Mountz, S. (2014). Negative and positive factors associated with the well-being of lesbian, gay, bisexual, transgender, queer, and questioning (LGBTQ) youth. *Youth & Society, 46*, 663–687.
19. Killoren, S., & Roach, A. (2014). Sibling conversations about dating and sexuality: Sisters as confidants, sources of support, and mentors. *Family Relations, 63*(2), 232–243.
20. Kowal, A., & Blinn-Pike, L. (2004). Sibling influences on adolescents' attitudes toward safe sex practices. *Family Relations, 53*(4), 377–384.
21. Kosciw, J., Greytak, E., Giga, N., Villenas, C., & Danischewski, D. (2015). *The 2015 national school climate survey: The experiences of lesbian, gay, bisexual, transgender, and queer youth in our nation's schools*. GLSEN. https://files.eric.ed.gov/fulltext/ED574780.pdf
22. Sterzing, P., Ratliff, G., Gartner, R., McGeough, B., & Johnson, K. (2017). Social ecological correlates of polyvictimization among a national sample of transgender, genderqueer, and cisgender sexual minority adolescents. *Child Abuse & Neglect, 67*, 1–12.
23. Shilo, G., & Savaya, R. (2011). Effects of family and friend support on LGB youths' mental health and sexual orientation milestones. *Family Relations, 60*(3), 318–330
24. Snapp, S., Watson, R., Russell, S., Diaz, R., & Ryan, C. (2015). Social support networks for LGBT young adults: Low cost strategies for positive adjustment. *Family Relations, 64*(3), 420–430.
25. Hall, K., McDermott, J., Komro, K., & Santelli, J. (2016). The state of sex education in the United States. *The Journal of Adolescent Health, 58*(6), 595–597. The new source lists eleven states. They are California, Colorado, Connecticut, Delaware, Iowa, Maryland, New Jersey, New Mexico, Oregon, Rhode Island, Washington.
26. Demissie, Z., Brener, N., Mcmanus, T., Shanklin, S., Hawkins, J., & Kann, L. (2015). *School health profiles 2014: Characteristics of health programs among secondary schools*. Center for Disease Control and Prevention. www.cdc.gov/healthyyouth/data/pro-files/pdf/2014/2014_profiles_report.pdf.
27. Kosciw, J.G., Clark, C.M., Truong, N.L., & Zongrone, A.D. (2020). *The 2019 national school climate survey: The experiences of lesbian, gay, bisexual, transgender, and queer youth in our nation's schools*. A Report from GLSEN. Gay, Lesbian and Straight Education Network (GLSEN).

28. Newman, P., Fantus, S., Woodford, M., & Rwigema, M. (2018). 'Pray that God will change you': The religious social ecology of bias-based bullying targeting sexual and gender minority youth—A qualitative study of service providers and educators. *Journal of Adolescent Research, 33*(5), 523–548.
29. Quinn, K., & Dickson-Gomez, J. (2016). Homonegativity, religiosity, and the intersecting identities of young black men who have sex with men. *AIDS and Behavior, 20*(1), 51–64.
30. Smallwood, S., Spencer, M., Ingram, L., Thrasher, J., & Thompson-Robinson, M. (2017). Examining the relationships between religiosity, spirituality, internalized homonegativity, and condom use among black men who have sex with men in the deep south. *American Journal of Men's Health, 11*(2), 196–207.
31. Acosta, K.L. (2020). Religion in the Lives of LGBTQ-Parent Families. In A.E. Goldberg, & K. R. Allen (Eds.). *LGBTQ-Parent Families: Innovations in Research and Implications for Practice* (pp. 215–227). Springer.
32. Arrington-Sanders, R., Harper, G., Morgan, A., Ogunbajo, A., Trent, A., & Fortenberry, D. (2015). The role of sexually explicit material in the sexual development of same-sex-attracted black adolescent males. *Archives of Sexual Behavior, 44*(3), 597–608.
33. Nelson, K.M., Golden, M., & Nelson Glick, S. (2016). Measuring exposure to sexually explicit media among young men who have sex with men: A pilot study. *Sexual Health, 13*(1), 93–95.
34. Harper, G., Serrano, P., Bruce, D., & Bauermeister, J. (2016). The Internet's multiple roles in facilitating the sexual orientation identity development of gay and bisexual male adolescents. *American Journal of Men's Health, 10*(5), 359–376.
35. Nelson, K.M., Pantalone, D.W., & Carey, M.P. (2019). Sexual health education for adolescent males who are interested in sex with males: An investigation of experiences, preferences, and needs. *The Journal of Adolescent Health: Official publication of the Society for Adolescent Medicine, 64*(1), 36–42.
36. Nelson, K.M., & Carey, M.P. (2016). Media literacy is an essential component of HIV prevention for young men who have sex with men. *Archives of Sexual Behavior, 45*(4), 787–788.

4

MEMORABLE MESSAGES FOR MORE PRODUCTIVE FAMILY CONVERSATIONS WITH LGBTQ YOUTH

Valerie Rubinsky and Angela Cooke-Jackson

Family conversations, especially between parents and children, about dating relationships, reproductive health, sexual activity, sexual health, and sexuality lead to healthier attitudes and behaviors about those same subjects.[1,2] Despite the benefit of routinely talking about these subjects, many parents feel unprepared to engage their children and adolescents in such conversation. When families don't have ongoing conversations about sex, young people are likely to recall isolated and sometimes harmful messages in their place.[3,4] This is especially true for young lesbian, gay, bisexual, transgender, and queer (LGBTQ) women, who experience problematic messages about sex that most young people manage and messages that can make them feel bad about their emergent sexual or gender identities. In 2021, we published an article titled "It Would Be Nice to Know I'm Allowed to Exist: Designing Ideal Familial Adolescent Messages for LGBTQ Women's Sexual Health" in the *American Journal of Sexuality Education*.[5] This chapter will explain the background research that informed the study and discuss the study's findings in plain language. We will also explore why this type of research matters to sexuality educators.

Sex Talk Matters—Families Rarely Have It

Even though parents are ideal figures to guide their kids as they explore their sexuality, research shows that many parents are hesitant to talk to their kids about sex. Reviews of the research on parent-child communication about sex suggest that typical barriers, or reasons why parents avoid communicating with their children about sex, involve (1) their own limited sexual health knowledge, (2) false beliefs that adolescents are not ready for the talk, (3) personal discomfort, and (4) demographic and cultural factors.[1] Sexual communication researcher Amanda Holman

DOI: 10.4324/9781003189787-5

suggests that we consider not only why parents do not talk to their kids about sex but why they aren't talking about sex in-depth, effectively, or holistically.[6] Holman conducted an interview study to explore these barriers from the perspective of parents, finding that parents also note that they never had such conversations with their own parents and feel they lack accurate information. Specifically, Holman categorized the barriers to effective family sex talk as informational, emotional, or cultural. Similar to the barriers that other researchers[1] have described for avoiding *any* conversation about sex, Holman's study found that parents may not have *productive* conversations with their kids about sex because they don't know the information themselves, they find the conversations uncomfortable, they believe their kids would find them uncomfortable, or for reasons like religion and culture.

Sexual Health Communication for LGBTQ Adolescents

Previous research suggests that regardless of an adolescent's sexual or gender identity, they likely did not have very productive conversations with their parents about sex and sexual health. In addition to these generally ineffective or altogether absent conversations, young people who identify as LGBTQ have to navigate how these same messages erase, contradict, or criticize their emergent identities.[7] Previous research has considered the specific parent-child conversations that gay, bisexual, or queer (GBQ) male adolescents recall. Findings from that study report that similar to the general population, conversations occur sparingly, but when they do, they tend to perpetuate heteronormativity and stereotype GBQ people.[8] Heteronormativity is an ideological assumption that heterosexuality is the natural, normal, and desired state. Heteronormative messages are broadly harmful to people regardless of their sexual or gender identity but may be especially harmful to people whose experiences do not align with heterosexuality, like queer youth.[3,4]

Memorable Messages About Sex

In the absence of more holistic conversations about sex, young people may recall specific, isolated moments, comments, or even the fact that no conversation at all took place.[9] Because parents don't talk to their children and adolescents about sex in ongoing ways that promote a culture of dialogue, young people *really* hang on to whatever was or wasn't said. These messages become "sticky" and influential in sometimes problematic ways. These messages tend to be common among people of similar age or cultural demographics. For instance, if you ask most cisgender women between 18 and 30 to recall the message from their youth about sex or sexual health that stuck with them over time, they will likely report "Use a condom"; "Don't have sex until marriage"; "Sex is dangerous"; or other messages about sustaining purity.[9,4] Communication scientists call these kinds of messages that are long-lasting and influential *memorable messages*.[10]

Memorable messages are typically defined as any type of communication that someone recalls or remembers for a long period of time and believes has been influential in some way.[11] They can take a number of forms, including verbal messages (e.g., a phrase, use of language, advice, a conversation), nonverbal (e.g., a mean look, not feeling listened to), or even the absence of any message at a time when communication was needed. Although they are most effective when delivered interpersonally in face-to-face settings,[12] research finds that they occur in a number of communication modes and contexts, including through books, blogs, or mediated communication like texts or emails.[11] Memorable messages most often come from an important other like a parent, teacher, partner, or close friend.[11] Memorable messages are critical because they influence how a person feels about themselves, they influence how individuals develop and assess their identities, they influence the relationship between the sender and receiver of the message, and they can predict attitudes and behaviors about sex.[11]

Over the last few years, our research lab has studied the forms and functions of memorable messages, specifically about intimacy and intimate health. Although not all memorable messages are negative, and early memorable message research focused more on positive and encouraging messages that people are likely to recall from influential others,[13,14] in the context of sex, sexuality, and sexual health, we find in most situations people recall a variety of negative and harmful memorable messages.[15] Memorable messages about sex, sexuality, and dating are often fear- and shame-based, encourage abstinence and purity, and promote traditional gender roles.[11,4,16]

At best, these messages fail to provide practical *or* emotional support for navigating changing bodies and desires and early relationships.[17] At worst, these messages tell young people to be ashamed of their bodies and desires, encourage dangerous and problematic practices, and maintain a cycle of trauma in sexual navigation. This may be because memorable messages are often a form of anticipatory socialization.[14,18] *Anticipatory socialization* occurs when we receive messages that prepare us for something to happen in the future. One study that we conducted about six years ago found that messages LGBTQ women recall about sex and sexuality normalize rape as a part of the female experience.[3] In the same study, the most common themes among LGBTQ women's memorable messages about sex and sexuality were that homosexuality is wrong or doesn't exist, or that sex is for men and women don't enjoy sex.[3] Rather than messages that promote agency and empowerment, these particularly harmful memorable messages serve to prepare young women and girls for a sexual experience in which they will not have agency. Rather than messages that explore the diversity of sexualities and genders and the many healthy avenues toward intimacy and fulfilling relationships, these messages tell young LGBTQ women that anything other than heterosexual experience is invalid and wrong. In addition to doing harm, fear and shame messages are ineffective at accomplishing their intended goals in the context of sexual communication.[19]

Another emerging line of research has explored the potential for memorable messages to be interrupted. In line with our lab's work on memorable messages, we have proposed the Theory of Memorable Messages (ToMM). ToMM formalizes what researchers have observed in four decades of studying the construct: (1) memorable messages are long-lasting and influential; (2) they take a number of forms; (3) they influence both how we form our identities and how we evaluate them; and (4) they influence the messages we send to others.[11,10] Since working with this theory, we have observed that although many people recall and experience harm from early ineffective memorable messages, they also recognize those messages *as* harmful.[10] For example, someone might note that their memorable message was "sex is bad" but acknowledge that this wasn't a good message to receive. In addition, people can articulate what messages would have been better to receive in place of the ones that they did.

These designed messages, which we term *ideal memorable messages*, can lay the groundwork for what kinds of conversations are most appropriate and what kinds of messages parents may want to prioritize. It was with this in mind that we conducted this research study, asking the research question: "What messages do LGBQ women and people of diverse genders wish they had received in place of existing memorable messages about intimate health?"[5]

Research Methodology and Summary of Findings

Methods

In our article, we used a survey methodology. A survey method assesses attitudes, beliefs, and behaviors among some sample of people. Our survey was a part of a larger study looking at sexual communication behaviors among women and people who were assigned female at birth. The data presented in this article broke apart a particular set of questions from that survey and pulled the participants who identified as LGBTQ. Participants were asked to reflect on their early conversations with their parents and family system about sexual and reproductive health. Then, specifically, participants answered this question:

> Please think, as an adult, if there are any conversations or messages you wish had been present during these early conversations about sexual and/or reproductive health, but were not? That is, if you could design any message to hear from your family as a child and/or adolescent about sexual and/or reproductive health, what would it be?[5]

Of the larger survey, 103 LGBTQ women or people of marginalized genders responded to that question. They were between 18 and 45, with an average age of about 27, and were mostly white. About half of the sample were cisgender women, with the other half identifying under the transgender or nonbinary umbrellas. Sexual orientations included gay, lesbian, bisexual, pansexual, asexual, and queer; some transgender participants identified as heterosexual.[5]

To analyze this data, we conducted a kind of thematic analysis. Thematic analysis is a data analysis technique for drawing conclusions from qualitative data, which is data that is not numeric. That is, we read over participants' open-ended responses, which were sometimes a short sentence and sometimes a few paragraphs in length, and assessed the common themes among these responses.

Findings—Constructing Ideal Familial Memorable Messages About Sexual Health

Themes from this data suggest that ideal memorable messages about sexual health from parents to adolescent LGBTQ women would be (1) positive, affirming, and validating; (2) contain practical information; and (3) prioritize pleasure. Most participants identified parents as the appropriate source of these messages and wanted, more so than isolated messages, an ongoing and open dialogue that was supportive and warm. However, some of our participants did note that they would prefer these messages, although similar in content, to come from the school system, as they believed their parents were likely misinformed and would be an "awkward" message source. These were relatively rare in this data set.

First, ideal sexual health messages are positive in tone and directly validating and affirming of diverse sexual and gender identities. That is, our participants identified wanting to hear that LGBTQ people exist, that there are many ways to do relationships and have sex, and that no matter whatever way ended up being their way, their parents would love and support them.[5] Recall our earlier discussion of how memorable messages often function as a form of anticipatory socialization—telling people what to expect in the future. In this way, participants embrace that function of memorable messages—they did want messages that prepare them for their sexual lives and identities. However, rather than being prepared for a sexuality that would be rejected and a body that would be harmed, they wanted to be prepared to be loved, validated, and accepted no matter how they ultimately identified.[5] Beyond the findings from this particular study, we see this theme in much of our research. In our perspective, validation and support are the most vital aspects of these messages and, when done well, allow room for error in the other components.

Second, participants wanted what we broadly term "practical information." This includes practical information about the biomedical aspects of sex, development, and reproduction and practical information for navigating intimate relationships.[5] While some participants identified wanting messages that provided clinical information, more often than not, this theme was characterized by participants not wanting parents to know the clinical terminology or biological explanations for how menstruation, reproduction, or infections worked but rather that they would help their adolescent navigate those experiences. That is, young people wanted their parents to take them to a gynecologist or help them talk to a gynecologist. They wanted to be told it was okay to take contraceptives, provided options for doing so, and supported in the process. This point was especially common in this study and other research our lab conducts regarding contraception communication. In essence, participants wanted their parents to acknowledge that parents are gatekeepers. For most young people, parents are the means to access medical attention, medication, or funds for contraception. So, rather than parents being a point of explanation, they saw their parents as a point of access and would have preferred their parents embrace and explicitly acknowledge support for this role. For sexuality educators, this is an especially useful detail. Parents may feel pressure to know everything, but it might be more productive to teach them how to find information than what information is worth knowing.

In addition, this study found that young LGBTQ women desired more conversation surrounding how relationships function.[5] Largely, they wanted their parents, mostly their mothers, to share their own relational and sexual experiences—good and bad. For the most part, participants framed these desires as wanting to know what to expect as they moved through their own life stages, another anticipatory socialization function of memorable messages—people want to know what to expect and largely felt unprepared by the memorable messages they did receive.[5]

Third, our study found that participants did want a more explicit discussion of the "fun" parts of sex from their parents.[5] They wanted specifically some discussion surrounding masturbation, discussions of female pleasure (messages that counter the cultural messages of "women don't enjoy sex"), and encouragement that sex was not supposed to be shameful. Generally, participants alluded to general societal messages (e.g., from media, friends, other members of the family system) that treat sex as something not "for" women. Participants wanted their parents to help them prepare to reject these messages by encouraging them to consider and prioritize their own pleasure, and at minimum, emphasize that masturbation is okay, and that sex is supposed to feel good.

Key Takeaways

There are two conclusions that we believe are especially critical for sexuality education. First, there is a need for home-focused sexuality education, and parents are part of that target audience. Regardless of what kids are learning at school or from their doctor, parents are a part of their sexual socialization, and an influential part at that. Second, parents can take a breath. At the end of the day, adolescents did not need their parents to be clinical experts, but rather they wanted them to provide a support system as they grow into their sexual identities and begin navigating more adult relationships. We offer several key recommendations from this and related research on the subject:

1. Parents should acknowledge that LGBTQ people exist to their children and that there are many ways to have relationships. Further, they should explicitly tell their children, even if they assume their child is heterosexual, that they will be loved and supported by their family no matter how they identify with or express their gender or sexuality.
2. They should maintain ongoing conversations about reproductive health, sex, sexual health, and sexuality. Young people don't want one memorable message; they want dialogue and a space where they feel comfortable being vulnerable and sharing parts of themselves. This is not accomplished through one weighted talk but rather by ongoing conversations over the course of years.
3. Parents and guardians are gatekeepers between adolescents and many of their sexual and reproductive health needs. Young people appreciate parents acknowledging and embracing this role. By that, we mean that it may be effective for parents to say outright that they can take their child to a gynecologist or help them decide which gynecologist they might want to see. Young people want their parents to say they will help them acquire preferred contraceptives and help them find one that meets their needs. They want these acknowledgments to be common and free of judgment and shame. In addition, they desire an ongoing reminder that parents are available not only as someone who prevents them from acquiring their needs but as someone who will help them navigate these sometimes complicated choices (and, of course, give them a ride and financial help as needed).
4. It's okay to share stories—good and bad. Many of our participants highlighted that they wanted to know more about how relationships developed across the lifespan so that they can be aware of what to expect at different life stages. They also noted that it would be especially helpful if parents provided this information in the form of stories rather than lectures or advice. Sharing relational experiences with their kids, good and bad, helps explain relational development without giving advice that can sometimes feel shaming and dismissive.

Future Directions and Conclusion

Our research found common themes among the conversations and messages that LGBTQ women would have preferred hearing from their family systems during adolescence. Those themes suggest that messages should be (1) positive, (2) affirming gender and sexual diversity, (3) free of shame and judgment, and (4) helpful to young people learning about their bodies and developing relationships.[5] Importantly, the messages did not have to be filled with specific clinical information but instead provided a space for conversation and curiosity, free of judgment and/or assumptions of promiscuity. Young people wanted their parents to be navigators—in partnership with sex and sexuality education and practitioners—not necessarily to have all the answers themselves.

Future Directions for Memorable Message Research

We are interested in two new directions for ToMM. First, we are interested in how new memorable messages disrupt old ones. What we have termed *message disruption*[10] is a phenomenon that takes place when a new memorable message contradicts or overrules an old one. For example, as a child, someone might hear that "homosexuality is a sin" and internalize that as a memorable message. But, as an adult, life shifts, events and situations change, bringing maturity and a new perspective. The old messages are disrupted by new messages. For example, that same person might join a community that celebrates the diversity of people's sexualities. The messages they receive now contradict each other, and the new one can disrupt or problematize the old one. We commonly observe this and believe that understanding what kinds of messages are so meaningful that they can disrupt deeply ingrained ones will help educators craft the kinds of curricula that reach people no matter where they are.

Another future direction for ToMM is exploring the generational nature of memorable messages and how messages become repeated or altered between generations. Earlier research has found that folks tend to transmit similar messages that they heard themselves about love and relationships.[20] We are currently furthering this by considering the trigenerational (three-generation) family communication about intimate health in Latina and Latinx families. Much memorable message research explores the messages people between 18 and 30 remember receiving in childhood and adolescence. Our research is useful because it allows one to learn more about older adults and how they think about sexual health. It also provides insight into where they received their memorable messages and if and how they are passed onto young adults and adolescents within family systems and kinship relationships—from one generation to another generation.

Takeaways for Sexuality Educators

Our study and the body of research around memorable messages and sex suggest a few ways that this work might benefit sex and sexuality educators. First, sexuality educators must be comfortable moving between simple messages to more complex ones. Listening and being responsive to young people is critical. There is no one size fits all. Maturity happens on different levels and in different ways for emerging young adults. We recommend providing a range of opportunities to have conversations that feel safe and genuine and transparent. If working with parents, this again reflects the importance of acknowledging their role as a gatekeeper by paying attention, asking open-ended questions, and giving space for conversations.

Families and caregivers need to understand that curiosity about sex does not equate to sexual activity. It is essential to help them recognize that for some young adults, curiosity may be nothing more than curiosity. We often miss opportunities to talk or offer resources because we (mistakenly) believe curiosity is the gateway to sexual promiscuity. We must be careful of this assumption and misinterpretation of a young person's interest in sexual health. Start with open-mindedness and curiosity, and meet the young person where they are, which is far more valuable toward understanding them.

One major takeaway from our study was that young people understand that adults are gatekeepers in their lives. This might be because of your title, your position in the school system, the role you hold as their teacher, and so on. You must acknowledge that this expected role is yours whether you want to be seen that way or not. It is important to acknowledge this role, have healthy conversations, provide adequate materials and resources, and set clear boundaries. We know from the research that if you do not function in the role of the gatekeeper, something or someone else will. This often comes in the form of their peer group or information from digital platforms, which they have in abundance.

It is critical that sexuality educators help adolescents and emerging young adults be smart, critical consumers of media.[21] We see more and more that early intervention programs in media literacy are transformative for young adults and provide a sense of agency over behavioral habits.[22] For example, in an all-male focus group of 15- to 17-year-olds, participants were asked where they learned about sex.[21] While a few stated they learned about sex from school sexuality education or their parents, without hesitation, the majority stated "from pornography." Sexuality educators must understand that media consumption has shifted exponentially over the past two decades, while education around how to consume media has not kept track of the range of content that has emerged. It is imperative that we as gatekeepers help adolescents and teens develop critical thinking skills and the ability to discern, find, evaluate, and interpret quality media content, especially on sex and sexuality. This doesn't mean they will not engage with poorly curated content, but it can mean that when and if they do, they will understand what they are seeing and how to process and/or disregard that content. This developmental process gives them a robust and comprehensive sexual health tool kit for developing their bodies, puberty, reproductive health, and the numerous other aspects that impact one's sexuality.

Finally, it seems basic, but we must encourage parents and kinship members to create and maintain open conversations in the household that are candid, honest, fun, and—yes—normal. Our adolescents and teens have powerful instincts, which can be easily dismantled if not respected. Our goal is to help them learn how to discern honest and trustworthy people and keep those quality family members, friends, and mentors around them during their formative years.

We should also work to ensure that in school and at home, they can engage in open conversations to increase agency.

To conclude, the work might seem herculean, but if done over time, at younger ages, and in collaboration with families and kinship relationships, we can see young adults emerge who are better decision-makers, better consumers of media, who have a more comprehensive perspective on their bodies and sexual health, and who have more fluid understanding of sexuality and relationship construction.

References

1. Flores, D., & Barroso, J. (2017). 21st century parent—child sex communication in the United States: A process review. *The Journal of Sex Research, 54*(4–5), 532–548. http://doi.org/10.1080/00224499.2016.1267693
2. Mustanski, B., & Hunter, J. (2012). Parents as agents of HIV prevention for gay, lesbian, and bisexual youth. In W. Pequegnat, & C. Bell (Eds.), *Family and HIV/AIDS*. Springer. https://doi.org/10.1007/978-1-4614-0439-2_12
3. Rubinsky, V., & Cooke-Jackson, A. (2016). "Where is the love?" Expanding and theorizing with LGBTQ memorable messages of sex and sexuality. *Health Communication, 32,* 1472–1480. http://doi.org/10.1080/10410236.2016.1230809
4. Rubinsky, V., & Cooke-Jackson, A. (2017). Tell us something other than to use a condom and that sex is scary: Memorable messages women and gender minorities wish for and recall about sexual health. *Women's Studies in Communication, 40*, 379–400. http://doi.org/10.1080/07491409.2017.1368761
5. Rubinsky, V., & Cooke-Jackson, A. (2021). "It'd be nice to know I'm allowed to exist": Designing ideal familial adolescent messages for LGBTQ women's sexual health. *American Journal of Sexuality Education, 16*(2), 221–237. https://doi.org/10.1080/15546128.2021.1880346%20.
6. Holman, A. (2021). "Why don't all parents talk about this stuff": Informational, emotional, and cultural barriers to meaningful parent-child conversations about sex. In A. Cooke-Jackson, & V. Rubinsky (Eds.), *Communicating intimate health* (pp. 19–32). Lexington Books.
7. Malacane, M., & Beckmeyer, J.J. (2016). A review of parent-based barriers to parent—adolescent communication about sex and sexuality: Implications for sex and family educators. *American Journal of Sexuality Education, 11*(1), 27–40. http://doi.org/10.1080/15546128.2016.1146187
8. Flores, D.D., Meanley, S.P., Bond, K.T., Agenor, M., Relf, M.V., & Barroso, J.V. (2020). Topics for inclusive parent-child sex communication by gay, bisexual, queer youth. *Behavioral Medicine*, 1–10. http://doi.org/10.1080/08964289.2019.1700481
9. Holman, A., & Koenig Kellas, J. (2018). "Say something instead of nothing": Adolescents' perceptions of memorable conversations about sex-related topics with their parents. *Communication Monographs, 85*(3), 357–379. http://doi.org/10.1080/03637751.2018.1426870
10. Cooke-Jackson, A., & Rubinsky, V. (2021). Theory of memorable messages: Theorizing message disruption. In A. Cooke-Jackson, & V. Rubinsky (Eds.), *Communicating intimate health* (pp. 89–98). Lexington Books.
11. Cooke-Jackson, A., & Rubinsky, V. (2017). Deeply rooted in memories: 30 years of memorable message research. *Health Communication, 33*, 409–422. http://doi.org/10.1080/10410236.2016.1278491
12. Miczo, N., Danhour, E., Lester, K.E., & Bryant, J. (2013). Memorable messages and the H1N1 flu virus. *Western Journal of Communication,* 77(5), 625–644. http://doi.org/10.1080/10570314.2013.776099
13. Knapp, M.L., Reardon, K.K., & Stohl, C. (1981). "Memorable" messages. *Journal of Communication, 31*, 27–41. http://doi.org/10.111/j.1460-2466.1981.tb00448.x.

14. Stohl, C. (1986). The role of memorable messages in the process of organizational socialization. *Communication Quarterly, 34*(3), 231–249. http://doi.org/10.1080/01463378609369638
15. Gunning, J., Cooke-Jackson, A., & Rubinsky, V. (2019). Negotiating shame, silence, abstinence, and period sex: Women's shift from harmful memorable messages about reproductive and sexual health. *American Journal of Sexuality Education, 15*, 111–137. http://doi.org/10.1080/15546128.2019.1669511
16. Heisler, J.M. (2014). They need to sow their wild oats: Mothers' recalled memorable messages to their emerging adult children regarding sexuality and dating. *Emerging Adulthood, 2*(4), 280–293. https://doi.org/10.1177/2167696814550196
17. Rubinsky, V., Gunning, J., & Cooke-Jackson, A. (2020). "I thought I was dying": (Un)Supportive communication surrounding early menstruation experiences. *Health Communication, 35*, 242–252. http://doi.org/10.1080/10410236.2018.1548337
18. Dallimore, E.J. (2003). Memorable messages as discursive formations: The gendered socialization of university faculty. *Women's Studies in Communication, 26*. http://doi.org/10.1080/07491409.2003.10162460
19. Noland, C.M. (2010). *Sex talk: The role of communication in intimate relationships*. Praeger.
20. Koenig Kellas, J.K. (2010). Transmitting relational worldviews: The relationship between mother—daughter memorable messages and adult daughters' romantic relational schemata. *Communication Quarterly. 8*(4), 458–479. http://doi.org/10.1080/01463373.2010.525700
21. Cooke-Jackson, A., & Ringiewicz, A. (2016). *#RealTalk* Beta: A digital mosaic of insights and advice on sexual health from real teens. *Media Education Research Journal, 7*, 1.
22. Cooke-Jackson, A. (2015). Calling Dr. Google: Health literacy and media agency for at-risk urban youth. In J. Yamaskai, P., Geist-Martin, & B.F. Sharf (Eds.), *Communicating health: Personal, cultural, and political complexities* (pp. 120–122). Waveland Press Inc.

5

PROTECTING CHILDREN FROM SEXUAL ABUSE

Mixed Messages and Cultural Challenges

Kathleen P. Allen, Jennifer A. Livingston and Amanda B. Nickerson

CSA Protection and Prevention

Parents and educators are well situated to protect children from child sexual abuse (CSA) and, as such, are logical targets for CSA prevention programming. One such program is the Child Protection Unit (CPU), developed by the Committee for Children to be implemented by parents and school-based educators. We were engaged by the Committee for Children to evaluate this program. Focus group interviews were held separately with parents to discuss their responses to four educational videos and with educators to assess their experiences teaching the CPU.[1,2] The goal of these focus groups was to gain insight into participants' perceptions of the intervention materials and understand their perspectives on teaching children about sexual abuse and personal safety. The detailed findings specific to these focus groups have been reported elsewhere.[1,2] For this chapter, we re-examine two of the primary themes and issues raised in the focus groups that have implications for sexual abuse prevention programming in general: (1) confusing messages about sexual abuse prevention education for children and (2) challenges to protection as faced by parents because of racism, poverty, and sexism. We then build upon this prior work by offering new directions for sexual abuse prevention.

Confusion About Educating Children about CSA

Safety Messages and Confusion

Conventional sexual abuse prevention education teaches children rules about touching that focus on safe, unsafe, and unwanted touches.[2] Unsafe touches are generally considered to include aggressive behaviors (e.g., hitting, kicking,

DOI: 10.4324/9781003189787-6

punching, slapping) and touching private body parts, which are covered by a bathing suit. The CPU lessons locate private body parts between a child's legs and, in the case of females, the vicinity of the chest, primarily the nipples. The euphemism "private body parts" thus refers to different things depending on whether the child is a boy or girl because a bathing suit does not cover boys' nipples. Teachers are encouraged to use anatomically correct terms for genitalia but are not required to do so.

Early proponents of CSA prevention education noted that the underlying messages implicit in the rules about touching are inherently negative. One problem is that not naming the genitalia with anatomically correct terms sends the message that something is wrong with these parts and that they may be "bad" or "dirty." Another is that a one-piece bathing suit suggests that the stomach area is a "private" body part on a girl but not on a boy. Confusion also arises when a girl's breasts are deemed private but not a boy's. A "titty-twister" (pinching the nipple between the thumb and forefinger and twisting the skin) to a boy is invasive and hurtful, even if it is meant to be playful. If someone gives a girl a titty-twister, is it sexual abuse, but not when it's done to a boy?

Children are taught that no one should touch their "private body parts," except a parent or a doctor, for the purpose of keeping them healthy. These messages are often first extended to children during well-child visits to the pediatrician in the presence of the child's parent/guardian. However, these rules about parents and physicians come with inconsistencies that generate confusion. As one parent noted in a focus group evaluating CSA prevention videos for parents, the doctor said "no one should touch your private body parts" to her daughter without any qualifications, then attempted to examine the child's genitalia. The child promptly responded to the doctor's attempt by saying, "But you just said no one can touch me there."

In addition to being confusing, the private body parts rules and exceptions do not address the problem that some parents and doctors sexually abuse children. How are young children supposed to know the difference between a safe or unsafe touch to their "private body parts" from a parent or physician even if it does appear to qualify as being needed for the child's health? In addition, children often need help cleaning their genitalia as they go through toilet training and beyond. Children as old as 5 may genuinely need help from a parent with bathing or toileting as they may not be capable of adequate hygiene. Similarly, people with disabilities depend on assistance from aides to perform all forms of hygiene throughout their lives. These situations may be opportunities that an adult uses to molest a child, which can be misinterpreted or excused as an appropriate touch to assist with hygiene.

Messages about touches involving the mouth, including kissing, are often missing from discussions or rules about private body parts. Certainly, kissing, hugging, and handholding are ways of showing affection as a normal and important component of human development. The problem for children is that they are expected to develop a sense of appropriate touch that is normatively affectionate yet within the bounds of appropriate displays of affection between adults and children, and children and other children. This can be quite difficult for most children, making them vulnerable to sexual contact disguised as appropriately affectionate touch. Situations like this illustrate the confusion and ambiguity around CSA prevention messages and the difficulty of qualifying what is and what is not abusive.

An additional complication with the rules about touching and private body parts is that abusers often trick children into posing for nude pictures or watching pornography. These activities may not involve any kind of touching at all yet become part of the grooming process for future sexual contact. Children who are very literal may not think of these interactions as inappropriate if they are conducted with a favorite adult who rewards silence and secrecy with gifts. Additionally, children can experience sexual arousal when watching pornography or being touched. Children may experience guilt or shame when these experiences produce pleasant sensations, and following disclosure, they need to be reassured that they are not responsible for the violation—the perpetrator is.

Not only are the rules about touching confusing, but they may also have unintended negative consequences. These rules do not address children's natural curiosity about their bodies and those of their peers, including interest in genitalia. The rule that "no one should ever touch" implies that later sexual contact is prohibited and bad. In other words, "never means never"; thus, sexual activity, whatever it might mean in the mind of a child, is a bad thing. Unfortunately, no longitudinal data on the long-term effects of CSA prevention education exist to address the possibility of negative outcomes on sexual intimacy. The challenge of imparting accurate and helpful information that ensures safety in unambiguous ways is complicated.

Safety Education

Safety education seeks to prevent harm to children in its many manifestations, including CSA. The materials evaluated in this research included environmental safety concerns such as crossing the street, wearing a bike helmet or a seat belt, ingesting substances that might be poison, animal/pet safety, gun safety, and fire safety.[3] Avoiding injury is often connected to rules about asking adults for permission/help, paying attention to uncomfortable feelings, and saying "no" to dangerous situations.[3] Thus, in the context of safety education, body safety is one facet.

In their advocacy for CSA prevention, the American Academy of Pediatrics recommends that children be taught the correct anatomical terms for their genitalia from the time they are learning to talk. This recommendation is made because it eliminates much of the confusion about safety messages inherent in rules that use euphemisms. Pediatricians support this type of straightforward discussion because it eliminates confusion if a child needs to describe inappropriate or abusive touch. It also normalizes these body parts and removes feelings of guilt or shame children might develop about their genitalia.[4]

Cultural and Structural Challenges in CSA Prevention Education

With the aid of community partners (e.g., YMCA, child advocacy centers), we conducted 24 focus groups with parents from four different regions in the United States (northeast, southeast, west, southwest). Of these 24 groups, 21 were conducted in working- and middle-class communities. We were also invited to conduct three groups in low-income housing communities in the southeastern US. This offered a unique opportunity to hear the voices of parents who are often excluded from research studies. Parents in all groups viewed the family video materials and provided feedback about the videos, their messaging, and their perspectives on CSA prevention programming in general. As reported,[1,2] the *Second Step* CPU materials were well received by working- and middle-class parents but not those located in low-resourced communities, where people live in inexpensive or subsidized housing and need supplemental sources of free food.

The challenges of protecting children were amplified in these three groups compared to other focus groups conducted in communities that were less segregated and better resourced. Unlike most groups, issues of structural racism, poverty, sexism, and traumatic sexual histories loomed over women's efforts to keep children safe.

Structural Racism

Two of the three focus groups were held in predominantly Black communities. Participants were female except for one man in each focus group. The women were remarkably candid about their reasons for participating. They talked about their own experiences with CSA and how they wanted to keep these wrongs from being repeated with their beloved children and grandchildren. Yet, from the stories that unfolded, it became clear that structural racism was a deeply rooted factor in keeping them trapped in cycles of intergenerational abuse.

Historically, the African American man has been the target of systemic violence and imprisonment,[5] which has led to African American families being anchored and raised by Black women.[5] Several participants' experiences mirrored the research literature that describes the culture of secrecy whereby Black women must not disclose their abuse or the abuser for fear that the results will be deadly violence against the perpetrator and incarceration for his killer.[6] This dynamic ensures that Black women remain silent about their own abuse so as not to shoulder the responsibility of losing Black men to violence and jail.[5,6,7]

The Role of Poverty

Poverty is a risk factor for multiple negative outcomes, including continued poverty, exploitation, and abuse.[8] Children who live in poverty and experience CSA or other forms of abuse are significantly more likely to continue to be abused and have worse life outcomes than children who do not grow up in poverty.[9] One of the characteristics of families that live in poverty that increases the risk of CSA is the constant chaos and disorder of daily life. A chaotic home environment makes it easier for abusers to take advantage of a mother beset by multiple daily problems, responsibilities, and demands.[10] It also increases the chances that child protective services will become involved in these families' lives.

Participants in our low-resourced focus groups indicated that they distrust law enforcement and child support services because they fear these entities will look for and find reasons to remove their children from their homes.[2] Because of this, they are hesitant to ask for help or report abuse when it occurs. This fear also promotes silence and secrecy when it comes to educating children by giving them explicit body safety information. For cultural, social, or religious reasons, children having knowledge about anything sexual is taboo and dangerous for low-resourced families because it may be construed as a sign of having been abused.[2]

Sexism and Traumatic Sexual Histories

Women disproportionally carry the burden of protecting their children from CSA. This responsibility is connected to long-held sexist views about the designated role of women as childcare providers in society. When children are abandoned, abused, injured, neglected, or poorly monitored, their mothers are blamed, often without consideration of the structural roadblocks many of these women face. These challenges include poor education, low-paying/nonexistent jobs, inadequate childcare, lack of family support and transportation, and poor/inaccessible medical care. Women are held accountable for not leaving dangerous relationships instead of blaming the men for their abusive, exploitive behavior. Ironically, this makes it easier for men to trap vulnerable women and children into these dependent situations because severing the relationship and notifying authorities brings more shame and blame on the mother.[11]

Many of the women we interviewed in these three focus groups alluded to or openly described their own childhood sexual abuse. The stories seemed to tap into traumatic memories of painful experiences that were still unresolved. As childcare providers, they wanted to find out how to prevent what had happened to them from happening to their children or grandchildren. They intuitively sensed that their own histories of victimization had left them vulnerable, and they wanted it to be different for the children in their care.

Improving CSA Prevention Education for All Children

What Should the Messages Be?

Teaching children to be safe from unwanted or unsafe touching of any kind, including CSA, requires support for comprehensive and unambiguous body safety education. Changing the practices by which we educate children to be safe and have healthy sexual lives is vital to successful human development. This means talking to children about their bodies early in life. When speaking to children—even babies—parents and pediatricians must name body parts including genitalia with accurate, anatomically correct terms: anus, breasts, penis, scrotum, vagina, and vulva. This does not mean describing sexual behaviors; it means naming these parts without embarrassment, fear, or suggestions that they are bad or dirty, and doing it often enough so that neither children nor adults are uncomfortable. One parent commented that if you talk to your child about why they shouldn't wear flip-flops when riding a bike and why they should wear a helmet when biking, then you should be able to talk about sexual abuse, as "It's another facet of safety."

Children must be taught that they have control over their bodies, and if they feel uncomfortable with the way anyone touches them or violates their boundaries, they must say so to that person and talk to a trusted and accessible adult about it. This is essentially an issue of consent, a concept closely linked to sexual activity, but one that needs to be developed for children in a much broader sense. In other words, when children are empowered to exercise consent regarding any kind of touch, they are in control of their bodies. As one teacher put it, "This is so important to be talking about, and we are really empowering our children."

The issue of consent and body integrity extends to affection and whether children have the freedom to accept or reject it. Our conversations with children can support a sense of body ownership coupled with discussions of how feelings help them recognize when that sense of ownership is breached; again, this broadly addresses the notion of consent. These conversations do not need to involve sexuality education explicitly, but when those discussions occur, the concept of consent will be readily available to children. Body safety education lays the foundation for successful sex education and promotes successful human development.

CSA perpetrators often tell children they are in trouble, that the abuse is their fault, that they must keep it a secret, and that no one will believe their story if they tell. Hence, parents/guardians need to tell their children that they will always believe them and they won't get in trouble even if the incident involves breaking a family or safety rule or divulging a secret. When children are honest, adults need to give reasonable consequences and discuss the situation calmly.

Half of CSA is perpetrated by individuals under age 18,[12] and being sexually abused as a child increases the risk of becoming an abuser.[13] Those who abuse report that abusing gives them a sense of power and control and that these actions make them feel affirmed.[12] One feature seldom addressed in CSA prevention education for parents, children, and educators is the possibility that safety messaging and sexuality education directed to those who might abuse others may support restraint or desisting abusive behavior. Adolescents who have been treated for sexual abuse offending indicate that learning about appropriate and healthy sexual behaviors, and learning about consent and each person's right to invoke consent, may have inhibited their inclination to act on sexually abusive behaviors.[13] Most abused children will never abuse others, but some will. Efforts to address CSA need to go beyond teaching children how not to become victims but also how to respect others' personal boundaries.[12,13]

Whom Do We Train and Educate?

Teaching children about sensitive subjects, especially ones that make adults uncomfortable, has generally been handed off to parents, pediatricians, and educators. While parents are often billed as the primary educators of children on topics such as CSA prevention or sexuality education, nothing requires them to do so. However, because the problems caused by CSA or lack of knowledge about sexuality fall to society to solve, professionals in the medical field and governmental entities have taken it upon themselves to insist on proactive efforts to educate parents and children on these subjects.

Parents

Most parents in our evaluation research acknowledged that it was their responsibility to keep their children safe from CSA, but a number of them described considerable barriers. We observed that some focus groups participants voiced mistaken ideas about CSA and children's natural sexual development and disagreed with the recommendations made in the educational videos. In at least one instance when this occurred, other parents provided accurate information and reassured their peers who disagreed with or were skeptical of the program content. Thus, trusted and knowledgeable parents can be a resource to challenge some of the barriers that less informed parents face.

Pediatricians

Physicians and public health professionals are unanimous in supporting CSA prevention education. Pediatric providers (i.e., pediatricians, nurse practitioners, physician's assistants) are well positioned to discuss normal sexual development and comprehensive body safety with parents and children beginning in infancy. Pediatric providers are often highly respected for their knowledge, skill, and professional status, increasing the likelihood of parents following their advice. Additionally, pediatric providers can mobilize their influence to promote government policies that advocate for universal, comprehensive body safety education. One challenge, however, is that doctor visits are short, and CSA is only one of several topics that providers need to address with parents. Hence, the discussion about preventing and recognizing CSA may be limited or not take place at all.

Educators

While schools have often been the focus of efforts to provide children with both CSA prevention education and sex education, their enthusiasm has not always been universal. However, educators today realize that adverse childhood experiences such as CSA and exposure to sexual violence negatively affect children's academic and social success in schools. While there is some apprehension among educators for comprehensive CSA prevention education, teachers and principals can support such efforts.[1] Again, however, time during the school day is limited, and CSA is one of several safety concerns that educators need to cover. They may also face backlash from some parents. Nevertheless, as a large constituency, educators can advocate for comprehensive body safety education because it improves children's chances for success in school.

Others

While parents, pediatricians, and educators can provide the necessary information to support children's sexual health and body safety, there are entities that exert significant influence on what is communicated to children, when it is communicated, and how it is communicated. These entities include politicians, law enforcement officers, child protective workers, mental health providers, and faith leaders. Politicians are the key to implementing sensible policies that can educate parents, children, and professionals, so efforts to effect change ultimately need to focus on legislative action. However, policy is driven by the voices of experts who can influence public opinion and exert pressure to bring about change. Law enforcement, physicians, mental health providers, child protective workers, and faith leaders all have multiple, large professional organizations through which they can exert influence on policy, perspectives, and practices.

What Do We Need to Change?

Challenge Structural Inequalities Based on Sex and Race

Sexist and racist stereotypes of women keep women trapped in abusive, desperate, and untenable situations which endanger their children. Regardless of race, women are often judged and blamed for their circumstances, while the men who fail to meet their spousal and parental obligations are exonerated. Stereotypes that reflect these racial and sexist judgments include the "welfare queen" who has too many children, the woman who is labeled "lazy" if she can't secure childcare so that she can work, and the woman who is "stupid" and "culpable" if she stays with an abusive partner. These sexist and racist stereotypes influence policy and need to be challenged by accurate information on why women make the choices they do.[14]

Challenge Assumptions

The thinking around who is responsible for CSA needs to move away from the sexist view that women must control men's sexual urges and behaviors. It is a fallacy that men sexually abuse children because they aren't "getting enough sex." Men and women who sexually abuse children are responsible for their behaviors. Until social norms put the blame squarely on the abuser, women will continue to struggle to keep their children safe. Additionally, society must acknowledge that poor people, particularly women, are not necessarily ignorant, lazy, or promiscuous. Rather, they are often trapped in poverty that is cyclical and generational. Stereotypes that blame women for circumstances they cannot change without help need to be challenged.

Build Trust

Women from socioeconomically disadvantaged backgrounds, of any ethnic or racial background, are often deeply suspicious of law enforcement, child protective services, and medical providers. This is because these are the people who often believe the stereotypes and will find a way to take their children away from them.[2] Another risk that many women speak of is the tendency of pedophiles to move into the very same low-income housing that is affordable to single mothers with limited incomes. Professionals who work with and offer support to these women should be especially cognizant of the risks children face in these communities and understand that mothers are not willingly complicit in their own children's abuse. Pedophiles not only groom children; they also groom their mothers.[11] Just as with children, abusers can be charming, generous with gifts and time, and appear to be quite trustworthy. They also are good at choosing vulnerable women. Efforts to build trust between protective agencies and community members may help those dealing with abuse to reach out for help without fear of reprisal.

Involve Men in Prevention

Men can help change the way we educate and protect children, but they often fear being accused of negative motives or inappropriate behaviors with children.[1,2] Men can help protect children by publicly taking a stand against CSA, inviting men to contribute to children's education on CSA prevention, and challenging other men to do the same. High-profile male public figures and respected experts can use their bully pulpit to put this need front and center. Men need to tell ***men*** to become full partners in protecting children.

Men need to challenge the heteronormative script that shames and blames women because it reinforces their need for silence and makes it harder for them to leave the men who abuse their children. Instead, men, particularly policy-makers, faith leaders, and high-profile celebrities, can advocate making more supports available to women. These include measures that make it economically and legally feasible for women to end relationships with fathers, stepfathers, and boyfriends who may seek revenge for their perceived betrayal by a mother.[11]

Talk to Children

Sexual predators themselves speak about what can be done to prevent CSA.[13–15] Perpetrators avoid children who have strong relationships with their parents. This supports the research that children who communicate well with their parents are less vulnerable to CSA.[16] Talking to children about sexuality and safety is a major factor in protecting youth, especially when these messages come from parents. When parents start talking to their children about sexual safety in positive and honest ways when they are very young, it lays the groundwork for a strong relationship where children delay the onset of sexual activity and are less likely to be manipulated into sex by others. They are also less likely to be sexually abused and more likely to disclose it to their parents. Caring parenting that fosters good communication may be the best CSA prevention possible.[16,17]

Conclusion

As a society, we need to do better for children. The cycle of child abuse, including CSA, is perpetuated by the persistent and often intergenerational repetition of sexual, physical, and emotional abuse and neglect that too many children experience. If we want our own children to be safe, we need to ensure the safety of all children. It means addressing the deep structural inequalities that keep women from under-resourced, marginalized, and isolated communities silent about their own and their children's CSA. It means stopping the ways that policies and norms punish women for not controlling the sexual behaviors of men. It requires that women be made aware of the misleading and inaccurate information they subscribe to that makes their children more vulnerable and less safe. It means changing our messages to children to receive information that respects their agency and facilitates their ability to develop into healthy, successful adults.

References

1. Allen, K.P., Livingston, J.A., & Nickerson, A.B. (2019). Child sexual abuse prevention education: A qualitative study of teachers' experiences implementing the Committee for Children's *Second Step* Child Protection Unit. *American Journal of Sexuality Education*. https://doi.org/10.1080/15546128.2019.1687382

2. Livingston, J.A., Allen, K.P., & Nickerson, A.B. (2020). A parental perspective on child sexual abuse prevention: Barriers and challenges. *Journal of Child and Family Studies*. https://doi.org/10.1007/s10826-020-01796-0
3. Committee for Children. (2014). *Second step child protection unit*. Author.
4. American Academy of Pediatrics. (n.d.). *Sexual abuse*. www.healthychildren.org/English/safety-prevention/at-home/Pages/Sexual-Abuse.aspx
5. Broussard, P.A. (2013). Black women's post-slavery silence syndrome: A twenty-first century remnant of slavery, Jim Crow, and systemic racism—who will tell her stories? *The Journal of Gender, Race & Justice, 16*, 373–421.
6. Long, L.L., & Ullman, S.E. (2013). The impact of multiple traumatic victimization on disclosure and coping mechanisms for Black women. *Feminist Criminology, 8*(4), 295–319. 10.1177/1557085113490783
7. Bell, E.L. (2004). Myths, stereotypes, and realities of Black women: A personal reflection. *The Journal of Applied Behavioral Science, 40*(2), 146–159. 10.1177/0021886304263852
8. Merrick, M.T., & Guinn, A.S. (2018). Child abuse and neglect: Breaking the intergenerational link." *American Journal of Public Health, 108*(9), 1117–1118. doi: 10.2105/AJPH.2018.304636
9. Oshima, K.M.M., Jonson-Reid, M., & Seay, K.D. (2014). The influence of childhood sexual abuse on adolescent outcomes: The roles of gender, poverty, and revictimization. *Journal of Child Sexual Abuse, 23*, 367–386. 10.1080/10538712.2014.896845
10. Grubesic, T.H., Murray, A.T., & Mack, E.A. (2008). Sex offenders, housing and spatial restriction zones. *GeoJournal, 73*, 255–269. 10.1007/s10708-008-9197-x
11. McLaren, H.J. (2013). (Un)-blaming mothers whose partners sexually abuse children: In view of heteronormative myths, pressures and authorities. *Child & Family Social Work, 18*, 439–448. 10.1111/j.1365-2206.2012.00863.x
12. McKibbin, G., Humphreys, C., & Hamilton, B. (2017). "Talking about child sexual abuse would have helped me": Young people who sexually abused reflect on preventing harmful behavior. *Child Abuse & Neglect, 70*, 210–221. https://doi.org/10.1016/j.chiabu.2017.06.017
13. Sullivan, J., & Sheehan, V. (2016). What motivates sexual abusers of children? A qualitative examination of the spiral of sexual abuse. *Aggression and Violent Behavior, 30*, 76–87. https://doi.org/10.1016/j.avb.2016.06.015
14. Windsor, L.C., Dunlap, E., & Golub, A. (2011). Challenging controlling images, oppression, poverty, and other structural constraints: Survival strategies among African-American women in distressed households. *Journal of African American Studies, 15*, 290–306. 10.1007/s12111-010-9151-0
15. Sprengelmeyer, M.E, & Vaughan, K. (2000, October 8). Stalking children. *Denver Rocky Mountain News*, pp. 5a, 41–45a.
16. Smith, S.G., & Cook, S.L. (2008). Disclosing sexual assault to parents: The influence of parental messages about sex. *Violence against Women, 14*(11), 1326–1348. 10.1177/1077801208325086
17. Longmore, M.A., Eng, A.L., Giordano, P.C., & Manning, W.D. (2009). Parenting and adolescents' sexual initiation. *Journal of Marriage and Family, 71*, 969–982.

6

"THERE HAS TO BE A REASON FOR DOING IT"

Emerging Adults' Insights and Explanations of Male Circumcision

Michelle M. Murray and Katherine R. Allen

Male circumcision has been occurring in nations around the world for centuries and is frequently practiced.[1] Globally, nearly 40% of boys 15 and younger are known to be circumcised, and these rates vary greatly based on ethnicity, race, region, religion, and socioeconomic status.[2] In the United States in 2010, an estimated 58% of newborn boys were circumcised in hospitals.[3] This percentage is well above the global estimates and does not account for boys circumcised in settings other than the hospital or circumcised older. Though it is still prevalent, circumcision rates in the United States are declining slowly[4,5] and have dropped from 65% in 1979.[3]

With over half of newborn boys being circumcised in hospitals,[3] it is safe to say that the procedure remains popular in the United States. Over half of parents participating in one study on circumcision reported they would choose circumcision if they had sons, and only about 25% would not due to the risks.[6] Parents choosing circumcision for their newborn sons cite a variety of reasons, including health risks and benefits, peer response, and father's circumcision status.[6,7] These decisions are largely made without discussion with doctors,[8] suggesting that opinions formed early in life could impact circumcision decisions and, in turn, influence rates of circumcision over time. This study aimed to explore perceptions of circumcision in the United States to understand what emerging adults know about the procedure, how they developed their opinions, and how they will apply this information in the future.

Ideas about male circumcision are often engrained in cultural beliefs,[9] which contribute to some variation in rates. Differences in rates of circumcision between racial and ethnic groups reflect that White, non-Hispanic men tend to be circumcised more often than Black, non-Hispanic men and that Mexican-Americans tend to be circumcised less often than either group.[4] Socioeconomic status may

DOI: 10.4324/9781003189787-7

also play a role in circumcision rates, as insurance coverage and cost could limit access for some.[10,11] There are also regional differences within the United States; rates of circumcision tend to be higher in the Midwest and Northeast and slightly lower in the South and West.[3]

These differences in rates likely impact how parents think about circumcision. Social factors may be just as influential, if not more influential than, as health factors when it comes to parents making circumcision decisions.[7] This indicates perceptions of others and predicted perceptions of circumcision status may mean more to parents than potential health risks and benefits.

Parents consider their future sons' self-image when deciding whether to circumcise.[7] Concerns about self-image could be justified, as circumcised teenage boys in one study said they were happier with their circumcision status than intact boys.[12] Another study refutes this finding, claiming that intact men were more satisfied with their penises.[13] However, when it comes to overall body image, circumcised and intact boys indicated similar satisfaction levels.[12] Though parents may have concerns about their sons' future self-esteem, it seems that opinions about one's own circumcision status have a greater impact on self-image than the actual circumcision status.[14]

Though circumcision involves the removal of foreskin and alteration of the penis, it is often considered to enhance masculinity rather than detract from it.[15] In one study, participants demonstrated how circumcision is closely linked to masculinity by reporting they felt more masculine and claiming improved sexual functioning after a voluntary adult circumcision, possibly due to the social meaning attributed to the procedure.[16] The social understanding of circumcision as a procedure that enhances sexual performance and masculinity shapes the way men view their gender and masculinity[17] and will certainly influence how they view circumcision. This could illuminate how circumcision became and has remained popular in a society where the penis is valorized. If the social process of circumcision is prevalent, men might define this process as one that helps them fit the masculine ideal.

Parents may be relying on their perceptions of circumcision, shaped through their social and cultural interactions, to make decisions about circumcising their sons rather than seeking out information about the procedure. Learning about and discussing circumcision is recommended before making decisions,[18] but few parents choose to talk about circumcision with their doctors.[8] Further, information about the procedure's risks and benefits does not seem to impact parents' decisions about circumcision.[19] This, as well as the findings that few parents state they are undecided about whether to circumcise,[8] means that parents may be making decisions based on their perceptions formed before they were expecting a son.

The topic of male circumcision garners strong responses, both for and against the procedure.[20,21] Advocates tout the potential health benefits of circumcision, such as the lowered risk of penile cancer, sexually transmitted infections, and urinary tract infections.[8] Opponents question the validity of findings indicating the health benefits of circumcision[22] and have stated that infant circumcision violates the infant's rights because he cannot consent to the procedure.[23] These polarizing views may impact how parents draw conclusions about circumcision and may garner some confusion about the facts of the procedure, as well as may make it difficult for them to make circumcision decisions for their sons.

Our Study

To explore emerging adults' perceptions on male circumcision, we asked undergraduate students enrolled in a human sexuality course to complete voluntary extra-credit assignments. Students enrolled in the course had attended a guest lecture on male anatomy given by a biology professor and were asked to read a textbook chapter on male anatomy, which contained the definition of male circumcision and a one-page passage on circumcision worldwide. All other information students referenced in their narratives was discovered outside the context of the course. Students would choose one of the prompts and write a one-page narrative using their own voices to earn extra credit. The prompt related to circumcision asked students to discuss their overall perspectives on male circumcision, as well as how they talk about circumcision with their peers and families. Participants were also asked to describe when they became aware of circumcision, whether they would circumcise their sons, and whether male participants were satisfied with their circumcision status.

Thirty-four students responded to this prompt, seven male and 27 female. None of the participating students identified as nonbinary. The average age of the students who responded was 20, though ages ranged from 18 to 23. The university Institutional Review Board, through which this study was approved, prohibited the collection of additional information about the participants' backgrounds, but the entire student body is made up of 72% White, 7% Asian, 4% African-American, 2% Hispanic, 2% International, less than 1% Native American, and 12% students of unknown races.

Both authors read and analyzed the 34 narratives, sorting information into categories to understand the consensus on participants' overall perspectives and responses to each of the questions asked in the prompts. We assigned each participant a pseudonym to protect their confidentiality. We sorted the information revealed by participants into five main themes: overall perceptions of circumcision, sources of knowledge, explanations of circumcision, justifications for circumcision, and would you circumcise your son.

Findings

Most students who participated in this study were either completely in favor or mostly in favor of circumcision. Twelve participants completely approved of circumcision, stating, "I believe males should be circumcised," and expressing no doubts about the procedure. Thirteen participants mostly agreed with circumcision while expressing some doubts or questions. "Belle" illustrated these doubts by writing, "On the contrary, when thinking about the actual procedure, it could be considered barbaric. When I think of female circumcision I believe that it is wrong. Which makes me think twice about my feelings about male circumcision."

Four participants, all female, expressed that they were unsure about whether they were in favor of circumcision. These participants acknowledged benefits and drawbacks of the procedure, and forming an opinion on circumcision was not needed at this point in their lives. This may indicate that some emerging adults do not feel the need to research and carefully consider circumcision until it impacts their lives.

Only five participants were against circumcision, with four female participants being mostly against circumcision and one male participant completely against it. Those mostly against circumcision shared major doubts about the procedure but shared certain circumstances in which they would consider it. "Isabel" conveyed, "I do not care how old you are, I could not imagine cutting off any part of me, especially in that area. It bothers me when parents do things that children should decide when they are older" and later stated, "The only good reason for circumcision is when it is done for hygienic reasons." "Ethan" described the procedure as "abhorrent" and posited, "one would think that parents who willfully mutilated their child or allowed someone else to do so by cutting off some part of the child's body would be arrested and charged with child abuse."

Sources of Knowledge

Most participants cited friends and family as sources of information about circumcision, with 24 saying they learned about circumcision from friends and 19 saying they learned about it from their families. Participants mentioned learning about circumcision through formal education settings; 16 reported they learned about the procedure in the human sexuality class they were taking when they wrote their narratives; and 13 stated they learned about circumcision in classes they took before coming to university. Four participants learned about circumcision through internet research, six through entertainment media, six through religious teachings, and 11 through personal experiences. Interestingly, eight participants stated they did not know much about circumcision when they wrote their narratives.

Seeking to Explain Circumcision

To understand how emerging adults form an overall perception of circumcision, we searched their narratives for information about how they explain the procedure. We categorized these explanations into four discourses revealing the participants' beliefs about circumcision. Every participant referenced at least one of these explanations in their narrative, signaling their pervasiveness among emerging adults. These are not exclusive categories; many participants used multiple explanations for circumcision in their narratives.

Cleanliness

Participants were very concerned about cleanliness and hygiene and used these concepts to explain circumcision in their narratives. Twenty-five participants mentioned cleanliness as an argument for circumcision, claiming that circumcision is "cleaner and healthier" and citing concerns about infections. "Kylie" wrote, "Some guys who are not circumcised do not properly care for the under portion of the foreskin and nasty bacterial growth occurs." The consensus among participants was that circumcised penises are clean and that intact penises are not, and they used this opinion to explain their support for circumcision.

Tradition

Twenty-five participants explained their support for circumcision by explaining its significance in terms of religious or cultural significance. "Dava" stated, "I am from a conservative Jewish family and circumcision has been the norm in my culture for thousands of years." "Amanda" stated that circumcision is consistent with "Christian tradition," and "Hana" claimed family tradition as a reason to circumcise by stating, "It is such a cultural and traditional thing in each society, and all of the males in my family are circumcised, so my upbringing says that it is the natural thing to do." For these participants, the custom of circumcision seemed to have a deeper meaning than the procedure itself, and they saw it as a way to connect to their larger culture, religion, or family. Participants supported what has been done in the past and were hesitant to not support circumcision as others in their life have done.

"Corine" described experiencing a cultural shift when moving to America:

> I was brought up in a culture, where male circumcision was performed on around high school students; therefore, I always believed that male circumcision was not a necessity. But now exposed to American culture, my old perspective on male circumcision was changed.

It seems she saw circumcision as a procedure engrained in American culture that she needed to support to fit in.

Aesthetic

Twenty-one participants cited aesthetic reasons for supporting circumcision, describing intact penises as "weird" and "unappealing." Kylie explained, "the extra skin/foreskin on the uncircumcised penis looks different and is less appealing, simply because fewer men in our culture are uncircumcised." "Ursula" noted foreskin would be a "turn off," and "Carl" said he would have been "extremely self-conscious about my own genitalia" if he had not been circumcised. He further explained, "I'd hate to be in a sexual situation with someone only to have them recoil at the sight of my genitalia." To these participants, appearance seemed to be incredibly important and was a major explanation for their support of circumcision.

Social Acceptability

Twenty-eight participants considered social acceptability when developing opinions about circumcision. They wrote that circumcision is seen as the norm and that those who are intact are likely to be teased due to their circumcision status. A few participants shared stories about knowing someone who had not been circumcised and reported those individuals seemed to be embarrassed or struggled with their circumcision status. Quinn shared that she did not have an opinion on circumcision until witnessing her boyfriend's "intense insecurity about the appearance of being uncircumcised." Carl shared he would have felt "out of place" with an intact penis and described the importance of circumcision status to his ability to fit in with peers. Several participants described circumcised penises as "natural" and "normal" and conversely referred to intact ones as "foreign."

Rationalizing Risks

As well as explaining their support for the procedure, participants also wrote about potential risks that may accompany circumcision. Most participants acknowledged potential risks and drawbacks of circumcision in their narratives, yet they quickly dismissed these risks and rationalized their support for circumcision.

Fear of Peer Rejection

Participants in this study were incredibly concerned about the perceived social acceptability of circumcision status. Eighteen participants wrote that they were willing to overlook risks of circumcision in favor of being accepted by peers. Amanda wrote:

> Many cultures do not circumcise. I think if I were a man I would like to be born in a different country so I could keep my foreskin. I know if they gave out clitorectamys (sp) at birth, later in life I would be upset that my pleasure zone was cut off. But in fear of being different, or judged, I would rather not live in the United States, where circumcision is considered normal and necessary.

Amanda wrote about the drawback of potentially reduced pleasure after being circumcised and shared that she would not want to be circumcised if she were a man. Yet, she concluded that in the United States, circumcision is "normal and necessary" despite the drawbacks. Rosie recounted her parents' opinions before clarifying her own:

> My father, being a doctor, disagrees with circumcisions. His opinion is that there is no medical reason that one MUST be circumcised and that it is cruel to inflict such pain on an infant for no reason. . . . After listening to both of my parents about their opinions on circumcision I think that I will give my son a circumcision. I believe that it will resolve any teasing and/or embarrassment when he gets older and that as a baby, although it may hurt, it is better for the long run.

This young woman acknowledged her father's opinion about circumcision and dismissed his concern about the pain inflicted on an infant in favor of avoiding potential future embarrassment. Although participants were knowledgeable about the risks and drawbacks of the procedure, they were supportive of circumcision because of its benefits when it comes to social acceptability.

Infancy

Nine participants shared their beliefs that though circumcision could cause some pain, they did not believe this pain was meaningful because it is performed in infancy and will therefore not be remembered. "Dennis" stated, "I personally feel it is a great idea to circumcise infants soon after birth because there is no way they will remember the pain or trauma." These participants acknowledged that the procedure is not without risk and advocated for circumcision on infants because the infant will not remember, and the risk may increase later in life.

Irrelevant

Five female participants reported they did not feel circumcision was relevant to their lives. Dava shared, "Personally, I am indifferent and think that as long as my son is fully functioning and happy that it really does not matter too much." These female participants saw themselves as unrelated to the issue of circumcision, which could indicate a reluctance to seek out information or gather multiple perspectives before making circumcision decisions. This may lead women to make circumcision decisions based on their own experiences rather than educational materials.

Parents' Rights

Twelve participants, all female, pointed out that parents should be able to make circumcision decisions for their sons. These participants defended the rights of the parents when it came to making circumcision decisions and stated those decisions should be respected and not questioned. Neva described her thoughts on how parents should make this decision, "I believe that parents of male children should make their own decision based on their religious morals, own personal opinions, and values." These participants viewed circumcision decisions as personal ones akin to any other parenting decision.

Rarity of Side Effects

Many participants acknowledged the side effects of circumcision in their narratives and dismissed their seriousness using their own experiences. Seven participants brought up the loss of nerve endings and shared information from their personal lives to refute potential concerns about lack of feeling. "Gemma" shared, "I have heard some opinions that uncircumcised men have better sex because their foreskin is still intact, but I have never once heard my boyfriend complain that the quality of sex is lessened by the lack of foreskin." "Fred" discussed the medical risks of the procedure by writing, "There can be problems with removing too much or too little skin, scars, or minor infections that can be treated easily." These participants acknowledged a potential risk and dismissed them because they seemed to be rare or easily handled.

Personal Satisfaction

Of the seven male participants, all were circumcised. Of these participants, five were either completely in favor or mostly in favor of circumcision and used their personal experiences and satisfaction with their circumcision status to justify their position. "Bret" summarized by writing, "if I were to have a son, I would have him circumcised because that is how I grew up and I now have a bias toward it."

Making Circumcision Decisions

Participants' narratives included information about how they learned about, thought about, and justified circumcision. They used this information to share their thoughts on whether they would choose to circumcise if they had a son. Eighteen participants stated they definitely would circumcise, seven said they would most likely circumcise, seven were unsure, one female participant stated she would most likely not circumcise, and one male participant said he would definitely not circumcise. Most participants stated they would circumcise their sons, using explanations and rationalizations to justify their decisions.

Discussion

The emerging adults participating in this study were overwhelmingly in favor of circumcision. However, many of them noted they did not know much about the procedure or had not thought about circumcision much before writing their narratives. They explained their support of circumcision using the four discourses of cleanliness, aesthetics, tradition, and social acceptability. Participants acknowledged the risks of circumcision and dismissed them for a variety of reasons: fear of rejection, not remembering infancy, circumcision is not relevant, parents should be able to have circumcision decisions respected, side effects are rare, and male participants' satisfaction with their circumcision status. Participants used the four discourses and rationalizations of risk to explain why most of them planned to circumcise their future sons.

While over half of infant boys were circumcised in hospitals in 2010,[3] participants' perceptions that circumcision is an absolute may be more reflective of their upbringing and communities. All seven male participants had been circumcised, and many of the female participants had experiences with circumcised partners or had male friends who were circumcised. Further, the university attended by all participants is made up of mostly White students from more privileged socioeconomic backgrounds, which could mean that they were more likely to have access to circumcision.[10]

Consistent with previous research suggesting parents make circumcision decisions based on personal experience instead of informational materials,[19] participants reported they had not considered circumcision carefully but would choose to circumcise their sons. The participants rationalized risks and explained their reasoning for favoring the procedure, but not without expressing some doubts. One participant questioned how circumcision gained popularity by stating, "So the reason why circumcision was ever invented is beyond me, since males are so sexually driven in the first place." Another pondered, "My immediate reaction to circumcision would have to be why? What benefits are gained? There has to be a reason for doing it." It seems these participants did not completely understand the reasons for circumcision's popularity in American culture and perhaps did not completely understand their support for the procedure.

We posit that the concept of masculinity could help to explain why participants were so in favor of circumcision. Given the status of the penis as a symbol of power, it was surprising that many emerging adults were unworried about the removal of the foreskin. The removal of the foreskin could act to sexualize the penis, rendering it more masculine, by drawing attention to a newborn boy's penis as a sexual object and readying it for sexual activity through the removal of the foreskin, which would retract when erect.[15] The body, and therefore the penis, is closely tied to the exploration and performance of masculinity.[17] We may also understand this phenomenon using the theory of cognitive dissonance, which states that individuals tend to settle any differences between beliefs and observations by rationalizing what they observe.[24] For the participants in this study, it seems they were confused about the discrepancy between what they believed (the penis is powerful and valued) and what they observed (the popularity of surgically altering the penis) and believed "there must be a reason for it." They settled that discrepancy by rationalizing the risks and drawbacks so that they may feel more comfortable supporting circumcision. In the end, participants seemed to make their decisions about circumcision emotionally, mainly considering the social consequences of circumcision decisions.

Of course, the participants in this study do not represent all emerging adults. We were unable to collect much information about the participants' backgrounds. Still, the university they all attended suggests that the participants may be mostly White and from higher socioeconomic backgrounds. We suggest that future research includes a more varied sample and explores how circumcision is discussed in educational, family, and peer settings to gather more information and assess how we may increase knowledge on this procedure.

Implications for Sex Education

This study provided a peek into the minds of emerging adults, which may provide some insight into American perspectives on circumcision. Emerging adults may find themselves in the position of making circumcision decisions for their children, and their support for the procedure may indicate that circumcision will remain popular among parents of infant boys. Our participants indicated some confusion and a lack of informational sources about circumcision, which could indicate a need for sexuality education to change how circumcision is introduced and discussed.

Sexuality education may address this confusion about circumcision by including a description of the procedure in primary school discussions on anatomy and physiology. Less than 40% of participants in this study had learned about circumcision in a formal education setting before their university human sexuality course. Learning straightforward information about circumcision when learning about other aspects of male anatomy may help children, teens, and young adults make sense of the procedure and prevent confusion about the benefits and risks. Reading materials and the guest lecture in the undergraduate human sexuality course participants were enrolled in did explain that circumcision has been controversial and outlined some risks and benefits of the procedure. Participants acknowledged some of these risks and benefits in their narratives, though it seemed social consequences were most influential in shaping their perceptions. If more participants had received education on circumcision earlier in their educations, they might be better poised to weigh information from educational sources and social ones while making future circumcision decisions.

References

1. World Health Organization. (2016). *Male circumcision: Global trends and determinants of prevalence, safety, and acceptability.* http://data.unaids.org/pub/report/2007/jc1360_male_circumcision_en.pdf
2. Morris, B.J., Bailis, S.A., & Wiswell, T.E. (2014). Circumcision rates in the United States: Rising or falling? What effect might the new affirmative pediatric policy statement have? *Mayo Clinic Proceedings, 89*, 677–686. doi:10.1016/j.mayocp.2014.01.001

3. Centers for Disease Control and Prevention (2013). *Trends in circumcision for male newborns in U.S. hospitals: 1979–2010*. www.cdc.gov/nchs/data/hestat/circumcision_2013/circumcision_2013.pdf
4. Introcaso, C.E., Xu, F., Kilmarx, P.H., Zaidi, A., & Markowitz, L.E. (2013). Prevalence of circumcision among men and boys aged 14 to 59 years in the United States, national health and nutrition examination surveys 2005–2010. *Sexually Transmitted Diseases, 40*, 521–525. doi:10.1097/01.OLQ.0000430797.56499.0d.
5. Mor, Z., Kent, C., Kohn, R., & Klausner, J. (2007). Declining rates in male circumcision amidst increasing evidence of its public health benefit. *PLoS One, 2*(9), e861–e865. doi:10.1371/journal.pone.0000861
6. Rediger, C., & Muller, A.J. (2013). Parents' rationale for male circumcision. *Canadian Family Physician, 59*(2), e110–e115.
7. Brown, M.S., & Brown, C.A. (1987). Circumcision decision: Prominence of social concerns. *Pediatrics, 80*, 215–219. doi:10.1016/s0022-5347(17)42482-7.
8. American Academy of Pediatrics Task Force on Circumcision (2012). Circumcision policy statement. *Pediatrics, 130*, 585–586. doi:10.1542/peds.2012-1990
9. Renshaw, D.C. (2006). Male and female circumcision today. *The Family Journal, 14*, 283–285. doi:10.1177/1066480706287894
10. Leibowitz, A.A., Desmond, K., & Belin, T. (2009). Determinants and policy implications of male circumcision in the United States. *American Journal of Public Health, 99*, 138–145. doi:10.2105/AJPH.2008.134403.
11. Warner, L., Cox, S., Whiteman, M., Jamieson, D., Macaluso, M., Bansil, P., Kuklina, E., Kourtis, A.P., Posner, S., & Barfield, W. (2015). Impact of health insurance type on trends in newborn circumcision, United States, 2000 to 2010. *American Journal of Public Health, 105*, 1943–1949. doi:10.2105/AJPH.2015.302629
12. Schlossberger N.M., Turner R.A., & Irwin C.E. Jr. (1992). Early adolescent knowledge and attitudes about circumcision: Methods and implications for research. *Journal of Adolescent Health, 13*, 293–297. doi:10.1016/1054-139x(92)90162-5
13. Loehle, B., McKie, R.M., Levere, D., Bossio, J.A., Humphreys, T.P., & Travers, R. (2017). Predictors of men's genital self-image across sexual orientation and geographic region. *Canadian Journal of Human Sexuality, 26*, 130–141. doi:10.3138/cjhs.262.a7
14. Bossio, J.A., & Pukall, C.F. (2018). Attitude toward one's circumcision status is more important than actual circumcision status for men's body image and sexual functioning. *Archives of Sexual Behavior, 47*, 771–781. doi:10.1007/s10508-017-1064-8
15. Harrison, D.M. (2002). Rethinking circumcision and sexuality in the United States. *Sexualities, 5*, 300–316. doi:10.1177/1363460702005003003
16. Fleming, P.J., Barrington, C., Pearce, L.D., Lerebours, L., Donastorg, Y., & Brito, M.O. (2017). "I feel like more of a man": A mixed methods study of masculinity, sexual performance, and circumcision for HIV prevention. *Journal of Sex Research, 54*, 42–54. doi: 10.1080/00224499.2015.1137539
17. Connell, R. (2012). Gender, health and theory: Conceptualizing the issue, in local and world perspective. *Social Science and Medicine, 74*, 1675–1683. doi: 10.1016/j.socscimed.2011.06.006
18. Kaufman, M.W., Clark, J.Y., & Castro, C.L. (2001). Neonatal circumcision: Benefits, risks, and family teaching. *MCN, the American Journal of Maternal/Child Nursing, 26*, 197–201. doi:10.1097/00005721-200107000-00009
19. Binner, S., Mastrobattista, J., Day, M., Swaim, L., & Monga, M. (2002). Effect of parental education on decision-making about neonatal circumcision. *Southern Medical Journal, 95*, 457–461. doi:10.1097/00007611-200204000-00016
20. Brady, M.T. (2016). Newborn male circumcision with parental consent, as stated in the AAP circumcision policy statement, is both legal and ethical. *The Journal of Law, Medicine & Ethics, 44*, 256–262. doi:10.1177/1073110516654119

21. Earp, B.D. (2016). Infant circumcision and adult penile sensitivity: Implications for sexual experience. *Trends in Urology & Men's Health,* 7, 17–21. doi:10.1002/tre.531
22. Bossio, J., Pukall, C., & Steele, S. (2014). A review of the current state of the male circumcision literature. *Journal of Sexual Medicine, 11*, 2847–2864. doi:10.1111/jsm.12703
23. Svoboda, J.S., Adler, P.W., & Van Howe, R.S. (2016). Circumcision is unethical and unlawful. *The Journal of Law, Medicine & Ethics, 44*, 263–282. doi:10.1177/1073110516654120
24. Festinger, L. (1962). *A theory of cognitive dissonance.* Stanford, CA: Stanford University Press.

7

SEXUALITY EDUCATION FOR PARENTS OF CHILDREN WITH INTELLECTUAL AND DEVELOPMENTAL DISABILITIES

Deborah L. Rooks-Ellis and Nicole Achey

Sexuality is a natural and healthy part of life and encompasses knowledge, beliefs, attitudes, values, and behaviors. Yet, parents and caregivers encounter prevailing stereotypes and false beliefs and may find it difficult to communicate about sexuality-related topics with their child diagnosed with intellectual and developmental disabilities (IDD).[1–3]

Perspectives on Sexuality by Parents of Individuals With IDD

Parents may hold conservative or reserved views about the sexuality of their child with IDD when compared to siblings or individuals without disabilities.[4–6] Individuals with IDD report being aware of the differences between their parents' responses to their sibling's intimate relationships and their own intimate relationships. This inequity may be related to parents' lack of understanding of educating or communicating with their child with IDD about sexuality and sexuality education content. Likewise, parents may believe that their child with IDD is incapable of sexual feeling because of developmental, cognitive, or social delays or that their child is unable to consent to sexual expression or relationships.[1,7,8] Since individuals with IDD may need to rely on others to arrange intimate activities, restrictions about their sexual lives may be placed inadvertently upon them by others (e.g., parents, caregivers), denying sexual rights and rights to privacy. These misunderstandings may result in hesitation from family members to provide education on sexually related issues.

DOI: 10.4324/9781003189787-8

Perspectives on Sexuality by Individuals With IDD

Individuals with IDD categorize their parents' perspectives as an inequality existing between themselves and their families.[9] Contrary to the myths and false beliefs held by parents and caregivers, individuals with IDD seek ways to gain more control over their lives and assert their rights to make choices related to their sexuality and form relationships.[10] Some men and women with IDD want to have and be able to talk about loving relationships; they seek intimacy passion, and romance.[11] Furthermore, individuals with IDD want to be more in charge of their sexuality and relationships rather than being controlled by others. For example, both men and women with IDD report that their needs, opinions, views, and rights to self-determination are, in some cases, not recognized and even ignored. They are often excluded from opportunities to actively explore and develop their sexuality.[12]

A common experience shared by individuals with IDD is a lack of control in what information they are provided and therefore able to understand. Specifically, adults with IDD indicate that their parents and care providers would not permit a steady partner because "that's not right" and "you can't do that sort of thing."[13] Individuals with IDD report being misinformed of sexual information, stating they wanted to have an intimate relationship but did not know how to pursue such a relationship.[14] Others report not having the confidence to speak to their romantic interest and are more comfortable loving someone secretly. When an individual is excluded from certain information or intentionally misguided about content, there is a lack of control in what information a person may access. The misinformation, direct orders, or the void of information results in a skewed version of the truth for individuals with IDD. For example, an individual with IDD self-disclosing as female was told, "a man and woman cannot get physically close to each other."[14] Others share that they never talked about masturbation or sexual intercourse and that "this is a very private issue; parents do not talk about it or let us know about it."[14] The sexual needs of adults with IDD are often neglected or strictly controlled by their families and caregivers.[14,15] Individuals with IDD may have a lack of understanding of sexuality and limited access to sexuality education;[1,16,17] they may want to know how to start relationships, as well as to understand safe sex practices,[1] and may be denied the right to experience sexuality because of a lack of education and information.[18] These recurring experiences indicate a need for sexuality education.[12]

Lack of Sexuality Education at Home

A lack of understanding exists about what and how much sexuality education occurs at home.[19] Parents of children with IDD may often "overlook the responsibility of sex education because they do not know what to talk about, when to talk about it, or how to modify the content so their child will understand."[20]

Parents are the primary sexuality educators for their children with disabilities, and research indicates that parents want to have this role.[20] However, available resources for parents are limited and include independent learning curricula or are limited to a few in-person training sessions.[21] Furthermore, parents seeking to educate their children about sexual health and relationships may find that the scope of topics to be taught is extremely broad and ill-defined.[22] These beliefs are perpetuated with abstinence-based sexuality education programs, which heavily focus on sexual abuse prevention with minimal focus on skill development of positive relationships.[23] Caregivers express a need for guidance and support to integrate comprehensive sexuality education into their children's educational programs and formal instructional goals.[24] Unfortunately, the majority of sexuality education curricula for individuals with IDD focus on protection and prevention. Therefore, the parents of children with IDD are faced with these conflicting initiatives.[25]

Regardless, parents are the major source of sexuality education for children with IDD through formal and informal communication and social experiences to practice emerging sexuality skills.[20] When parental involvement is minimal, the child will likely be less successful acquiring, generalizing, and maintaining the skills needed for positive sexual health and relationships.[22] Likewise, it is essential to support and include parents of children with IDD in providing sexuality education, as relying solely on school-based sexuality education alone would be insufficient.[26]

Lack of Sexuality Education in Educational Settings

The American Academy of Pediatrics recommends that age-appropriate education about sexual health be implemented to help develop safe and positive views of sexuality throughout the lifespan.[27] Furthermore, it is recommended that sexuality education address the biological, psychological, sociocultural, and spiritual dimensions of sexuality within the affective learning domain, the behavioral learning domain, and the cognitive learning domain.[28] However, most states have no standard policy that ensures individuals with IDD have access to accurate, comprehensive, inclusive information and education in schools or community settings to support their healthy sexual development and lifelong sexual health and well-being. At present, less than 60% of states mandate that school personnel teach sexuality education, and the requirements vary widely. Even fewer states have legislation requiring culturally appropriate and unbiased language, information about contraception and healthy relationships, and medical accuracy.[29] To date, three states explicitly include youth with disabilities within their sexuality education requirements, five states mandate the health curriculum be accessible to youth with disabilities, and six states and the District of Columbia include mandates requiring the provision of optional resources pertaining to sexuality education curricula for youth with disabilities.

Furthermore, many teachers do not view educating students with disabilities about sexuality as part of their professional responsibility, nor do they think that students with IDD would benefit from the sexuality education if provided.[30] In fact, due to inappropriate teaching modalities such as reliance on verbal explanations for abstract concepts, adolescents with IDD may not retain the information presented in sexuality education classes.[31,32] Sexuality education, therefore, ought to be tailored, potentially on an individual level, as the group setting may limit the educator's ability to ensure individuals achieve understanding.[6,32,31] Additionally, teachers report little to no training regarding sexuality education and urge parents and family members to become involved with the sexuality education of their child with IDD.[30] A strong evidence base exists demonstrating that individuals with IDD can learn daily living and self-care skills, including sexuality.[33–35]

Sexuality Education Tools and Resources

Commercially produced sexuality education programs exist; however, these vary widely in the accuracy of content, effectiveness, and emphasis, ranging from abstinence-only to comprehensive sexuality education curricula. Access to evidence-based information, parent training options, and reliable resources may be another barrier for families who are supporting the sexuality education of their child. We present some of the more commonly used educational tools and resources. The first set of resources provides sexuality education to children and adolescents, and the second set includes more advanced sexuality education concepts suitable for adults.

Educational Tools for Minors

Recognizing that families may likely have concerns about how best to protect their child with IDD from sexual abuse, curricula such as the *Circles* strategy are often used to teach physical boundaries based on relationships.[36] The *Circles* strategy helps families categorize their child's real-life relationships. Using the six color-coded concentric circles, families and individuals with disabilities define the various levels of intimacy and social relationships that may be experienced. Social narratives, another strategy, have been shown effective for teaching choice-making and self-care skills for children with autism and developmental disabilities.[37] Other online resources include Do2Learn, a free online program that provides thousands of free pages of social skills and behavioral regulation activities.[38] The *Home-Based Adolescent Sexuality Education for Intellectual Disabilities (Home B.A.S.E.)* educational curriculum was designed to increase parents' comfort and confidence in discussing sexuality and healthy relationship topics with their adolescents with IDD. This curriculum has unique features for parents to consider, including (1) the belief that sexuality is a human right for individuals with IDD; (2) the perspective of individuals with disabilities speaking about their sexual rights and relationships; (3) activities based on adult, social, and transformational learning theories; and (4) a small interactive group format over multiple sessions.[20]

Ready-made products are available for purchase. For example, the James Stanfield Company offers an extensive line of multimedia products addressing sexuality education and relationship issues for individuals with IDD, including these separate curricula: *Circles, Date Smart, LifeFacts*, and *Life Horizons*.[39] Another option is the online developmental disabilities and sexuality curriculum *Elevatus*. This program is meant to be used with teens and adults with IDD and includes 22 lesson plans with scripts, handouts in English and Spanish, teaching tools, and an instructor's manual. The curriculum helps professionals, educators, parents, and self-advocates skillfully and confidently navigate the topic of sexuality by offering evidence-based and trauma-informed curricula, in-service training, online training, and workshops.[40] The *Life Horizons I & II* comprehensive education series was designed by Winifred Kempton. This classic and comprehensive sexuality education series uses DVDs and teaching scripts. Part I focuses on the physiological and emotional aspects and includes topics such as the parts of the body, sexual development, human reproduction, and sexually transmitted infections. Part II emphasizes the moral, social, and legal aspects of sexuality and discusses self-esteem and relationships, dating skills and learning to love, marriage and other lifestyles, and parenting. The *PossAbilities* training is designed to help individuals with disabilities understand and embrace their sexuality by accepting responsibility for making personal choices. The program comes with an instructor's manual, student manual, and handouts providing step-by-step guidance for examining relationship and self-esteem issues, including attitudes, emotions, health, self-image, positive adult behavior, relationships, safety, sexuality, and values.[41]

Additional recommended print resources include *The Facts of Life . . . and More: Sexuality and Intimacy for People with Intellectual Disabilities*.[42] In this book, parents will find tips for talking about sexuality with their adolescent or adult children with intellectual disabilities. Author Terri Couwenhoven is a well-known expert in the field who has also published *Boyfriends & Girlfriends: A Guide to Dating for People with Disabilities* and *Teaching Children with Down Syndrome about Their Bodies, Boundaries, and Sexuality*.[43,44] Readers can gain expert dating advice and helpful information on a child's sexual development within these books.

Educational Tools for Adults

Just as there are targeted sexuality education trainings for children and adolescents with IDD, there are similar educational series for adults with IDD that would be considered more developmentally and chronologically appropriate. One ready-made sexuality curriculum is *Elevatus*, previously mentioned in the educational tools for minors. The program includes developmentally appropriate topics for adults such as sexual self-advocacy, rights to sexuality, lessons on the use of the

Internet and social media, STI/STD/HIV/AIDS, feelings about sexual acts and decision, cost of raising a child, prevention of pregnancy and contraception.[40] Additionally, the *Life Horizons I and II* programs,[39] specifically *Part II*, are relevant to adults with IDD. *Part II* emphasizes the moral, social, and legal aspects of sexuality, including self-esteem and relationships, dating skills, learning to love, marriage and other lifestyles, and parenting.

Curricula that are not specifically designed for adults with IDD but can be used to facilitate the learning of sexuality with the help of a parent include the *Sexuality Education for Adults With Developmental Disabilities* by Planned Parenthood of Greater Northern New England and Green Mountain Self Advocates.[45] This unique and comprehensive curriculum is designed to help all people establish sexuality education. It focuses primarily on relationships—both friendships and romantic relationships—and the skills and responsibilities needed. This content is beneficial for adults with IDD and can be modified and taught to include more visual content and longer discussion times to ensure learning outcomes are met. There may be situations when a curriculum or books proposed for adolescents would also be appropriate for an adult with IDD.

Strategies to Support Families as Sexuality Educators

Empowering parents and caregivers to become their child's primary sexuality educator effectively increases parent-child communication and supports the child in making healthy decisions about sexual behavior.[46,47] Families are appropriate educators, and meaningful communication and learning can happen when provided helpful and appropriate tools to do this important work. When a parent or family member is trained and prepared to teach curricula or adapt sexuality education content for individuals with IDD, the gap in the sexuality education of individuals with IDD can be minimized or closed altogether.

Sexuality education among parents may increase their knowledge and change their attitudes, beliefs, and behaviors about educating their child about sexuality.[20,46,48] Likewise, sexuality education may encourage parents to communicate more about these topics with their children. However, there is limited research on models of sexuality education for parents to support their child with IDD in the United States. For example, the authors of this chapter, along with our colleagues, implemented a brief sexuality education training for parents and caregivers who have children diagnosed with IDD, including autism. A pre-post questionnaire examined parents' and caregivers' attitudes and beliefs about sexuality education, their comfort level in communicating about sexuality topics with their child, and their perceived competence for teaching sexuality education topics. Statistically significant positive changes were observed post-training for each area. Results indicated that parents benefit from sexuality education training and that they want and need guidance on how to provide developmentally appropriate sexuality education for their child with IDD.[48] Likewise, results from the *Home B.A.S.E.* workshop showed a significant decrease in negative attitudes surrounding sexuality and disability and a significant increase in parents' self-efficacy discussing sexuality topics. Additionally, international studies have demonstrated that parents of children with IDD participating in educational workshops have reduced parental concerns, increased communication about sexuality topics, and improved confidence in addressing sexuality issues.[21,49–51] Parents can benefit from educational workshops and training to support their role in providing sexuality education in the home.

Parents require strategies to initiate and maintain sexuality education at home.[52,53] Evidence-based practical strategies to support the specific needs of individuals with IDD promote understanding and generalization of sexuality content. For example, behavior modeling is a strategy that parents can use to demonstrate important concepts and topics, such as the importance of a safe space to practice or role-play modeled scenarios. This modeling technique supports use of those skills by the child in other environments.[54] Likewise, improved generalization outcomes have been demonstrated when parents use evidence-based interventions paired with literal language.[7,55] Using literal medical terms rather than metaphorical language such as "birds and bees" to describe intercourse and reproduction promotes a deeper understanding of these concepts.

Limited reading skills are often identified as a characteristic of individuals with IDD. Therefore, families will need to accommodate text-based resources and use visuals with their children to support understanding of the sexual actions described. Individuals with IDD often need repetition of information. Parents can support their children by providing multiple opportunities to practice modeled behaviors pertaining to sexual hygiene, such as using menstrual health products and proper self-cleansing when toileting. The use of comprehensive, evidence-based strategies (e.g., behavior modeling, literal language), modified appropriately, and multiple media (e.g., images, models, and other visual supports) to address the spectrum of topics relating to sexuality can improve sexual health knowledge for individuals with IDD.[48,56,57]

The Promise of Parent-Mediated Interventions

Even brief trainings, such as those described earlier by the chapter authors and the *Home B.A.S.E.* study, give parents the permission and the skills to engage with the complex and sensitive topic of sexuality. Parent-mediated intervention supports the parent to learn the skills and strategies needed to teach their child with IDD about sexuality. When paired with professional coaching (e.g., sexuality educator, related service provider, interventionist), ongoing opportunities are provided to the parent to practice the strategies with the child. These strategies, used within the families' everyday routines and activities, increase the likelihood of generalization across people and settings. These types of interventions build parent capacity and are a promising practice to train and teach parents about the importance of sexuality for their child with disabilities.[48]

Future Directions

We commend SIECUS: Sex Ed for Social Change for its *Comprehensive Sex Education for Youth with Disabilities: A Call to Action* and agree that more research is needed on effective instructional practices for sexuality education for individuals with disabilities.[58] We advocate that parents and caregivers, in partnership with professionals, seek opportunities to participate in training and be involved in the development and implementation of school-based curricula designed to address the unique needs of individuals with disabilities, particularly individuals with IDD.

References

1. Sinclair, J., Unruh, D., Linstrom, L., & Scanlon, D. (2015). Barriers to sexuality for individuals with intellectual and developmental disabilities: A literature review. *Education and Training in Autism and Developmental Disabilities, 50*(3), 3–16
2. Travers, J., & Tincani, M. (2010). Sexuality education for individuals with autism spectrum disorders: Critical issues and decision making guidelines. *Education and Training in Autism and Developmental Disabilities, 45*(2), 284–293.
3. Tissot, C. (2009). Establishing a sexual identity: Case studies of learners with autism and learning difficulties. *Autism, 13*(6), 551–566
4. Cuskelly, M., & Bryde, R. (2004). Attitudes towards the sexuality of adults with an intellectual disability: Parents, support staff, and a community sample. *Journal of Intellectual & Developmental Disability, 29*, 255–264
5. Ćwirynkało, K., Byra, S., & Żyta, A. (2017). Sexuality of adults with intellectual disabilities as described by support staff workers. *Hrvatska Revija Za Rehabilitacijska Istraživanja, 53*, 77–87
6. Healy, E., McGuire, B.E., Evans, D.S., & Carley, S.N. (2009). Sexuality and personal relationships for people with an intellectual disability. Part I: Service-user perspectives. *Journal of Intellectual Disability Research, 53*(11), 905–912.
7. Ballan, M.S. (2012). Parental perspectives of communication about sexuality in families of children with autism spectrum disorders. *Journal of Autism and Developmental Disorders, 42*(5), 676–684
8. Holmes, L.G., & Himle, M.B. (2014). Brief report: Parent—child sexuality communication and autism spectrum disorders. *Journal of Autism and Developmental Disorders, 44*, 2964–2970
9. Senne, E. (2016). *Experiences of direct support professionals supporting sexuality for individuals with developmental disabilities*. Clinical Research Paper, St. Catherine University, SOPHIA. https://sophia.stkate.edu/msw_papers/678/.
10. Kelly, G., Crowley, H., & Hamilton, C. (2009). Rights, sexuality and relationships in Ireland: It'd be nice to be kind of trusted. *British Journal of Learning Disabilities, 37*(4), 308–315.
11. Wheeler, P. (2007). 'I count myself as normal, well, not normal, but normal enough' men with learning disabilities tell their stories about sexuality and sexual identity. *Tizard Learning Disability Review, 12*(1), 16–27.
12. Brown, M., & McCann, E. (2018). Sexuality issues and the voices of adults with intellectual disabilities: A systematic review of the literature. *Research in Developmental Disabilities, 74*, 124–138.
13. Gil-Llario, M.D., Morell-Mengual, V., Ballester-Arnal, R., & Díaz-Rodríguez, I. (2018). The experience of sexuality in adults with intellectual disability. *Journal of Intellectual Disability Research, 62*(1), 72–80.

14. Chou, Y., Zxy-Yann, J.L., & Pu, C. (2015). Attitudes toward male and female sexuality among men and women with intellectual disabilities. *Women & Health, 55*(6), 663–678.
15. Servais, L. (2006). Sexual health care in persons with intellectual disabilities. *Mental Retardation and Developmental Disabilities Research Reviews, 12*(1), 48–56
16. Saxe, A., & Flanagan, T. (2014). Factors that impact support workers' perceptions of the sexuality of adults with developmental disabilities: A quantitative analysis. *Sexuality and Disability, 32*(1), 45–63
17. Swango-Wilson, A. (2008). Caregiver attitude of sexuality of the intellectually disabled population and implications for sex education. *Sexuality and Disability, 26*(3), 167–174.
18. O'Sullivan, L.F., Byers, E.S., Brotto, L.A., & Majerovich, J. (2015). Access to and use of sexual health care services among young Canadians with and without a history of sexual coercion. *Canadian Family Physician, 61*, 467–473.
19. Fader Wilkenfeld, B., & Ballan. M.S. (2011). Educators' attitudes and beliefs towards the sexuality of individuals with developmental disabilities. *Sexuality and Disability, 29*(4), 351–361.
20. Frank, K., & Sandman, L. (2021). Parents as primary sexuality educators for adolescents and adults with Down syndrome: A mixed methods examination of the Home B.A.S.E for Intellectual Disabilities workshop. *American Journal of Sexuality Education, 16*(3), 283–302.
21. Kok, G., & Akyuz, A. (2015). Evaluation of effectiveness of parent health education about the sexual developments of adolescents with intellectual disabilities. *Sexuality and Disability, 33*, 157–174.
22. Wolfe, P.S., Wertalik, J.L., Domire Monaco, S., Gardner, S., & Ruiz, S. (2019). Review of sociosexuality curricular content for individuals with developmental disabilities. *Focus on Autism and Other Developmental Disabilities, 34*(3), 153–162.
23. Anderson, S. (2015). Sex education programs focused on 'protection' and 'prevention' with little attention given to supporting people to develop healthy, positive sexual relationships. *Research and Practice in Intellectual and Developmental Disabilities, 2*(1), 98–100.
24. Aunos, M., & Feldman, M.A. (2002). Attitudes towards sexuality, sterilization and parenting rights of persons with intellectual disabilities. *Journal of Applied Research in Intellectual Disabilities, 15*(4), 285–296.
25. Schaafsma, D., Kok, G., Stoffelen, J.M.T., van Doorn, P., & Curfs, L.M.G. (2014). Identifying the important factors associated with teaching sex education to people with intellectual disability: A cross-sectional survey among paid care staff. *Journal of Intellectual & Developmental Disability, 39*(2), 157–166.
26. Rowe, B., & Wright, C. (2017). Sexual knowledge in adolescents with intellectual disabilities: A timely reflection. *Journal of Social Inclusion, 8*(2), 42–53.
27. Breuner, C.C, Mattson, G., Committee on Psychosocial Aspects of Child and Family Health, & Committee on Adolescence (2016). Sexuality education for children and adolescents. *Pediatrics, 138*(2), 1348.
28. Future of Sex Education Initiative (2020). *The future of sex education*. https://futureofsexed.org/
29. Guttmacher Institute. (2021). *Sex and HIV education*. www.guttmacher.org/state-policy/explore/sex-and-hiv-education.
30. Treacy, A.C. (2016). *A mixed methods study of sexual health education for students with disabilities*. ProQuest Dissertations Publishing.
31. Finlay, W.M.L., Rohleder, P., Taylor, N., & Culfear, H. (2015). 'Understanding' as a practical issue in sexual health education for people with intellectual disabilities: A study using two qualitative methods. *Health Psychology, 34*(4), 328–338
32. Corona, L.L., Fox, S.A., Christodulu, K.V., & Worlock, J.A. (2016). Providing education on sexuality and relationships to adolescents with autism spectrum disorder and their parents. *Sexuality and Disability, 34*(2), 199–214.

33. Bouck, E.C. (2010). Reports of life skills training for students with intellectual disabilities in and out of school. *Journal of Intellectual Disability Research, 54*(12), 1093–1103
34. Cobb, R.B., & Alwell, M. (2009). Transition planning/coordinating interventions for youth with disabilities: A systematic review. *Career Development for Exceptional Individuals, 32*(2), 70–81
35. Schaafsma, D., Kok, G., Stoffelen, J.M.T., & Curfs, L.M.G. (2015). Identifying effective methods for teaching sex education to individuals with intellectual disabilities: A systematic review. *The Journal of Sex Research, 52*(4), 412–432.
36. Walker-Hirsch, L., & Champagne, M.P. (1991). The circles concept: Social competence in special education. *Educational Leadership, 49*(1), 65.
37. Test, D.W., Richter, S., Knight, V., & Spooner, F. (2011). A comprehensive review and meta-analysis of the social stories literature. *Focus on Autism and Other Developmental Disabilities, 26*(1), 49–62.
38. Do2Learn. (2021). *Educational resources for special needs.* https://do2learn.com/
39. James Stanfield Company (n.d.). *Life horizons: Family life and sex education programs.* https://stanfield.com/product/life-horizons-family-life-program/
40. Elevatus Training. (n.d.). www.elevatustraining.com/.
41. Koller, R., & Kempton, W. (2007). *PossAbilities.* Program Development Associates. www.disabilitytraining.com/product-info.php?PossAbilities_Book_Package-pid666_html=/asc_action=SetCurrentProduct/prod_id=666
42. Walker-Hirsch, L. (2007). *The facts of life . . . . and more: Sexuality and intimacy for people with intellectual disabilities.* Brookes Publishing.
43. Couwenhoven, T. (2007). *Boyfriends & girlfriends: A guide to dating for people with disabilities.* Woodbine House
44. Couwenhoven, T. (2007). *Teaching children with Down syndrome about their bodies, boundaries, and sexuality: A guide for parents and professionals.* Woodbine House.
45. Planned Parenthood of Northern New England and Green Mountain Self Advocates (n.d.). *Sexuality Education for People with Developmental Disabilities Curriculum.* www.plannedparenthood.org/planned-parenthood-northern-new-england/population-health-and-education/community-resources/sexuality-education-people-developmental-disabilities-curriculum.
46. Klein, J.D., Sabaratnam, P., Pazos, B., Matos Auerbach, M., Graff Havens, C., & Brach, M.J. (2005). Evaluation of the parents as primary sexuality educators program. *Journal of Adolescent Health, 37*(3), S94–S99.
47. McDaniels, B., & Fleming, A. (2016). Sexuality education and intellectual disability: Time to address the challenge. *Sexuality and Disability, 34*(2), 215–225.
48. Rooks-Ellis, D.L., Jones, B., Sulinski, E., Howorth, S., & Achey, N. (2020). The effectiveness of a brief sexuality education intervention for parents of children with intellectual and developmental disabilities. *American Journal of Sexuality Education, 15*(4), 444–464
49. Dupras, A., & Dionne, H. (2014). The concern of parents regarding the sexuality of their child with a mild intellectual disability. *Sexologies: European Journal of Sexology, 23*(4), e79–e83
50. Lafferty, A., McConkey, R., & Simpson, A. (2012). Reducing the barriers to relationships and sexuality education for persons with intellectual disabilities. *Journal of Intellectual Disabilities, 16*(1), 29–43
51. Stein, S., Kohut, T., & Dillenburger, K. (2018). The importance of sexuality education for children with and without intellectual disabilities: What parents think. *Sexuality and Disability, 36*(2), 141–148.
52. Clatos, K., & Asare, M. (2016). Sexuality education intervention for parents of children with disabilities: A pilot training program. *American Journal of Health Studies, 31*(3), 151–162

53. O'Donnell, L., Stueve, A., Agronick, G., Wilson-Simmons, R., Duran, R., & Jean-baptiste, V. (2005). Saving sex for later: An evaluation of a parent education intervention. *Perspectives on Sexual and Reproductive Health, 37*(4), 166–173.
54. Wong, C., Odom, S.L., Hume, K.A., Cox, A.W., Fettig, A., Kucharczyk, S., Brock, M.E., Plavnick, J.B., Fleury, V.P., & Schultz, T.R. (2015). Evidence-based practices for children, youth, and young adults with autism spectrum disorder: A comprehensive review. *Journal of Autism and Developmental Disorders, 45*(7), 1951–1966.
55. Blanchett, W.J., & Wolfe, P.S. (2002). A review of sexuality education curricula: Meeting the sexuality education needs of individuals with moderate and severe intellectual disabilities. *Research and Practice for Persons with Severe Disabilities, 27*(1), 43–57.
56. Sala, G., Hooley, M., Attwood, T., Mesibov, G.B., & Stokes, M.A. (2019). Autism and intellectual disability: A systematic review of sexuality and relationship education. *Sexuality and Disability, 37*(3), 353–382
57. Schmidt, E.K., Brown, C., & Darragh, A. (2020). Scoping review of sexual health education interventions for adolescents and young adults with intellectual or developmental disabilities. *Sexuality and Disability, 38*(3), 439–453.
58. SIECUS: Sex Ed for Social Change (2021). *Comprehensive sex education for youth with disabilities: A call to action.* https://siecus.org/wp-content/uploads/2021/03/SIECUS-2021-Youth-with-Disabilities-CTA-1.pdf.

8

IMPROVING ACCESSIBILITY OF SEXUALITY EDUCATION FOR LEARNERS WITH INTELLECTUAL AND DEVELOPMENTAL DISABILITIES

Elizabeth Koss Schmidt, Megan E. Dougherty, Natalie Robek, and Anna E. Murray

Introduction

Developmental disabilities are a group of conditions present at birth and persist throughout a person's life. Examples of developmental disabilities include autism spectrum disorder, cerebral palsy, Down syndrome, intellectual disability, and Prader Willi syndrome. Individuals with developmental disabilities may have limitations in behavior, cognition, language, learning, and/or physical function. The characteristics and severity of these disabilities are widely variable. Some people may experience a physical disability with no cognitive involvement, and vice versa. Some people require high levels of support during daily life, while others require minimal support. To encompass this wide range of disabilities and characteristics, *intellectual and developmental disability* is often used as an umbrella term.

There is a misconception that people with intellectual and developmental disabilities are asexual, unaffected by human sexuality, or lack desire for relationships and sexual activity. Contrarily, adolescents and young adults with intellectual and developmental disabilities are sexually mature beings who experience the same desires for relationships and intimacy as their non-disabled peers.[15,16] Yet people with intellectual and developmental disabilities are often excluded from conversations about sexual health. It is essential to recognize that people with intellectual and developmental disabilities have an inherent right to sexual education, expression, and exploration. Providing sexuality education accessible to people with disabilities is imperative to affirming and respecting those rights.

At school, students with disabilities are less likely to receive formal sexuality education than the general student body.[2] At home, parents are less likely to talk about sex with their children if their child has a disability.[17] This education gap can have detrimental effects on health, knowledge, and safety. Adolescents and

DOI: 10.4324/9781003189787-9

young adults with intellectual and developmental disabilities often miss out on crucial information and may look to unreliable sources (e.g., the Internet, movies, pornography) to fill in the gaps.[9] Beyond a general lack of knowledge about sexual health topics, there are alarming health disparities among people with intellectual and developmental disabilities. They face an increased risk of sexual abuse and sexually transmitted infections (STIs) compared to the general population.[3,4] Comprehensive sexuality education has the potential to curb these adverse outcomes, as it teaches people about boundaries, consent, and safe practices. It has also been found to improve appreciation of sexual diversity (e.g., reduced homophobia and homophobic bullying, improve understanding of gender norms and gender equity, rights, and social justice), prevent dating and intimate partner violence and child sexual abuse, and increase knowledge and skills associated with healthy relationships (e.g., communication) among the general population of adolescents.[18] Comprehensive sexuality education addresses a wide range of topics and allows learners to explore traditional sexual health subjects, along with relational or social-emotional topics.

Traditional sexuality education subjects (such as anatomy, reproduction, and safe sex) are necessary to increase body awareness and understand how bodies work. Additionally, many social and emotional influencers of sexual health should be considered. Adolescents benefit from instruction on dating, gender expression, gender identity, healthy communication, relationships, and sexual orientation. Individuals with intellectual and developmental disabilities often experience difficulties with adaptive behaviors, communication, and social interaction, making it particularly beneficial to deliver sexuality education that emphasizes the social-emotional aspects of sexuality. Individuals with intellectual or developmental disabilities are also more likely to identify as LGBTQIA+,[19–22] emphasizing the importance of addressing gender expression, gender identity, and sexual orientation.[23–25] There are commercially available curricula and guidelines for comprehensive sexuality education, but few programs employ a Universal Design for Learning (UDL). There is a lack of accessible and effective programs for people with intellectual and developmental disabilities.[26,27]

To learn more about how to effectively deliver sexuality education to individuals with intellectual and developmental disabilities, researchers interviewed key groups to learn about their perspectives on sexuality education.[7,14] Interviews were completed with adolescents and young adults, ages 15 to 24, with intellectual and developmental disabilities. Researchers asked a flexible set of questions to learn about preferred learning modalities and settings.[14] For example, participants identified whether they liked learning through games, lectures, videos, visuals, or worksheets. They were also asked about their group, in-person, one-on-one, and online course preferences. Researchers completed additional interviews with people who may provide sexuality education, including nurses, parents, physicians, social workers, and therapists.[7,14] Through these interviews, researchers identified common themes and preferred ways to deliver sexuality education to individuals with intellectual and developmental disabilities. Additionally, the authors reviewed the available literature to provide an overview of strategies that can improve the accessibility of sexual education for students with intellectual and developmental disabilities, as described below.

Accessible Sexuality Education

Strategies/Modalities

In general, best practices for sexuality education still apply to individuals with intellectual and developmental disabilities. Specifically, educators should include age-appropriate, medically accurate information to address a comprehensive set of health, relationships, and sexuality topics.[9,14] This education should start proactively, ideally before the onset of puberty, and should continue throughout the individual's lifetime.[7] A baseline formal education should be provided, and the information should be reiterated throughout a person's life, as it relates to their life stage since repetition is beneficial for individuals with intellectual and developmental disabilities.[28,29] For example, a person with Down syndrome may learn about sexual health topics in high school but would benefit from continued instruction as they enter their first romantic relationship as an adult. This means that sexual health information should be provided by a variety of professionals throughout an individual's lifetime.[7] This chapter focuses on recommendations to improve the accessibility of formal sexuality education for youth with intellectual and developmental disabilities.

As previously stated, all information should be age-appropriate; however, youth with intellectual and developmental disabilities may need some accommodations in how this information is taught to maximize understanding. There are a variety of strategies that can be utilized to help promote understanding and access for students with intellectual and developmental disabilities, although none have been tested or compared in large-scale, randomized trials.[26,30] It is recommended that educators start with didactic teaching, including clear instructions, opportunities for discussion, structured routines, and clear, explicit examples.[14,26,29,30] Instructions should be broken down into small steps to ensure that students can participate in the curriculum. Some students may need additional adaptations to understand the instructions thoroughly. For example, educators may need to provide written and verbal instructions or images next to each written step. Expectations for participation in the curriculum should also be clear. It may be useful for educators to offer the opportunity to review the "rules" and expectations of the sexuality education program, including an opportunity for students to help establish the rules.

Further, engaging students in discussion throughout the sexuality education program can offer opportunities for educators to identify additional questions or topics that need to be further explored and elaborated on and check for understanding. Finally, educators should utilize clear, explicit examples of all content covered in the program. This may include elaborating on slang terms used to describe certain body parts, sexual activities, and/or relationship types to ensure that students can generalize information discussed in other contexts outside of the classroom.

There are some necessary considerations for promoting an inclusive environment for discussions. First, the language used should respect diverse abilities, cultures, genders, and sexual orientations. Educators are responsible for respecting a student's preferred language when talking about their disability. Some people prefer person-first language (e.g., person with intellectual disability), while others prefer identity-first language (e.g., autistic person). Educators can ask their students what language they prefer if/when they talk about their disability and respect those preferences. They should avoid making assumptions about students' sexuality based on their disability. Finally, educators may need to allow more time for students when responding or ensure that any adaptive, augmented communication devices they utilize are programmed with the appropriate language to participate in discussions about sexual health topics.[29]

Other strategies to promote accessibility for students with intellectual and developmental disabilities include utilizing pictures, videos, and models to help illustrate various concepts, parts, or actions.[14,26,30] For example, anatomy may be a particularly useful topic to illustrate using pictures or models, whereas someone may need videos or models to demonstrate the proper application of condoms to promote safe sexual practices. All videos should include closed captioning, and educators may want to slow videos down or pause them to discuss further and clarify any questions.[29] Educational guides, handouts, and worksheets are handy for traditional classroom-based sexuality education settings.[14] Educators may need to read them aloud, dependent on their students' needs.[29] Printed materials should be in large fonts and use appropriate contrast for students with low vision.[29] Role-playing is recommended for students to practice applying information learned in sexuality and relational health programs.[14,29] This can help students retain the information and may help them generalize it to settings outside the classroom.

Each of the strategies described earlier can be useful for any student, regardless of whether they also have an intellectual or developmental disability. The use of a variety of strategies in a sexual health curriculum may help a variety of students. This aligns with UDL,[31] ensuring that the materials will also be accessible to students with intellectual and developmental disabilities.[14] The paucity of literature on strategies to promote understanding of sexuality education for youth with intellectual or developmental disabilities suggests UDL is an important modification for sexuality education programs.[14,32,33] Educators can incorporate principles of UDL by first removing distractions and barriers to learning, adapting learning materials to be clear, concise, and incorporating multiple modalities (e.g., auditory, tactile, visual).[28,31] For example, handouts should focus on key points and include pictures to summarize the information provided in each session.[28,29]

Sexuality educators should also consider how caregivers are involved in their sexuality education curricula. Caregivers of individuals with intellectual and developmental disabilities often want to support their children when learning about sexuality education but often lack the tools and support to do so successfully.[17] Further, some individuals with intellectual and developmental disabilities have suggested they would prefer to learn about sensitive topics from their parents.[34] Educators can support their students' parents/caregivers by providing educational guides and handouts to demonstrate the topics covered in their course and tips for discussing these topics further at home. Again, this practice would likely benefit all students, not only students with intellectual and developmental disabilities.

Arguably, the most important consideration when providing sexuality education to individuals with intellectual and developmental disabilities is the inclusion of these individuals in the development and delivery of the content. Inclusion of individuals with intellectual or developmental disabilities in the development and delivery of sexuality education aligns with both the "engagement" principle of UDL and the "Nothing About Us Without Us" disability rights movement.[28,35] The use of peer educators can facilitate educators in providing inclusive sexuality education for other youth with intellectual and developmental disabilities. Peer educators ensure individuals with intellectual or developmental disabilities voices are incorporated into the development of the program, influencing *what* is taught and *how* it is taught. It is hypothesized that this format may improve the comfort of students with intellectual and developmental disabilities when learning sensitive information and ensure that the material is relevant and appropriate for these youth. Additional research is needed to test this format compared to other more traditional education formats, but the limited available evidence demonstrates positive effects on peer educators.[36]

Clinical Application/Settings

Knowledge of the most effective modalities for individuals with intellectual and developmental disabilities can be applied in a variety of clinical and non-clinical settings. This includes, but is not limited to, community outreach programs, family units, foster systems, hospitals, religious organizations, and schools. Research suggests that the type of modalities utilized depends on where education is provided. For example, healthcare providers typically introduce sexuality education using handouts and worksheets.[14] Worksheets that use simple language, incorporate clear visuals, and are easy to comprehend are more successful among clients with diverse strengths. However, not all individuals learn best from written text, which can be a limiting factor of this modality. Educators often utilize modeling and role-play activities when addressing sexuality education with individuals with intellectual and developmental disabilities.[14] This may be done in a large group setting, such as a classroom, small group, or one-on-one with a professional and the individual.

To promote effective learning and carryover of skills, sexuality education should be presented proactively by multiple trusted adults. Further, early and consistent exposure to sexuality education helps empower the individual, normalize the topics, promote independence, and help decrease negative or unhealthy sexual health experiences. Sexuality education has been successfully delivered to individuals with intellectual and developmental disabilities in group settings, one-on-one, in-person, and virtually. A delivery method should be selected based on the setting, resources (i.e., access to a computer or Wi-Fi), and student needs. Second, the learning preferences and strengths of the individual should be taken into consideration. For example, authors have found some people may prefer to discuss sexuality education topics virtually. Students reported that meeting virtually allowed for increased written communication as opposed to verbal communication. They felt less discomfort typing sexual health questions than verbally asking an adult. Virtual communication also can reduce environmental stimuli (eye contact, lighting, loud noises) that may be stressful to an individual. Considering the COVID-19 pandemic, virtual sexuality education provides an alternative method for teaching this information while adhering to social distancing and quarantining safety guidelines. This allows students to continue to learn without risking their or their family members' health.

All clinical and non-clinical settings that regularly work with individuals with intellectual and developmental disabilities should consider current practices on sexuality education. It may benefit care providers to consider the following questions: Is there access to medically accurate and accessible sexuality education at my current workplace? Is sexuality education being prioritized? What can be done to increase access or quality of programming for people with intellectual and developmental disabilities? Do people with intellectual and developmental disabilities feel empowered to explore sexuality-related topics of interest? A variety of resources are available to help ensure people with intellectual and developmental disabilities receive high-quality sexuality education.

Resources

Below is a compilation of sexuality education resources developed by the authors or sourced from freely available resources and tested for usability, usefulness, and desirability among individuals with intellectual and developmental disabilities and sexuality educators.[37] Although this list is not exhaustive and additional testing is needed, the following resources were found to be accessible, useful in improving sexual health knowledge in the related content area, and enjoyable to engage with for individuals with intellectual and developmental disabilities.[37] These activities are freely available at ekschmidt.com/resources.

- Visuals: The visuals found to be useful, usable, and desirable included contraceptives infographics, visual representation of adolescent development and puberty, and the gender unicorn. Specific recommendations to improve accessibility included simplifying graphics, including real photographs or sketches, emphasizing efficacy over failure rates, prioritizing key points, and narrating information while using the visuals.[37]
- Videos: The videos found to be useful, usable, and desirable included interviews with actual people with intellectual and developmental disabilities, those that use fun animations and cartoon-style illustration with voice-overs, and those that use captioning and other methods to improve accessibility.

Other resources that the authors have utilized during the provision of sexuality education to individuals with intellectual and developmental disabilities include educational websites, freely available sexuality education curricula, and educational YouTube channels. Examples of websites used are listed here:

- Planned Parenthood: plannedparenthood.org/learn/teens/tools-for-teens
- FLASH Program Curriculum: https://kingcounty.gov/depts/health/locations/family-planning/education/FLASH/special-education.aspx
- YouTube Channels: www.youtube.com/user/watchwellcast/videos and www.youtube.com/user/watchwellcast/videos

Here are examples of other activities that incorporate concepts of UDL, including multimodal approaches, for teaching sexuality education.

- Contraceptive Demonstration: Bring in condoms and other forms of birth control for the students to see and touch as they learn about contraceptive options. Educators can demonstrate appropriate condom application using anatomical models.
- Kahoot!: This website allows teachers to create a trivia game for their students using various question formats such as true or false, multiple-choice, or short response. The students can sign in with the unique game code and compete against each other to answer questions about the material. This is always a fun and user-friendly way to end a session or topic.
- Post-It-Notes: This activity can be used for a variety of content areas. For example, when teaching about internet safety, it is often helpful to first explore the concept of public and private information. A t-chart can be drawn on a whiteboard with "public" and "private" written on either side. Each student is given four Post-It notes and asked to write two pieces of information about themselves that should be kept private and two that are public. For example, their social security number and address are private information, where public information could be pictures of their pets or food they like. The teacher or aide can assist students who need cognitive or

physical support writing the answers down. When all the students are done, the teacher collects the Post-It notes, sticks them under each category on the board, and reads them aloud with the class. This provides the opportunity to start conversations about answers on the board while allowing students to stay anonymous.

Sample Lesson

Often, the authors start class with a video from one of the above sources and follow the video with a discussion about what the students noticed and what questions they have. This serves as a segue into the lessons and activities of that class session and helps people feel more comfortable. Each lesson covers basic terminology and themes using language appropriate for the student's cognitive ability. Throughout the lesson, the authors typically incorporate examples and interactive activities to further enhance comprehension of the material. Finally, the lesson ends with a group quiz or review of the key takeaways.

For example, a lesson about internet safety and online dating starts with a video from AMAZE that introduces internet safety. After viewing the video, the students engage in a brief discussion and make comments or ask questions. Next, the educator gives a direct lecture on internet safety using a visual aid (e.g., slideshow presentation). To assess each student's understanding of the covered material, the lecture is followed by an interactive learning activity in which the students sort information based on whether it is safe to share on the Internet or not. Next, educators may lead role-playing or use worksheets to cover topics such as cyberbullying, identifying fake profiles, online dating, and social media. Finally, the lesson ends with true or false questions that the class answers together. This final activity can be beneficial to identify any areas that students are still having difficulty with and can be further addressed in the moment and the next class if necessary. Of course, every teacher and group of students are different and may benefit from other tools and structures. Teachers should adapt their lessons and teaching approaches to best meet the abilities and needs of their students.

Key Takeaways

People with intellectual and developmental disabilities are often excluded from conversations about sexual health. Understanding modality recommendations will enhance current sexuality education programming. Additionally, research on best practices for teaching sexuality education to people with intellectual and developmental disabilities can be used as a tool to advocate for curriculum enhancement. Multiple resources are available for people with intellectual and developmental disabilities to learn sexual health information. Resources include community programs, infographics, group activities, videos, visuals, and websites. Educators should provide accommodations as needed and adapt educational materials to the learner's strengths. Sexuality education should always be age-appropriate, medically accurate, and comprehensive. An inclusive environment should make all students feel safe and respected. The role of the caregiver should also be emphasized to reinforce information at home. Finally, it is best practice for individuals with intellectual and developmental disabilities to be included in the development and delivery of sexuality education.

References

1. Kahn, N.F., & Halpern, C.T. (2018). The relationship between cognitive ability and experiences of vaginal, oral, and anal sex in the United States. *The Journal of Sex Research, 55*(1), 99–105. https://doi.org/10.1080/00224499.2016.1247149
2. Barnard-Brak, L., Schmidt, M., Chesnut, S., Wei, T., & Richman, D. (2014). Predictors of access to sex education for children with intellectual disabilities in public schools. *Intellectual and Developmental Disabilities, 52*(2), 85–97. https://doi.org/10.1352/1934-9556-52.2.85.
3. Mandell, D.S., Eleey, C.C., Cederbaum, J.A., Noll, E., Hutchinson, M.K., Jemmott, L.S., & Blank, M.B. (2008). Sexually transmitted infection among adolescents receiving special education services. *Journal of School Health, 78*(7), 382–388.
4. Jones, L., Bellis, M.A., Wood, S., Hughes, K., McCoy, E., Eckley, L., Bates, G., Mikton, C., Shakespeare, T., & Officer, A. (2012). Prevalence and risk of violence against children with disabilities: A systematic review and meta-analysis of observational studies. *The Lancet, 380*(9845), 899–907. https://doi.org/10.1016/S0140-6736(12)60692-8.
5. Spencer, N., Devereux, E., Wallace, A., Sundrum, R., Shenoy, M., Bacchus, C., & Logan, S. (2005). Disabling conditions and registration for child abuse and neglect: A population-based study. *Pediatrics, 116*(3).
6. Sullivan, P.M., & Knutson, J.F. (2000). Maltreatment and disabilities: A population-based epidemiological study. *Child Abuse & Neglect, 24*(10), 1257–1273.
7. Schmidt, E.K., Hand, B.N., Havercamp, S., Sommerich, C., Weaver, L., & Darragh, A. (2021). Sex education practices for people with intellectual and developmental disabilities: A qualitative study. *American Journal of Occupational Therapy, 75*, 7503180060. https://doi.org/10.5014/ajot.2021.044859.
8. Campbell, M., L€ofgren-Mårtenson, C., & Martino, A.S. (2020). Cripping sex education. *Sex Education, 20*(4), 361–365. https://doi.org/10.1080/14681811.2020.1749470
9. Frawley, P., & Wilson, N.J. (2016). Young people with intellectual disability talking about sexuality education and information. *Sexuality and Disability, 34*(4), 469–484. https://doi.org/10.1007/s11195-016-9460-x
10. Nelson, B., Odberg Pettersson, K., & Emmelin, M. (2020). Experiences of teaching sexual and reproductive health to students with intellectual disabilities. *Sex Education, 20*(4), 398–412. https://doi.org/10.1080/14681811.2019.1707652
11. Ferrante, C.A., & Oak, E. (2020). "No sex please!" We have been labelled intellectual disabled. *Sex Education, 20*(4), 383–397. https://doi.org/10.1080/14681811.2020.1719579.
12. Swango-Wilson, A. (2009). Perception of sex education for individuals with developmental and cognitive disability: A four cohort study. *Sex & Disability, 27*, 223–228. https://doi.org/10.1007/s11195-009-9140-1
13. Lofgren-Mårtenson, L. (2013). € "Hip to be crip?" About crip theory, sexuality and people with intellectual disabilities. *Sexuality and Disability, 31*(4), 413–424. https://doi.org/10.1007/s11195-013-9287-7

14. Schmidt, E.K., Robek, N., Dougherty, M., Hand, B.N., Havercamp, S., Sommerich, C., Weaver, L., & Darragh, A. (2020). Recommendations to improve accessibility of sexuality education for individuals with intellectual or developmental disabilities: A qualitative study. *American Journal of Sexuality Education,* 1–20. https://doi.org/10.1080/15546128.2020.1860177
15. Ward, K.M., Bosek, R.L., & Trimble, E.L. (2010). Romantic relationships and interpersonal violence among adults with developmental disabilities. *Intellectual and Developmental Disabilities, 48*(2), 89–98. https://doi.org/10.1352/1934-9556-48.2.89
16. Leutar, Z., & Mihoković, M. (2007). Level of knowledge about sexuality of people with mental disabilities. *Sexuality and Disability, 25*(3), 93–109. https://doi.org/10.1007/s11195-007-9046-8
17. Pownall, J.C., Jahoda, A., & Hastings, R.P. (2012). Sexuality and sex education of adolescents with intellectual disability: Mothers' attitudes, experiences, and support needs. *Intellectual and Developmental Disabilities, 50*(2), 140–154. https://doi.org/10.1352/1934-9556-50.2.140.
18. Goldfarb, E.S., & Lieberman, L.D. (2020). Three decades of research: The case for comprehensive sex education. *Journal of Adolescent Health, 68,* 13–27. https://doi.org/10.1016/j.jadohealth.2020.07.036.
19. Bejerot, S., & Eriksson, J.M. (2014). Sexuality and gender role in autism spectrum disorder: A case control study. *PLoS One, 9*(1), Article e87961. https://doi.org/10.1371/journal.pone.0087961
20. George, R., & Stokes, M.A. (2018). A quantitative analysis of mental health among sexual and gender minority groups in ASD. *Journal of Autism and Developmental Disorders, 48*(6), 2052–2063. https://doi.org/10.1007/s10803-018-3469-1
21. George, R., & Stokes, M.A. (2018). Sexual orientation in autism spectrum disorder: Sexual orientation in ASD. *Autism Research, 11*(1), 133–141. https://doi.org/10.1002/aur.1892
22. Gilmour, L., Schalomon, P.M., & Smith, V. (2012). Sexuality in a community based sample of adults with autism spectrum disorder. *Research in Autism Spectrum Disorders, 6*(1), 313–318. https://doi.org/10.1016/j.rasd.2011.06.003
23. McCann, E., Lee, R., & Brown, M. (2016). The experiences and support needs of people with intellectual disabilities who identify as LGBT: A review of the literature. *Research in Developmental Disabilities, 57,* 39–53. https://doi.org/10.1016/j.ridd.2016.06.013
24. Sitter, K.C., Burke, A.C., Ladhani, S., & Mallay, N. (2019). Supporting positive sexual health for persons with developmental disabilities: Stories about the right to love. *British Journal of Learning Disabilities, 47*(4), 255–263. https://doi.org/10.1111/bld.12287
25. Wilson, N.J., Macdonald, J., Hayman, B., Bright, A.M., Frawley, P., & Gallego, G. (2018). A narrative review of the literature about people with intellectual disability who identify as lesbian, gay, bisexual, transgender, intersex or questioning. *Journal of Intellectual Disabilities, 22*(2), 171–196. https://doi.org/10.1177/1744629516682681
26. Schmidt, E.K., Brown, C., & Darragh, A. (2019). Scoping review of sexual health education for adolescents and young adults with intellectual or developmental disabilities. *Sexuality and Disability, 38*(3), 439–453. https://doi.org/10.1007/s11195-019-09593-4
27. Sexual Health Equity for Individuals with Intellectual/Developmental Disabilities (SHEIDD) Project. (2019). *SHEIDD review of sexual health education curricula designed for people with disabilities.* www.ohsu.edu/sites/default/files/2019-08/Review%20of%20Sexual%20Health%20Education%20Curricula%20Designed%20for%20People%20with%20Disabilities%208.2019.pdf

28. Roden, C.R., Schmidt, E.K., & Holland-Hall, C. (2020). Sexuality education for individuals with intellectual and developmental disabilities: Recommendations for accessible sexual and reproductive health information. *The Lancet, 4,* 699–708.
29. DiGioia, M.K. (n.d.). *Taking a special education approach.* www.uua.org/sites/live-new.uua.org/files/owl_specialed.pdf.
30. Schaafsma, D., Kok, G., Stoffelen, J.M.T., & Curfs, L.M.G. (2015). Identifying effective methods for teaching sex education to individuals with intellectual disabilities: A systematic review. *Journal of Sex Research, 52*(4), 412–432. https://doi.org/10.1080/00224499.2014.919373
31. CAST (2018). *Universal design for learning guidelines version 2.2.* http://udlguidelines.cast.org
32. Sala, G., Hooley, M., Attwood, T., Mesibov, G.B., & Stokes, M.A. (2019). Autism and intellectual disability: A systematic review of sexuality and relationship education. *Sexuality and Disability, 37*(3), 353–382. https://doi.org/10.1007/s11195-019-09577-4
33. Grove, L., Morrison-Beedy, D., & Kirby, R. (2018). The birds, bees, and special needs: Making evidence-based sex education accessible for adolescents with intellectual disability. *Sexuality and Disability, 36,* 313–329. https://doi.org/10.1007/s11195-018-9547-7
34. Schmidt, E.K., Dougherty, M., Robek, N., Weaver, L., & Darragh, A. (2021). Sexual experiences and perspectives of adolescents and young adults with intellectual and developmental disabilities. *Journal of Adolescent Research,* 1–26. doi:10.1177/07435584211028225.
35. Frawley, P., & O'Shea, A. (2019). "Nothing about us without us": Sex education by and for people with intellectual disability in Australia. *Sex Education, 20*(4), 413–424. https://doi.org/10.1080/14681811.2019.1668759
36. Frawley, P., & Bigby, C. (2014). "I'm in their shoes": Experiences of peer educators in sexuality and relationship education. *Journal of Intellectual & Developmental Disability, 39*(2), 167–176. http://dx.doi.org/10.3109/136682420.2014.890701.
37. Schmidt, E.K., Dougherty, M., Robek, N., Darragh, A., Hand, B.N., Havercamp, S.M., Weaver, L.L., & Sommerich, C. (2021). Usability, usefulness, and desirability of learning activities for sexual health education for individuals with intellectual and developmental disabilities. *American Journal of Sexuality Education,* 1–24.

9

TALKING TO CHILDREN ABOUT PORNOGRAPHY

Insights and Future Directions

Jessica D. Zurcher

With a seemingly overnight shift in education from in-person to online settings combined with possible negative implications of prolonged social isolation, some question if the recent months of the novel form of coronavirus disease (COVID-19) led to increases in adolescent pornography consumption. Indeed, research infers a possible connection between numerous psychosocial outcomes derived from the pandemic (such as higher levels of depression and anxiety, problematic technology use, loneliness, and post-traumatic stress disorder) and growing pornography use among adults.[1] And such ramifications may not differ for adolescents. Beyond facing augmented social stressors for some adolescents, the pandemic created educational settings where the Internet became the primary instructor and non-supervised time on the computer amplified, thus providing greater opportunities and accessibility for online pornography engagement.

Although we may still be several years out from beginning to unearth the effects of COVID-19 on today's adolescents, parent-child communication about pornography (perhaps now more than ever) is crucial in assisting adolescents in navigating through an ever-changing—and even revamped—technological world. As such, I offer five insights observed from my previous work on parent-child pornography communication[2,3] in conjunction with recent research to inform and promote future conversations.

Should We Be Concerned? Adolescents, Pornography, and the Digital Age

Educators and parents are beginning to discover how common it is for children to encounter pornography. Indeed, research indicates that the average age of adolescent exposure to pornography is about age 14 for boys and 17.5 for girls.[4,5]

DOI: 10.4324/9781003189787-10

This is not necessarily surprising, particularly considering that about 92% of US adolescents ages 13–17 use the Internet daily.[6] And the Internet provides space for what is known as the "triple-A engine effect," where users are offered potentially unlimited access, availability, and anonymity via personalized computers to online pornography.[7]

Although research related to general adult pornography use is mixed, findings addressing adolescent impacts are more consistent despite some concerns regarding the methodological approaches used. A summary of the literature suggests several negative outcomes of adolescent pornography consumption, including decreased sensitivity toward women, distorted and unhealthy views about sexuality, increased risk of developing a negative body image, and increased risk of developing sexually compulsive behavior.[8]

A more recent narrative review[9] offers additional implications to adolescent pornography use, such as the following: declines in individual self-esteem and sexual satisfaction;[10] increased participation in adolescent sexting;[11] increased victimization and assault;[12] and legal consequences as dictated by state and federal laws.[13] The narrative study also cites two studies that assert little to no specific effects related to adolescent pornography engagement.[9,14,15] A scholarly commentary explains varying impacts related to adolescent pornography engagement, suggesting that such engagement is mediated by "what consumers bring to this, how they negotiate its meanings, the media in question, and the organization and contexts of use."[16]

Communicating About Pornography to Protect Children

Though evidence concerning the impacts of pornography is mixed, few doubt the need for increased analytical, critical, and media literacy skills among adolescents concerning both sexualized and non-sexualized media content.[17] Parents may be a strong and central force in building adolescent media literacy. One scholar gave this testimony to the Congressional Committee on Government Reform: "A warm and communicative parent-child relationship is the most important nontechnical means that parents can use to deal with the challenges of the sexualized media environment."[18]

Specific to media conversations and pornography use, this communicative environment might be defined as *active mediation*, or "parent-child discussion of the media or media content that is intended to impact how and the extent to which children are influenced by media exposure."[19] A study of college students reflecting on parent-child pornography conversations retroactively illustrated that when parents consistently discussed pornography during adolescence, attitudes toward pornography in young adult years were significantly less positive; indeed, negative attitudes toward pornography were associated with a reduction in young adult pornography use.[20] Moreover, parental active media served as a protection to the self-esteem of one whose romantic partner regularly engaged with pornography.

This concludes that active mediation may be "one way to reduce negative indirect effects of pornography exposure and prevent future pornography use."[20]

The benefits of parent-child communication extend to multiple attributes of adolescent sexual education. For instance, one study reported that adolescents whose parents discussed pornography with them within the last year were half-as likely to view pornography as a central sex educator compared to those parents and children who had not.[21]

Five Insights

Derived from my ongoing research on parent-child pornography communication, I generated the following insights to assist parents and educators in these conversations by contextualizing my research with recent studies. I also offer suggestions for future research.

Increase Parents' Education About Pornography Prior to Discussions With Children

Patterns in the literature posit parental sexual knowledge as a central predictor of whether parents address sexual topics with their children. This means that parents need more information about adolescent pornography exposure rates and vulnerable populations, accessibility types, and the types of pornography content available to teens.

Exposure Rates and Vulnerable Populations

Although there is disagreement on the exact number of adolescents who view pornography and the age of first exposure,[22] there is general agreement that a significant number of adolescents view it.[9,23–27] For instance, one study found that by the age of 19, 80% of British adolescents included in the sample had viewed pornography.[28] Studies from Scandinavian countries report some of the highest numbers of adolescent views, with reports of 99% of samples having viewed pornography.[27,29] In Italy, a study encompassing 1,163 adolescents reported that 70% of the sample encountered pornography.[30] Other research observed that due to increasing online accessibility, "pornography use has now become both normative and widespread across most parts of the modern world."[31]

The literature provides further information concerning adolescent populations who may be considered more likely to consume pornography. A summative review points to the variables of gender, age, and family functionality as influential factors.[9] For instance, in a review of 20 years of research on adolescents and pornography, one study suggests that males, older adolescents (or those of high school age), and adolescents who experience dysfunction in their familial environment are prone to higher pornography use.[32] Further, the narrative report notes that adolescents who struggle with limited self-regulation and increased susceptibility to peer pressure are also higher risk groups.[33] Lastly, the narrative report outlines research related to adolescents' interest in sexual activities as a possible risk factor. Particularly among boys, *perceived realism* (or the perception that pornography portrays realistic content) and stronger sexual interests were linked to increased adolescent pornography use.[34,35] Interestingly, another study revealed that adolescents who had not had sex by the age of 18 were less likely to engage in pornography consumption.[36]

Accessibility versus Exposure

Related to exposure rates and demographics, it becomes crucial for parents to comprehend the differences between the terms accessibility and exposure. Findings distinguish between the two engagement types, with the term *access* referring to a deliberate viewing of pornography—with adolescents actively seeking out pornography.[37] Research suggests that young males are more likely to access pornography deliberately.[38–40] Conversely, the term *exposure* refers to a non-deliberate encounter of pornography by adolescents, which can occur by accident, by design of the pornography industry, or through peer-to-peer distribution.[22] Exposure frequently occurs when an adolescent seeks information non-related to sex;[28,41] consequently, exposure can be shocking and upsetting for adolescents as pornography consumption was not the original intent, and the adolescent was psychologically unprepared for the encounter.[42]

The Sharing of Pornography

The nature of how pornography is created and distributed continues to evolve; what used to be shared primarily through print magazines and video has transformed to numerous formats due to advancing internet technologies. These formats now include unsolicited emails, pop-ups, and texts; search engine keywords similar to children's non-sexualized content; homework and/or popular music star names;[28] and "mouse trapping," or when exiting a website the user is automatically taken to another.

Educators, parents, and professionals face increasing difficulties in combatting the availability of pornography online.[43] Indeed, with reconstructions to technologies that offer pornography, rapid advances occur that create a workaround either by young people and/or the industry itself. Consider the following examples from the article "Young People, Sexuality, and the Age of Pornography": [44]

> An example of this is the hopes held by many professionals who work with young people that Snapchat could be used to send personal or sexual images without the possibility of them being shared. However, the ability of phones to take a screenshot means that even a temporary or disposable

> image can be captured, saved and shared. However, the ability of phones to take a screenshot means that even a temporary or disposable image can be captured, saved and shared. In addition to this, there is evidence to suggest that government measures to limit this effect—such as encouraging households to opt in or out of parental controls—had little effect, as young people are often entrusted with orchestrating any technology changes and so know how to bypass safeguards.[22]

Several scholars admit that an answer to adolescent pornography engagement is not necessarily through the removal or disabling of technology. While filters may assist parents, many adolescents find means to bypass such safeguards.

So, where does this leave parents and educators? Again, the conversation turns toward parental mediation and communication with children to build porn literacy. Parental education can be a crucial first step in approaching parent-child pornography communication. For instance, parents may approach a conversation about pornography with an adolescent very differently if they know the following: (1) globally, many adolescents encounter pornography, (2) some adolescent populations are more likely to engage in pornography than others, (3) there's a difference between access and exposure, and (4) the nature of pornography is continuously shifting and evolving, making it difficult for adolescents to avoid exposure and parents to use technology as a primary filtering tool.

Parents can consider forming an active mediation conversation about pornography with adolescents with the right educational context. If parents can first understand rather than go on the defensive or attack, this response may go a long way in promoting ongoing conversations. The next set of suggestions focuses on insights within parent-child pornography communication and offers areas for future research.

Build Parental Definitions of the Term "Pornography"

The literature notes that the concept of "pornography" is ambiguous and complex, and my research findings convey a similar view. When asked to define the word "pornography," parents may talk *around* the content of pornography itself by concentrating on some of the following: (1) the specific media used to access pornography (e.g., inappropriate pictures in magazines or videos online), (2) the "taboo" culture that surrounds pornography, (3) emotionally driven terms such as "fear" or "curiosity," and/or (4) more generalized terms such as "nudity" to define pornography (e.g., "pornography is nudity").[2,3] Rarely did the parents I interviewed convey direct definitions of pornography, such as sexually explicit content that is "intended primarily for the purpose of sexual arousal,"[45] or for younger audiences, "bad pictures of people with little or no clothes on."[46] Bolstering parental knowledge concerning the definition of pornography may build parental self-efficacy—which, in turn, may build parental self-efficacy that can act as a confidence booster in having conversations with children.[47]

One suggestion to combat the complexity of the word "pornography" is to encourage parents to use the word itself instead of more ambiguous terms that do not accurately describe the content; don't disguise it—call pornography for what it is. As observed in my research, if parents struggle to define pornography directly, children may leave the conversation with greater confusion. Moreover, how parents and children approach sexual topics can be passed on to future generations.[48] If parents use fear, avoidance, and/or shame-based language, adolescents will likely use a similar approach with future children. Fostering parental confidence in how parents define and discuss pornography and its related contexts (i.e., exposure rates, access, availability, etc.) are key first steps.

Prepare Adolescents to Encounter Pornography—Don't Be Victim to the "Third-Person Effect"

An adolescent will likely encounter pornography, yet several of the parents I interviewed perceived a social norm that "good kids don't encounter pornography." Extending this idea, parents also sometimes experience what I call the "not my kid" descriptive norm, or the idea that while pornography impacts many adolescents, "my child is a 'good kid' and therefore won't reach him/her."[2,3] This notion ties into the third-person effect,[49] or the theory that media holds a greater impact on those around us compared to ourselves. Adolescent pornography exposure statistics imply that this is inaccurate. Just as parents should prepare children to encounter pornography, they should also prepare to discuss pornography with their children.

One observation that could perpetuate the "not my kid" descriptive norm is the fear of parental judgment from influential others. Some of the parents I interviewed expressed fear and distress if other parents, friends, family members, close work, and/or religious associates learned that a parent's child engaged in pornography. At times, this fear of judgment from influential others created parental burdens surrounding the topic of pornography, leading to increased feelings of shame and fear. Such emotions became barriers to parent-child communication and parents' efforts to reach out to others for additional resources.

Understanding that third person effects on adolescent pornography engagement may exist can be freeing for some parents who fear discussing it. My research observed that positive peers could be one of the greatest assistants to parents seeking support, particularly as some parents perceive close associates as more credible than authoritative sources.[50]

Remove Shame-Based Messaging

Research tells us that when adolescents experience pornography for the first time, some express distress, fear, and shock. Likewise, parents may also experience a negative response. One study categorizes parental responses to children encountering pornography into the following classifications: (1) "anger, shame or punitive," (2) "being calm and providing facts," (3) "panic or fear," (4) "ignoring, minimizing, or denying that it happened," and (5) "lying to the child about what the child viewed."[51] Correspondingly, findings from my research suggest that some parents blame and punish their children for encountering pornography.[2]

Negative parent reactions are harmful to parent-child communication environments, particularly if children perceive adverse consequences from discussing pornography with trusted adults. Imagine the following scenario: a 10-year-old child encounters pornography while doing homework. She was not actively searching for this content. After the encounter, she is frightened, confused, but also curious about what she saw. Her mother enters the room, sees the image, and immediately begins to chastise her daughter and threaten to "take away the computer and ground her for the week." This response leaves little room for parent-child discussions, the expression of feelings, openness to questions, nor promotes opportunities for parents to serve as primary educators.

Let's take the same scenario from another possible parent response. Mom enters the room, sees the pornographic image, but also observes that her daughter is distressed. The mother sits down and asks her child how she feels about what she saw and what questions she may have. The two create an action plan for future encounters of pornography so that the daughter understands the options allotted to her. Action items could include (1) naming pornography for what it is, (2) turning it off and turning away, and (3) talking to a trusted adult.[46] Such a response encourages conversation with instances of future pornography encounters and sets the stage for when other difficult topics may arise.

Educators and parents alike must prepare their response to children encountering pornography. Acts that illustrate positive communication (such as a parent thanking a child for confiding in them and asking questions and/or encouraging further open dialogue) may shift conversations to warmer communication climates. Again, through a realization and further understanding of context and research, parents may become empowered to promote communication channels that travel beyond sexualized media content into open communication patterns in everyday life.

Build an Ongoing, Open, Positive Relationship with Children

I am unaware of any specific research exploring relevant parent-child conversations about pornography scripts, nor a longitudinal study that examines parental scripts or educational scaffolding for various parent-child pornography communication approaches. Other research echoes this claim, purporting a great need for age-appropriate and "culturally relevant scripts" that could be tested over time.[51] One study argues for the development and testing of a question guide on how to ask children if they've viewed pornography preemptively instead of "catching" an adolescent in the act.[51] I agree that these directions would be helpful to the field as a deep analysis of varying communicative responses, conversation structures, question types, and so on surrounding parent-child pornography communication has yet to be undertaken.

We do, however, have some understanding relating to the influence of active mediation and adolescents, or in a more generalized construct as it relates to parenting, the integration of *positive parenting* and the *authoritative* parenting style within parent-child relationships. *Positive parenting* associates characteristics such as parental support, involvement, warmth, and open communication to increase adolescent overall well-being and self-esteem.[52] Similarly, research on *parenting styles* (or approaches that influence children's behaviors through the expression of control) highlights implications of varying parental responses. For example, parents who are responsive to children but are relaxed in enforcing rules and discipline are categorized as having a *permissive parenting style*. Conversely, the *authoritarian parenting style* mandates high obedience from children without offering reasoning for the associated behavior. Nonetheless, the *authoritative parenting style* straddles between permissive and authoritarian approaches by offering adolescents firm expectations mixed with an understanding of *why* certain behaviors and expectations are important.[53]

A study evaluating parenting styles and internet risk prevention strategies records that permissive parents had difficulty addressing the dangers of the Internet with their children.[54] It further suggests that parents who engaged in an authoritarian style (where children were provided a set of rules without further communication) expressed an easier time speaking with children. Yet, authors contend that the most productive prevention method involved using the *authoritative parenting style*, which consists of a blend of the positives of both authoritarian and permissive (e.g., "a balance of open communication and control").[54] Simply put, "the more both parties found it difficult to talk to one another, the more likely the kids were to resist the idea of their parents accessing their Internet worlds."[54]

This statement emphasizes parents' abilities to communicate with adolescents, or what some scholars identify as levels of openness. *Openness* may be defined as the "disclosing or discussing thoughts, feelings, or viewpoints about the self, others, or events."[55] Assessing the implications of parent-child openness, adolescents frequently react more positively to "responsive and accepting parents" in comparison to "rejecting and judgmental parents"; such responses set the stage of adolescent openness in younger ages. Adolescents play a larger role "in creating the relational climates as well as their own openness" and, subsequently, should not be discounted as key players.[55]

Authoritative parents experience the greatest success in both parental communication of internet mediations and child compliance with this communication; the authoritative approach holds further benefits as it works to increase children's ability to critically assess media.[54] Future research should work to develop parent-child pornography communication scripts that contain elements of openness and the authoritative parenting style as a means to test parent-child pornography communication strategies and best practices empirically.

Conclusion

There are numerous benefits of positive parent-child communication. Developing an open communication pattern with children on multiple subjects—not just pornography—is crucial to assist children's navigation of online content in an ever-changing, ever-increasing technological world. To develop greater open communication, my research points to a need for increasing parental education concerning the pervasiveness and topic of pornography prior to parent-child conversations; such education may better empower parents with tools to promote positive parent-child relationships. Moreover, parenting tools often expressed through an authoritative parenting style can be useful in building a positive rapport with children, and children may become more likely to approach parents and trusted adults with questions about pornography rather than seek information about sex or sexuality from external (and untrusted) sources. These actions, along with future research regarding parent-child pornography communication scripts and educational approaches, are useful in understanding parents' roles to actively mediate children's pornography exposures.

References

1. Marchi, N.C., Fara, L., Gross, L., Ornell, F., Diehl, A., & Kessler, F.H.P. (2021). Problematic consumption of online pornography during the COVID-19 pandemic: Clinical recommendations. *Trends Psychiatry Psychotherapy, 21*, 34043899
2. Zurcher, J. (2017). Exploring descriptive norms of parent-child communication about pornography among parents of middle-schoolers in the US. *Journal of Children and Media, 11*(4), 381–398, doi:10.1080/17482798.2017.1312471
3. Zurcher, J. (2019). The interplay between peer and authoritative norms of parents discussing pornography with adolescents. *American Journal of Sexuality Education,* 1–17. doi:10.1080/15546128.2019.1635059.
4. Herbenick, D., Fu, T., Wright, P., Paul, B., Gradus, R., Bauer, J., & Jones, R. (2020). Diverse sexual behaviors and pornography use: Findings from a nationally representative probability survey of Americans aged 18 to 60 years. *The Journal of Sexual Medicine, 20*, 623–633.
5. Other research has suggested even younger ages ranging from 12 to 15. See, for example, Bischmann A., Richardson C., Diener J, Gullickson M., Davidson M., Gervais S. (2017). Age and experience of first exposure to pornography, relations to masculine norms. InPoster presented at the annual American Psychological Association convention 2017 Aug. and Carnevali, D., Cavazzana, L., Grimoldi, L., Magnoni, P., Principi, N., Pellai, A. (2022). The use of online pornography among minors: Epidemiological analysis of the phenomenon. *Minerva Pediatrics, 2022.* doi:10.23736/s2724-5276.19.05342-8. PMID: 35166482.
6. Lenhart, A. (2015). *Teens, social media and technology overview 2015.* www.pewinternet.org/2015/04/09/teens-social-media-technology-2015/

7. Cooper, A., Delmonico, D.L., & Berg, R. (2000). Cybersex users, abusers, and compulsives: New findings and implications. *Sexual Addiction & Compulsivity: The Journal of Treatment & Prevention,* 7, 5–29. doi:10.1080/10720160008400205
8. Owens, E.W., Behun, R., Manning, J., & Reid, R. (2012). The impact of Internet pornography on adolescents: A review of the research. *Sexual Addiction and Compulsivity, 19*, 99–122.
9. Field, T., (2020). Adolescent pornography: A narrative review. *International Journal of Psychological Research and Reviews, 3*(36). doi: 10.28933/ijprr-2020-03-0505
10. Koletić, G. (2017). Longitudinal associations between the use of sexually explicit material and adolescents' attitudes and behaviors: A narrative review of studies. *Journal of Adolescence, 57*, 119–133. doi:10.1016/j.adolescence.2017.04.006
11. Van Ouystel, J., Ponnet, K. & Walrave, M. (2014). The associations between adolescents' consumption of pornography and music videos and their sexting behavior. *Cyberpsychology, Behaviors and Social Networking, 17*, 772–778.
12. Maas, M.K., Bray, B.C. & Noll, J.G. (2019). Online sexual experiences predict subsequent sexual health and victimization outcomes among female adolescents: A latent class analysis. *Journal of Youth and Adolescence, 48*, 837–849.
13. Lorang, M.R., McNiel, D.E. & Binder, R.L. (2016). Minors and sexting: Legal implications. *Journal of American Psychiatry and Law, 44*, 73–81.
14. Hokby, S., Hadlaczky, G., Westerlund, J., Wasserman, D., Balazs, J., Germanvicius, A., Machín, N., Meszaros, G., Sarchiapone, M., Värnik, A., Varnik, P., Westerlund, M., & Carli, V. (2016). Are mental health effects of Internet use attributable to the web-based content or perceived consequences of usage? A longitudinal study of European adolescents. *JMIR Mental Health, 13*(3), e31. doi:10.2196/mental.5925.
15. Stulhofer, A., Tafro, A. & Kohut, T. (2019). The dynamics of adolescents' pornography use and psychological well-being: A six-wave latent growth and latent class modeling approach. *European Child and Adolescent Psychiatry, 2019*. doi: 10.1007/s00787-019-01318-4.
16. Crabbe, M., & Flood, M. (2021). School-based education to address pornography's influence on young people: A proposed practice framework. *American Journal of Sexuality Education, 16*(1), 1–37. https://doi. org/10.1080/15546128.2020.1856744
17. Rothman, E.F., Daley, N., & Alder, J. (2020). A pornography literacy program for adolescents. *American Journal of Public Health, 110*(2), 154–156.
18. Greenfield, P.M. (2004). Inadvertent exposure to pornography on the Internet: Implication of peer-to-peer file-sharing networks for child development and families. *Applied Developmental Psychology, 25*, 741–750
19. Rasmussen, E.E. (2013). Theoretical underpinnings of reducing the media's negative effect on children: Person-centered, negative-evaluative mediation within a persuasion framework. In E.L. Cohen (Ed.), *Communication yearbook 37* (pp. 379–406). Routledge.
20. Rasmussen, E.E., Ortiz, R.R., & White, S.R. (2015). Emerging adults' responses to active mediation of pornography during adolescence. *Journal of Children and Media, 9*(2), 160–176. doi:10.1080/17482798.2014.997769
21. Rothman, E.F., Beckyeyer, J.J., Herbenick, D., Tsung-Chief, F., Dodge, B., & Fortenberry, J.D. (2021). The prevalence of using pornography for information about how to have sex: Findings from a nationally representative survey of U.S. adolescents and young adults. *Archives of Sexual Behavior, 50*, 629–646. https://doi.org/10.1007/s10508-020-01877-7
22. Massey, K., Burns, J. & Franz, A. (2021). Young people, sexuality and the age of pornography. *Sexuality and Culture, 25*, 318–336. https://doi.org/10.1007/s12119-020-09771-z
23. Cowell, A., & Smith, E. (2009). *Streetwise pornography research*. Streetwise Young People's Project.

24. Häggström-Nordin, E., Tydén, T., Hanson, U., & Larsson, M. (2009). Experiences of and attitudes towards pornography among a group of Swedish high school students. *European Journal of Contraception and Reproductive Health Care, 14,* 277–284.
25. Kim, Y.H. (2011). Adolescents' health behaviours and its associations with psychological variables. *Central European Journal of Public Health, 19,* 205–209.
26. Papadopoulos, L. (2010). *Sexualisation of young people review.* Department of Health.
27. Tydén, T., & Rogala, C. (2004). Sexual behaviour among young men in Sweden and the impact of pornography. *International Journal of STD and AIDS, 15,* 590–693.
28. Livingstone, S., & Bober, M. (2004). *UK children go online: Surveying the experiences of young people and their parents.* London School of Economics and Political Science/EU Kids Online.
29. Sørensen, A.D., & Knudsen, S.V. (2006). *Unge, kon og pornografi i Norden. Slutrapport* (Youth, gender and pornography in the Nordic countries. Final report). The Nordic Council of Ministers, ANP (Vol. 749).
30. Pizzol, D., Bertoldo, A. & Foresta, C. (2016). Adolescents and web porn: A new era of sexuality. *International Journal of Adolescent Medical Health, 28,* 169–173.
31. Willoughby, B.J., Young-Petersen, B., & Leonhardt, N.D. (2018). Exploring trajectories of pornography use through adolescence and emerging adulthood. *The Journal of Sex Research, 55*(3), 297–309.
32. Peter, J. & Valkenburg, P.M. (2016). Adolescents and pornography: A review of 20 years of research. *Journal of Sex Research, 53,* 509–531.
33. Efrati, Y. & Gola, M. (2018). Understanding and predicting profiles of compulsive sexual behavior among adolescents. *Journal of Behavioral Addiction, 7,* 1004–1014.
34. Doornwaard, S.M., van den Eijden, R.J., Overbeek, G. & ter Bogt, T.F. (2015). Differential developmental profiles of adolescents using sexually explicit Internet material. *Journal of Sex Research, 52,* 269–281.
35. Doornwaard, S.M., den Boer, F., Vanwesenbeeck, I., van Nijnatten, C.H.C.J., Ter Bogt, T.F.M. & van den Eijnden, R.J.J.M. (2017). Dutch adolescents' motives, perceptions, and reflections toward sex related internet use: Results of a web-based focus-group study. *Journal of Sex Research, 54,* 1038–1050.
36. Kastbom, A.A., Sydsjo, G., Bladh, M., Priebe, G. & Svedin, C.G. (2016). Differences in sexual behavior, health, and history of child abuse among school students who had and had not engaged in sexual activity by the age of 18 years: A cross-sectional study. *Adolescent Health, Medicine and Therapeutics, 7,* 1–11.
37. Flood, M. (2007). Exposure to pornography among youth in Australia. *Journal of Sociology, 43,* 45–60.
38. Alexy, E.M., Burgess, A.W., & Prentky, R.A. (2009). Pornography use as a risk marker for an aggressive pattern of behaviour among sexually reactive children and adolescents. *Journal of the American Psychiatric Nurses Association, 14,* 442–453.
39. Bleakley, A., Hennessy, M., Fishbein, M., & Jordan, A. (2011b). Using the integrative model to explain how exposure to sexual media content influences adolescent sexual behaviour. *Health Education and Behavior, 38,* 530–540.
40. Bonino, S., Ciairano, S., Rabaglietti, E., & Cattelino, E. (2006). Use of pornography and self-reported engagement in sexual violence among adolescents. *European Journal of Developmental Psychology, 3,* 265–288.
41. Livingstone, S., & Bober, M. (2005). *UK children go online: Final report of key project findings.* London School of Economics and Political Science/EU Kids Online.
42. Buckingham, D., & Bragg, S. (2003). *Young people, media and personal relationships.* Advertising Standards Authority, British Board of Film Classification, British Broadcasting Corporation, Broadcasting Standards Commission, Independent Television Commission.
43. Kirkup, J. (2012, January 6). Parents worry about sexualised children, one year after David Cameron promised cracking down on advertising. *The Telegraph.* www.

telegraph.co.uk/women/mother-tongue/9311970/parents-worry-about-sexualised-children-one-year-after-David-Cameronpromised-crackdown-on-advertising.html.

44. Livingstone, S., & M. Bober (2003). *UK Children Go Online. Listening to young people's experiences*. London School of Economics and Political Science/EU Kids Online.
45. McManus M. (1986). *Final report of the Attorney general's commission on pornography*. Rutledge Hill Press.
46. Burchett, S. (2015, November 2). *New church video helps parents talk to children about pornography*. www.churchofjesuschrist.org/church/news/new-church-video-helps-parents-talk-to-children-about-pornography?lang=eng
47. Jerman, P., & Constantine, N.A. (2010). Demographic and psychological predictors of parent—adolescent communication about sex: A representative statewide analysis. *Journal of Youth and Adolescence, 39*, 1164–1174. doi:10.1007/s10964-010-9546-1
48. Lehr, S.T., Demi, A.S., DiIorio, C., & Facteau, J. (2005). Predictors of father—son communication about sexuality. *Journal of Sex Research, 42*(2), 119–129.
49. Davison, P.W. (1983). The third-person effect in communication. *Public Opinion Quarterly, 47*(1), 1–15
50. Bute, J.J., & Jensen, R.E. (2010). Low-income women describe fertility-related expectations: Descriptive norms, injunctive norms, and behavior. *Health Communication, 25*(8), 681–691. doi:10.1080/10410236.2010.521909
51. Rothman, E.F., Paruk, J., Epsensen, A., Temple, J., Adams, K. (2017). A qualitative study of what US parents say and do when their young children see pornography. *Academic Pediatrics, 17*(8), 844–849.
52. Lereya, S., Samara, M. & Wolke D. (2013). Parenting behavior and the risk of becoming a victim and a bullying/victim: A meta-analysis study. *Child Abuse and Neglect, 37*, 1091–1108.
53. Baurmind, D. (1991). Effective parenting during the early adolescent transition. In P.A. Cowan, & E.M. Hetherington (Eds.), *Advances in family research*, vol. 2. Erlbaum.
54. Byrne, S., & Lee, T. (2011). Toward predicting youth resistance to Internet risk prevention strategies. *Journal of Broadcasting and Electronic Media, 55*, 90–113. doi: 10.1080/08838151.2011.546255
55. Dailey, R.M. (2006). Confirmation in parent-adolescent relationships and adolescent openness: Toward extending confirmation theory. *Communication Monographs, 73*(4), 434–458.

10

THE CONTENTS AND CONSUMPTION OF PORN

Who Is Watching What Exactly?

Dan J. Miller

Introduction

Sex educators might consider two broad approaches to pornography: (1) "pedagogy about porn," that is, teaching porn literacy to encourage critical reflection on the contents of porn, and (2) "porn as pedagogy," that is, the use of porn to promote sexual learning (primarily among adults).[1] The pedagogy about porn approach often focuses on the harms of pornography—the assumption being that, unless educated on the unrealistic nature of porn, some consumers may internalize problematic messages contained within pornography. It is often assumed that negative outcomes may be especially likely among younger people, who have less real-world sexual experience to contextualize what they see in pornography and may seek out porn to fill in knowledge gaps not addressed by traditional sex education.[1] Many young adults indicate using pornography as a source of information about sex, more so than friends, healthcare professionals, media, parents, and sexual partners.[2] The porn as pedagogy approach is less harm-focused, acknowledging potential benefits of pornography for consumers.

Although these approaches differ in the assumed effects of pornography, both require sex educators to have a thorough knowledge of the contents of pornography and the prevalence of porn use. After all, without knowledge of the contents of porn, it would be difficult to know what "inaccuracies" a porn literacy program would need to address or what aspects of sexual health could be enhanced through engagement with pornographic texts. Similarly, knowledge of the prevalence of porn use can provide sex educators context as to the need to address pornography in sex education programs.

The following chapter presents the takeaway findings of two review articles. One of these articles reviews studies into the contents of porn.[3] The other reviews

DOI: 10.4324/9781003189787-11

studies into the prevalence of porn use.[4] In this way, the first half of this chapter aims to give insight into the messages that porn users are exposed to through their consumption of pornography. The second half of this chapter then aims to contextualize this information, outlining who is exposed to such messages, how frequently, and under what circumstances.

What Is Being Watched? The Contents of Pornography

To gain insight into the contents of pornography, many researchers have employed a technique called "content analysis." This technique involves analyzing the contents of a "text" (e.g., advertisements in fashion magazines). In porn research, this typically entails collecting a sample of pornographic videos (e.g., a random selection of clips from Pornhub). Trained coders then view sample videos to record the frequency of target behaviors. For some target behaviors (e.g., condom use), this coding process is relatively objective (i.e., either the male performer is wearing a condom or he is not). Other target behaviors are far more "in the eye of the beholder" and require researchers to develop a comprehension definition of the behavior under investigation. This section gives an overview of this literature, broken down in terms of the major thematic areas addressed by this research.

Violence and Aggression

A major focus within this content analytic literature is violence within pornography. This is perhaps not surprising given the public concern with the effects of violent pornography on consumers. The most fundamental question here is *What percentage of porn contains depictions of violence?* But even a question that is as straightforward as this is difficult to answer. The crux of the matter comes down to what one counts as "violence." In this literature, there are two schools of thought. One is that we should count any act capable of harming *regardless* of the intention of the person performing the act or the reaction of the person receiving the act. Using this definition, a scene depicting rape (simulated or otherwise) would be categorized as "violent," but so would a scene in which a male performer inserts his penis very far into the mouth of a female co-star, causing her to gag—even if the female character is clearly enjoying this and asking the male character to "go deeper." Even a playful slap on the buttocks would be categorized as "violent" if taking this approach. Proponents of this school of thought argue that this approach better captures aggressive acts which have been normalized. This is especially important if one believes that the problem with violent pornography is that it communicates to consumers that aggressive sex is "the norm" and pleasurable for all.

The alternative school of thought argues that categorizing acts like consensual spanking or deep throating as "violent" is incongruent with what the average person means when talking about violent pornography. It also runs the risk of stigmatizing those who engage in BDSM or even just rough sex, which, according to a recent survey of undergraduate students, is a practice that many younger adults engage in and enjoy.[5]

As an example of how different approaches to defining violence can influence findings, one study in the *harm regardless of intention* camp reports 88% of best-selling pornographic film scenes to contain violence.[6] Another study, which takes the alternative approach to defining violence, reports 2% of best-selling pornographic film scenes contain violence.[7]

The importance of this different philosophical approach to understanding violence has led some authors of more recent papers to report the prevalence of "visible aggression, regardless of consent" alongside the prevalence of "non-consensual aggression" (acts which are met with verbal or physical resistance). If focusing only on mainstream heterosexual porn, somewhere between 1%[8] and 15%[9] of scenes contain non-consensual aggression, whereas between 13%[10] and 45%[11] of scenes contain visible aggression of any kind.

The literature is consistent in the findings that the vast majority of aggressive acts depicted in pornography consist of spanking, slapping, or gagging. These behaviors are typically directed at women by men.[11,12] Women most typically react with pleasure in response to these behaviors.[11] According to one study, visible and non-consensual aggression occurs more frequently in videos of gay male partners as compared to videos of heterosexual partners.[10] The literature consistently indicates that extreme sexual violence (e.g., depictions of rape) is rarely depicted in mainstream pornography.[3]

Objectification and Degradation of Women in Pornography

Of course, depicting violence is not the only way pornography may model problematic behavior for consumers. Some researchers analyze pornographic texts for depictions of objectification and degradation, especially of female characters. The idea is that exposure to these messages could promote non-egalitarian attitudes. As you might imagine, the concepts of "objectification" and "degradation" are even more difficult to pin down than "violence." Accordingly, different authors take different approaches to examining objectification and degradation in pornography. For example, some researchers focus on markers of sexual agency, as it is argued that a lack of sexual agency indicates objectification. When considering sexual agency, researchers may look at who initiates sex, who appears to control the direction of the sexual encounter, and the relative social status of sexual partners (e.g., a boss would be categorized as being of a higher social status than an employee).

A few studies have found that male and female characters are equally likely to initiate sex in pornography,[13,14] equally likely to be of a higher social status,[13] and typically share control of the direction of the sexual encounter.[13] When power is not shared equally, men are more likely to be depicted as the dominant partner, and women are more likely to be depicted as submissive.[13] One research team indicates that about a third of internet porn videos portray domination by a man, and about half portray submission by a woman, with 22% of scenes depicting sexual reciprocity between partners.[15]

It is worth noting that genre may play an important role in how male and female characters are portrayed. Men are more likely to initiate sex, control the direction of sex, and be of a higher social status in "teen" videos. The reverse is true for videos featuring older female performers.[9,16] This said, another study found that sexual agency of female characters did not markedly differ between heterosexual feminist, "for-women," and mainstream videos.[17]

Other researchers code for the presence of sexual acts which they believe to be degrading to the receiving partner. Acts that researchers have used to index degradation include ass-to-mouth (i.e., oral sex immediately following anal sex), double penetration, and ejaculation onto the face or body. Although double penetration and ass-to-mouth are far from ubiquitous in mainstream pornography, they appear to occur with some frequency—double penetration in 17% of mainstream internet porn videos[17] and ass-to-mouth in 4% of internet porn scenes.[14] By contrast, external ejaculation is more common, with multiple studies indicating that around half of heterosexual internet porn videos depict ejaculation onto the partner.[15,16] Critics of this approach might question the appropriateness of researchers making blanket determinations about the legitimacy of particular sexual acts. It also ignores the context in which acts occur. Whether the recipient of external ejaculation interprets this behavior as degrading likely depends on the context of the situation.

Another approach is to examine whose pleasure is privileged in porn. The answer to this question would appear to be men's. Male performers are much more likely to be depicted reaching orgasm than female performers,[13,17,18] and female-to-male oral sex is depicted significantly more frequently than male-to-female oral sex.[12,19] This said, it would be inaccurate to claim that pornography is devoid of female orgasm or cunnilingus. A 2020 review found that female orgasm is depicted in around 15–20% of mainstream videos, with cunnilingus occurring in just under half of videos.[12] The point is merely that there appears to be a bias toward men's pleasure in porn.

Finally, some researchers[7,20] investigate the issue of objectification within pornography by analyzing videos for film conventions used to humanize characters and convey agency (e.g., looking directly into the camera). From this lens, it appears that female performers are more likely to be presented in a way that implies agency. For example, compared to male performers, female performers are more likely to be centrally located within the camera frame, to look directly into the camera, and to speak.[20] One study reports that pornographic films are equally likely to be presented from the point of view of a male or female character, but female performers are more likely to speak to the camera.[7] Conversely, male performers are "actively hidden from view and often silent,"[20] which has been interpreted as dehumanizing male characters.

Safe Sex and Consent Communication

Sex educators might also be interested in portrayals of safe sex practices and consent communication in porn. Multiple studies have examined condom use in mainstream pornography. The consensus finding is that condom use is infrequently depicted in heterosexual pornography, occurring in between under 1%[15] and 11% of scenes.[6] Discussions of safe sex occur even less frequently.[6,21] In contrast to heterosexual pornography, condom use is relatively common in gay male pornography, with protected anal sex being depicted as frequently as unprotected anal sex—depicted in 34% and 36% of scenes, respectively[22] (this said, a recent trend toward condomless "bareback" sex in gay male porn has been noted by scholars).[23]

Only one study has examined consent communication in mainstream pornography.[24] Here researchers examined whether and what kind of consent was garnered for each sexual behavior shown in top-selling pornographic films. In around a quarter of cases, no consent communication was shown (i.e., the scene starts with the performers mid-coitus). Explicit verbal consent was uncommon; however, it was not absent, making up about 12% of the consent cues. Nonverbal consent communication (e.g., bodily touching in a sexual way) was more common than verbal consent communication. Female characters were found to use fewer explicit verbal consent cues than male characters. The authors argue that, for these reasons, pornography may promote some problematic ideas around consent: that explicit verbal consent isn't normal and that men are direct, while women are indirect when it comes to communicating consent.

Who Is Watching? Consumers of Pornography

The review of content analytic studies would suggest that mainstream pornography models some problematic behaviors, for example, unprotected casual sex. The content analytic evidence could also indicate that mainstream pornography is not as dangerously problematic as some critics of porn claim. Knowledge of the contents of pornography naturally results in questions around the consumption of porn use. How common is porn use? How many people are frequently exposed to the potentially problematic messages contained within porn? The chapter will now attempt to provide a picture of what is typical in terms of porn use by reviewing surveys into porn use behavior.

Prevalence of Porn Use

A few large-scale surveys are available to draw on for information about the prevalence of porn use. Two particularly useful large-scale surveys are the General Social Survey (GSS)[25] and Relationships in America (RIA) survey.[26,27]

The GSS has been ongoing since the 1970s. The GSS assesses porn use via a single question "Have you seen an X-rated movie in the past year?" In 2018, 39%

of male participants and 20% of female participants answered in the affirmative to this question. Among participants ages 18–26, 59% of men and 38% of women answered yes. In contrast, far fewer older participants (ages 64+) indicated that they had seen an X-rated movie in the past year (13% of males and 4% of females).

A major strength of the GSS is its sample. The survey samples households at random, meaning it produces a sample that is a good representation of the general population. However, some researchers query the adequacy of the question used to assess porn use. The term "X-rated movie" is somewhat outdated. (Is a 10-minute clip on Pornhub a "movie"?) The timeframe specified by the item ("the past year") is also very broad. Such a measure cannot distinguish between participants who use porn once a year and those who use porn once a day.

The RIA study surveyed US adults ages 18–39. The study, conducted in 2014, assessed the use of porn with the question "When did you last intentionally look at pornography?"[27] Response options related to different time periods (e.g., "today," "3–4 weeks ago"), allowing researchers to get a sense of the percentage of participants that have intentionally viewed porn in the past week, month, and year. Around half of male participants indicated they had intentionally viewed porn in the past week and month (46% and 56% of participants, respectively), with 69% reporting doing so in the past year. Among female respondents, 16%, 26%, and 40% indicated intentionally viewing porn in the past week, month, and year, respectively.

You may have noticed that considerably more males than females indicated consuming pornography in the GSS and RIA studies. (You may have also noticed that neither the GSS nor RIA surveys report on porn use among nonbinary people.) The robust gender gap in the consumption of porn is consistently observed in the research.[28] For this reason, our team's 2020 review focused on men's use of pornography specifically.[4]

Many smaller surveys into pornography use have also been conducted. These smaller studies tend to have less representative samples than the GSS and RIA studies. Many of these studies used "convenience sampling" of college students, meaning that their samples tend to be younger and more educated than the general population. However, these studies can still provide useful information in that they tend to be more thorough in their measurement of porn use and related behaviors.

Our review identified 19 studies reporting the percentage of male respondents who consume pornography on a close-to-weekly basis. (Some studies ask about "viewing at least weekly," others ask about "viewing at least several times per week.") These percentages were combined to produce a cross-study estimate of the percentage of men to be weekly porn users: 45%. Notably, this figure is close to the RIA survey's estimate of the percentage of males to have consumed porn in the past week (46%). This should give us some confidence that around half of younger men are frequent (meaning at least weekly) porn users. Regarding the amount of exposure, one study reports that the men sampled viewed an average of three hours of pornography per week,[29] although other studies report figures in the one to two hours per week range.[30,31]

A few studies have formally compared porn use among heterosexual and gay and bisexual men. These have found higher rates of porn consumption among gay and bisexual men compared to heterosexual men.[31,32] If gay and bisexual men use more pornography than their heterosexual counterparts, this may indicate that gay and bisexual men get something out of pornography that heterosexual men do not. For example, porn may be useful in helping sexual minority men come to understand their sexuality.

The Internet is the most common method for accessing pornography.[4] Most consumers primarily access free pornography, with only about 10% of men having a paid subscription to a pornographic website.[31] About 30% of gay and bisexual men report having used a live webcam service.[33]

Sexual Behaviors Associated With Porn Use

Perhaps unsurprisingly, pornography use appears to be closely tied to solitary masturbation among men.[34,35] The majority of men, ranging from 74% to 98% in different studies, report having masturbated while watching pornography.[36,37] Men most typically masturbate on occasions that they view pornography—although this is not to say that men do not also masturbate without the aid of pornography.[38] When asked their motivations for using pornography, men's most commonly given responses imply masturbation, for example, *for solo sexual stimulation*,[39] *for sexual satisfaction, to feel arousal, to achieve orgasm*,[29] *horny at the time*, and *wanting to orgasm*.[33]

Using porn with a sexual partner occurs less frequently than solitary porn use.[40] However, partnered porn use is still relatively common. Around 5% of university-aged men and women report using porn with a sexual partner in the past month,[29] and just under half (46%) of coupled-but-unmarried men and women report ever having done so.[41] Around 35% of gay and bisexual men report having used porn with a sexual partner at some point.[33]

Women are far more likely to report only, or primarily, viewing porn with a sexual partner, compared to men, who are far more likely to report only viewing porn alone.[42] Interestingly, although solitary porn use is associated with sexual and relationship dissatisfaction, at least among men,[35] using porn with a romantic partner appears to be associated with less sexual boredom,[43] greater sexual satisfaction,[41] and more intimacy.[44]

Conclusion

It is hoped that this chapter will be of use to sex educators, whether they are adopting a porn as pedagogy or pedagogy about porn approach. The available literature reveals the widespread use of pornography, especially among younger men, about half of whom appear to be frequent porn users. The high prevalence of porn use suggests a need for sex educators to consider the role and influence of porn on clients.

The review identifies some potentially problematic aspects of pornography that developers of porn literacy programs may seek to address—for example, porn's bias toward men's pleasure over women's, its portrayal of sex acts that some may perceive to be demeaning or violent (e.g., external ejaculation and gagging) as being highly sexually gratifying for both partners, its eschewal of condoms (at least in pornography aimed at heterosexual audiences), and its lack of overt discussions of consent. The review also highlights some ways in which pornography could be utilized to promote sexual learning. Despite its bias toward men's pleasure, depictions of female pleasure are not absent in pornography. Thus, there is a potential to use porn as a starting point for discussions of female sexual agency and pleasure. The fact that partnered pornography use is associated with greater sexual satisfaction would also lend support for using porn for sexual learning within relationships. Additionally, the frequency with which gay male porn depicts condom use would suggests that porn has potential for use to promote safe sex practices among this population.

References

1. Albury, K. (2014). Porn and sex education, porn as sex education. *Porn Studies, 1*(1–2), 172–181. https://doi.org/10.1080/23268743.2013.863654
2. Rothman, E.F., Beckmeyer, J.J., Herbenick, D., Fu, T.C., Dodge, B., & Fortenberry, J.D. (2021). The prevalence of using pornography for information about how to have sex: Findings from a nationally representative survey of US adolescents and young adults. *Archives of Sexual Behavior, 50*(2), 629–646. https://doi.org/10.1007/s10508-020-01877-7
3. Miller, D.J., & McBain, K.A. (2021). The content of contemporary, mainstream pornography: A literature review of content analytic studies. *American Journal of Sexuality Education*. Advance online publication. https://doi.org/10.1080/15546128.2021.2019648
4. Miller, D.J., Raggatt, P.T., & McBain, K.A. (2020). A literature review of studies into the prevalence and frequency of men's pornography use. *American Journal of Sexuality Education, 15*(4), 509–529. https://doi.org/10.1080/15546128.2020.1831676
5. Herbenick, D., Fu, T.C., Valdivia, D.S., Patterson, C., Gonzalez, Y.R., Guerra-Reyes, L., Eastman-Mueller, H., Beckmeyer, J., & Rosenberg, M. (2021). What is rough sex, who does it, and who likes it? Findings from a probability sample of US undergraduate students. *Archives of Sexual Behavior, 50*(3), 1183–1195. https://doi.org/10.1007/s10508-021-01917-w
6. Bridges, A.J., Wosnitzer, R., Scharrer, E., Sun, C., & Liberman, R. (2010). Aggression and sexual behavior in best-selling pornography videos: A content analysis update. *Violence against Women, 16*, 1065–1085. http://dx.doi.org/10.1177/1077801210382866
7. McKee, A. (2005). The objectification of women in mainstream pornographic videos in Australia. *The Journal of Sex Research, 42*, 277–290. http://dx.doi.org/10.1080/00224490509552283
8. Shor, E., & Seida, K. (2019). "Harder and harder"? Is mainstream pornography becoming increasingly violent and do viewers prefer violent content? *The Journal of Sex Research, 56*, 16–28. https://doi.org/10.1080/00224499.2018.1451476

9. Shor, E. (2019). Age, aggression, and pleasure in popular online pornographic videos. *Violence against Women, 25*, 1018–1036. https://doi.org/10.1177/1077801218804101
10. Seida, K., & Shor, E. (2019). Aggression and pleasure in opposite-sex and same-sex mainstream online pornography: A comparative content analysis of dyadic scenes. *The Journal of Sex Research*. Advance online publication. https://doi.org/10.1080/00224499.2019.1696275
11. Fritz, N., Malic, V., Paul, B., & Zhou, Y. (2020). A descriptive analysis of the types, targets, and relative frequency of aggression in mainstream pornography. *Archives of Sexual Behavior, 49*(8), 3041–3053. https://doi.org/10.1007/s10508-020-01773-0
12. Carrotte, E.R., Davis, A.C., & Lim, M.S. (2020). Sexual behaviors and violence in pornography: Systematic review and narrative synthesis of video content analyses. *Journal of Medical Internet Research, 22*(5), e16702. http://dx.doi.org/10.2196/16702
13. Klaassen, M.J., & Peter, J. (2015). Gender (in) equality in Internet pornography: A content analysis of popular pornographic Internet videos. *The Journal of Sex Research, 52*, 721–735. http://dx.doi.org/10.1080/00224499.2014.976781
14. Zhou, Y., & Paul, B. (2016). Lotus blossom or dragon lady: A content analysis of "Asian women" online pornography. *Sexuality & Culture, 20*(4), 1083–1100. http://dx.doi.org/10.1007/s12119-016-9375-9
15. Gorman, S., Monk-Turner, E., & Fish, J.N. (2010). Free adult Internet web sites: How prevalent are degrading acts? *Gender Issues, 27*, 131–145. http://dx.doi.org/10.1007/s12147-010-9095-7
16. Vannier, S.A., Currie, A.B., & O'Sullivan, L.F. (2014). Schoolgirls and soccer moms: A content analysis of free "Teen" and "MILF" online pornography. *The Journal of Sex Research, 51*, 253–264. http://dx.doi.org/10.1080/00224499.2013.829795
17. Fritz, N., & Paul, B. (2017). From orgasms to spanking: A content analysis of the agentic and objectifying sexual scripts in feminist, for women, and mainstream pornography. *Sex Roles, 77*(9), 639–652. http://dx.doi.org/10.1007/s11199-017-0759-6
18. Séguin, L.J., Rodrigue, C., & Lavigne, J. (2018). Consuming ecstasy: Representations of male and female orgasm in mainstream pornography. *The Journal of Sex Research, 55*(3), 348–356. https://doi.org/10.1080/00224499.2017.1332152
19. Zhou, Y., Paul, B., Malic, V., & Yu, J. (2019). Sexual behavior patterns in online sexually explicit materials: A network analysis. *Quality & Quantity, 53*(4), 2253–2271. https://doi.org/10.1007/s11135-019-00869-7
20. Mazandarani, F. (2021). Between a camera and a hard place: A content analysis of performer representation in heterosexual pornographic content. *The Journal of Sex Research, 58*(3), 305–313. https://doi.org/10.1080/00224499.2020.1754747
21. Sun, C., Bridges, A., Wosnitzer, R., Scharrer, E., & Liberman, R. (2008). A comparison of male and female directors in popular pornography: What happens when women are at the helm? *Psychology of Women Quarterly, 32*, 312–325. http://dx.doi.org/10.1111/j.1471-6402.2008.00439.x
22. Downing, M.J., Jr., Schrimshaw, E.W., Antebi, N., & Siegel, K. (2014). Sexually explicit media on the Internet: A content analysis of sexual behaviors, risk, and media characteristics in gay male adult videos. *Archives of Sexual Behavior, 43*(4), 811–821. http://dx.doi.org/10.1007/s10508-013-0121-1
23. Tollini, C. (2019). How two holdouts went bareback: CockyBoys and Men.com's initial transition to producing videos without condoms. *Porn Studies, 6*(3), 282–300. https://doi.org/10.1080/23268743.2019.1602958
24. Willis, M., Canan, S.N., Jozkowski, K.N., & Bridges, A.J. (2020). Sexual consent communication in best-selling pornography films: A content analysis. *The Journal of Sex Research, 57*(1), 52–63. https://doi.org/10.1080/00224499.2019.1655522
25. Smith, T.W., Davern, M., Freese, J., & Morgan, S. (2021). *General Social Surveys, 1972–2018* [machine-readable data file]/Principal Investigator, Smith, Tom W.; Co-Principal Investigators, Michael Davern, Jeremy Freese, and Stephen Morgan; Sponsored by

National Science Foundation. --NORC ed.-- Chicago: NORC, 2018: NORC at the University of Chicago [producer and distributor]. Data accessed from the GSS Data Explorer website at gssdataexplorer.norc.org.

26. The Austin Institute for the Study of Family and Culture. (2014). *Relationships in America survey* [report]. https://relationshipsinamerica.com/
27. Regnerus, M., Gordon, D., & Price, J. (2015). Documenting pornography use in America: A comparative analysis of methodological approaches. *The Journal of Sex Research, 53*, 873–881. http://dx.doi.org/10.1080/00224499.2015.1096886
28. Petersen, J.L., & Hyde, J.S. (2010). A meta-analytic review of research on gender differences in sexuality, 1993–2007. *Psychological Bulletin, 136*, 21–38. http://dx.doi.org/10.1037/a0017504
29. Wéry, A., & Billieux, J. (2016). Online sexual activities: An exploratory study of problematic and non-problematic usage patterns in a sample of men. *Computers in Human Behavior, 56*, 257–266. http://dx.doi.org/10.1016/j.chb.2015.11.046
30. Blais-Lecours, S., Vaillancourt-Morel, M.P., Sabourin, S., & Godbout, N. (2016). Cyberpornography: Time use, perceived addiction, sexual functioning, and sexual satisfaction. *Cyberpsychology, Behavior, and Social Networking, 19*, 649–655. http://dx.doi.org/10.1089/cyber.2016.0364
31. Downing Jr., M., Schrimshaw, E.W., Scheinmann, R., Antebi-Gruszka, N., & Hirshfield, S. (2017). Sexually explicit media use by sexual identity: A comparative analysis of gay, bisexual, and heterosexual men in the United States. *Archives of Sexual Behavior, 46*, 1763–1776. http://dx.doi.org/10.1007/s10508-016-0837-9
32. Rissel, C., Richters, J., de Visser, R.O., McKee, A., Yeung, A., & Caruana, T. (2017). A profile of pornography users in Australia: Findings from the second Australian study of health and relationships. *The Journal of Sex Research, 54*, 227–240. http://dx.doi.org/10.1080/00224499.2016.1191597
33. Nelson, K.M., Simoni, J.M., Morrison, D.M., George, W.H., Leickly, E., Lengua, L.J., & Hawes, S.E. (2014). Sexually explicit online media and sexual risk among men who have sex with men in the United States. *Archives of Sexual Behavior, 43*, 833–843. http://dx.doi.org/10.1007/s10508-013-0238-2
34. Böhm, M., Franz, P., Dekker, A., & Matthiesen, S. (2014). Desire and dilemma: Gender differences in German students' consumption of pornography. *Porn Studies, 2*, 76–92. http://dx.doi.org/10.1080/23268743.2014.984923
35. Miller, D.J., McBain, K.A., Li, W.W., & Raggatt, P.T.F. (2019). Pornography, desire for porn-like sex, masturbation, and men's sexual and relationship satisfaction. *Personal Relationships, 26*(1), 93–113. https://doi.org/10.1111/pere.12267
36. Shaughnessy, K., Byers, E.S., & Walsh, L. (2011). Online sexual activity experience of heterosexual students: Gender similarities and differences. *Archives of Sexual Behavior, 40*, 419–427. http://dx.doi.org/10.1007/s10508-010-9629-9
37. Rosenberg, H., & Kraus, S. (2014). The relationship of "passionate attachment" for pornography with sexual compulsivity, frequency of use, and craving for pornography. *Addictive Behaviors, 39*, 1012–1017. http://dx.doi.org/10.1016/j.addbeh.2014.02.010
38. Træen, B., & Daneback, K. (2013). The use of pornography and sexual behaviour among Norwegian men and women of differing sexual orientation. *Sexologies, 22*, e41–e48. http://dx.doi.org/10.1016/j.sexol.2012.03.001
39. Bridges, A.J., & Morokoff, P.J. (2011). Sexual media use and relational satisfaction in heterosexual couples. *Personal Relationships, 18*, 562–585. http://dx.doi.org/10.1111/j.1475-6811.2010.01328.x
40. Donevan, M., & Mattebo, M. (2017). The relationship between frequent pornography consumption, behaviours, and sexual preoccupancy among male adolescents in Sweden. *Sexual & Reproductive Healthcare, 12*, 82–87. http://dx.doi.org/10.1016/j.srhc.2017.03.002

41. Maddox, A.M., Rhoades, G.K., & Markman, H.J. (2011). Viewing sexually-explicit materials alone or together: Associations with relationship quality. *Archives of Sexual Behavior, 40*, 441–448. http://dx.doi.org/10.1007/s10508-009-9585-4
42. Carroll, J.S., Busby, D.M., Willoughby, B.J., & Brown, C.C. (2017). The porn gap: Differences in men's and women's pornography patterns in couple relationships. *Journal of Couple & Relationship Therapy, 16*, 146–163, http://dx.doi.org/10.1080/15332691.2016.1238796
43. Grov, C., Gillespie, B.J., Royce, T., & Lever, J. (2011). Perceived consequences of casual online sexual activities on heterosexual relationships: A US online survey. *Archives of Sexual Behavior, 40*(2), 429–439. https://doi.org/10.1007/s10508-010-9598-z
44. Huntington, C., Markman, H., & Rhoades, G. (2020). Watching pornography alone or together: Longitudinal associations with romantic relationship quality. *Journal of Sex & Marital Therapy*. Advance online publication. https://doi.org/10.1080/0092623X.2020.1835760

11

IN SEARCH OF PLEASURE

An Examination of the Current State of Sexual Pleasure Education and Research in the United States

Susan Milstein, Genevieve Hunter, Gina M. Lepore, Taylor E. Hilliard, and Scott S. Hall

Why Talk About Pleasure?

A study by the majority of the authors of this chapter was completed to better understand how college students experience sexual pleasure and satisfaction. Sexual pleasure is self-defined and heavily influenced by sexual scripting starting in childhood and continuing throughout our lives. The study found that hookups gave respondents less pleasure compared to those in committed and emotionally involved relationships.[1] It was also discovered that factors like age, ethnicity, race, religiosity, and sexual orientation were not related to self-reported sexual pleasure and satisfaction. However, people in relationships for at least six weeks reported having greater levels of pleasure than those in shorter relationships and hookups.

This study raised questions about how people learn about pleasure and healthy sexual relationships as part of sex education, and whether the education that currently exists is serving the needs of all students. To answer these questions, we need to better understand the current status of sex education in the United States.

Status of Sex Education in the United States

Before we begin to discuss the current state of sexual pleasure in the United States, it would help to understand the current state of sex education. If a person tried to summarize the state of sex education in the United States in two words, *inconsistent* and *incomplete* would be accurate descriptors. Currently, only Washington, DC, and 29 states require sex education.[2] Additionally, 15 states do not require that the sex education provided be medically accurate, age-appropriate, or evidence-based. The sex education programs available in public schools are often brief, perhaps one or two classes during an entire term of health education.[2]

DOI: 10.4324/9781003189787-12

What is actually taught in sex education classes in middle and high schools is often left up to the states and the local communities. Most sex education classes tend to focus solely on disease and pregnancy, though there are more comprehensive programs that strive to include pleasure amongst other topics. Local municipalities and school boards influence the content and delivery of sex education, and school boards often have the power to remove valuable information such as condom demonstrations or additional resources for students who want more information on a certain topic. This could prevent students from getting access to information that helps promote a healthy sense of sexuality, and helps them have happy, healthy sex lives.

For an idea of what could be offered in sex education programming, one can look at the Scandinavian model. Sweden made sex education mandatory in schools in 1955 and has since continued to revise and update requirements on content.[3] Unlike in the United States, where sex education typically doesn't begin until middle school or high school, sex education in Sweden begins in grades four through six.[3] Students continue to receive sex education throughout their schooling, not just on disease and pregnancy prevention but also on orientation and gender identity, relationships, and love. In many ways, what is happening in Sweden is similar to what was outlined in the first edition of the *National Sexuality Education Standards* released in the United States almost a decade ago.[4] These standards called for age-appropriate sex education starting in kindergarten and continuing until grade 12. One of the major differences between the Swedish model and the *National Sexuality Education Standards* is that the Swedish model integrates sex education into classes other than health.[3] The curriculum in Sweden encourages the exploration of topics like relationships and identity in classes such as history and religion. In the United States, formal sex education is not integrated into history classes, and religion is not taught in public schools, although some teachers cover discrimination, equality, and laws about sex and gender minorities, especially if they are in the news. The second edition of the *National Sex Education Standards*[5] has examined this approach and says that "a coordinated and concerted effort to teach and reinforce important sexual health concepts throughout other areas of the curriculum is a promising strategy."[6] Furthermore, it also states, "Many of the positive outcomes and promising approaches that worked toward creating affirming, inclusive school environments occurred not in traditional health or sex education classes, but in social studies, English, physical education, mathematics, music, and art."[6]

While the first *National Sexuality Education Standards* attempted to outline and explain how comprehensive sex education could look in the United States, no state currently requires the standards to be implemented. Particularly relevant to this chapter, there is no mention of the word "pleasure" in the standards, although being sex-positive is included. Sexual pleasure is indeed missing in most sex education around the world.[7] The United Nations Educational, Scientific, and

Cultural Organization's *International Technical Guidance on Sexuality Education*[8] is more explicit about sexual pleasure in sex education. For example, for ages 9–12, there is a focus on how physical touch (including sexual contact) brings pleasure. There is messaging for ages 12–15 that sexual feelings and desires are natural, not shameful. And for ages 15 and older, there is a focus on sexual behavior being pleasurable and taking responsibility for one's well-being. While evidence shows that safer sex campaigns and educational programs that focus on pleasure contribute to more consistent condom use by young people, which lowers rates of sexually transmitted infections (STIs) and unintended pregnancies, this approach is not typically used in K-12 settings in the United States.[9]

Talking About Sexual Pleasure

Pleasure is important because it is part of how we experience all things in life, including sex and sexuality. Sexual pleasure is a way to express our bodies, multiple emotions, and satisfy desire. It is crucial to talk about pleasure because it informs our relationship with sexual experiences. As vital as it is, our impression is that many adults in the United States do not openly discuss sexual pleasure, especially with younger children. And it is not surprising that many teens aren't quite sure how to talk about it either.

In "Pleasure and Sex Education: The Need for Broadening Both Content and Measurement," the authors argue that the lack of content on healthy relationships and pleasure in sex education programming negatively impacts young people's sexual well-being and inadequately addresses continued rates of sexual coercion and violence among young adults.[10] They also note that national surveys designed to assess the quality and breadth of sex education programming and young people's perceptions of such are inadequate. The same could probably be said about what occurs in the home.

Parents and Their Children

All people, including children, are sexual beings. Children explore their bodies through their own touch at very young ages. Due to religious upbringing or past experiences, adults and parents might hesitate to use the word pleasure because they see it as inherently sexual or hedonistic. Taboo topics like masturbation and fears of child sexual exploitation in mainstream American culture further complicate discussion about pleasure, but teaching that sex could be pleasurable actually helps reduce the likelihood of child sexual abuse and the exploitation of minors.[10] One author explains it well, citing a TED Talk by filmmaker Sue Jaye Johnson:

> In all the ways we touch our kids, play with our kids and engage their senses, Johnson argues that we can teach them "what it feels like to be present in their body and to know when they're not." These lessons can come

> in the simplest of forms. In her TED Talk, Johnson explained, "I realized that when I dry my daughter off in a towel tenderly, the way a lover would, I'm teaching her to expect that kind of touch." I see that. When I tickle my daughter and she's fully in charge of how far she wants [the] tickling to go, it reinforces the fact that her body is hers and hers alone.[11]

Adolescence is a time of rapid growth in multiple realms, including physical, sexual, social-emotional, and cognitive. Using Erik Erikson's stages of development, an example of the adolescent stage is understanding how individuals weigh out their previous experiences, societal expectations, and aspirations to establish values and "finding themselves."[12]

The United States still has a sexual understanding that appears to be highly fragmented. In terms of parents' expectations of their teens, some want their teens to remain abstinent, even if they were not. On the other end of the spectrum, some adults expect that their child will likely have sex sometime during high school or soon thereafter. Either way, are adults having conversations with their children about pleasure, desire, and, yes, passionate, *hot* sex? Researchers from West Virginia University School of Medicine say the answer is no. "Unfortunately, in many instances, 'sex talks' between parents and their children are less than optimal. Parents tend to exclude positive topics associated with sexuality, such as pleasure, love, and healthy relationships, in favor of negative topics and warnings."[13]

Many parents rely on schools to provide sex education for their children. A recent study found that parents *still* support sex education as they have for decades. Roughly 98% of American parents want their children to receive sex education in high school, and 89% support it for middle schoolers. Survey respondents also agreed that sex education should cover a range of topics, including birth control, STIs and HIV, puberty, consent, healthy relationships, sexual orientation, and abstinence.[14] But, did you notice that the subject of pleasure was not included in this list?

Not only are pleasure and desire often left out of formal sex education in the United States, but if they are discussed, they are often tagged with words of caution and risk related to unplanned pregnancy, STIs, and HIV. Feedback from young people indicates general dissatisfaction with this narrow focus on sexual education and the lack of emphasis on the positive elements of sexuality.[15]

So, where does that leave us as a country? As educators, we have found from experience that the answer may depend on context. If we ask parents if they want their teens to have pleasurable sexual relationships, the answer might be, "Of course!" However, some parents might add, "As long as it's safe, or as long as they love or care about each other." Other parents may say, "Hell NO!" And still other parents may completely ignore any possible talk because they think it would put ideas into their teen's mind. But parents aren't the only source of sexual information.

Adolescents and Social Media

US culture is highly sexualized in all realms, from online porn to music to the state of politics of our bodies. Yet, how openly do we talk about sexual pleasure in a healthy manner? Teens have instant and constant access to explicit sexual content and spend much of their days online. It is crucial to explore how adolescents use social media. What messages do they receive about sexual pleasure? More importantly, how are adolescents receiving information and processing it into their thinking and behavior? Recent research shows the

> majority of young adults, ages 18 to 29 say they use Instagram or Snapchat and about half say they use TikTok, with those on the younger end of this cohort—ages 18 to 24—being especially likely to report using Instagram (76%), Snapchat (75%) or TikTok (55%).[16]

But what messages are teens receiving? Are they empowering messages about teens' sexuality and pleasure, or are teens inundated with imagery and messaging that undermines their feelings of self-worth and self-expression? It's pretty much a mixed bag.

While some users on these platforms talk about sex, most are not experts in the field, and may not be sharing accurate information, though there are exceptions. Dr. Jennifer Lincoln, an OB-GYN based in Portland, Oregon, offers a safe online space for questions about sex. She built a large following on Instagram and then moved to TikTok after her doctor friends encouraged her to reach more millennials.[17] Other trained educators and organizations are starting to move into social media platforms, including Amaze.org, Sex Positive Families, and Unhushed.

College Students and Beyond

Since college students experience a pivotal life transition period from adolescence to adulthood, their experience with sexual pleasure is essential to consider. At least one large survey indicated that 70% of college students wanted sexual pleasure to be included in sexual health education.[18] Accordingly, universities generally appear to have at least some focus on sexual pleasure in sex education courses. One study of 150 college educators throughout the United States indicated that sexual pleasure was part of the sexual education curriculum in 91% of the courses.[19]

But what about outside of the classroom? What do college students learn about pleasure from each other and their own sexual experiences? Research has shown that being in a committed relationship corresponds with increased sexual pleasure compared to those in uncommitted relationships.[20] Yet, college students often report that hooking up among their peers is quite common. The idea that hookups are not only common but also desirable leads to inaccurate expectations among students. Studies that look at pleasure and hookups have found that students who engage in hookups report dissatisfaction with the experience and that the emotional fallout disproportionately affects females.

This problem is exacerbated by the common use of social media and texting among students, leading to further miscommunication and assumptions about expectations when hooking up.[21] It's important to note that a common problem with many of these findings is that the people responding to these surveys and questionnaires are usually white and heterosexual. It may be that young adults of color and those who are LGBTQIA+ have different experiences with both pleasure and hookup expectations.

Sexual satisfaction has become increasingly recognized as an indicator of health and well-being, and therefore, it is necessary to discuss when considering life outcomes.[22] Despite reservations about discussing this topic, recognition and support for sexual health and rights are rising.[23] Many grassroots movements have advocated for more discussion and promotion of individual rights and education on issues of affirmative consent, bodily autonomy, and pleasure. These movements include advocacy and programmatic work for sex workers' rights, the disability rights movement, the global women's health and rights movement, LGBTQIA+ movements, trans and intersex rights mobilization, and youth mobilizing on sexual and reproductive rights.

Where We Are Now

A number of researchers', educators', and writers' contributions to the national discourse on pleasure advocate for a shift in how we study, understand, and talk about pleasure. Attention to diverse sexual perspectives and experiences can add nuance to our understanding of sexual pleasure. Experts ask us to deepen our understanding of consent, desire, and pleasure and consider how these impact our relationships with ourselves and our partners, reframing how we talk about these concepts with young people in sex education programming.

In her companion books, *Girls and Sex* and *Boys and Sex*, Peggy Orenstein suggests that conversations about consent and pleasure in sex education are essential to empower the next generation to engage in the sex they both *want* and *enjoy*. Her interviews with (mostly heterosexual but socioeconomically and racially diverse) young women and men across the country reveal the subtle coercion that many young women experience in their early sexual encounters with male sexual partners.

The interviews in *Girls and Sex* illustrate the impact of generations of gender-based double standards around sex and indicate that while young women may be more empowered than their predecessors in their professional lives, genuine sexual empowerment is still elusive for many. Stories of early sexual experiences reveal themes of manipulation and pressure to please male partners through unreciprocated oral and/or anal sex. These experiences are described as consensual but not particularly enjoyable. Some women believed that women aren't entitled to pleasure, and even if they were that, they aren't able to achieve it in practice. Because masturbation may still be taboo for some, they often don't know how to pleasure themselves and thus cannot communicate their desires to their partners. Some reported spectatoring (critically observing oneself from a third-person perspective during sex) rather than enjoying sex due to insecurities about their bodies and genital appearance. Further, Orenstein reported that many of her interviewees, when asked to evaluate their sexual satisfaction, do so in terms of their partner's experience of pleasure rather than their own.

These challenges are compounded by young men's male-centric framing of sex and pleasure. In *Boys and Sex*, Orenstein's interviews with predominantly heterosexual young men illustrate how ill-prepared many are for connected, consensual, mutually pleasurable sex. Many report being raised on gendered expectations that discourage emotional vulnerability. Some are confused by competing messages about healthy versus toxic masculinity. Others are influenced by male-focused, misogynist, and violent depictions of sex that are the hallmark of mainstream porn (the type most adolescent boys can access freely and anonymously). Mystified by female sexuality and pleasure, and partnering with girls who are even less familiar with their own capacity for pleasure than they are, many young men are equally at a loss for navigating a sex life worth having and enjoying.

In her Ted Talk, "What Young Women Believe About Their Own Sexual Pleasure," Orenstein summarizes this neatly:

> If we truly want young people to engage safely, ethically, and yes, enjoyably, it's time to have an open, honest discussion about what happens after "yes," and that includes breaking the biggest taboo of all and talking to young people about women's capacity for and entitlement to sexual pleasure.[24]

Orenstein then cites research by Sara McClelland that revealed findings similar to her interviews with young women—that heterosexual women are more likely than their male counterparts to define their own sexual satisfaction by their partner's orgasm.

Our research with college students also revealed some gender differences related to sexual pleasure. Female students were less likely than male students to associate sexual pleasure and satisfaction with reaching orgasm and were less likely to have experienced an orgasm in their last sexual encounter. They also placed more focus on the emotional elements of the sexual relationship as a source of sexual pleasure. However, male students were somewhat more likely than female students to report that they focus on making sure their partner is sexually satisfied. This focus could reflect pervasive messages and pressures regarding masculinity and sexuality, or perhaps the female students believing that the male is more in control of bringing about his sexual satisfaction than they are. We also noticed that those who identified as a sexual minority were more open than heterosexual students with their partners about the levels of sexual pleasure and satisfaction they experience.

In her *Intimate Justice* framework, McClelland calls for research on sexual satisfaction that better articulates the subtle and not-so-subtle ways that systems of power and oppression impact individuals' sense of their rights to and experiences of sexual pleasure and satisfaction.[22] McClelland argues that many current satisfaction ratings inadequately account for the negative impact of stigma, marginalization, and oppression on the sexual self-esteem of LGBTQIA+ folks and women in general. Only when research methods and measures of sexual satisfaction more accurately address the impact of the socio-political domain on sexual identity and rights will researchers obtain a clear portrait of the true antecedents of sexual pleasure and satisfaction for these populations. This clarity will have broad implications for educators, policymakers, and researchers alike.

In *Come As You Are: The Surprising New Science that Will Transform Your Sex Life* (referred to as *CAYA* by the author), Emily Nagoski discusses concepts that explain the relationship between pleasure, desire, and arousal.[25] One of these is *the Dual Control Model of Sexual Response* (developed by Kinsey Institute researchers Erick Janssen and John Bancroft in the late 1990s), which frames sexual response as an interaction between two key brain mechanisms: excitatory responses and inhibitory responses. It asserts that different degrees of sensitivity to these responses account for individual variability in sexual arousal, desire, and responsiveness. It also considers the impact of individuals' sexual self-concept, relationship dynamics, and history of trauma on their experiences of pleasure and satisfaction. For example, research indicates that women who have more difficulty reaching orgasm also report more sexual inhibition and fewer erotic thoughts in general and more negative affect while engaged in sexual activity.[26]

CAYA also explains that humans have both spontaneous and responsive desires and that both are normal and healthy. Spontaneous desire arises suddenly, randomly, or perhaps unexpectedly from several potential stimuli, whereas responsive desire generally arises from specific stimuli in anticipation of pleasure. This framing of desire challenges a dominant narrative that recognizes and legitimizes only spontaneous desire and suggests that a lack thereof indicates that something is missing or broken, either with the person or the relationship.

The third concept that Nagoski introduces is that of *arousal non-concordance*, which distinguishes genital response to sex-related stimuli from subjective experiences of desire and pleasure (wanting and liking) and reminds us that "a person's genitals do not tell us whether or not they like what's happening, their words do."[25]

Nagoski's work presents multiple implications for future sex research, the legal system, sex education, and sexual medicine. Suppose the concepts presented in *CAYA* were offered in a developmentally appropriate manner as part of relationships and sex education at the high school level. In that case, young people might be more empowered to better advocate for and understand their bodies, desires, and limits as they embark on their journeys of sexual self-discovery. They would also possess crucial information and language to better negotiate consent in their relationships, language that many lack and do not see modeled in the relationships of their parents and caregivers.

The concepts and perspectives in the works described earlier offer educators concrete, evidence-based, medically accurate language to engage young people in conversations about everything from puberty, to experiences of pleasure during masturbation and partnered sex, to conversations about consent and satisfaction in their relationships. We have the language. We have the research. We also have plenty of well-educated and trained sex educators able to deliver this content in an inclusive, developmentally appropriate manner. Young people thirst for this information and would be less likely to turn to porn for answers to their questions if they had the opportunity to have such conversations in the classroom.

What Can We Do Next?

Could framing sexual pleasure differently in the United States encourage adolescents to openly talk about pleasure and desire? If so, what would be the consequences? We know that countries in Europe discuss sex in a positive manner and have many teens who talk openly about sexual pleasure precisely because the culture sets it up that way. At the same time, those countries have lower teen pregnancy rates, teen birth rates, and STI rates, to boot! The United States can and should take the same approach.

What if a new American value system included sexual pleasure as part of finding oneself? How different would it be if adolescents could learn about sexual pleasure without shame? What if they could discover what brings them sexual pleasure if and when they are authentically ready rather than due to peer pressure or cultural norms. Might they transition to adulthood and have an increased sense of sexual agency?[27] Would this lead to a huge shift in thinking, youth culture, and norms in the United States? We think it can!

Many norms are already changing. Sex education programs are making a notable impact in multiple areas. According to recent research that examined the past 30 years of sex education in the United States, there have been improvements in both students' knowledge and attitudes about sex and an effort to make sex education more inclusive and more comprehensive. It also found that it needs to start in middle school for education to be effective.[28] However, data about sexual pleasure in sex education is difficult to come by.

Many educators and researchers believe that more should be taught about pleasure precisely because sex education is promoted primarily as a teen pregnancy and STI/HIV prevention tool rather than a way for adolescents to learn about their bodies and sexuality. The movement for more pleasure education is here and will continue to grow as more people support sexuality as a complex but positive aspect of being human. The 2020 *National Sex Education Standards* include a sex-positive lens that supports equity for all young people with revisions that focus on the needs of young people in the 21st century.[6] Moreover, the standards support sex education that will "present sexual development as a normal, natural, healthy part of human development that every school district should address."

The shift toward fully responsive sex education is happening in many parts of the country. We hope that schools across the United States will offer more comprehensive sex education curricula and follow the lead of experts in the field while using the standards backed by sound research. Youth and parents must also demand this of their school systems. This work is far from over, but the authors hope that the next ten years will continue to be a decade led by both researchers and changemakers, where the topic of sexual pleasure is here to stay for this generation and the ones still to come.

References

1. Milstein, S., Hilliard, T., Hall, S., Knox, D., & Hunter, G. (2019). Factors that impact college students' perceptions of sexual pleasure and satisfaction. *American Journal of Sexuality Education, 15*(1), 99–110.
2. SIECUS (n.d.). *The SIECUS state profiles 2019/2020.* https://siecus.org/state-profiles-2019-2020
3. Skolverket (2014). *Sex education. Gender equality, sexuality and human relationships in the Swedish curricula.* Swedish National Agency for Education.
4. Future of Sex Education Initiative. (2012). *National sexuality education standards: Core content and skills, K-12 [a special publication of the Journal of School Health].* www.futureofsexeducation.org/documents/josh-fose-standards-web.pdf.
5. Note that there was a change in the title between the first and second editions.
6. Future of Sex Education Initiative (2020). *National sex education standards: Core content and skills, K-12.* Future of Sex Education Initiative.
7. Allen, L., & Carmody, M. (2012). 'Pleasure has no passport': Re-visiting the potential of pleasure in sexuality education. *Sex Education, 12*(4), 455–468.
8. United Nations Educational, Scientific and Cultural Organization (2018). *International technical guidance on sexuality education: An evidence-informed approach.* Rev ed. www.unaids.org/sites/default/files/media_asset/ITGSE_en.pdf.
9. Philpott, A., Knerr, W., & Maher, D. (2006). Promoting protection and pleasure: Amplifying the effectiveness of barriers against sexually transmitted infections and pregnancy. *The Lancet, 368*(9551), 2028–2031.
10. Kantor, L.M., & Lindberg, L. (2020). Pleasure and sex education: The need for broadening both content and measurement. *American Journal of Public Health, 110*(2), 145–148.
11. Woo, M. (2018, January 17). *Give kids specific words to talk about pleasure.* Lifehacker. https://offspring.lifehacker.com/give-kids-specific-language-to-talk-about-pleasure-1822150699.
12. Orenstein, G.A., & Lewis, L. (2020). Erikson's stages of psychosocial development. *StatPearls [Internet].* National Library of Medicine.
13. Ashcraft, A.M., & Murray, P.J. (2017). Talking to parents about adolescent sexuality. *Pediatric Clinics of North America, 64*(2), 305.
14. Eisenstein, Z. (n.d.). *Survey says (again): People overwhelmingly support sex ed.* SIECUS. https://siecus.org/survey-says-people-support-sex-ed/
15. Pound, P., Langford, R., & Campbell, R. (2016). What do young people think about their school-based sex and relationship education? A qualitative synthesis of young people's views and experiences. *BMJ open, 6*(9).

16. Auxier, B., & Anderson, M. (2021, April 7). *Social media use in 2021*. PEW Research Center. www.pewresearch.org/internet/2021/04/07/social-media-use-in-2021
17. Mooney, K. (2020, September 29) Welcome to the corner of TikTok where sex ed is actually cool; It's the hipper, sex-positive Schoolhouse Rock. *Bustle*. www.bustle.com/wellness/obgyn-educators-tiktok-sex-ed-accessible
18. Canan, S.N., & Jozkowski, K.N. (2017). Sexual health education topics in schools: Inclusion and timing preferences of a sample of southern US college students. *Sexuality Research and Social Policy, 14*(2), 143–156.
19. Oswalt, S.B., Wagner, L.M., Eastman-Mueller, H.P., & Nevers, J.M. (2015). Pedagogy and content in sexuality education courses in US colleges and universities. *Sex Education, 15*(2), 172–187.
20. Barnett, M.D., & Melugin, P.R. (2016). Reported sexual pleasure among heterosexual men and women: An empirical investigation. *Personality and Individual Differences, 98*, 62–68. doi:10.1016/j.paid.2016.03.061.
21. Klinger, L. (2016). Hookup culture on college campuses: Centering college women, communication barriers, and negative outcomes. *College Student Affairs Leadership, 3*(2), 5.
22. McClelland, S. (2010). Intimate justice: A critical analysis of sexual satisfaction. *Social and Personality Psychology Compass, 4*(9), 663–680. doi: 10.1111/j.1751-9004.2010.00293.x.
23. Gruskin, S., Yadav, V., Castellanos-Usigli, A., Khizanishvili, G., & Kismödi, E. (2019). Sexual health, sexual rights and sexual pleasure: Meaningfully engaging the perfect triangle. *Sexual and Reproductive Health Matters, 27*(1), 29–40.
24. Orenstein, P. (2017, April 5). What young women believe about their own sexual pleasure. *TEDTalk*. www.youtube.com/watch?v=mWA2uL8zXPI
25. Nagoski, E. (2021). *Come as you are: The surprising new science that will transform your sex life, revised and updated*. Simon and Schuster.
26. Moura, C.V., Tavares, I.M., & Nobre, P.J. (2020). Cognitive-affective factors and female orgasm: A comparative study on women with and without orgasm difficulties. *Journal of Sexual Medicine, 17*(11), 2220–2228.
27. Sexual agency is one's ability to have control over their bodies and their sexuality.
28. Goldfarb, E.S., & Lieberman, L.D. (2020). Three decades of research: The case for comprehensive sex education. *Journal of Adolescent Health, 68*(1):13–27.

12

A CALL FOR AN EXPANSIVE COMPREHENSIVE SEXUAL HEALTH EDUCATION MODEL

Juyeon Son and Cindy Draws

Introduction

According to the annual Sexually Transmitted Disease Surveillance Report by the Centers for Disease Control and Prevention (CDC), the United States reached an all-time high number of combined cases of the three most common sexually transmitted infections (STIs): chlamydia, gonorrhea, and syphilis in 2018.[1] These STIs disproportionately impact our youth. People aged 15–24 make up about a quarter of the sexually active population but account for a much higher proportion of new STI cases. For example, 70% of all gonorrhea, 63% of chlamydia, and 45% of genital herpes cases were found in this age group in 2018. In addition to the youth group, women and gay, bisexual, and other men who have sex with men (MSM) are also at a higher risk for STIs.[2,3] The US federal government invests over 175 million dollars annually in "abstinence-only-until-marriage" programs. There is a federal eight-point definition of abstinence-only education under Section 510 of Title V of the Social Security Act, while a federal definition for comprehensive sex education is still yet to be established.[4] Both at the national and the state levels, more than two-thirds of those affected by one of the most common STI infections, chlamydia, are in the youth group aged 15–24. Thus, the insufficient attention paid to comprehensive sexual health education and the lack of a governmental-level mandate to provide and guide sexual health education at an institutional level are of serious concern.[5]

One way to address this concerning public health and safety trend is by providing a solid sexual health education curriculum in our public schools. Research has persistently pointed to the fact that a lack of knowledge and understanding of sexual health leads to a multitude of issues for our youth and our communities.[6–8] Yet the extent to which the contents of sexual health curriculum would

DOI: 10.4324/9781003189787-13

be acceptable and desirable has been contentious among different groups. These discontents have sometimes been impediments to preparing our youths with the knowledge and skills to better protect them from the risks. The risk factors for sexual health are largely preventable. According to a CDC report, the disproportionate rate of STIs among youth derives from a lack of screening, reluctance to disclose due to confidentiality concerns, biological factors, lack of access to health care services, and multiple sex partners. Good sexual health education is not a solution to all the problems associated with the STI epidemic but should be emphasized as a preventable measure.

As we looked into the current sexual health curriculum contents, we found that many sexual health curricula rely heavily on heteronormative assumptions of human development and anatomic information regarding puberty and human reproduction. The commonly used sexual health curriculum also tended to lack inclusive content related to human sexuality and gender identity and expressions.[9,10] A comprehensive sexual health curriculum refers to content coverage that could fill the existing gap in sexual health education as it expands beyond the core-knowledge components of human development. A comprehensive curriculum underscores the importance of educating and opening up lines of communication regarding sexual health and relationships, both on the personal and social levels. The National Sexuality Education Standards (NSES) is an example of a comprehensive curriculum framework developed by the Future of Sex Education based on National Health Education Standards. The NSES consists of seven major categories of learning outcomes: anatomy and physiology, puberty and adolescent development, identity, pregnancy and reproduction, STIs and HIV, healthy relationships, and personal safety.

Many studies have pointed out that a non-comprehensive understanding of sexual well-being can be detrimental to creating a safer community. In fact, the abstinence-only model contains inaccurate information, distorts data, and reinforces gender stereotypes.[4] Strategies to avoid sexual risks are ineffective in protecting youth and can be pernicious.[11] In contrast, comprehensive sexual health programs or active intervention programs effectively reduce risky behaviors by delaying sex initiation, reducing the number of partners, and increasing the use of condoms and contraceptives during sexual encounters. Existing research has also informed us of the importance of early sexual health education in institutional settings.[4,6] For example, a review of research regarding school-based comprehensive sex education for the last three decades found strong empirical evidence for implementing it in our schools.[12] They found that existing research clearly showed the effectiveness of comprehensive sex education for facilitating the healthy growth of our children. Especially, comprehensive sex education starting in elementary schools with contents continuing to scaffold in the following years appears to significantly improve various characteristics that we would need to promote for our children. They include an appreciation of sexual diversity, reduced sexual abuse and violence, and aiding in the development of healthy relationships and sexuality.

The lack of systematic education on sexual health can be costly for youth but even more so for lesbian, gay, bisexual, transgender, queer/questioning (LGBTQ+), and other youth with non-heterosexual identities. Existing research shows that the social and cultural contexts in which young people are positioned during their developmental stages profoundly impact their physical, psychological, social, and mental well-being. Suicidal thoughts and suicide attempts are more prevalent among LGBTQ+ youth. Young people questioning and exploring their sexuality and gender identities are subject to varying forms of marginalization and harassment, such as verbal abuse and physical assault, which increases the likelihood of self-harm and attempted suicide.[13–15] Victimization of LGBT young adults is also strongly associated with poorer mental well-being, leading to depression and suicidal ideation among young men, higher risk for STIs and HIV exposures, and self-harm and suicide.[16,17]

This study asked whether the types of sexual health curricula taught result in differences in students' knowledge, attitudes, and perceptions regarding sexual health and development. We examined the learning outcomes of the existing curriculum and found that it had a heavy weight on human anatomy and development, which differed significantly from the new curriculum that contained more expanded content as proposed by NSES.[18]

Methods

This project was a community-based, collaborative research endeavor[19] wherein a county public health department partnered with the principal investigator.[20] The project team comprised the principal investigator, the county public health department staff, and a representative from the school district's health education teachers. The study site was a small city surrounded by rural communities in the Midwest.

The school district that participated in this study provided two opportunities for sexual health education: one for seventh graders and the other for 11th graders. A weekly general health education class was offered at each school during these two grades, with about a month dedicated to covering sexual health. We decided to conduct this study for the seventh graders because we aimed to see the effects of curriculum differences before the students reach their teen years when they are more likely to become sexually active. In addition, focusing on seventh graders could also be used to assist in improving the sexual health curriculum for earlier age groups.

Participants

All seventh-graders enrolled in health education classes in all five middle schools in the study site's school district were invited to participate in the online survey. Three of the five health education teachers volunteered to teach the new curriculum. The remaining two continued teaching the class according to their existing curriculum, which did not include a comprehensive sexual health education model. The new curriculum group teachers participated in one day-long training session on a structured, comprehensive sexual health education curriculum hosted by a professional training center, Cardea.

Instrument Development

The survey's broad goal was to examine the effect of a new comprehensive sexual health curriculum on the students' learning in two areas: knowledge and attitudes on issues of sexual health. Survey questions were developed in consultation with the school district's head of health teachers. Special care was exercised to ensure that the questions measured the primary learning outcomes outlined by the NSES and their seven learning categories. The survey instrument included questions to measure at least one designated learning outcome for each category. As the existing curriculum used assessments focusing heavily on only two NSES categories: anatomy and physiology and puberty and adolescent development, additional questions were added to measure the students' learning in all categories. The instrument also included questions measuring students' perceptions and attitudes about sexual health.

As a result, the final survey instrument was comprised of the following specific subject areas:

- Basic demographic data: homeownership, parent education, race, religiosity, sex, and vacation.
- Knowledge about Sexual Health: anatomy and physiology, puberty and adolescent development, identity, pregnancy and reproduction, STIs and HIV, healthy relationships, and personal safety.
- Perceptions and Attitudes: preventive sexual behaviors, sexual orientation, healthy relationships, pregnancy, and STIs.

Procedure

At the onset of this study, all participating schools' existing seventh-grade sexual health curricula were examined and compared to the NSES by consultants at ANSWER.[21] The analysis identified significant gaps in the existing curriculum in three topic areas: healthy relationships, identity, pregnancy, and reproduction. In addition, we also researched potential comprehensive sexual health curricula and selected Family Life and Sexual Health (FLASH) as the base comprehensive sexual health curriculum for this study.[22]

For the new curriculum group teachers to have consistent and sufficient content coverage for teaching the contents, they received a day-long systematic training led by an expert from Cardea, a professional training organization. The teachers then revised their course curriculum to meet the recommended sexual health content of the NSES.

The five participating schools taught either the new or existing sexual health curriculum. All students enrolled in health education classes were invited to participate in the online survey shortly after completing the sexual health unit.

Data Analysis

A total of 260 surveys were completed, and the total number of correct responses was pooled to construct the final measurement of knowledge. Additional questions were added to estimate further students' attitudinal tendencies, distinct from fact-based knowledge, regarding various topics such as access to services and other resources on sexual health, pregnancy and STIs, sexual identities and orientation, and safety on using online and on relationships. Demographic characteristics of the two curricula groups were mainly similar except for family homeownership, where the existing curriculum schools had higher homeownership (92%) compared to the new curriculum group (78%).

Results

Curriculum Effects on Sexual Health Knowledge

First, we examined the students' sexual health knowledge between the two groups through 42 questions on sexual health knowledge in four categories: anatomy, puberty, reproduction, STIs, and sexual orientation. When looking at the number of correct answers in those categories, the existing curriculum group performed better in anatomy and puberty and the new curriculum group in the reproduction, STIs, and sexual identity components. Students from families with homeownership, non-white race, and male students' scores were higher than their counterparts.

The outcome showed differences in the performance between the two curricula groups in gaining particular types of sexual health knowledge. The higher scores for the existing curriculum group in human anatomy and puberty are consistent with the heavy focus on these subjects found in the initial curricula content review.

Curriculum Effects on Student Perception and Attitude

We also examined whether the more comprehensive sexual health curriculum would affect students' perceptions and attitudes regarding various sexual health issues to be distinguished from a fact-based understanding of these topics. This was assessed through questions gauging perceptions and attitudes regarding preventive sexual behaviors, pregnancy and STIs, sexual orientation, and healthy relationships. We asked them their level of being at ease with saying that they do not want to have sex, with discussing contraception use, and their level of agreement with statements such as "Before I decide to have sex, I should learn how to prevent an STI and getting pregnant," "When someone is raped or sexually assaulted, she or he is at fault," "It is important for a couple to talk about STIs and pregnancy prevention before having sex," and "If I thought I had an STI, I would not get tested because of fear."

The results showed a significant difference between the two curricular groups regarding the students' attitudes toward diversity in sexual orientation. Overall, the students that were taught the new curriculum displayed more open attitudes toward diversity in sexual orientation. The survey asked how the students perceived their openness toward diverse sexual orientations using the following questions: How much do you agree with "I am accepting of people of all sexual orientations" and "I am respectful to people of all genders and sexual orientations?" Most students (at least 85%) agreed with both statements, but the new curriculum students were more likely to agree with both statements than the existing curriculum students. The new curriculum group students were also more likely to disagree with "When someone is raped or sexually assaulted, she or he is at fault" than the existing curriculum students. Students who scored high in the sexual identity segment displayed more acceptance toward diverse sexual orientations. Overall, the outcomes indicated that the new curriculum resulted in students displaying a higher level of acceptance of people of all sexual orientations, being respectful of all genders and sexual orientations, and being less likely to victim-blame sexual assault cases.

Lessons From the Study

As previously stated, our goal for this study was to see the learning outcomes differing sexual health education curricula produce for seventh-grade students, including their effect on attitudes and perceptions regarding sexual health and well-being. As the comprehensive sexual health curriculum stresses these aspects, unlike commonly taught curriculum contents, we were curious to see if the added components in the comprehensive content would produce different learning outcomes for students. In this regard, the most important outcome of this study would be the role that comprehensive sexual health education could play in creating a more open atmosphere in our schools, possibly contributing to bringing positive changes in students' attitudes and behaviors later regarding sexual diversity.

Health education classrooms are one of the most vital venues for students to have much-needed discussions regarding sexual well-being. Although exploratory, these outcomes point to the potential effectiveness of a comprehensive curriculum in public schools creating inclusive community environments. Students demonstrated more accepting and respectful attitudes toward diverse sexual orientations and a lower tendency for sexual assault victim-blaming. The superior performance of the comprehensive curriculum students in sexual diversity attitudes holds meaningful and critical implications. The new curriculum's students had increased awareness and openness toward diverse sexual identities and gender equality and a reduced level of victim-blaming of sexual assault victims compared to the old curriculum.

This outcome is especially significant when considering the numerous challenges LGBTQ+ youths face. For example, they are more likely to experience violence[23–25] at a higher risk of having suicidal thoughts and behaviors, attempting suicide, and committing suicide than heterosexual youth.[15,26,27] There is no doubt that creating safer and more supportive schools and communities for LGBTQ+ youth is imperative to ensuring a healthy learning and growing environment.[16,28] If a one-day training of health teachers, combined with assistance from the county health department for supplemental materials, can yield such a significant increase in students' positive perceptions and attitudes toward sexual orientation and diversity, a more thoroughly planned and implemented comprehensive sexual health curriculum has much potential to create an increased level of acceptance and respect for diverse identities among students. Creating a more diverse and safer environment will benefit not only LGBTQ+ students but also all students. This implication is further related to the need for providing an effective and comprehensive sexual health education program and doing so before students enter puberty.[29,30] Recent research shows that insufficient sexual health knowledge and diversity training could put our youths at a greater risk for sexual health issues and aggravate the risks for high-risk groups such as LGBTQ+ youth. This, in part, is due to students that lack the educational opportunity on sexual health often resorting to unreliable and dangerous sources on the Internet as an alternative, exposing them to even riskier environments.[9]

From this project, we also see the significance of a broader, more inclusive, more systematic sexual health education design, which goes beyond the curriculum for our students. We find that providing educational resources and opportunities for health education teachers and parents is imperative. While the study goal was to identify the difference between different sexual health curricula contents in students' learning, it quickly became evident that barriers to effective education were not just about students. During our research, we frequently heard from teachers about their discomfort discussing more comprehensive sexual health content, especially sexual identity and orientation. Any effort to improve sexual health education for youth must include and recognize the role of the health education teachers' own beliefs, attitudes, and comfort level with the subject matter. The teachers that participated in the training shared that it helped them feel a little more at ease with delivering the content to the students as they felt more comfortable with the materials. Yet they also expressed concerns about limited resources and support from the schools and the community, including parents willing to expose their kids to comprehensive sexual health curriculum content. The teachers feared parents pulling their children from health education classes if they were to go beyond the topics they deemed acceptable. The teachers have been dealing with resistance from some parents even to enroll their children in sexual health education. Some parents chose to opt their kids out of health education classes as they preferred no sexual health education or abstinence-only option for their children. This points to the need to involve the family and community to narrow the gap between research and the reality of sexual health education. Existing research has provided ample evidence for providing comprehensive sexual health education for youths. Still, it does not directly translate into having the parents and communities on board with such directions and goals.

Efforts to identify the best content for sexual health education are an essential task, as we have attempted in this study. However, a good sexual health curriculum can only go so far if health educators who teach the materials continue to have insufficient support and a sense of discomfort in delivering the contents and if parents are not supportive of sexual health education in the first place. Health education teachers could benefit from having access to comprehensive sexual health materials and more training on LGBTQ+ education to ease their discomfort and better their communication with the school community and families.

The known adverse effects of insufficient sexual health knowledge and diversity training have been published, but not enough actions have been followed to influence the students and school atmosphere.[31] As a starting point, schools and community leaders could first utilize local resources to identify existing sexual health curriculum gaps to build a more comprehensive curriculum that meets the community's needs. Many teachers tend to work from a list of objectives that rely heavily on physiological knowledge of the human body and development because alternatives and improvements are deemed unavailable. Providing resources for teachers to expand their curriculum cores to match national guidelines such as the NSES could greatly help increase comfort in the subject matter and create consistency. We could also invest in developing and implementing a separate sexual health education program for parents and a training opportunity for health education teachers. A curriculum designed more specifically for high-risk youth groups such as LGBTQ+ could also be another essential factor to employ.

We strongly recommend that all policymakers seek ways to enhance further and provide an extensive and more comprehensive sexual health curriculum. For schools and teachers needing assistance to improve sexual health education, it is crucial to improve access and availability of resources and guidelines such as those outlined by the NSES. Making such efforts can start with a thorough review of the existing sexual health curriculum and providing institutional-level guidance and resources for health education teachers. Institutional-level efforts to involve family members in sexual health education and well-structured teacher training for dealing with sensitive sexual content can yield far more effective outcomes in learning than merely providing a single class.

At the societal level, much discussion has been taking place on creating a more inclusive and safer school environment for all students in the 21st century. Finding ways to promote a more inclusive learning community will require us to act promptly to implement policies that are proven to be effective. Suppose a trial run promoting comprehensive sexual education content leads to greater openness and respect toward sexual diversity. In that case, there is much to say about how this outcome could guide us, as it points to one of the various tasks we can take on to ensure a safer and more inclusive atmosphere in our schools.

A lack of sexual health education exposes our youth to greater risk. LGBTQ+ students face and struggle with prejudice and discrimination from heteronormative social environments and are at a greater risk of engaging in self-harm and suicidal attempts. A purposive, systematic, and longitudinal effort to provide comprehensive sexual health education can be a powerful tool for educators, school administrators, policymakers, and communities to create a safer and more harmonious society for all.

References

1. Centers for Disease Control and Prevention. (2019). *Sexually transmitted disease surveillance 2018*. www.cdc.gov/std/stats18/default.htm
2. Centers for Disease Control and Prevention. (2014). *Lesbian, gay, bisexual, and transgender health: LGBT youth*. www.cdc.gov/lgbthealth/youth.htm
3. Centers for Disease Control and Prevention. (2017). *What gay and bisexual men need to know about sexually transmitted diseases*. www.cdc.gov/std/life-stages-populations/MSMandSTDs-Dec-2017.pdf
4. Ott, M.A., &. Santelli, J.S. (2007). Abstinence and abstinence-only education. *Current Opinion in Obstetrics and Gynecology, 19*(5), 446–452.
5. Wisconsin state health profile 2015 (2019, July 10). www.cdc.gov/nchhstp/stateprofiles/pdf/Wisconsin_profile.pdf.
6. Carter, D. (2012). Comprehensive sex education for teens is more effective than abstinence. *American Journal of Nursing, 112*(3), 15.
7. Chin, H.B., Sipe, T.A., Elder, R., Mercer, S.L., Chattopadhyay, S.K., Jacob, V., Wethington, H.R., Kirby, D., Elliston, D.B., Griffith, M., Chuke, S.O., Briss, S.C., Ericksen, I., Galbraith, J.S., Herbst, J.H., Johnson, R.L., Kraft, J.M., Noar, S.M., Romero, L.M., Santelli, J., & Community Preventive Services Task Force. (2012). The effectiveness of group-based comprehensive risk-reduction and abstinence education interventions to prevent or reduce the risk of adolescent pregnancy, human immunodeficiency virus, and sexually transmitted infections: Two systematic reviews for the *Guide to Community Preventive Services. American Journal of Preventive Medicine, 42*(3), 272–294.
8. Grossman, J.M., Tracy, A.J., Charmaraman, L., Ceder, I., Erkut, S. (2014). Protective effects of middle school comprehensive sex education with family involvement. *Journal of School Health, 84*(11), 739–747.
9. Bittner, R. (2012). Queering sex education: young adult literature with LGBT content as complementary sources of sex and sexuality education. *Journal of LGBT Youth, 9*(4), 357–372.
10. Pingel, E.S., Thomas, L., Harmell, C., & Bauermeister, J.A. (2013). Creating comprehensive, youth centered, culturally appropriate sex education: What do young gay, bisexual, and questioning men want? *Sexuality Research and Social Policy, 10*, 293–301.

11. Santelli, J.S., Kantor, L.M., Grilo, S.A., Speizer, I.S., Lindberg, L.D., Heitel, J., Schalet, A.T., Lyon, M.E., Mason-Jones, A.J., McGovern, T., Heck, C.J., Rogers, J., Ott, M.A. (2017). Abstinence-only-until-marriage: An updated review of U.S. policies and programs and their impact. *Journal of Adolescent Health, 61*(3), 273–280.
12. Goldfarb, E.S., & Lieberman L.D. (2021). Three decades of research: the case for comprehensive sex education. *Journal of Adolescent Health, 68*(1), 13–27.
13. Cochran, S.D., & Mays, V.M. (2000). Lifetime prevalence of suicide symptoms and affective disorders among men reporting same-sex sexual partners: Results from NHANES III. *American Journal of Public Health, 90*(4), 573–578.
14. Hershberger, S.L., & D'Augelli, A.R. (1995). The impact of victimization on the mental health and suicidality of lesbian, gay and bisexual youth. *Developmental Psychology, 31*(1), 65–74.
15. McDermott, E., Roen, K., & Scourfield, J. (2008). Avoiding shame: Young LGBT people, homophobia and self-destructive behaviors. *Culture, Health & Sexuality: An International Journal for Research, Intervention and Care, 10*(8), 815–829.
16. Russel, S.T., Ryan, C., Toomey, R.B., Diaz, R.M., & Sanchez, J. (2011). Lesbian, gay, bisexual, and transgender adolescent school victimization: implications for young adult health and adjustment. *Journal of School Health, 81*(5), 223–230.
17. Scourfield, J., Roen, M., & McDermott, L. (2008). Lesbian, gay, bisexual and transgender young people's experiences of distress: Resilience, ambivalence and self-destructive behaviour. *Health and Social Care in the Community, 16*(3), 329–336.
18. Future of Sex Education Initiative. (2012). *National sexuality education standards: Core content and skills, K-12 [a special publication of the Journal of School Health]*. http://futureofsexed.org/documents/josh-fose-standards-web.pdf
19. Israel, B.A., Schulz, A.J., Parker, E.A., & Becker, A.B. (1998). Review of community-based research: Assessing partnership approaches to improve public health. *Annual Review of Public Health, 19*, 173–202.
20. This study is supported by the Wisconsin Partnership Program development grant from the School of Medicine and Public Health, University of Wisconsin-Madison.
21. ANSWER of Rutgers University, Family Life Education experts (n.d.). http://answer.rutgers.edu/page/aboutusintro
22. Family Life and Sexual Health Curriculum (FLASH). King County Seattle Public Health. (2019, July 10). www.kingcounty.gov/depts/health/locations/family-planning/education/FLASH.aspx
23. Lombardi, E., Wilchins, R., Priesing, D., & Malouf, D. (2001). Gender violence: Transgender experiences with violence and discrimination. *Journal of Homosexuality, 42*(1), 89–101.
24. Savin-Williams, R.C. (1994). Verbal and physical abuse as stressors in the lives of a lesbian, gay male, and bisexual youths: Associations with school problems, running away, substance abuse, prostitution, and suicide. *Journal of Consulting and Clinical Psychology, 62*(2), 261–269.
25. Wyss, S.E. (2004). 'This was my hell': the violence experienced by gender non-conforming youth in US high schools. *International Journal of Qualitative Studies in Education, 17*(5), 709–730.
26. Almeida, J., Johnson, R.M., Corliss, H.L., Molnar, B.E., & Azraelet, D. (2009). Emotional distress among LGBT youth: The influence of perceived discrimination based on sexual orientation. *Journal of Youth & Adolescence, 38*(7), 1001.
27. Szalacha, L.A. (2003). Safer sexual diversity climates: lessons learned from an evaluation of Massachusetts safe schools program for gay and lesbian students. *American Journal of Education, 110*(1), 58–88.
28. Birkett, M., Espelage, D.L., & Koenig, B. (2009). LGB and questioning students in schools: the moderating effects of homophobic bullying and school climate on negative outcomes. *Journal of Youth & Adolescence, 38*, 989.

29. Ma, Z., Fisher, M.A, & Kuller, L.H. (2014). School-based HIV/AIDS education is associated with reduced risky sexual behaviors and better grades with gender and race/ethnicity differences. *Health Education Research, 29*(2), 330–339.
30. Gay, G., & Howard, T.C. (2000). Multicultural teacher education for the 21st century. *The Teacher Educator, 36*(1), 1–16.
31. Campa, M.I., Leff, Z.L., & Tufts, M. (2018). Reaching high-need youth populations with evidence-based sexual health education in California. *American Journal of Public Health, 108*(S1), S32–S37.

13

GRASSROOTS HEALTH

A Sports-Based Health Promotion Program for Middle School Students

Tyler Spencer, Jane Wallis, Alexandra McAuliffe, and Dahanah Josias Sejour

Founding Story and Initial Motivation for Grassroots Health

By Tyler Spencer

I met a professor during my sophomore year of college who opened my mind to the field of social medicine, an approach to health that privileged a wide range of non-clinical perspectives on the meanings of health, disease, and community. A few months after meeting her, I traveled to Limpopo Province in northeastern South Africa, where I was exposed to the complexities of HIV/AIDS, a preventable disease afflicting nearly one in four residents. Perhaps worse than the virus itself, the stigma associated with HIV and AIDS often precluded people living with the virus from accessing care, disclosing their status to friends and family members, and pursuing better health.

After that experience, I returned to South Africa each year for four years, volunteering to coordinate and evaluate HIV prevention programs that used soccer as an avenue to teach youth about HIV. During my third year visiting South Africa, a friend asked me about HIV in the United States. I hastily told him that AIDS was a problem in the 1980s and 1990s but that the United States had developed treatment, promoted condoms for HIV prevention, and figured out a way to stem the epidemic. I was wrong.

A few months later, while doing a research project on HIV in Washington, DC, I learned that one in 20 adult residents was estimated to be living with HIV. This rate was more than ten times the national average, and it was on par with capital cities in some Sub-Saharan African countries. Despite HIV being considered a chronic, non-life-threatening disease in many developed countries, people

DOI: 10.4324/9781003189787-14

were still dying of AIDS-related illnesses in Washington, DC. This was largely because they were either not getting tested soon enough or were not adhering to antiretroviral treatment.

I tell this story to set up this chapter on Grassroots Health, an organization I founded with 39 other college athletes to promote sexual health and prevent teen HIV infections in Washington, DC. In this chapter, my team and I discuss the rationale for creating Grassroots Health, our theory of change, and our model to promote sexual health in Washington, DC, schools. We also share some of the findings from our initial program evaluations and offer our insights on the challenge of conducting and evaluating sexual health education in schools.

This chapter could not have been written if not for the contributions of multiple authors, including Jane Wallis, Grassroots Health's director of programs and the architect of our organization's comprehensive pipeline of health promotion programs, Alexandra McAuliffe, who has managed the piloting and evaluation of our programs for the past three years, and Dahanah Josias Sejour, who conducted a third-party analysis of our impact evaluation data and advised us on future directions for evaluation research. The programs described here are also the product of a community-wide effort involving the leadership, critical feedback, and participation of youth and adult residents of Washington, DC, university researchers, middle school health and physical education teachers, and hundreds of Washington, DC, college student-athlete volunteer health educators.

Grassroots Health's Sexual Health Education Program

By Tyler Spencer, Jane Wallis, Alexandra McAuliffe, and Dahanah Josias Sejour

In 2009, there was a documented need for comprehensive sexual health promotion programs in Washington, DC, and there was a unique political window of opportunity to improve the response to HIV/AIDS in Washington, DC. New leadership in the DC Department of Health's HIV/AIDS, Hepatitis, STD, and TB Administration helped to provide unprecedented data on the HIV epidemic in DC, showing a marked increase in infections among teenagers and a city-wide estimated adult HIV prevalence of 5% (five times the magnitude needed for the CDC to declare the epidemic as "severe and generalized"). While HIV incidence was high among teenagers, schools often struggled to provide HIV prevention programs during the school day.

Grassroots Health was founded in 2009 as a student-led organization that aimed to educate Washington, DC, youth about HIV prevention, testing, and treatment. Our vision was to mobilize college athletes to facilitate sports-based sexual health promotion programs in DC schools, using both their status as near-peers and an innovative curriculum to address DC's HIV epidemic. We used a modified version of the Grassroot Soccer intervention developed and piloted in several Sub-Saharan African countries. The intervention, based on social learning theory and diffusion of innovation theory, uses sports as an avenue to both instill key health literacy messages (e.g., through kinesthetic learning) and to break the ice surrounding stigmatized sexual health topics. We also believed that, with the right training, local college athletes could be idea program facilitators and role models for youth because of the transferable skills they had picked up in pursuing a college degree and high-level sports participation. Given that our curriculum is sports-based, we also felt that college athletes could be particularly effective lead facilitators. We adapted this curriculum for use in Washington, DC, following three months of focus groups with DC teenagers and HIV educators.

Our intervention involves the following core components:

1. Recruiting NCAA college athletes to become trained as volunteer health educators for middle school students.
2. Training athletes as health educators through a four-day training-of-facilitators course.
3. Building partnerships with local middle schools to host weekly sexual health promotion sessions.
4. Grouping athletes into facilitation teams and matching them with partner middle school classrooms.
5. Supporting athletes to facilitate our curriculum during middle school physical education and health classes once per week for eight to ten weeks.
6. Providing a two-session supplementary health communication workshop for parents and caregivers of middle school students after school.
7. Building partnerships with local healthcare organizations and providing a three-hour linkage-to-care event for all student participants at the culmination of the curriculum.

Our current curriculum includes ten lessons, or "practices," implemented during physical education and health classes. These modules cover the topics listed in Table 13.1.

Curriculum Iterations

While the present-day intervention is detailed in Table 13.1, it went through several iterations in its infancy. The original curriculum included between six and eight sessions that varied from 45 to 90 minutes, depending on the timing that schools offered. Most of the original lessons were focused on HIV prevention, testing, and treatment. As our work grew and we became more responsive to the broader needs of the youth in our city's schools, we added additional lessons that covered HIV, sexually transmitted infections, unplanned pregnancies, and a range of other life skills related to sexual health (bodily awareness, consent, healthy relationships, etc.).

TABLE 13.1 Scope and Sequence for Grassroots Health's Sexual Health Promotion Curriculum

PRACTICE 1: CHOICES	**GOALS**
• Choices • Pre-Game Speech	Introduce the theme of personal choice: It is important make our own choices amongst our peers, and it's okay to make different choices from others. Making choices based on factual information can promote our own health and the health of our communities.
PRACTICE 2: RISKS & RESILIENCY	**GOALS**
• Cat & Mouse • Goal Setting	Discuss risks, and how risks can impact health. Learn life skills to help avoid risks and overcome challenges. Use these skills to set personal goals. Define resiliency and the concept of "bouncing back"
PRACTICE 3: JUGGLING OUR HORMONES	**GOALS**
• Hormone Monster • Juggling My Life	Define types of sexual intercourse, and how puberty/bodily changes connect to sex. Understand that there are things in life that we choose to do, and there are things in life that we have to do: sex is a choice. Understand that there are risks related to having sex.
PRACTICE 4: SEX ED BASICS	**GOALS**
• Fact or Nonsense • Coach's Story	Dispel myths and learn the facts about sex, STIs, HIV, etc. Understand the risks related to having sex. Apply the concept of resiliency to real-life, and build trust between students & coaches.
PRACTICE 5: HIV BASICS	**GOALS**
• HIV Attacks • High Risk, Low Risk, No Risk	Review risks that lead to HIV, STIs, and unwanted pregnancy. Introduce higher-level knowledge around HIV (how it is transmitted, how it works in the body, how to evaluate risk of transmission in real life and prevent it, how to treat it, etc). Explain the concept of treatment as prevention.
PRACTICE 6: PREVENTING TRANSMISSION	**GOALS**
• Transmission Tree • Find the Ball	Demonstrate that HIV & STIs spread quickly when having unprotected sex. Teach the ABCs of HIV & STI prevention (Abstinence, Be Mutually Faithful, Condoms). Eliminate the myth that someone with HIV/STIs looks sick. Establish where people can get tested for HIV/STIs.
PRACTICE 7: UNPLANNED PREGNANCY PREVENTION	**GOALS**
• Prevention Soccer	Understand that there are different forms of contraception that reduce the risk of unplanned pregnancy. Explore which forms of contraception do/do not protect against HIV/STIs. Understand the impact of alcohol/substance use on contraception use.
PRACTICE 8: INFLUENCES & PEER PRESSURE	**GOALS**
• Pressure Tug of War	Explore factors that influence our values and choices around sex and relationships. Discuss different sources of pressure we may feel. Demonstrate that pressure to have sex increases with age. Demonstrate the effect of substance use on decision-making
PRACTICE 9: CONSENT	**GOALS**
• Crossing the Line • Condom Communications	Demonstrate what consent really is: No always means no. Reflect on personal values & beliefs about boundaries and communicating in relationships. Practice communication skills with a partner (e.g. using health facts learned in TGP to communicate around condom use, set boundaries, and respond to a partner rejecting condom use.

Our approach has always offered students age-appropriate, comprehensive, and medically accurate information. We offer students a full menu of options to protect their sexual health and to make informed decisions throughout their lives, but the curriculum is designed such that facilitators are encouraged not to pressure students to choose any single prevention measure over another.

Our curriculum development process at the time of this writing is a three-step process of (1) assessing evidence-based approaches to adolescent health promotion,

(2) facilitating, coding, and analyzing a series of health-related focus group discussions with community stakeholders, including middle and high school students, parents and caregivers, and school health and physical education instructors, and (3) considering insights from the first two steps, assembling a team of our staff and athletes to create and pilot test physical-activity-based games that teach critical health learning methods. Once these steps are complete, our curriculum development team continually evaluates and adapts our curriculum on an ongoing basis.

Recruiting Middle School Partner Sites

In 2009, we recruited four schools as partner sites by traveling from school to school and asking for meetings with school leaders. Middle schools were chosen because students are at a critical stage for developing health-related knowledge and health-promoting behavior before entering high school and becoming more independent. During the creation of the curriculum, Grassroots Health's founder also observed the receptiveness of the middle school age group to Grassroots Health's games-based curriculum. Our initial pitch was to implement our sexual health promotion curriculum after school, as we did not feel that schools would offer us instructional time during the day. After our first year, the principal at our first implementation site asked us to provide programming during the school day rather than after school so that all students could participate. He also reached out to his peers at other schools to foster additional partnerships. Our reach grew exponentially through this type of word-of-mouth partnership recruitment.

In our first several years of programming, we grew too fast, saying "yes" to partnerships at more schools than we could reasonably provide high-quality programs without a full-time staff. Then, after noting a dip in the quality/fidelity of programming, we made the intentional decision to adopt a school prioritization and selection process. We utilized a mechanism developed by our DC's Office of the State Superintendent of Education (OSSE) in combination with our assessment of schools' readiness to partner with us meaningfully. We also fundraised to hire a more robust program staff to support high-quality volunteer training workshops and ensure implementation fidelity at our program sites. As of the writing of this chapter, we are operating in between 10 and 15 schools and providing sexual health programming for 500 students annually.

Recruiting and Training Volunteer Health Educators

In the first iteration of programs, student-athlete volunteer facilitators were recruited by our organization's founder, who was also a student-athlete. Athletes were used as facilitators because they were considered near-peers of middle school students and because the curriculum itself was based around sports and sports metaphors. One early Grassroots Health participant pointed out that athlete role models were considered "cooler than our parents, but not as judgmental as our peers."

Over time, our recruitment method for new student-athlete volunteer health educators evolved into word-of-mouth recruitment from existing volunteers, recruitment meetings with university officials, and in-person informational sessions delivered within university athletic departments. We learned that a successful recruitment effort should be tailored to our target volunteer demographic—college student-athletes. We recognized that Division I athletes are often committed to their sports teams because of the immense discipline, sacrifice, and teamwork skills required to compete at a high level. We felt that these skills could be effectively translated into positive social impact with the proper training and support. We communicated our recruitment messaging accordingly, explaining to athletes that we did not want them to volunteer unless they were fully committed to the hard work required to make a difference in adolescent sexual health.

Grassroots Health's volunteers have always been trained through intensive four-day training sessions that teach thematic proficiency and facilitation techniques. Our training curricula also engage all participants in sessions related to cultural competency and social justice themes that underpin our work (health equity, racial justice, and other social determinants of health). We offer these modules in collaboration with DC community activists, medical educators, and school teachers.

Reach

Grassroots Health has operated in more than 60 schools and community centers across the Washington, DC, Metropolitan Area, reaching more than 10,000 youth with health promotion programs. We have also mobilized more than 1,300 college athletes to become volunteer health educators. These athletes have been undergraduate students at American University, Howard University, Georgetown University, George Washington University, and the University of Maryland. Our athletes have contributed more than 50,000 volunteer hours teaching health in our city's schools.

Impact

From the first set of programs that we facilitated, evaluating our impact has been a priority. We administer pre-program and post-program surveys to all participants, and these surveys assess participant growth from baseline to program completion, using a range of indicators. Our surveys have evolved in tandem with changes to our curriculum and improvements in our organizational capacity to manage evaluation data.

The first iteration of our evaluation survey was a short scale that assessed students' HIV-related knowledge and attitudes, including attitudes related to HIV stigma. In those first few years, we saw gains in students' HIV-related knowledge, but we lacked the funding, staffing, and systems to generate more sophisticated insights into the impact we were having on students (e.g., to assess behavior changes, utilize more complex attitudinal scales).

We set out to assess our impact using a quasi-experimental design, which we understood to be considered as a design that yielded results of high scientific quality. We recruited seven schools to participate in the study, but we encountered significant barriers to gaining permission for long-term follow-up of students. Principals whose students were in our control group asked us to offer our program within the same academic year as students in the treatment group, which limited our follow-up period to just one month post-intervention. Ultimately, our study indicated that Grassroots Health created promising improvements in students' sexual health-related attitudes and increased self-efficacy in a limited number of areas, but it was not able to assess whether these changes had a correlational or causational relationship with students' sexual behaviors and sexual health outcomes over time. We emerged from this study recognizing that we would need a large research grant and more buy-in from school administrators to conduct research to assess long-term changes in students' health outcomes.

Later, we worked with researcher Dahanah Josias Sejour on a pro-bono project to rigorously analyze data from our most recent semester of programs. The data set included matching pre-program and post-program surveys that assessed 160 students' sexual health-related knowledge, attitudes, and beliefs from sixth-grade participants of Grassroots Health's programs, 55% of whom were female, 40% male, 4% not self-identifying with any of our listed gender options, and less than 1% "other." The participants' self-reported race included 57% identifying as Black/African American, 27% as Hispanic/Latino, 10% as mixed/multiple races, 3% as American Indian/Alaskans, and less than 1% each as Asian, Hawaiian/Pacific Islander, and White. The remainder of the participants (2%) did report their race. The results of pre-program and post-program analyses suggested that participation in Grassroots Health's increased students' sexual health knowledge, attitudes and beliefs about healthy relationships, self-efficacy to refuse/delay sexual activity, positive attitudes toward the topic of sexual health, and communication with a parent and/or caregiver around sexual health.

Insights From the Early Years

To build a longer-term strategic plan, we reflected on our footprint, partnerships, impact, and lessons learned over our first decade of programs, as well as changes in the broader environment in which our work is situated. This process resulted in key realizations that guided our thinking about our organization's future.

The Prevailing Approach to HIV Prevention Has Become Medicalized in Recent Years

With the dawn of the era of treatment-as-prevention for HIV, we have seen a sweeping shift in the strategic and funding environments related to HIV/AIDS and, in turn, many other sexual health promotion programs. Many stakeholders have re-focused their programs on targeting "high-risk" populations at the expense of supporting broader interventions that work at the population level. Instead of focusing on changing norms, attitudes, and behaviors, we have seen many stakeholders become laser-focused on more downstream interventions that aim to reduce viral loads and usher patients through the HIV continuum of care. While we appreciate the new scientific tools available for HIV prevention and treatment and recognize the need to support them, we also see a persistent and urgent need to address the larger factors that drive sexual health risks—fragmented social support systems for health-seeking, racial and socioeconomic inequalities, and stigma.

Quantitative Data and Randomized Trials Dominate the Policy-Level Discourse Around HIV and Sexual Health in the United States

Earlier in the evolution of Grassroots Health, we embarked on a rigorous impact evaluation with an ambitious goal of using an experimental design. We came to realize that experimental research in social settings presents a range of ethical, political, and pragmatic challenges that make it difficult to do well with a limited budget and without a large, seasoned research team. We wondered if other organizations might have encountered similar barriers, and we recognized the challenge of homegrown, community-based, and innovative organizations to access the resources needed to become part of the CDC's compendium of evidence-based interventions.

In Schools, Addressing Only One Disease Misses the Mark. There Needs to Be a Unified Call to Re-Think Adolescent Health and the Role of Health Promotion in Our Students' Core Curriculum

Perhaps most of all, we recognized that addressing HIV in schools was a drop in the bucket, and many of our students and teachers requested that we use our unique curriculum model to address other adolescent health topics.

Expanding Our Curricula

In our first few years, we noticed that students wanted us to come back and spend more time in their classrooms and that teachers encouraged us to think about how our model could be used to address other areas of health promotion. In DC, the government approved a new law that mandated schools to teach a specified set of physical education and health education activities for students, and the coordinated school system established age-appropriate, medically accurate health learning standards for all DC students. Our team decided to embark on a strategic effort to build new curricula, and in the process, we created our curriculum development process, detailed below.

Step 1: Literature review: Grassroots Health's program team analyzed relevant literature, particularly focusing on meta-analyses of health education reviews, by topic area (mental health, nutrition, physical health, and sexual health promotion) to identify key topic areas for a comprehensive approach to adolescent health promotion.

Step 2: Community focus groups: Using the key topics areas, Grassroots Health designed community focus group sessions with various stakeholders to gain insight into the community perspective on each topic area. Grassroots Health held focus groups for each curriculum with volunteer program facilitators, middle school students, high school students, parents/caregivers, and school teachers. The primary motivation behind these focus groups was to make the curriculum as specific to the community's needs as possible. Each focus group was designed to follow an open-ended interview guide that helped Grassroots Health assess community perceptions of health issues and the barriers students face to sustaining healthy lives and accessing health services. Grassroots Health's model is built not only on building students' health knowledge but also on helping them apply it to their own lives and communities. This component of the curriculum relies on the information gained from focus groups.

Step 3: Review of health standards: Grassroots Health reviewed National Health Standards and OSSE Health Education Standards to align the literature review findings and the community focus groups to the grade-level standards.

Step 4: Gamify key topic areas: Grassroots Health's staff, volunteers, and teachers then synthesize the information gained in the first three steps and develop a series of movement-based games that will underpin the lessons in the curriculum. All games align with the program's targeted health objectives and the health education and physical education standards. Lessons are designed to engage students in a variety of sports drills and classic physical education games, using sports-related metaphors to teach difficult health concepts and life skills. Grassroots Health created a nutrition and physical activity curriculum for sixth-grade students, a comprehensive sexual health curriculum for seventh-grade students, and a mental health promotion curriculum for eighth-grade students. Each curriculum focuses on core health knowledge around each topic area while also providing an opportunity to discuss the nuances of social determinants of health, barriers to healthy decision-making, and practical application at each grade level.

Using this approach, we developed two new curricula—one 10-session curriculum in nutritional/physical health and one 10-session curriculum for mental health promotion. We piloted each of these curricula in five schools over one semester, proactively soliciting feedback from students, volunteer program facilitators, middle school physical education teachers, and our staff.

The Future for Grassroots Health: Supporting Schools to Reimagine Health Education

Promoting school-based health education and physical activity have long been national priorities, given the purview of school systems. Schools enroll approximately 95% of US youth[1] and are responsible for their academic, social, emotional, and behavioral development.[2,3] Importantly, these areas of development are intricately tied to health and physical activity, centering schools in a unique position to promote health and wellness amongst their students. In response, public health and education leaders have called on schools to provide the bulk of health-promotion opportunities, recommending 225 minutes of in-school moderate physical activity for middle and high schoolers per week and a minimum of 40 hours of health education each year.[4,5] Distributing health information, changing health behaviors, and linking students to care should therefore be fundamental to the mission of schools. Yet, in practice, the current landscape reflects an erosion to this commitment, and the proportion of schools meeting recommended targets is nominal.

A national assessment by the Centers for Disease Control and Prevention found that only half of school districts at the middle and high school levels and just over a third at the elementary level meet their health education standards.[6] Furthermore, only about 24% of youth meet the daily recommended physical activity standards, a rate that decreases with age, most notably among girls.[7] Even within the nation's capital, schools struggle to meet recommended targets, with fewer than 5% of Washington, DC, schools providing adequate health education and physical activity programs for their students, as mandated by the DC Healthy Schools Act.[8]

It is evident that schools across the country are facing steep barriers to providing comprehensive physical and health education and are cutting these programs from their curricula at staggering rates. Despite evidence that school wellness programming increases time spent in physical activity without deterring from academics,[9] the pervasive culture of high-stakes standardized testing, coupled with budget shortfalls and conflicting federal and state policies, pressures schools to prioritize tested subject areas above all else.[10] The prioritization of tested subjects is reflected in allotted funding, instructional time and space, professional development, staffing, and administrative support, resulting in diminished resources and capacity to provide health and physical activity programs.[6,10] This has disproportionate effects, with lower-income and majority Hispanic/African American schools implementing local wellness policies at lower rates.[10]

When health and physical education teachers are cut, the burden often falls on untrained staff or uncomfortable with teaching this content.[5,11] Research has highlighted that psychosocial factors among teachers (e.g., low perceived capability and/or pessimistic affect) are major barriers to implementation.[10] Coupled with little administrative accountability and bureaucratic and political hurdles, this results in cookie-cutter curricula that, at best, emphasize content knowledge but place little value on students' priorities or cultivating life skills needed to make healthy choices across the lifespan.[5]

In stark contrast to the declining resources for health and physical activity programs, the body of research recognizing their benefit is ever-increasing. Physical activity promotes positive physical outcomes and is associated with enhanced mental, psychosocial, behavioral, and academic outcomes. A dose-response relationship exists between physical activity and academic-related outcomes,[12] and classroom-based physical activity has been linked to improved self-concept, social behaviors, goal orientation, self-efficacy, focus and memory, on-task behavior, and reduced absenteeism.[1,12–15] The potential of physical activity to reduce symptoms of depression and anxiety also makes it a promising mental health promotion and early intervention strategy.[16,17] Integrated with health education and healthy lifestyle curricula, outcomes such as improved cognitive functioning and academic achievement; enhanced quality of life; improved health knowledge, attitudes, and practices; and other long-term benefits such as increased employability have been found.[5,16,18,19]

The widening gap between research and practice in health and education points to the need for reinvigorated health education programming and school-based physical activity and innovative solutions to persistent resource and implementation problems. Community-school partnerships are a potential solution to achieve greater collaboration between fields.[1] These cross-system partnerships blend school-owned and community-owned resources to provide a continuum of health interventions within school-based settings while expanding students' "support teams" beyond just school-based staff.[2,3] However, little has been published to explore how these school-community partnerships are cultivated and leveraged to support the design, implementation, and evaluation of sustainable and effective interventions in meeting state health requirements, improving health knowledge, changing behaviors, and improving access to health services.

This chapter has provided one example of how our community-based organization reimagined traditional health promotion interventions (beginning with sexual health) using school-community partnerships to address this pressing need. We hope our story might be useful reading for other instructors, school administrators, public health practitioners, and social entrepreneurs interested in improving adolescent health through school-based programs.

References

1. Giles, W., Hunt, H., Lewallen, T., Potts-Datema, W., & Slade, S. (2014). *Whole school, whole community, whole child: A collaborative approach to learning and health*. ASCD and Centers for Disease Control and Prevention. www.cdc.gov/healthyschools/wscc/WSCCmodel_update_508tagged.pdf
2. Stephan, S.H., Sugai, G., Lever, N., & Connors, E. (2015). Strategies for integrating mental health into schools via a multitiered system of support. *Child and Adolescent Psychiatric Clinics of North America, 24*(2), 211–231. https://doi.org/10.1016/j.chc.2014.12.002
3. Adelman, H.S. and, & Taylor, L. (2006) Mental health in schools and public health. *Public Health Reports, 121*(3), 294–298.
4. U.S. Department of Health and Human Services. (2018). *2018 Physical activity guidelines for Americans*, 2nd ed. U.S. Department of Health and Human Services.
5. Benes, S., Boyd, K.M., Cucina, I., & Alperin, H.L. (2020). School-based health education research: Charting the course for the future. *Research Quarterly for Exercise and Sport*, 1–16. https://doi.org/10.1080/02701367.2020.1712315
6. Mann, M.J., & Lohrmann, D.K. (2019). Addressing challenges to the reliable, large-scale implementation of effective school health education. *Health Promotion Practice, 20*(6), 834–844. doi:10.1177/1524839919870196
7. National Physical Activity Plan Alliance. (2018). *The 2018 United States report card on physical activity for children and youth*. National Physical Activity Plan Alliance. http://physicalactivityplan.org/projects/PA/2018/2018%20US%20Report%20Card%20Full%20Version_WEB.PDF?pdf=page-link
8. Heim, J. (2018, December 2). D.C. schools are still a long way from meeting physical education targets. *The Washington Post*. www.washingtonpost.com/local/education/dc-schools-are-still-a-long-way-from-meeting-physical-education-targets/2018/12/02/38e986c6-ec4b-11e8–96d4–0d23f2aaad09_story.html
9. Bublitz, M.G., & Rhodes, J. (2017) Activity in the classroom: Interventions to increase activity and help fight childhood obesity. *Journal of Childhood Obesity, 2*(1), 3.
10. Weatherson, K.A., McKay, R., Gainforth, H.L., & Jung, M.E. (2017). Barriers and facilitators to the implementation of a school-based physical activity policy in Canada: Application of the theoretical domains framework. *BMC Public Health, 17*, 835.
11. Long, C. (2017, March 28). When physical education is cut, who picks up the slack? *National Education Association Today*. https://neatoday.org/authors/cindylong
12. Watson, A., Timperio, A., Brown, H., Best, K., & Hesketh, K.D. (2017). Effect of classroom-based physical activity interventions on academic and physical activity outcomes: A systematic review and meta-analysis. *International Journal of Behavioral Nutrition and Physical Activity, 14*(1). https://doi.org/10.1186/s12966-017-0569-9
13. SHAPE America—Society of Health and Physical Educators. (2016). Shape of the nation: Status of physical education in the USA. In *SHAPE America* (pp. 1–142). www.shapeamerica.org/uploads/pdfs/son/Shape-of-the-Nation-2016_web.pdf
14. Kohl, H.W. III, & Cook, H.D. (2013). Physical activity and physical education: Relationship to growth, development, and health. In *Educating the student body: Taking physical activity and physical education to school* (pp. 97–160). National Academies Press.
15. Roberts, C.K., Freed, B., McCarthy, W.J. (2010). Low aerobic fitness and obesity are associated with lower standardized test scores in children. *The Journal of Pediatrics, 156*, 711–718, 718 e1.
16. Pascoe, M., Bailey, A.P., Craike, M., Carter, T., Patten, R., Stepto, N., & Parker, A. (2020). Physical activity and exercise in youth mental health promotion: A scoping review. *BMJ Open Sport & Exercise Medicine, 6*(1), e000677. https://doi.org/10.1136/bmjsem-2019-000677

17. Institute of Medicine. (2013). *Educating the student body: Taking physical activity and physical education to school*. National Academies Press.
18. Centers for Disease Control and Prevention. (2010). *The association between school-based physical activity, including physical education, and academic performance*. U.S. Department of Health and Human Services.
19. Kopkin, N., Martin, M.L., & Hollar, D. (2018). Improvements in standardised test scores from a multi-component nutrition and healthy living intervention in a US elementary-school setting. *Health Education Journal*, 77(5), 527–541. doi: 10.1177/0017896917741510.

14

QUEERING SEXUALITY EDUCATION

Current Research and Future Directions

Steven Hobaica, Kyle A. Schofield, Gregory H. Keiser, and Paul Kwon

Introduction

As most readers of this book are aware, sexuality education often occurs at a critical time in youth development. By providing essential information about the body, identities, and sexuality, education can help children and adolescents understand bodily changes and become aware of their sexuality and gender. In addition, sexuality education can help alleviate anxiety, shame, and other negative feelings as youth become aware of their body and identity.

For children and adolescents who identify as heterosexual and cisgender (individuals whose gender identity aligns with their assigned sex at birth), sexuality education typically affirms their sexual orientation and gender identity. Curricula will typically cover heterosexual identities and intercourse, as well as anatomy and experiences that correspond to a cisgender student's body. However, what is the experience of lesbian, gay, bisexual, transgender, and other queer (LGBTQ+) students in sexuality education? To what extent does sexuality education acknowledge and affirm students who are LGBTQ+? What are the consequences when sexuality education fails to affirm LGBTQ+ youth?

This chapter will address these questions with a set of research studies performed by the authors while summarizing past literature. We will conclude with policy recommendations that support the health of LGBTQ+ youth through the provision of comprehensive and inclusive sexuality education.

Vulnerability and Resilience among LGBTQ+ Youth

It has been well-demonstrated that LGBTQ+ individuals are at higher risk for mental health problems than heterosexual and cisgender individuals. Throughout one's lifetime, gay men and lesbian women are two and a half times more likely

DOI: 10.4324/9781003189787-15

to have a mental disorder compared to heterosexual individuals.[1] LGB youth and adults report thinking about suicide and attempting suicide significantly more than their heterosexual counterparts.[2] Transgender (trans or gender diverse) people also have higher rates of mental health problems compared with cisgender people.[3] More specifically, trans people have a rate of suicide attempts that is particularly disturbing: it is ten times higher than the general population's rate.

The main cause of these mental health problems in stigmatized populations, including LGBTQ+ people, has been termed *minority stress*.[1] We all experience stress as a part of daily life; minority stress refers to additional stress because of one's stigmatized identity. The most visible type of minority stress is an individual's experiences with prejudice and discrimination. For LGBTQ+ people, this can include being bullied, called derogatory names, rejected by one's family of origin, denied housing or employment because of one's identity, and other negative experiences. LGBTQ+ people are also at greater risk for multiple types of violence throughout their lives, including sexual assault.[3,4]

Other types of minority stress are less visible but are just as damaging. For example, LGBTQ+ individuals may expect rejection in interactions with others, which can become a chronic source of stress.[1] When this occurs at school, youth may feel "on guard" and hypervigilant with students they encounter due to an expectation of rejection. Relatedly, LGBTQ+ people may adopt the negative attitudes they encounter from other people and the media, a process called internalized homophobia or internalized transphobia. Finally, when there is a disaffirming atmosphere, resulting in the development of shame and guilt, LGBTQ+ individuals may choose to conceal their identity.[5] Suppression of any kind tends to backfire: when we push away our emotions, we experience more distress than if we were to accept our emotions.[6] For LGBTQ+ individuals, suppressing a core aspect of their identity is painful and stressful. Concealment also suppresses immune functioning[7] and interferes with forming a support network, which is essential for proper development in youth.[1]

Despite the greater challenges that they face, many LGBTQ+ people thrive. A review of the research literature on resilience found that social support was the most crucial resilience variable for LGBTQ+ individuals.[8] There are two different ways that social support benefits us.[9] First, when we have a bad day, we are often comforted by sharing our experience with a supportive person in our life. By processing the negative events aloud in a safe atmosphere, we can think about things differently, easing our stress and negative emotions. Second, social support gives us a sense of belonging with others and a sense of community. For LGBTQ+ people, these general benefits of social support come with one important caveat. Social support is most beneficial when it affirms one's sexual orientation and gender identity.[8] Such affirmative support is necessary for helping LGBTQ+ people process stress related to their sexuality or gender identity.

Given what we know about vulnerability and resilience in LGBTQ+ youth, we can profile those youth that are most at risk and those that are least at risk.

Most at risk are youth who conceal their identity, harbor negative beliefs about their sexual orientation or gender identity, and have little social support. Least at risk are youth who are out, have positive beliefs about their sexual orientation or gender identity, and have a supportive network. This supportive network would include a school with an affirmative atmosphere, including a Gay-Straight-Alliance or Gender-Sexuality-Alliance and affirming teachers.

Sexuality educators play an especially important role in building resilience in their LGBTQ+ students. The education they provide can affirm the identities of LGBTQ+ students, encouraging less concealment and more self-acceptance. When made comprehensive and inclusive of all students, sexuality education curricula can be relevant for everyone in the classroom, regardless of each student's identity. Finally, these affirming educators would become easily identifiable adult support figures for LGBTQ+ students at the school.

In our research at Washington State University, located in Eastern Washington, we sought to learn more about the importance of sexuality education experiences among LGBTQ+ individuals. We interviewed and carefully listened to members of the LGBTQ+ community. Based on their words, we created a questionnaire to understand further the impact of sexuality education on identity development and health outcomes for LGBTQ+ students.

Sexually Diverse Students in Heteronormative Sexuality Education

Our first study explored the impact of school sexuality education on sexually diverse students.[10] Hour-long, semi-structured interviews were conducted with sexually diverse individuals (e.g., lesbian, gay, bisexual, pansexual, asexual, queer). Interviewed participants, who were all current or prior students, were asked about their identity, coming out, health, experiences with sexuality education, possible impacts of sexuality education, and recommendations for change.

Unsurprisingly, students reported strikingly similar experiences regarding their school sexuality education and its impact on their lives. As one participant shared, "[Sexuality education] was kind of like . . . this is how you hetero." Generally, participants described experiencing heteronormative sexuality education in school (e.g., curricula geared toward heterosexual students) that was full of scare tactics ("If you have sex, you'll get AIDS and die"), which led to the development of insufficient and often stigmatizing knowledge about their sexual identities and behaviors. Sexuality education made many students feel uncomfortable and isolated: "I couldn't relate to anybody or anything they were talking about. [My sexual orientation] was just not discussed." Participants linked their education with risky sexual behaviors (e.g., reduced sexual protection), internalized homophobia and shame regarding their sexual identity ("It was horrible, because for the longest time, I thought there was something wrong with me"), hesitance with sexual interactions and coming out, and being able to put a name to experiences of sexual violence (e.g., nonconsensual sexual interactions, sexual assault, sexual abuse) due to having limited education on consent. One participant, a sexual assault survivor, shared, "At first, I didn't even know that [a sexual assault] happened. It actually happened on multiple accounts because I didn't even know what was considered rape." Another survivor stated that with inclusive and comprehensive sexuality education, and increased understanding of consent, multiple assaults "definitely wouldn't have happened. I would've walked sooner."

Participants struggled with both physical (e.g., STIs) and mental health problems (e.g., depression, anxiety, suicidality) that they argued could have been alleviated with more inclusive and comprehensive sexuality education. To make up for the failure of their education, they self-educated through reading, surfing the Internet, and asking LGBTQ+ identified friends for information and support, which produced variable results, given that these sources are not always reliable. Furthermore, several students felt confused after sexuality education ("It's difficult to even try to be with a [member of the same sex] because I wouldn't know what to do") and identified participating in trial-and-error sexual experiences, where they would try something out with a partner and face possible consequences to learn about their identity, sexual behaviors, and risk for STIs. Another participant artfully shared, "Our sexuality education focused on what happens when a penis is involved with a vagina, and I was with a woman and there was no penis in the room. We had no clue what we were doing. [I had] absolutely no knowledge about any risks involved." Without seeking out their own education, a participant shared, "I would not have been prepared at all. I would be really awkward and ignorant of what goes where, how to do what . . . everything. Besides how to put on a condom. . . . What happens now?"

Given that students had comparable experiences, they also provided similar suggestions to include sexually diverse students of all ages. They advocated for more inclusive and comprehensive sexuality education that covers all LGBTQ+ identities, sexual behaviors, methods of contraception and protection, and consent education. Participants reported that more comprehensive and inclusive sexuality education would make LGBTQ+ identities and sexual behaviors visible and normalized ("If you talk about it, people can start to form their own opinions and start to be knowledgeable") while providing accurate and applicable information to all students, regardless of their identity. With adequate information, students argued that safer and more pleasurable sexual experiences would be expected ("If somebody had ever told me that sex was supposed to feel pleasurable for everyone involved, it would've been a little easier for me to not rationalize my [sexual assault]"). Additionally, according to participants, healthier relationships, an increased sense of community with classmates, increased resilience, and improved self-confidence and esteem could be expected. Furthermore, these improvements could improve sexually diverse students' mental and physical health outcomes, especially because they would likely experience less minority stress if they felt more included in curricula and were accepted by their teachers and peers.

Finally, participants noted that inclusive and comprehensive sexuality education could assist heterosexual students with understanding and accepting their sexually diverse peers. They stated that it could help all students feel prepared and confident while engaging in a variety of sexual behaviors, possibly leading to more frequent and effective use of protection and decreased frequency of nonconsensual sexual interactions. Thus, according to our participants, comprehensive and inclusive sexuality education would benefit all students, regardless of identity.

Gender Diverse Students in Cisnormative Sexuality Education

Our second study examined trans and other gender diverse individuals' experiences with sexuality education.[11] Trans individuals are people whose gender assigned at birth does not match their gender identity (e.g., a person who was assigned female at birth but identifies as nonbinary or as a man). Gender identity is different from sexual identity, which is when someone identifies as being lesbian, gay, bisexual, or as another sexual identity. Trans individuals may identify with any sexual identity while also identifying as transgender, non-binary, or another gender diverse identity. As in our first study, we conducted hour-long interviews, now with individuals who identified as transgender. Students answered similar questions to our first study, except we also explored experiences with gender identity development and transition.

Few students reported learning about transgender identities in sexuality education, with most saying they were completely excluded. One participant said, "There [was] no acknowledgment of trans people in my school, K—12, that I can recall." Another said that her only memory of discussing trans identities in high school was with peers, which was marked by confusion given that they did not understand what this identity meant. When LGBTQ+ identities were mentioned, participants shared that most examples were limited to gay men and focused on stigmatizing information, such as the risk for HIV/AIDS.

Many reported that their classrooms were split by sex (e.g., boys in one room and girls in another) and contained only information related to one's assigned sex. This led to a limited understanding of reproductive systems and the experiences of individuals with other gender identities; in one student's case, this also resulted in lacking appropriate knowledge about one's anatomy following gender affirmation surgery. Many participants noted that their sexuality education relied on binary understandings of gender, such as only educating "girls" about puberty and gendered messages about personality and personal strengths. One student described the overall message received in sexuality education as: "Boys have penises, girls have vaginas. . . . Sexuality education confines people into, 'you are a boy,' or, 'you are a girl,' [which is] really damaging to people who don't identify as a boy or a girl."

Most participants did not identify as transgender at the time they experienced sexuality education, but nonetheless, many reported being fearful and apprehensive of puberty. Some shared, in retrospect, that puberty was a gender dysphoric time for them. Gender dysphoria is best termed as the distress that can occur due to a mismatch between one's assigned sex and gender identity. Not having representation of transgender people in classroom discussions led the students to believe that they would inevitably go through the pubertal changes described in their class. None were made aware of medical treatments that could delay these changes or allow them to make different choices for their bodies.

Participants generally believed that their sexuality education had a negative effect on their identity development. Several described their gender dysphoria as being confusing and destructive during adolescence. One student said,

> there was no room for variance . . . it left a huge void in my knowledge. They never acknowledged [what] I was feeling at the time. So, I just felt really lost. I think having the words to describe what I was feeling earlier would have saved me.

Several also reported delaying their gender transition due to having limited knowledge of transition options available to them. Some were just beginning gender transition at the time of their interview; in fact, one trans woman told us that she would be starting hormone replacement therapy the day after her interview. Sexual relationships and sexual health may have been affected, too. Almost half of those interviewed reported engaging in unsafe sex (e.g., not using protection and not communicating about STI status or other sex-related concerns). Further, some individuals noted that after receiving sexuality education, they were unsure whether barrier methods were necessary for same-sex interactions.

Ultimately, our trans interviewees determined that their sexuality education was harmful and incomplete. They generally sought other sexual health information to supplement the information received in their sexuality education, such as asking friends and romantic partners; reading books, blogs, and articles; watching videos (e.g., informational videos, television shows, and pornography); and engaging in social media. They had three main suggestions for improving sexuality education: including all identities, comprehensive sexual health information, and structural changes to the classroom and curricula. They wished that a variety of identities could be explored, both in terms of possibilities for their own identities and for understanding their partners and peers. Additionally, they argued that information about both gender transition and consent is essential to sexual health, resulting in positive health outcomes for all students. Finally, students shared that the largest structural change was to always base education on scientific research to discourage students from seeking information from alternative sources, which can vary in accuracy.

Ultimately, interviewed students hoped that a trans-inclusive curriculum would result in a multitude of positive effects, including improvements in mental health, sexual health and relationships, identity development, and acceptance of transgender and other gender diverse identities among the general population, which could result in less trans-related violence and bullying.

Measuring the Consequences of Heteronormative and Cisnormative Sexuality Education

After our interviews revealed the common experiences of LGBTQ+ students in sexuality education and its possible consequences on their development and health, we developed a questionnaire to measure individuals' perceptions of their sexuality education.[12]

This measure, the Perceived Inclusivity of Sexuality Education Scale (PISES), was designed to capture the important aspects of sexuality education revealed by our interview work. It initially aimed to measure the extent to which individuals believed their sexual orientation was acknowledged, made visible, and normalized in their sexuality education, and to what degree their sexuality education provided them with relevant and applicable information about sex. Example items included whether participants' sexuality education "affirmed my orientation as normal and acceptable, and equal to other orientations," "made me feel prepared and comfortable for future sexual experiences," and "made me feel visible in the curriculum and in the classroom."

Developing this scale to measure students' perceptions of their sexuality education was important because previous research on sexuality education inclusivity had only measured instructors' beliefs about their abilities to include sexually diverse students in curricula.[13] In contrast to instructors' relatively high confidence in their ability to provide inclusive sexuality education, sexually diverse students have historically reported very low satisfaction levels in their sexuality education.[14] We expected that sexually diverse students who reported more exclusive, heteronormative sexuality education would have poorer mental and sexual health outcomes. In this study, we included our PISES measure in addition to measures of anxiety, depression, suicidality, sexual risk behaviors, and other sexual health outcomes.

We recruited a large sample of 263 sexually diverse participants for this study, allowing us to draw broader conclusions about the experiences of sexually diverse students in heteronormative sexuality education. Our results showed that sexually diverse students who experienced more exclusionary, heteronormative sexuality education tended to have more anxiety, depression, and suicidality. However, we did not see a difference in sexual health outcomes based on perceived inclusivity of sexuality education.

Participants reported low scores on the PISES, indicating that, on average, our participants had received exclusive, heteronormative sexuality education.

However, a few of our participants reported a maximum score on this scale, showing that it is entirely possible to provide inclusive sexuality education that is satisfactory to sexually diverse students. These results were consistent with our interview-based research, which found almost uniformly insufficient, exclusionary, and heteronormative sexuality education curricula and climate.

Our results help to demonstrate many of the powerful impacts of exclusionary sexuality education on sexually diverse students that we had heard in our interviews. Among the most striking results were the rates of suicidality found in our sample: 70% of the sample reported suicidal ideation in high school, 42% reported having made a suicide plan, and 28% reported having attempted to die by suicide. Among our participants, greater inclusion in sexuality education was related to lower rates of planning or attempting to die by suicide. The lesson from these findings is clear: inclusive sexuality education may help save lives.

Currently, we are conducting a similar study with gender diverse individuals to assess the consequences of cisnormative sexuality education. We adapted the PISES to assess perceptions of how well participants' sexuality education included content and language relevant to and inclusive of their gender identity. We also included other outcome measures such as desire to and age of transition and congruence with one's gender identity. Initial results suggest that greater perceived inclusion of gender diverse individuals in sexuality education may be related to lower depression among gender diverse students, a younger age of transition, and greater gender congruence.

Conclusions and Discussion

These studies have helped demonstrate across a large sample of sexually and gender diverse students that exclusionary, heteronormative, and cisnormative sexuality education is associated with adverse mental health outcomes for LGBTQ+ students. Thus, sex educators play a vital role in the well-being and health of their students. Sex educators' may overestimate their abilities to include LGBTQ+ students in their curricula and classroom climates and may benefit from critically examining how they include LGBTQ+ students in their instruction. They may also benefit from improving the visibility, normalization, and applicability of their material to LGBTQ+ students. It is of note that having more policy supportive of comprehensive sexuality education can likely help sex educators in their efforts to include, validate, and respect sexual minority and gender minority students.

The samples in our first two studies were college-educated, with each participant being out to at least some of their friends and most of them out to their families. Most described having informative conversations and moments of education during college. Several of them described being a privilege as they could finally be out to others in college. This is important, especially considering the disproportionate number of LGBTQ+ students who drop out of high school due to victimization and the striking number of LGBTQ+ individuals who are homeless,[15] who may never attend college. Additionally, they described that accessing education through their computers and the Internet was a privilege. Many LGBTQ+ individuals may not have access to technology to provide crucial information for positive sexual and gender identity development and safe, consensual sex.

Rather than expecting sexually and gender diverse students to seek out their own knowledge or for their families to teach them, students argued that all public schools should be required to provide inclusive and comprehensive sexuality education to all students. New data in our lab suggests that nearly 20% of youth identify as LGBTQ+.[16] Thus, in a classroom of 30, six students will identify as LGBTQ+ and in a classroom of 500, 100 of those students will be LGBTQ+, which is a substantial size for a "minority" group. Considering the size of this community and the impact that inclusive and comprehensive sexuality education can have on LGBTQ+ youth health, state- and federal-level policy change is recommended.

According to SIECUS (Sex Ed for Social Change), more than 20 states do not require sexuality education, and 35 states require a focus on abstinence during sexuality education when administered. Additionally, during sexuality education, only 16 states require instruction on condoms and contraception, and nine states require a discussion on consent. Even more disturbing, only seven states require sexuality education that is inclusive of LGBTQ+ youth, while nine states require education that discriminates against LGBTQ+ people.[17]

Recently published research reviewed 30 years of research on sexuality education. The authors report that comprehensive sexuality education has been found to help reduce sexual violence (e.g., child abuse, intimate partner violence), develop healthier relationships, and improve socio-emotional learning and media literacy. They also found that sexuality education should be scaffolded over numerous years and begin in elementary school for all youth. Finally, they found that LGBTQ+ inclusive, socially just sexuality education is essential when considering the health of our youth. In conclusion, they argue that multiple decades of research support long-term and scaffolded comprehensive sexuality education that is LGBTQ+ inclusive at a national level in all public schools.[18]

In 2020, after years of effort, the state of Washington (WA) effectively passed a bill that will require all public schools in WA to administer comprehensive, LGBTQ+ inclusive, and culturally sensitive sexuality education in the 2022–2023 school year.[19] For states interested in doing something similar, see SIECUS' Community Action Toolkit, which includes a guide to help individuals improve sexuality education in their local communities.[20]

It will be important for WA and other states that effectively pass similar bills to gather data on the impact of newly mandated comprehensive, inclusive, and culturally sensitive sexuality education. We hope that these efforts will eventually inform federal policy that mandates similar sexuality education in all public schools to affirm and protect all students, regardless of their sexual or gender identity. The data are clear, and policy is lagging. Comprehensive and inclusive sexuality education helps save lives, especially for underserved and marginalized groups, such as LGBTQ+ students. It is our duty to pass legislation that protects all youth.

As one of our participants beautifully shared:

> By not talking about it, there's the assumption that it doesn't exist, or it's not worthy or valid enough to talk about in the classroom. It's deviant. It's not normal. I think those messages happen at an early age. When you don't talk about these kinds of things, people just assume that it doesn't happen . . . or if it does happen, then you're weird. I think that schools can be a place of liberation, where you introduce different ideas and thoughts, and open people's minds . . . or it can be a place where you just continue to produce the status quo. Introduce those things [to students] because people identify as gay, bisexual, and trans at elementary school ages. It exists, it happens, and it should be talked about in the classroom.

References

1. Meyer, I.H. (2003). Prejudice, social stress and mental health in lesbian, gay and bisexual populations: Conceptual issues and research evidence. *Psychological Bulletin, 129*, 674–697. doi:10.1037/0033-2909.129.5.674
2. Plöderl, M., Wagenmakers, E.J., Tremblay, P., Ramsay, R., Kralovec, K., Fartacek, C., & Fartacek, R. (2013). Suicide risk and sexual orientation: A critical review. *Archives of Sexual Behavior, 42*(5), 715–727. doi:10.1007/s10508-012-0056-y
3. James, S.E., Herman, J.L., Rankin, S., Keisling, M., Mottet, L., & Anafi, M. (2016). *The report of the 2015 U.S. transgender survey*. National Center for Transgender Equality.
4. Herek, G.M., Gillis, J.R., & Cogan, J.C. (1999). Psychological sequelae of hate-crime victimization among lesbian, gay, and bisexual adults. *Journal of Consulting and Clinical Psychology, 67*, 945–951. doi:10.1037/0022-006X.67.6.945
5. D'Augelli, A.R., & Grossman, A.H. (2001). Disclosure of sexual orientation, victimization, and mental health among lesbian, gay, and bisexual older adults. *Journal of Interpersonal Violence, 16,* 1008–1027. doi:10.1177/088626001016010003
6. Pennebaker, J.W. (1997). *Opening up: The healing power of expressing emotions*, Rev. ed. Guilford.
7. Petrie, K.J., Booth, R.J., & Davison, K.P. (1995). *Repression, disclosure, and immune function: Recent findings and methodological issues.* In J.W. Pennebaker (Ed.), *Emotion, disclosure, & health* (pp. 223–237). American Psychological Association.
8. Kwon, P. (2013). Resilience in lesbian, gay, and bisexual individuals. *Personality and Social Psychology Review, 17*, 371–383. doi:10.1177/1088868313490248
9. Cohen, S. (2004). Social relationships and health. *American Psychologist, 59*, 676–684. doi:10.1037/0003-066X.59.8.676
10. Hobaica, S., & Kwon, P. (2017). "This is how you hetero": Sexual minorities in heteronormative sexuality education. *American Journal of Sexuality Education, 12*(4), 423–450. doi:10.1080/15546128.2017.1399491
11. Hobaica, S., Schofield, K.A., Kwon, P. (2019). "Here's your anatomy. . . Good luck": Transgender individuals in cisnormative sexuality education. *American Journal of Sexuality Education, 14*(3), 358–387. doi:10.1080/15546128.2019.1585308

12. Keiser, G.H., Kwon, P., & Hobaica, S. (2019). Sexuality education inclusivity and sexual minority health: The perceived inclusivity of sexuality education scale. *American Journal of Sexuality Education, 14*(3), 388–415. doi:10.1080/15546128.2019.1600448
13. Blake, S.M., Ledsky, R., Lehman, T., Goodenow, C., Sawyer, R., & Hack, T. (2001). Preventing sexual risk behaviors among gay, lesbian, and bisexual adolescents: The benefits of gay-sensitive HIV instruction in schools. *American Journal of Public Health, 91*(6), 940. doi:10.2105/ajph.91.6.940
14. Szalacha, L.A. (2003). Safer sexual diversity climates: Lessons learned from an evaluation of Massachusetts safe schools program for gay and lesbian students. *American Journal of Education, 110*(1), 58–88. doi:10.1086/377673
15. Corliss, H.L., Goodenow, C.S., Nichols, L., & Austin, S. (2011). High burden of homelessness among sexual-minority adolescents: findings from a representative Massachusetts high school sample. *American Journal of Public Health, 101*(9), 1683–1689. doi:10.2105/AJPH.2011.300155
16. Hobaica, S., Kwon, P., Reiter, S.R., Aguilar-Bonnette, A., Scott, W.D., Wessel, A., & Strand, P.S. (2021). Bullying in schools and LGBTQ+ youth mental health: Relations with voting for Trump. *Analyses of Social Issues and Public Policy, 21*(1), 960–979.
17. SIECUS (2020). *The SIECUS state profiles 2019/2020.* https://siecus.org/state-profiles-2019-2020/
18. Goldfarb, E.S., & Lieberman, L.D. (2020). Three decades of research: The case for comprehensive sex education. *Journal of Adolescent Health, 68*, 13–27. doi:10.1016/j.jadohealth.2020.07.036
19. SIECUS (2021). *Washington State profile.* https://siecus.org/state_profile/washington-state-profile/
20. SIECUS (2018). *Community action toolkit.* https://siecus.org/wp-content/uploads/2018/09/CAT-Sept-2018-Final.pdf

15

SEXUAL CONSENT IS MORE THAN A SIMPLE YES OR NO

Ways to Promote Positive Sexual Consent Attitudes and Behaviors

Kaylee P. Richmond, Mark A. Levand, and Zoë D. Peterson

Sexual consent, which can be defined as freely given verbal and/or nonverbal agreement without pressure or coercion to engage in sexual activity with an equally consenting partner or partners,[1–3] has been increasingly targeted in sexual assault prevention programming.[4] Because the absence of consent is a defining component of sexual assault,[5,6] it is assumed that training individuals to ask for consent clearly and to directly communicate their consent or non-consent might help reduce rates of sexual assault.

Beyond sexual violence prevention programming, though, sexual consent is increasingly recognized as a critical component of broader comprehensive sex education and as a useful tool in helping students understand the landscape of their sexuality and autonomy.[7,8] Currently, eight states and the District of Colombia require that school-based sex education include discussions of sexual consent, and seven of these nine requirements were passed in just the last five years.[9] Additionally, educational material from major sexuality organizations, including Advocates for Youth, The Center for Sex Education, Planned Parenthood, and SIECUS: Sex Ed for Social Change all include consent education, upholding it as a standard component in sex education curricula. For example, a lesson in the *Unequal Partners* curriculum discusses enthusiastic consent, stressing that consent should involve explicit affirmative agreement in the absence of pressure or manipulation.[10] An increased focus on sexual consent within general sex education likely grows out of heightened public attention to sexual assault, promoted, in part, by the #MeToo movement in 2017, in which women around the world used social media to share their experiences of sexual assault and harassment.[9]

This chapter aims to discuss why consent should be incorporated into comprehensive sex education and to address ways sex educators can better promote positive attitudes and behaviors about sexual consent. First, we summarize a recent research

DOI: 10.4324/9781003189787-16

paper from the *American Journal of Sexuality Education* that establishes a link between individuals' sexual knowledge and sexual consent. We discuss *why* sexual consent education incorporated into comprehensive sex education might be more effective than stand-alone consent education programs. Then, we discuss *how* sex educators can promote sexual consent attitudes and behaviors within comprehensive sex education.

Why Promote Positive Consent Attitudes and Behaviors in Sex Education?

Several authors have theorized that comprehensive sex education might be critical in promoting sexual consent even if that education is not explicitly focused on sexual assault prevention.[11,12] A recent article in the *American Journal of Sexuality Education* by two of the authors of this chapter, Kaylee P. Richmond and Zöe D. Peterson,[13] examined how general sexual knowledge was related to participants' (1) *attitudes toward* seeking consent, (2) *intentions to* seek consent, and (3) use of direct verbal communications of consent. This study included 315 participants recruited online and through college courses. Participants were over the age of 18 and grew up in the United States.

Objective sexual knowledge was measured through 20 multiple choice and true/false questions. The questionnaire included questions about birth control, sexual anatomy and physiology, and sexually transmitted infections (STIs). Importantly, no questions were explicitly related to sexual communication or giving/obtaining sexual consent. For example, one question was, "Also called the birth canal, what is the muscular passageway from the cervix to the outside of the female's body?" Participants were asked to select the correct answer from the following options: a) Vagina, b) Uterus, c) Vulva, or d) Fallopian tube.

In general, participants performed poorly on the sexual knowledge questionnaire—with an average score of only 62% correct, equivalent to a grade of a D if this were a test in a human sexuality course. Despite these low scores, sexual knowledge was still significantly related to sexual consent attitudes and behaviors. In other words, general sexual knowledge—related to birth control, sexual anatomy and physiology, and STIs—that did not include knowledge of sexual communication or giving/obtaining sexual consent was significantly related to sexual consent attitudes and behaviors. Specifically, results showed that higher scores on the objective sexual knowledge questionnaire were associated with using more direct verbal communication cues to obtain and give sexual consent in sexual encounters. Additionally, findings also demonstrated that, for men, higher scores on the objective sexual knowledge questionnaire were significantly associated with more positive attitudes toward establishing consent (i.e., viewing clear consent as important for any sexual act). This relationship was not significant for women in the sample; however, women's positive attitudes toward establishing consent were relatively high regardless of their levels of sexual knowledge. Participants' level of sexual knowledge was not associated with *intentions* to seek consent.

Richmond and Peterson's findings suggest that sexual knowledge may be influential in promoting positive sexual consent attitudes and behaviors even if that knowledge does not relate specifically to sexual consent or sexual assault. This research supports the theory that increasing sexual knowledge through general comprehensive sex education may improve sexual consent attitudes and skills, even if sexual assault and sexual consent are not the primary exclusive foci of that sex education.

There may be a variety of reasons that high-quality general sex education could increase consent communication. It may allow students to better understand their sexual wants and desires so that they are better positioned to communicate them to partners. It may increase students' comfort in talking about sex, making it easier to share their own and ask about their partners' sexual desires and values. It may undermine gendered stereotypes about sexual interactions (e.g., men always want sex and should initiate; women sometimes say "no" when they mean "yes"), which may contribute to the idea that explicit discussions of sexual consent are unnecessary.

The idea that promoting general sexual knowledge might also promote better consent communication offers some promising directions for intervention. Sexual consent education and sexual assault prevention programming may result in defensiveness among those at most risk for perpetrating sexual assault, thus reducing its effectiveness. Comprehensive sex education that is not *exclusively* focused on sexual assault prevention might be a more palatable way to promote the value and importance of consent. Consistent with this idea, in focus groups with college students, one study found that the students believed that traditional campus sexual assault prevention programming was ineffective and felt resentful about being mandated to complete it.[14] The participants also expressed a desire for more comprehensive information about sexual health. As one participant said, "I think [sexual assault prevention] programs spend so much time telling people what sex shouldn't look like that I think it would help if we discussed what sex should look like."

To be clear, the findings of Richmond and Peterson's study are correlational, not causal. We cannot definitively say, for example, that teaching students about sexual anatomy and physiology will result in better consent communication. Still, we do believe that, at the very least, the findings suggest that incorporating consent education into broader comprehensive education may be more effective than teaching it within a stand-alone sexual consent or sexual assault education program. Given that, for the rest of the chapter, we turn the focus to how consent education might best be incorporated into comprehensive sex education.

How to Promote Positive Consent Attitudes and Behaviors in Sex Education

Given that general sexual knowledge is related to positive sexual consent attitudes[13] and positive sexual consent attitudes are related to adopting consent behaviors,[15] it seems likely that incorporating specific teachings about sexual consent into sex education may foster even more positive consent attitudes and behaviors. As such, sex educators need to include discussions about sexual consent in their sex ed lessons and interventions. To better promote positive sexual consent attitudes and behaviors, we suggest that educators (1) move beyond an SAP framework, (2) promote intrapersonal reflection on sexual interests and values, and (3) frame consent as only one piece of sexual communication.

Sexual Assault Prevention (SAP) Framework

Much of consent education comes from an SAP framework, meaning that the reason we discuss sexual consent has philosophical roots in rape prevention education.[16] Approaching consent as SAP has its merits: raising awareness of sexual assault frequency, drawing attention to the sexual entitlement that may contribute to rape, and supplying communication skills about sexual activity. However, this frame and its interventions often are based on gendered assumptions of sexual aggression,[17] differ from the culture of sexual communication that widely exists,[6] and simplify consent in ways that may not foster an understanding of one's wants in a multi-layered context.[12]

An SAP framework, for example, often makes gendered assumptions about who is attempting to initiate sex (stereotypically men) and who is allowing or refusing sex (i.e., a "gatekeeper" role; stereotypically women). When educators teach about consent as SAP, interventions are often targeted in a gendered way, assuming that men are the initiators who must obtain consent and women are the gatekeepers who must communicate consent or non-consent. This may have unintended consequences such as placing men on the defensive, causing them to dismiss or ignore the content of the SAP.[18] Teaching in an SAP framework where gender stereotypes are often upheld and reinforced is problematic as research has identified that people who uphold gender stereotypes are more likely to accept rape myths. Rape myths are common and often inaccurate beliefs about rape, such as women who wear revealing clothes are asking for sex and men are sexually aggressive by nature, which allows individuals to inappropriately excuse sexual assault because of how their understandings of gender operate around consent. Consequently, teaching within an SAP framework may be unintentionally, but dangerously, promoting sexual assault-supportive attitudes and behaviors through perpetuating rape myths. One study indicated that when gender stereotypes are upheld in the roles of initiator versus gatekeeper, it may increase the endorsement of rape myths.[17] Gendered stereotypes about initiator and gatekeeper roles also promote heteronormativity, implying that sexual consent is only relevant in mixed-gender relationships.

Additionally, when consent education is framed as SAP, consent is often presented as easy, simple, and dichotomous ("yes" or "no"; permission or no permission). This approach is attractive in the context of SAP because it eliminates the possibility of miscommunication being used as an excuse for rape. In reality, consent is far more complex,[6] and individuals may encounter ambivalence when assessing their desires and ambiguity when interpreting their partners' desires. Enforcing an oversimplified dichotomous view of consent prevents educators from discussing the experience of ambivalence in desire and ambiguity in communication. At the same time, focusing on complexity alone can allow rapists to argue that communication was unclear as an excuse for an assault.[19]

To prevent this error of focusing on complexity alone, we address consent education as a piece of a system. In addition, researchers and scholars are beginning to note some of the issues with a dichotomous "yes/no" model of consent education. The "critical sexuality studies" model suggests that nuance is needed when examining issues of sexuality, which offers a lens through which we can challenge this dichotomy.[20] When we educate about consent, we are not educating in a void of identities and power differentials—our learners have identities and social powers and oppressions that will always be the lens through which they view the content. Affirmative consent policies may be unrealistic when considering sexual norms and alcohol consumption;[21,22] inadvertently culturally illiterate;[23] or insinuate a false dichotomy that once people have consent education, rape will be prevented.[19] These issues may act as barriers to affirmative consent practices and reduce the efficacy of educational sexual consent interventions.

Furthermore, an SAP frame that emphasizes the simplicity of consent comes from a "danger" paradigm (i.e., communicate clearly or you might be raped or accused of rape), as opposed to a sex-positive "pleasure" paradigm.[19] There are ways to reframe consent education more positively, rather than as a transactional imperative to prevent sexual assault.[19] Being mindful of the SAP frame and how it may impact the educational content and milieu (i.e., what students are expecting to hear when they show up) can help shift the conversation from danger to pleasure, possibly increasing the efficacy of educational interventions. For instance, students may enter a sex education class expecting broader discussions of sexual interactions; however, they may enter SAP expecting to be told how to avoid being raped or raping others. This is another argument for incorporating consent education into general "sex education" rather than including it only in SAP. Consequently, discussions of consent within sex education may feel more palatable and less threatening than a discussion of consent within SAP.

A final problem with the SAP framework is that consent scholars[4] point out that focusing on consent education in SAP has the potential to communicate that "rape would stop if everyone just communicated clearly," which is untrue. By moving consent education from SAP to general sex education, we can focus on the value of consent, not only for reducing sexual assault risk but also for promoting better sex.

Personal Interests and Values

Related to a more sex-positive frame in consent education, a model of sexual consent as transcendence stresses the importance of examining the intrapersonal experience of consenting—the internal, personal experience of assessing one's interests and values around sexual behaviors and communicating that with others.[24] Consent education often focuses on the verbal and nonverbal communication that can be seen or heard over the types of communication that occurs within oneself (i.e., self-reflection, self-talk) during sexual decision-making. Offering learners an understanding of how to weigh personal interests and values with sociocultural expectations allows them to examine consent more holistically, recognizing that some sexual decisions can be difficult and that they have the right to navigate their feelings differently in different contexts.

It is important to teach people how to understand their values and communicate with others about living out these values in sexual interactions. It is also critical for initiators to ensure they have obtained consent. Examining one's sexual interests and values is a shift toward sex-positive consent education by helping to name and normalize the experience of navigating the possible pros and cons of sexual interaction with a given person in a given context.

Interventions that address these intrapersonal interests and values can include:

- Providing a safe space for learners to develop, explore, and articulate their values about sexuality;
- Having discussions about how family, media, peers, and spirituality/religion shape and influence values about sexual consent and sexuality;
- Offering a space to reconsider those messages and how they align with personal values (e.g., critically evaluating messages about having sex with people you don't want to have sex with, non-heterosexual sex, pre-marital sex, and slut-shaming); and
- Discussing barriers that get in the way of living sexual life that aligns with one's values.

If these values and beliefs remain unexamined, it may be hard for learners to understand what they truly want from their own sexual decisions. Examining where values come from, what influences them, and if there are suppressed feelings around wants or desires can encourage learners to change, grow, and better articulate what they want and need to lead sexually healthy lives that best align with their values.

Consent as Part of Sexual Communication

Consent education is also broader than assessing whether one wants something and then telling someone. Consent is only one part—hopefully, an ongoing part—of sexual communication. Reflecting on interests and values, paired with communicating agreement or non-agreement to a potential partner, are critical pieces of sexual communication. Still, as sex educators, we should also help learners understand sexual communication more broadly—that consent is one type of sexual communication. Situating consent among other components of sexual communication such as communicating about adaptations to socially scripted behaviors, new sexual behaviors to try, pregnancy planning/prevention, sexual histories, and STIs helps learners frame consent as a necessary component of a healthy and intentional sex life. When consent is framed in this way, educators bring the focus from consent as a way to avoid sexual assault to consent as part of sexual wellness—a more positive framing that is likely to produce greater buy-in from learners.

Communication is a key component of any healthy relationship. General sexual communication skills are likely essential and necessary in helping individuals successfully give and obtain sexual consent. For example, it may be difficult for someone to give or ask for consent to specific sexual acts if they lack the terminology—or are too uncomfortable to use the terminology—to describe those acts.[12] Educators need to ensure learners are adequately equipped with the skills necessary to successfully communicate with their partners about their sexual concerns and desires. We recommend that educators normalize learners' emotions associated with sexual communication—noting that the anticipation of communicating sexual concerns and desires might bring about negative emotions (e.g., anxiety/worry). Interventions that address sexual communication might explore difficult sexual topics, such as discussions about sexual history and desires to engage in new sexual activities, to aid learners in navigating these conversations with their partners. In addition, educators should help learners understand barriers to sexual communication, such as fear of rejection, not wanting to hurt their partners' feelings, and lack of or problematic education about sexual communication. For example, an individual might have learned that it was "bad" or inappropriate to talk about anything related to sex. Talking with a partner about this underlying assumption of communication can help clear the air, making way for clearer communication.

Educators should provide learners with practical skills to improve their sexual communication, such as practicing communication with their partners about non-sexual topics, discussing sexual topics during non-sexual encounters, using "I" statements, and reflecting on their barriers to sexual communication. For instance, a learner that worries about rejection (a communication barrier) might hold the erroneous belief that sexual refusal means their partner does not love them anymore. It would be crucial for educators to help learners challenge these erroneous assumptions and beliefs.

Thus, goals for educators are to help learners recognize their own sexual beliefs, interests, and values. Additionally, educators should supply learners with tools to reflect on how their sexual beliefs were formed—this provides them with the autonomy to critically evaluate and potentially change some of their sexual beliefs/interests if they desire. Lastly, educators should equip learners with the skills necessary to successfully communicate with their partners about these sexual beliefs, interests, and values.

Of course, even if education on consent incorporates these three components as we are recommending, there are often complicating factors in sexual interactions—broader power dynamics at play in any sexual interaction such as past experiences of abuse, sexual scripts, and social norms, aspects of each interaction that cause individuals to weigh components differently in one situation than they would in another similar interaction.[20] For example, cultural prohibitions against sexual pleasure may be a barrier to healthy sexual communication. It is critical to name these dynamics in our education. Focusing on these aspects in consent education can offer an opportunity for educators to address and normalize these many factors during the learning process.

Making Consent Relatable: Embracing Complexity

Providing education related to sexual consent's complexity may aid in normalizing consent as complex, ambiguous, and requiring ongoing communication.[6] Educators need to incorporate contextual factors into consent discussions, helping individuals understand that communication varies in all contexts, including sexual consent communication. Educators should encourage individuals to be more attuned to the context and how context can impact sexual interactions. It is also important for educators to teach individuals how sexual consent interactions are embedded in the broader social, cultural, and historical context. For example, educators might note that how sexual consent is communicated and interpreted—and the extent to which it is freely given—may change based on any number of contextual factors: alcohol or drug use, the reasons for wanting or not wanting sex (e.g., to gain money, safety, shelter, social status, etc., to maintain a relationship; to please a partner), the social setting (e.g., bar, home, party), the type of sexual act, and the type or length of the relationship.[6] In addition, a partner's understanding of giving or obtaining consent may differ from one's own based on cultural differences,[23] gender role beliefs, or sexual scripts.[25] All of these factors illustrate why careful communication is so vital.

Teaching that sexual consent is a simple yes/no dichotomy ignores the complexity of intrapersonal values and beliefs, the experience of ambivalences, and the ambiguity that can occur in sexual communication.[6] If these things are left unaddressed, consent education can feel incomplete or unrealistic. However, heeding the warning that a hyper-focus on the complexity of consent can be used to excuse sexual assault and the critical sexuality studies noted earlier, we encourage educators to include the complexity as *part* of consent education.[19,20] Addressing *some* aspects of sexual consent as simple (e.g., expressing non-consent can be a simple "no"; if you aren't entirely sure of your partner's consent, simply stop) can help learners feel empowered and can avoid the use of miscommunication as an excuse for sexual assault. At the same time, acknowledging the complexities of other aspects of consent (e.g., How can you be sure consent is legitimate if alcohol or drugs are involved? What do you say if you aren't sure whether you agree? What nonverbal signals count as consent?) can normalize the feelings of ambivalence and experiences of ambiguity learners may have felt in past sexual experiences.

Conclusion

Although consent education has often been delivered as part of SAP programming, the findings of Richmond and Peterson illustrate that greater sexual knowledge is associated with more positive attitudes toward sexual consent and increased use of explicit verbal communication around consent. This highlights the values of incorporating consent education into broader sexual education curricula rather than delivering it only as a stand-alone program or as part of SAP. General sexual knowledge may provide a solid foundation to better support educational efforts surrounding sexual consent.

Taken together, sex educators must separate consent education from the context of an SAP framework. Instead, educators should promote consent communication not only as a form of SAP but also as a pathway to more pleasurable and enjoyable sex. Separating consent education from SAP may bypass many of the challenges of the SAP framework, including that SAP can promote defensiveness and may be dismissed as personally irrelevant (even individuals that perpetrate sexual aggression do not generally think of themselves as "rapists"[26]). Additionally, separating consent education from SAP may allow educators to address barriers to sexual consent communication that are generally ignored by the SAP framework (e.g., discomfort talking about sex, a lack of sexual terminology, and lack of self-awareness regarding one's sexual values and desires). Further, incorporating consent education into broader sex education allows for a more nuanced discussion of the complexities of consent. Although it is convenient from an SAP framework to teach that consent is easy and simple, a growing body of literature suggests that this message is inconsistent with people's own experiences.[6]

As sexual consent is increasingly incorporated into comprehensive sex education curricula, more research is needed on its effectiveness. Some scholars and SAP educators have argued that teaching about sexual consent will not necessarily reduce rates of sexual assault because most rapes are due to a perpetrator who actively ignores non-consent rather than a true miscommunication about consent.[4] More thorough evaluation of the impact of consent education on sexual assault victimization and perpetration is needed to evaluate this presumption. Beyond that, though, if consent education is part of general sex education rather than only a part of SAP, other outcomes might be relevant for determining the effectiveness of consent education. For example, does consent education lead to less sexual compliance (i.e., sex that is consensual but unwanted)?[27] Does consent education lead to more pleasurable sex because partners expand their discussion of what they do and don't like sexually? Does consent education lead to better general communication and thus create stronger relationships? Incorporating sexual consent education into broader sex education will allow educators and researchers to consider how sexual consent communication might be important and beneficial beyond the prevention of sexual assault.

Identifying the above components for sex-positive consent education places sex educators in the unique position of fostering positive cultural changes about sexual consent. We encourage education about sexual consent based on principles relevant to learners that can empower them to explore their understanding of sexuality and autonomy in their lives.

References

1. Beres, M. (2007). 'Spontaneous' sexual consent: An analysis of sexual consent literature. *Feminism & Psychology, 17*(1), 93–108. https://doi.org/10.1177/0959353507072914
2. Beres, M. (2010). Sexual miscommunication? Untangling assumptions about sexual communication between casual sex partners. *Culture, Health & Sexuality, 12*(1), 1–14. https://doi.org/10.1080/13691050903075226
3. Hickman, S.E., & Muehlenhard, C.L. (1999). By the semi-mystical appearance of a condom: How young women and men communicate sexual consent in heterosexual situations. *Journal of Sex Research, 36*(3), 258–272.
4. Beres, M. (2020). Perspectives of rape-prevention educators on the role of consent in sexual violence prevention. *Sex Education: Sexuality, Society and Learning, 20*(2), 227–238.
5. Beres, M. (2014). Rethinking the concept of consent for anti-sexual violence activism and education. *Feminism & Psychology, 24*(3), 373–389. https://doi.org/10.1177/0959353514539652
6. Muehlenhard, C.L., Humphreys, T.P., Jozkowski, K.N., & Peterson, Z.D. (2016). The complexities of sexual consent among college students: A conceptual and empirical review. *Journal of Sex Research, 53*(4/5), 457–487. https://doi.org/10.1080/00224499.2016.1146651
7. Degiuli, F., & Nowotny, J. (2020). The administration of consent: An exploration of how consent education is understood and implemented at a small private university. *Sexuality & Culture, 24*(3), 863–882. https://doi.org/10.1007/s12119-019-09669-5
8. MacDougall, A., Craig, S., Goldsmith, K., & Byers, E.S. (2020). #consent: University students' perceptions of their sexual consent education. *The Canadian Journal of Human Sexuality, 29*(2), 154–166. https://doi.org/10.3138/cjhs.2020-0007
9. Naide, S. (2020). State lawmakers say yes to consent education. *Guttmacher Institute*. www.guttmacher.org/article/2020/01/state-lawmakers-say-yes-consent-education
10. deFur, K. (2016). Selections from Unequal partners: Teaching about power, consent, and healthy relationships. *American Journal of Sexuality Education, 11*(2), 149–159. https://doi.org/10.1080/15546128.2016.1174025
11. Carmody, M. (2005). Ethical erotics: Reconceptualizing anti-rape education. *Sexualities, 8*(4), 465–480. https://doi.org/10.1177/1363460705056621
12. Peterson, Z.D. (2018). Teen and young adult sexual desire and the importance of yes. In C.B. Travis & J.W. White (Eds.), *APA handbook on the psychology of women* (vol. 1, pp. 273–295). American Psychological Association.
13. Richmond, K.P., & Peterson, Z.D. (2019). Perceived sex education and its association with consent attitudes, intentions, and communication. *American Journal of Sexuality Education*, 1–24. https://doi.org/10.1080/15546128.2019.1669512
14. Hubach, R.D., Story, C.R., Currin, J.M., Woods, A., Jayne, A., & Jayne, C. (2019). "What should sex look like?" Students' desires for expanding university sexual assault prevention programs to include comprehensive sex education. *Qualitative Health Research, 29*(13), 1967–1977. https://doi.org/10.1177/1049732319844502
15. Shumlich, E.J., & Fisher, W.A. (2019). An information-motivation-behavioural skills model analysis of young adults' sexual behaviour patterns and regulatory requirements

for sexual consent in Canada. *Canadian Journal of Human Sexuality, 28*(3), 277–291. https://doi.org/10.3138/cjhs.2018-0040
16. Levand, M.A. (2020a). *Is consent what we're talking about? The sexual assault history of consent education*. Global Sex Research Virtual Conference.
17. Willis, M., & Jozkowski, K.N. (2018). Barriers to the success of affirmative consent initiatives: An application of the social ecological model. *American Journal of Sexuality Education, 13*(3), 324–336. https://doi.org/10.1080/15546128.2018.1443300
18. Rich, M.D., Utley, E.A., Janke, K., & Moldoveanu, M. (2010). "I'd rather be doing something else": Male resistance to rape prevention programs. *The Journal of Men's Studies, 18*(3), 268–288. https://doi.org/10.3149/jms.1803.268
19. Harris, K.L. (2018). Yes means yes and no means no, but both these mantras need to go: Communication myths in consent education and anti-rape activism. *Journal of Applied Communication Research, 46*(2), 155–178. https://doi.org/10.1080/00909882.2018.1435900
20. Fahs, B., & McClelland, S.I. (2016). When sex and power collide: An argument for critical sexuality studies. *Journal of Sex Research, 53*(4–5), 392–416. https://doi.org/10.1080/00224499.2016.1152454
21. Curtis, J.N., & Burnett, S. (2017). Affirmative consent: What do college student leaders think about "yes means yes" as the standard for sexual behavior? *American Journal of Sexuality Education, 12*(3), 201–214. https://doi.org/10.1080/15546128.2017.1328322
22. Klein, L.B., Rizzo, A.J., Cherry, L.H., & Woofter, R.C. (2018). *Addressing alcohol's role in campus sexual assault: A toolkit by and for prevention specialists*. www.unh.edu/research/sites/default/files/media/2019/09/saalctoolkit.pdf
23. Levand, M.A. (2020b). Consent as cross-cultural communication: Navigating consent in a multicultural world. *Sexuality & Culture, 24*(3), 835–847. https://doi.org/10.1007/s12119-019-09667-7
24. Levand, M.A., & Zapien, N. (2019). Sexual consent as transcendence: A phenomenological understanding. *International Journal of Transpersonal Studies, 38*(1), 154–165. https://doi.org/10.24972/ijts.2019.38.1.154
25. Jozkowski, K.N., & Peterson, Z.D. (2013). College students and sexual consent: Unique insights. *Journal of Sex Research, 50*(6), 517–523. https://doi.org/10.1080/00224499.2012.700739
26. Strang, E., & Peterson, Z.D. (2017). Unintentional misreporting on self-report measures of sexually aggressive behavior: An interview study. *The Journal of Sex Research, 54*(8), 971–983. https://doi.org/10.1080/00224499.2017.1304519
27. Impett, E., & Peplau, L. (2003). Sexual compliance: Gender, motivational, and relationship perspectives. *Journal of Sex Research, 40*, 87–100. https://doi.org/10.1080/00224490309552169

16

SEXUALITY AND SAFER SEX COMMUNICATION

What Is Left Out of Sexuality Education in the United States?

Katherine L. Grasso and Lauren A. Trumbull

In the United States, about eight out of ten teenagers are exposed to sexuality education in which they learn about sexually transmitted infections (STIs), HIV/AIDS, and how to say no to sex.[1] However, just over half of US teenagers learn about birth control methods.[1] Students' sexuality education largely depends on their school location and type of sexuality education program. Depending on state law and differences across districts, schools, and instructors, students may not receive medically accurate and evidence-based information about sexual health. The shortcomings of sexuality education may help explain the sexual health problems affecting the United States, especially young people. Additionally, although safer sex communication (SSC) is related to safer sex,[2] it is rarely taught in sexuality education. Finally, many students report that their sexuality education programs ignore or condemn the LGBTQ+ community, leaving students who engage in same-sex encounters vulnerable.

Sexuality Education in the United States

Sexuality education in the United States is not providing young adults with consistent information on safer sex practices and communicating with a partner about consent, contraceptive use, sexual history, and preferences. Further, the mandates for and implementation of sexuality education across the United States are inconsistent, even at the state and local levels. As of April 10, 2022, 39 states and the District of Columbia mandate some form of sexuality education. Among states that provide sexuality education, 39 stress abstinence, 20 discuss contraception, 19 highlight the importance of sex only within marriage, nine states mandate culturally appropriate, non-biased instruction, and only 18 mandate that information be medically accurate.[3]

DOI: 10.4324/9781003189787-17

Misinformation is commonly presented about abortion (e.g., abortion causes fertility problems), abstinence (e.g., having sex at a young age will result in pregnancy), contraception (e.g., intrauterine devices are dangerous for adolescents), and sexual orientation (e.g., same-sex relationships lead to poor mental health).[4] Additionally, what is deemed "medically accurate" is state-dependent.[5] For example, Arizona stresses abstinence and medically accurate HIV education to clarify transmission myths, whereas California mandates medically accurate sex and HIV education.[3] Thus, one might assume any school-based educational program will be evidence-based, but students' sexuality education varies depending on location.

Abstinence-Only Sexuality Programming

Abstinence, which is the notion of abstaining from sexual activity (typically oral, anal, and vaginal), is the focus of abstinence-only (AO) or abstinence-only-until-marriage (AOUM) sexuality programming. As of August 2020, the US government outlines the goals of AO programs and cites that abstinence is the only way to avoid STIs, HIV, and unintended pregnancy.[6] Programs are eligible for US funding if they teach the following elements:

- the social, psychological, and health benefits from abstaining from sex;
- having sexual relations outside of marriage is not socially desirable;
- abstinence as the only way to avoid pregnancy outside of marriage and STIs;
- a faithful, monogamous relationship in marriage is expected;
- having an affair will result in harmful psychological and physical effects;
- teen pregnancy harms society, the baby, and the baby's parents;
- drugs and alcohol can increase sexual vulnerability; "just say no" to sexual advances;
- the importance of being self-sufficient before engaging in sex.[6]

In addition, these programs are barred from promoting or providing instruction regarding the use of birth control.[7] Although federally regulated, AO programs are highly variable, and students across the country are likely to receive vastly different information.

Comprehensive Sexuality Education

As the title suggests, comprehensive sexuality education (CSE) is more comprehensive and inclusive than AO. According to the Future of Sex Education (FOSE),[8] an organization that seeks to adopt CSE in public schools, the goal of CSE is to "build a foundation of knowledge and skills relating to human development, relationships, decision-making, abstinence, contraception, and disease prevention."[9] Thus, in addition to discussing the importance of contraception, CSE may discuss abuse and victim-blaming and teach refusal skills, boundaries, and that drugs and alcohol can impair sexual decision-making.[3,9,10] Similarly, The American College of

Obstetricians and Gynecologists (ACOG) recommends CSE be medically accurate, highlight the benefits of delaying sexual initiation, provide information on reproductive development, and discuss the importance of contraception in avoiding STIs and unintended pregnancy.[11] The ACOG recommendation indicates that this education should come in addition to covering consent, decision-making, gender identity, healthy relationships, intimate partner violence (IPV), and sexuality.[11] However, CSE is not regulated and, much like AO programs, is implemented differently across states and counties. For example, only 24 states discuss refusal skills and developing boundaries, and only nine discuss consent.[3]

No law outlines effective CSE, but FOSE developed *National Sexuality Education Standards (NSES)*, an evidence-informed, age-appropriate, theory-driven set of guidelines to address the inconsistent implementation of sexuality education in the United States.[9] Elements of this program include anatomy and physiology, consent and healthy relationships, gender identity, pregnancy, reproduction, personal safety, puberty and adolescent development, sexuality, and STIs/HIV.[9] As of 2016, 41% of school districts adopted *NSES*.[12]

Communication Barriers

Although both AO and CSE strive to teach students how to avoid unwanted sexual advances, it is unclear whether sexuality education teaches students how to discuss pregnancy, STIs/HIV, and contraceptive use with a sexual partner.[7,13] Additionally, such content is not outlined by the government or FOSE.[7,13] This is despite evidence that frequent and open communication about sexual health issues (e.g., STIs/HIV) with a partner can promote feeling informed about and confident in preventing sexual risks[14] and can promote safer sexual-decision-making, such as delaying sexual initiation and using condoms consistently after becoming sexually active.[2,15]

SSC offers clear health benefits to sexual partners, but conversations are often complicated. These complications may arise due to discomfort or not wanting to "ruin the mood."[16,17] Partners may not want to undermine their trust in each other[18] or may not feel that they are at risk for STIs/HIV or unintended pregnancy.[19] Or, someone may want to talk about safer sex practices but not know how.[20]

SSC often refers to talking about preventing STIs/HIV and unwanted pregnancy,[20,21] but it can also include partners' discussions of previous STI/HIV testing and sexual encounters/partners.[17] While these practices are important components of safer sex, sexuality education should offer more communication skills training. SSC should also consider the emotional, mental, and social components of sexual health. Sexual encounters should be mutually respectful and satisfying, which can be enhanced by communication. In fact, individuals' sexual assertiveness (i.e., ability to express sexual preferences and needs) improved sexual satisfaction.[22] Further, a positive relationship exists between disclosure of one's sexual preferences and sexual satisfaction.[23,24]

Despite the value of SSC, sexuality education programs do not consistently emphasize communication skills. In focus groups, both adolescents and their parents thought sexuality education lacked instruction on healthy relationships, including communication, honesty, trust, and respect.[25] Further, in a review of AO programs, researchers observed that skill-building included communication with only friends and parents.[26] AO programming likely excludes communication skills with a sexual partner because students are expected to remain abstinent. Certain CSE programs incorporate communication skills. For example, CSE laws in California and Oregon require that programming be medically accurate, develop negotiation tactics, decision-making skills, personal communication, and emphasize safety and consent.[27]

Additionally, in the most recent version of the *NSES*, FOSE outlines students' "ability to use interpersonal communication skills to enhance health and avoid or reduce health risks" as a key standard.[9] These SSC skills range based on age but include setting and respecting physical boundaries, demonstrating refusal skills, and expressing the decision to abstain from sexual behaviors. They also teach students to communicate about contraception and STI/HIV prevention and testing, foster healthy relationships, and decide when to engage in sexual behaviors.[9] However, recall that as of 2016, only 41% of school districts implemented *NSES*.[12] Further, CSE programming that does not follow *NSES* guidelines can be inconsistent or abstract. In a review of research on CSE, researchers observed four components of CSE programming: (a) rights, participation, and agency; (b) sexual and reproductive health-related concerns; (c) gender equality and power; and (d) positive sexualities and respectful relationships, but the importance of communication was never mentioned.[13]

In light of the fact that neither AO nor CSE emphasize SSC skills, the authors of this chapter conducted a study aiming to understand the rates of SSC among young and emerging adults who received either AO or CSE. We found that despite the lack of SSC training in sexuality education, about seven out of ten young and emerging adults (aged 18–28) reported engaging in SSC on a variety of topics (e.g., consent, sexual preferences), regardless of sexuality education.[28] Even the lesser common topics (e.g., previous sexual partners, sexual history, and what to do in case of pregnancy) were discussed by nearly six out of 10 respondents.[28] However, respondents only indicated whether the topics were discussed on a yes/no scale, so the extent or effectiveness of the conversations were not measured.[28] Additionally, up to ten years had passed since some respondents' sexuality education. Their sexual knowledge and experience were likely informed by other factors after middle or high school (e.g., family, higher education, media, peers).

As expected, conversations occurred less frequently among casual relationships and more often among committed relationships.[28] This raises concerns for young people who are not in committed relationships or engage in the "hookup culture." While engaging with a casual or one-time partner, individuals may be less comfortable communicating, which would inhibit discussions related to consent, desire, boundaries, etc. Although very few sexuality education programs focus on teaching SSC, many emerging adults report talking about sexually relevant issues with their partners. Thus, more research is needed to better understand the extent to which SSC takes place, how it impacts young people in casual and committed encounters, and how it may improve sexual health.

Effectiveness of Sexuality Education

Numerous studies comparing AO and CSE highlight the inconsistencies of both program types in helping teenagers abstain from sexual activity; however, there is a dearth of recent research. A six-year-long project published in 2007 measured the impact of sexuality education on students by evaluating 48 comprehensive programs and eight AO programs.[29] None of the AO programs effectively delayed sexual initiation, reduced the number of sexual partners, or improved contraceptive use.[29] The comprehensive programs were not without their flaws. Of the 48 CSE programs, 60% reduced unprotected sex and 40% delayed sexual initiation, and reduced the number of sexual partners.[29]

Although CSE programming is implemented inconsistently across state lines, it is more effective than AO in helping young adults delay first intercourse and avoid HIV/STIs and unintended pregnancy.[29,30-32] This is evident among males and females, a variety of ethnic groups, and for sexually experienced and inexperienced teens.[29] In addition, a systematic review evaluated whether CSE or AO programs effectively reduced sexual risk behaviors and activity and prevented STIs/HIV and pregnancy. Researchers found that CSE led to a reduction in sexual activity, number of sex partners, unprotected sex, and prevalence of STIs.[33] CSE also led to an increase in the use of condoms.[33] There was no reduction in sexual activity among those who received AO programming.[33] However, a meta-analysis of 14 studies examining the relationship between students' sexual attitudes and behaviors and AO programs found that AO was successful in reducing premarital sexual behaviors.[34]

CSE has had more consistent success considering outcomes beyond sexual debut, number of sexual partners, teen pregnancy, and STIs/HIV. A meta-analysis of 80 studies examining the effectiveness of CSE found that "CSE can lower homophobia and homophobic-related bullying, can increase understanding of gender and gender norms, can improve knowledge and skills that support healthy relationships, can build child sex abuse prevention skills, and can reduce IPV."[35]

Altogether, the literature is inconsistent regarding whether AO or CSE is more effective in teaching young adults to delay their first sexual encounter, but research suggests CSE is beneficial in combating STIs/HIV and making impactful changes related to safety, relationships, gender, and sexuality.

Barriers for LGBTQ Youth

The shortcomings of sexuality education are heightened for LGBTQ+ students whose issues continue to be disparaged[36] or overlooked.[37] AO programs exclude experiences of LGBTQ+ youth, which means that LGBTQ+ students are not learning how to have safer sex.[38] AO programs also reinforce heteronormativity, suggesting that relationships between a man and a woman are the expected societal standard.[38] As of September 2021, there are eight states with "No Promotion of Homosexuality" laws (i.e., NPH or "No Promo Homo").[39] These laws prohibit the promotion of homosexuality in health and sexuality education topics in public schools.[39,40] For example, Alabama state law says that educators must emphasize that homosexuality is not publicly acceptable and is punishable under Alabama law. Oklahoma mandates that HIV education teach that homosexuality is one of the reasons for coming into contact with AIDS.[3] The number of states enforcing NPH laws has slowly been decreasing. North Carolina and Utah repealed these laws in recent years.[3] Arizona repealed its law and then introduced a new bill.[3,41] Data indicate that 10 states and the District of Columbia (California, Colorado, Connecticut, Delaware, Iowa, Maryland, New Jersey, New Mexico, Oregon, Rhode Island, and Washington) require that sexuality education be inclusive of sexual orientation. Five states (Alabama, Florida, Illinois, South Carolina, and Texas) require that sexuality education portray sexual orientation negatively.[3]

Researchers conducted a thematic analysis of in-depth interviews with young gay, bisexual, and/or questioning men (YGBQM) aged 18–24 about their experiences with sexuality education in the United States.[42] They found that YGBQM felt left out of the curriculum and were unprepared to practice safe sex or advocate for their sexual needs and desires.[42] Due to a lack of classroom information, YGBQM turned to the Internet for questions about sex and sexual health, with most participants using WebMD for guidance.[42] More recently, the 2019 National School Climate Survey examined the sexuality education experiences of a sample of 16,713 students aged 13–21, 41% of whom identified as gay or lesbian.[43] The researchers found that of the students who received sexuality education, only 23% reported discussing LGBTQ+ topics.[43] Among those, only 28% reported discussing lesbian, gay, and bisexual topics, and only 19% of students received sexuality education on transgender and nonbinary topics.[43] Of the students who received lesbian, gay, and bisexual sexuality education, only 19% of the content was framed positively. Of the students who received transgender and nonbinary sexuality education, only 12% were positive.[43] Without relevant sexual education, many LGBTQ+ individuals experience their first sexual intercourse without knowledge of safer sex practices.[42] The current state of sexuality education relies on a limited conceptualization of sexual health, ignores entire populations, and overlooks communication as a crucial tool for safer sex and healthy relationships.

Sexual Health in the United States

As of 2019, rates of STIs reached a record high for the sixth consecutive year, and LGBTQ+ populations experience even higher rates of infection.[44,45] Early 2020 data suggests this trend continues; however, the COVID-19 pandemic interrupted STI testing and services in most of the country.[44] Additionally, although down

4% from 2018, the United States had 16.7 births for every 1,000 females aged 15–19 in 2019.[46] In states that stress AO programming, such as Kentucky, the pregnancy rate was 25 per 1,000 girls aged 15–19 in 2019.[47] In fact, the top five states (Arkansas, Mississippi,[48] Louisiana, Oklahoma, and Alabama) with the highest teen pregnancy rates (25.6–30 per 1,000 girls aged 15–19) require that sexuality education, if taught at all, emphasize AO.[3,47] In comparison, the five states (Connecticut, Maine, Massachusetts, New Hampshire, and Vermont) with the lowest rates of teen pregnancy (6.6–9.1 per 1,000 girls aged 15–19) cover abstinence rather than stress AO, except for Massachusetts, which does not specify whether AO is stressed or covered, and Maine, which stresses medically accurate AO programming.[3,47]

Young and emerging adults' sexual health is of particular concern as they engage in risky sexual behavior at high rates. In the United States, the median age at which people begin having penetrative sex or intercourse ranges between 16 and 17 years old.[49–52] Early initiation of sex is associated with a greater number of sexual partners,[53] increased risk of teen pregnancies, births, and abortion,[53] and increased risk for STIs.[54,55] In the United States, 15- to 24-year-olds comprise half of all newly transmitted STIs each year but only a quarter of the sexually active population.[56] Further, one-fourth of sexually active adolescent females have an STI.[56] In 2019, women aged 15–24 made up 3,728 per 100,000 reported chlamydia cases, and men aged 15–24 made up 1,449 per 100,000.[57] Among women aged 15–24, the rate for gonorrhea was 650 per 100,000, and in men aged 15–24, the rate was 540 per 100,000.[57] The United States experiences the highest rates of STIs and unintended pregnancies among developed nations,[58] which indicates a lack of knowledge and skills related to safer sex among young people.

The disproportionate effects of STIs are not limited to young people; they extend to the LGBTQ+ community. Sexually active gay, bisexual, and other men who have sex with men (MSM) have higher rates of syphilis than any other group. Between 2018 and 2019, almost half (47%) of primary and secondary syphilis cases in the United States were among MSM and bisexual men.[45] Despite a 33% decrease in HIV diagnoses among gay and bisexual men aged 13–24 from 2015 to 2019, sexually active gay, bisexual, and other MSM are disproportionately impacted by HIV.[45,59] In 2019, MSM made up 692,900 cases of HIV, 55% of whom were aged 13–24.[60]

Conclusion

The shortcomings within the current system of sexuality education are concerning. While the effectiveness of sexuality education is often measured by students' delay of sex, contraceptive use, and rates of STIs/HIV and pregnancy, neither AO nor CSE has shown consistent success on all fronts. Further, communication between sexual partners is not often promoted in sexuality education, although it plays a role in facilitating safer sex. In terms of sexual orientation, AO often ignores the needs of LGBTQ+ individuals, largely erasing or denigrating their experiences and leaving students uninformed about how to engage in safer sex. CSE has had more success in reducing homophobia and increasing understanding of gender-related issues, but shortcomings in addressing safer sexual behavior among LGBTQ+ individuals remain. Future research should broaden the notion of safer sex to include gender and sexuality-inclusive conversations around young people's willingness to talk with their sexual partners, their efficacy and comfort in doing so, and its potential to improve the safety and satisfaction in their sexual encounter(s). Additionally, considering the high rates of SSC among emerging adults and the lack of emphasis on communication training in sexuality education, researchers should explore how and through what sources individuals develop SSC skills.

References

1. Lindberg, L.D., Maddow-Zimet, I., & Boonstra, H. (2016). Changes in adolescents' receipt of sex education, 2006–2013. *Journal of Adolescent Health, 58*(6), 621–627. https://doi.org/10.1016/j.jadohealth.2016.02.004
2. Gause, N.K., Brown, J.L., Welge, J., & Northern, N. (2018). Meta-analyses of HIV prevention interventions targeting improved partner communication: Effects on partner communication and condom use frequency outcomes. *Journal of Behavioral Medicine, 41*(4), 423–440. https://doi.org/10.1007/s10865-018-9916-9
3. See Guttmacher Institute (2021, June 4). Sex and HIV education. *Guttmacher Institute*. www.guttmacher.org/state-policy/explore/sex-and-hiv-education#. For more information regarding state-by-state sexuality education mandates and curricula. Although this source is an advocacy organization, it provides credible data that are updated more regularly than academic publications.
4. California Healthy Youth Act Sexual Health Education Toolkit (n.d.). *Medical accuracy in comprehensive sexual health education*. ACLU Northern California.
5. National Conference of State Legislators [NCSL] (2020, October 1). *State policies on sex education in schools*. www.ncsl.org/research/health/state-policies-on-sex-education-in-schools.aspx
6. U.S. Department of Health (n.d.). *Impacts of four Title V, section 510 abstinence education programs. Title V, section 510 funding*. https://aspe.hhs.gov/report/impacts-four-title-v-section-510-abstinence-education-programs/title-v-section-510-funding
7. Planned Parenthood (2012). *Sex education in the United States*. www.plannedparenthood.org/files/3713/9611/7930/Sex_Ed_in_the_US.pdf
8. FOSE is a collective of three organizations: Advocates for Youth, Answer, and SIECUS—Sex Ed for Social Change.
9. Future of Sex Education Initiative [FOSE]. (2020). *National sexuality education standards: Core content and skills, K-12*, 2nd ed. www.advocatesforyouth.org/resources/health-information/future-of-sex-education-national-sexuality-education-standards/
10. Advocates for Youth (2019). *Understanding boundaries—A lesson plan from rights, respect, responsibility: A K-12 curriculum*. https://3rs.org/3rs-curriculum/3rs-curric-search/?_sft_grade=sixth-grade&_sft_topic=relationships
11. The American College of Obstetricians and Gynecologists (ACOG). (2020, November). *Comprehensive sexuality education*. www.acog.org/clinical/clinical-guidance/committee-opinion/articles/2016/11/comprehensive-sexuality-education
12. Centers for Disease Control and Prevention (CDC). (2016). *Results from the school health policies and practices study*. Division of Adolescent and School Health, National Center for HIV/AIDS, Viral Hepatitis, STD, and TB Prevention.

13. Miedema, E., Le Mat, M.L., & Hague, F. (2020). But is it comprehensive? Unpacking the 'comprehensive' in comprehensive sexuality education. *Health Education Journal,* 1–16, https://doi.org/1177/0017896920915960
14. Keene, L., & Boyd, D. (2021). Ending the epidemic: Assessing sexual health communication, personal agency, and HIV stigma among Black and Latino youth in the U.S. *International Journal of Environmental Research and Public Health, 18*(12), 6319. https://doi.org/10.3390/Ijerph18126319
15. Noar, S.M., Carlyle, K., & Cole, C. (2006). Why communication is crucial: Meta-analysis of the relationship between safer sexual communication and condom use. *Journal of Health Communication, 11*(4), 365–390. https://doi.org/10.1080/10810730600671862
16. Doull, M., Wolowic, J., Saewyc, E., Rosario, M., Prescott, T., & Ybarra, M.L. (2018). Why girls choose not to use barriers to prevent sexually transmitted infection during female-to-female sex. *The Journal of Adolescent Health, 62*(4), 411–416. https://doi.org/10.1016/j.jadohealth.2017.10.005
17. Horan, S.M. (2016). Further understanding sexual communication: Honesty, deception, safety, and risk. *Journal of Social and Personal Relationships, 33*(4), 449–468. https://doi.org/10.1177/0265407515578821
18. Troth, A., & Peterson, C.C. (2000). Factors predicting safe-sex talk and condom use in early sexual relationships, *Health Communication, 12*(2), 195–218. https://doi/org/10.1207/S15327027HC1202_5
19. Hickey, M.T., & Cleland, C. (2013). Sexually transmitted infection risk perception among female college students. *Journal of the American Association of Nurse Practitioners, 25*(7), 377–384. https://doi.org/10.1111/j.1745-7599.2012.00791.x
20. Cleary, J., Barhman, R., MacCormack, T., & Herold, E. (2002). Discussing sexual health with a partner: A qualitative study with young women. *Canadian Journal of Human Sexuality, 11.*
21. Donné, L., Hoeks, J., & Jansen, C. (2017). Using a narrative to spark safer sex communication. *Health Education Journal, 76*(6), 635–647. https://doi.org/10.1177/0017896917710967
22. Ménard, A.D., & Offman, A. (2009). The interrelationships between sexual self-esteem, sexual assertiveness and sexual satisfaction. *The Canadian Journal of Human Sexuality, 18*(1–2), 35.
23. Brown, R.D., & Weigel, D.J. (2018). Exploring a contextual model of sexual self-disclosure and sexual satisfaction. *The Journal of Sex Research, 55*(2), 202–213. https://doi.org/10.1080/00224499.2017.1295299
24. Coffelt, T.A., & Hess, J.A. (2014). Sexual disclosures: Connections to relational satisfaction and closeness. *Journal of Sex & Marital Therapy, 40*(6), 577–591. https://doi/org/10.1080/0092623X.2013.811449
25. Marshall, S.A., Hudson, H.K., & Stigar, L.V. (2020). Perceptions of a school-based sexuality education curriculum: Findings from focus groups with parents and teens in a southern state. *Health Educator, 52*(1), 37–51.
26. Wilson, K.L., Goodson, P., Pruitt, B.E., Buhi, E., & Davis-Gunnels, E. (2005). A review of 21 curricula for abstinence-only-until-marriage programs. *Journal of School Health, 75*(3), 90–98. https://doi.org/10.1111/j.1746-1561.2005.tb06648.x
27. SIECUS: Sex Ed for Social Change (2021). *The SIECUS State Profiles.* SIECUS.
28. Grasso, K.L., & Trumbull, L.A. (2021). "Hey, have you been tested?" The influence of comprehensive or abstinence-only sexuality education on safer sex communication and behavior. *American Journal of Sexuality Education, 16*(2), 257–281.
29. Kirby, D. (2007). *Emerging answers 2007: Research findings on programs to reduce teen pregnancy and sexually transmitted diseases.* National Campaign to Prevent Teen and Unplanned Pregnancy.
30. Fonner, V.A., Armstrong, K.S., Kennedy, C.E., O'Reilly, K.R., & Sweat, M.D. (2014). School based sex education and HIV prevention in low-and middle-income

countries: A systematic review and meta-analysis. *PLoS One, 9*(3), e89692. https://doi.org/10.1371/journal.pone.0089692
31. UNESCO. (2009). *International technical guidance on sexuality education: An evidence-informed approach for schools, teachers and health educators.* UNESCO
32. UNESCO. (2015). *Emerging evidence, lessons and practice in comprehensive sexuality education: A global review.* UNESCO.
33. Chin, H.B., Sipe, T.A., Elder, R., Mercer, S.L., Chattopadhyay, S.K., Jacob, V., Wethington, H.R., Kirby, D., Elliston, D.B., Griffith, M., Chuke, S.O., Briss, S.C., Ericksen, I., Galbraith, J.S., Herbst, J.H., Johnson, R.L., Kraft, J.M., Noar, S.M., Romero, L.M., & Sanrelli, J. (2012). The effectiveness of group-based comprehensive risk-reduction and abstinence education interventions to prevent or reduce the risk of adolescent pregnancy, human immunodeficiency virus, and sexually transmitted infections. *American Journal of Preventive Medicine, 42*(3), 272–294, https://doi.org/10.1016/j.amepre.2011.11.006
34. Jeynes, W.H. (2020). A meta-analysis on the relationship between student abstinence-only programs and sexual behavior and attitudes. *Education and Urban Society, 52*(1), 3–20. https://doi.org/10.1177/0013124519848045
35. Goldfarb, E.S., & Lieberman, L.D. (2020). Three decades of research: The case for comprehensive sex education. *Journal of Adolescent Health, 68,* 13–27. https://doi.org/10.1016/j.jadohealth.2020.07.036
36. Gay, Lesbian, & Straight Education Network (GLSEN). (2019). *"No promo homo" laws.* www.glsen.org/activity/no-promo-homo-laws
37. Gowen, L.K., & Winges-Yanez, N. (2014). Lesbian, gay, bisexual, transgender, queer, and questioning youths' perspectives of inclusive school-based sexuality education. *The Journal of Sex Research, 51*(7), 788–800. https://doi.org/10.1080/00224499.2013.806648
38. Elia, J.P., & Eliason, M.J. (2010) Dangerous omissions: Abstinence-only-until-marriage school-based sexuality education and the betrayal of LGBTQ youth, *American Journal of Sexuality Education, 5*(1), 17–35.
39. SEICUS: Sex Ed State Law and Policy Chart (2021). *SIECUS State Profiles: Aug. 2021.* SIECUS
40. Wille, L., & Parent, M.C. (2019). Association of no promotion of homosexuality laws and electronic cigarette use disparities for sexual minority youth. *JAMA Pediatrics, 173*(10), 991–993. 10.1001/jamapediatrics.2019.2729
41. Jones, D., & Franklin, J. (2022, April 10). Not just Florida. More than a dozen states propose so-called 'Don't Say Gay' bills. *NPR.* www.npr.org/2022/04/10/1091543359/15-states-dont-say-gay-anti-transgender-bills
42. Pingel, E.S., Thomas, L., Harmell, C., & Bauermeister, J.A. (2013). Creating comprehensive, youth centered, culturally appropriate sex education: What do young gay, bisexual, and questioning men want? *Sexuality Research & Social Policy* 10, 293–301. https://doi.org/10.1007/s13178-013-0134-5.
43. Kosciw, J.G., Clark, C.M., Truong, N.L., & Zongrone, A.D. (2020). *The 2019 national school climate survey: The experiences of lesbian, gay, bisexual, transgender, and queer youth in our nation's schools.* GLSEN.
44. Centers for Disease Control and Prevention (CDC). (2021). *Reported STDs reach all-time high for 6th consecutive year.* www.cdc.gov/media/releases/2021/p0413-stds.html
45. Centers for Disease Control and Prevention (CDC). (2021). *Syphilis & MSM (men who have sex with men)—CDC fact sheet.* www.cdc.gov/std/syphilis/stdfact-msm-syphilis.htm
46. Martin, J.A., Hamilton, B.E., Osterman, M.J.K., & Driscoll, A.K. (2021). Births: Final data for 2019. *National Vital Statistics Reports, 70*(2). https://dx.doi.org/10.15620/cdc:100472.
47. Centers for Disease Control and Prevention (CDC). (2021). *Stats of the state—Teen birth rates.* www.cdc.gov/nchs/pressroom/sosmap/teen-births/teenbirths.htm

48. With permission from the state Department of Education, some localities in Mississippi may incorporate contraception and STIs into their sexuality education; however, abstinence is still stressed (Guttmacher Institute, 2021).
49. Brouwer, A.F., Delinger, R.L., Eisenberg, M.C., Campredon, L.P., Walline, H.M., Carey, T.E., & Meza, R. (2019). HPV vaccination has not increased sexual activity or accelerated sexual debut in a college-aged cohort of men and women. *BMC Public Health, 19*(1), 821. https://link.springer.com/article/10.1186/s12889-019-7134-1
50. Centers for Disease Control and Prevention (CDC). (2017). *Key statistics from the national survey of family growth—S listing.* www.cdc.gov/nchs/nsfg/key_statistics/s.htm#sexualactivity
51. Fisher, M.L., Worth, K., Garcia, J.R., & Meredith, T. (2012). Feelings of regret following uncommitted sexual encounters in Canadian university students. *Culture, Health & Sexuality, 14*(1), 45–57. https://doi.org/10.1080/13691058.2011.619579
52. Vasilenko, S.A., Kugler, K.C., & Rice, C.E. (2016). Timing of first sexual intercourse and young adult health outcomes. *Journal of Adolescent Health, 59*(3), 291–297. https://doi.org/10.1016/j.jadohealth.2016.04.019
53. Heywood, W., Patrick, K., Smith, A.M., & Pitts, M.K. (2015). Associations between early first sexual intercourse and later sexual and reproductive outcomes: A systematic review of population-based data. *Archives of Sexual Behavior, 44*(3), 531–569. https://doi.org/10.1007/s10508-014-0374-3
54. Lowry, R., Dunville, R., Robin, L., & Kann, L. (2017). Early sexual debut and associated risk behaviors among sexual minority youth. *American Journal of Preventive Medicine, 52*(3), 379–384. https://doi.org/10.1016/j.amepre.2016.10.008
55. Upchurch, D.M., Mason, W.M., Kusunoki, Y., & Kriechbaum, M.J. (2004). Social and behavioral determinants of self-reported STD among adolescents. *Perspectives on Sexual and Reproductive Health, 36*(6), 276–287. https://doi.org/10.1363/3627604
56. Centers for Disease Control and Prevention (CDC). (2019). *STDs in adolescents and young adults.* www.cdc.gov/std/stats18/adolescents.htm
57. Centers for Disease Control and Prevention (CDC). (2021). *Figures—Sexually transmitted disease surveillance, 2019.* www.cdc.gov/std/statistics/2019/figures.htm
58. Walsh-Childers, K. (2016). *Mass media and health: examining media impact on individuals and the health environment.* Routledge.
59. Centers for Disease Control and Prevention (2020). *HIV and gay and bisexual men.* www.cdc.gov/hiv/group/msm/index.html
60. Centers for Disease Control and Prevention (CDC). (2021). Estimated HIV incidence and prevalence in the United States, 2015–2019. *HIV Surveillance Supplemental Report, 26*(1). www.cdc.gov/hiv/library/reports/hiv-surveillance.html.

17

THE POTENTIAL OF SOCIAL MARKETING CAMPAIGNS IN THE PREVENTION OF SEXUALLY TRANSMITTED INFECTIONS

Matej Sande

Introduction

Sexually transmitted infections (STIs) are still a relatively major public health issue in Europe and the United States (USA),[1–3] and understanding the attitudes of young adults toward STIs is important in terms of planning appropriate prevention as it is an important part of sexuality education. There were an estimated 68 million STIs in the USA in 2018, reaching an all-time high in reported cases for chlamydia, gonorrhea, and syphilis in 2019.[4] Almost half of the infections in 2018 were among young adults aged between 15 and 24 years. This means that we need to make a special effort to target young adults in our prevention programming, which requires tailored prevention messages. These messages must be delivered in a meaningful way through channels that young adults are close to or use. Data for the general population in Slovenia show that almost one in two 17-year-olds has had sexual intercourse, and 67% used a condom in their last sexual encounter.[5] Data from a survey of high school seniors on graduation trips showed that just under half of the respondents always would use a condom.[6] Findings from the large-scale Health Behavior in School Children (HBSC) survey for Europe and North America are of concern. A quarter of sexually active 15-year-olds did not use a contraceptive pill or condom during their last sexual intercourse.[5] Results from cross-sectional surveys of young people in Europe also show low levels of awareness and knowledge about STIs,[7] alongside high levels of awareness and knowledge about HIV and AIDS, which may be linked to the many awareness campaigns on the topic since the mid-1980s. In European Union and European Economic Area countries, around 30,000 people are infected with HIV each year,[2] and in the USA, the overall prevalence of sexually transmitted HIV infections in 2018 was 984,000,[3] so raising awareness about the risks associated with transmission and condom use remains highly relevant.

DOI: 10.4324/9781003189787-18

The research mentioned so far has looked at the problem of STIs in the general population, but specific environments such as nightlife can escalate the risk for transmissions. Nightlife can increase the risk of transmission, as unprotected sex is more likely when alcohol and other drugs are used. If we think of the more traditional nightlife as going to bars, clubs, and large events with electronic music, there has recently been more and more mention of chemsex parties when talking about STI prevention. Chemsex parties are attended mainly by men who have sexual relationships with men, and the focus is on sex under the influence of stimulants and other drugs and on changing sexual partners. Such parties pose a high risk of STI transmission due to the higher number of unprotected sexual contacts. As such parties are generally not public and are advertised in closed circles, prevention or harm reduction work in such settings is hampered. Thus, in addition to improving harm reduction in drug and alcohol use, it is essential to provide information on the risks and modes of transmission of STIs in nightlife. We need to provide information in relevant ways to young adults in traditional nightlife settings and those attending chemsex parties.

Since 1999, the DrogArt Association has been working to reduce drug and alcohol-related harm in nightlife and explore the various aspects of nightlife in Slovenia. Most of our prevention campaigns and nightlife activities have been based on research and studying the needs of drug and alcohol users. We have thus successfully developed a comprehensive model of field campaigns in nightlife, with outreach work, personal counseling and psychotherapy, and a day center for young people who use drugs. As sex is closely connected to nightlife, alongside music and drugs, we started planning our first social marketing campaign on STI prevention in 2017 and participated in a campaign on chemsex.

Social marketing is based on behavioral sciences and commercial marketing techniques to plan and implement social change.[8] Such campaigns have been effective in health promotion, STI prevention, and people adopting less risky sexual behaviors.[9] A well-designed social marketing campaign aims to change the target group's behavior, whether in terms of less risky drug use, safe driving, or less risky sexual relations using condoms. The key is to provide accurate and relevant information, dispersed through suitable channels and including the involvement of the target groups as much as possible. Such campaigns, if well planned, reach young adults repeatedly, not just once, e.g., via information on a website, a leaflet, or a billboard. A one-off piece of information or an advertisement can hardly be expected to change the target group's behavior. For a successful campaign, we have to reach the target group in the field, e.g., in traffic, if the campaign is about speed reduction or child safety in cars. Change will be more easily achieved if the target group is more involved; in this case, if their kindergarten or school involves them in workshops on the importance of wearing a seat belt in kindergarten or school.

Examples of successful Slovenia campaigns include the Slovenian Traffic Safety Agency program, which runs the Pasavček project to encourage children to fasten their seat belts while riding a car. Aimed at children between four and 12 years of age, the key message of the campaign, "Always wear your seat belt," is conveyed to children and their parents. The campaign reaches children and parents at different levels, the cornerstone of effective and well-planned social marketing. The message is conveyed through roadside advertisements, workshops in kindergarten and primary schools, and encouraging children to use their seat belts with a prize—a plush toy. The campaign has had a very good response, with an average of more than 94% of children wearing a seatbelt while riding in a car, compared to 2005 when the campaign was launched. Another high-profile campaign is the "40 Days without Alcohol" campaign, which aims to express solidarity with all those who suffer from the consequences of alcohol use and is organized annually by the Slovenian Karitas, the Slovenian Traffic Safety Agency, and the Med.over.net Institute. In Slovenia, the legal age to buy and drink alcohol is 18, so is the age limit to enter most nightclubs and other nightlife venues.

As part of the "I drive 0.0" campaign to reduce alcohol-related harm in traffic, DrogArt's "Choose by yourself" program has worked with police officers to measure alcohol in traffic, run workshops on alcohol and safe routes back from parties in secondary schools, developed an app to assess alcohol consumption and signpost young adults to taxis, and offered a scheme to provide free taxi rides for young adults at night with After Taxi[10] vouchers. All this had the clear aim of reducing the risks of alcohol-related nightlife. This allowed us to potentially contact young adults more than once: in workshops in secondary schools, with an online app, through a website, and by providing them a safer way home from parties with After Taxi vouchers. Some interpreted the campaign as a promotion for drinking alcohol to allow young adults to drink more than they would otherwise since they would be going home in a taxi. In 2012, we carried out an evaluation that found that 88% of young adults preferred to use After Taxi vouchers instead of drinking and driving. As many as 61% said they would take a taxi home more often after receiving an After Taxi voucher. This was a good result for us, as it let young adults communicate to us that they have accepted the message of the project and, therefore, the responsibility of not getting behind the wheel under the influence of alcohol and that they continue to use taxis as a less risky way of getting home even after the campaign. This indicates a change in behavior and the effectiveness of the social marketing campaign.

From 2017 to 2019,[11] we implemented the Chemsex project, the central part of which was a large-scale campaign targeting the population of men who have sex with men (MSM) and who use drugs at so-called chemsex parties. The risks of STI transmission at such parties required an innovative approach to risk reduction in a population that is difficult to reach. The project was based on a previously conducted survey and achieved good results with outreach and engagement for the target group. The central part of the campaign is a website that provides information on modes of transmission and harm reduction and the promotion of testing services. The website has been designed so that both the terms and the format are as close as possible to the target group. However, as stated previously, online information alone is not enough for campaigns of this kind, so the project focused on outreach work in bars, clubs, and saunas where MSM socialize, as well as on counseling and support. The campaign also achieved continuous contact with MSM, and some of them actively joined the project and participated in activities such as handing out information materials and outreach work. Studies have shown that less risky sexual behaviors that are peer-approved are better accepted and more sustainable,[12] so the involvement of peers or target group members in this type of project is well-received.

We have also tested the effectiveness of individual campaign elements in the past. In addition to outreach work in nightlife settings, the Dance Smart campaign has been providing young adults with leaflets containing information on harm reduction since 2000. Our research confirmed that those who follow the instructions on prevention leaflets also use drugs in a less harmful way.[13] In addition, we also confirmed that the Internet had become an essential source for young adults to obtain information about drugs.

When we studied the use of alcohol and other drugs in the general population of secondary school students, we first addressed the sexual behavior of secondary school students through a set of questions to identify the self-reported risks.[6] The reported risks associated with alcohol use included, among others, the posting of embarrassing photos on social media, sexual encounters that they would not have had in a sober state, and unwanted sexual experiences. Almost half of the respondents had used alcohol before their last sexual encounter on their graduation trip, and just under a tenth had used illicit drugs. We, therefore, concluded that our future work will need to focus more on raising awareness about less risky sex and, in particular, the link between alcohol, drugs, and sex.

The main purpose of our latest Sex and Nightlife survey, the results of which will be presented below, was to explore the characteristics of risky sexual behavior in nightlife and young adults' knowledge and attitudes toward STIs and their need for additional information. We wanted to directly apply the survey results to the HIV in Nightlife project to plan the "HIV is not picky" campaign and tailor it as much as possible to the target group's needs.

This study was not interested in specific nightlife subgroups, such as MSM or chemsex parties, but in risky sexual behavior and knowledge of STIs in the "general" nightlife population. We were interested in how young adults perceive infections to be and to what extent they protect themselves against STIs. In terms of planning a social marketing awareness campaign, we were interested in the extent to which young adults were informed about STIs, what additional information they would need, and through which channel they would be willing to receive them.

The sample included 1,103 respondents with an average age of 24.6 years. In the sample, 58% of respondents were under 25 and 85% under 30 years of age. Regarding sexual orientation, 83% of the sample was heterosexual, 11% bisexual, and 6% homosexual. Most respondents were attending high school or college at the time of the survey. Given the purpose of the survey, we included respondents who go out relatively often in the sample, with just under half going out at least once every 14 days. The following sections will briefly present the main findings on psychoactive substance use, risky sexual behavior, and STI awareness.[14] The online survey results cannot be generalized and therefore only apply to the sample studied. Still, they can give insights into the characteristics of risky sexual behavior in nightlife and allow us to plan prevention measures.

The Use of Alcohol and Other Drugs in Nightlife

As the survey focused on STIs and sexual behavior characteristics, drug use was measured on a smaller scale to monitor trends and the association with risky sexual behaviors. We were interested in the prevalence of use in the last 12 months or at the last "party" and the frequency of drug use.

Alcohol use in the 12 months before the survey was reported by 98% of respondents. In addition to alcohol, the most popular drugs in nightlife in Slovenia are still marijuana, methylenedioxymethamphetamine (MDMA, or ecstasy), cocaine, and amphetamines, as found by earlier research,[15,16] and there is still notable use of gamma-hydroxybutyrate (GHB) and gamma-butyrolactone (GBL). Marijuana had been tried in the last 12 months by 63% of respondents, MDMA by 38%, and cocaine by 31%. Alcohol, marijuana, MDMA, and cocaine were also the most commonly used drugs at the last party or on the last occasion. Both alcohol and illicit drugs were used more frequently by men in the sample. During the previous 12 months, nightlife drug use was higher in Slovenia than in the United States.[17] However, the use of synthetic cathinones, of which metaphedrone (3-MMC) became popular in Slovenia in the past after mephedrone (4-MMC), has recently decreased. According to our research, synthetic cathinones were popular among young adults in Slovenia between 2010 and 2016 due to their relative accessibility, low price, and stimulant effects. They are still used today (e.g., at chemsex parties) but to a much lesser extent. Users reported several side effects such as anxiety, concentration problems, cravings, depression, and use of increasing amounts.

The reported drug use might seem high, but we have to bear in mind that this is not the general population of young adults. It reflects those who go out more often to bars, clubs, and discos. Drug use in our survey is thus significantly higher than drug use in the general population of young people in Slovenia, where, for example, 33% of 17-year-olds in the HBSC survey had used cannabis in the last year, and 5% of young people in the HBSC survey had used MDMA at any time in their lives.[5]

The data on drug use is not directly helpful in planning the STI awareness campaign. Still, it has helped us examine possible links between drug use and risky sexual behavior and monitor trends in drug use in nightlife in the organization's other programs.

Characteristics of (Risky) Sexual Behavior

On average, respondents had had three sexual partners in the last year, and the highest percentage had had unprotected sex with one or two partners in their lifetime. Almost half of the respondents met their sexual partners in clubs and pubs, and a quarter met them through social networks. The majority of respondents still met their sexual partners among friends and acquaintances. Men had unprotected relationships with more sexual partners than women. Just over a quarter of respondents had had sex in a club or bar, a third of whom had used a condom. Of those who had not used a condom, a quarter reported having had sex with a steady partner.

Young adults who used drugs had unprotected sex more often compared to non-users. People who use drugs were more likely to report having unprotected sex and sex with strangers. These findings can be linked to a similar study of nightlife where people who use alcohol and drugs were more likely to adopt sexual risk behaviors.[18] Also, in the aforementioned survey of final-year secondary school students,[6] almost a quarter of young adults reported having had sex as a result of alcohol use, which they would refrain from if sober, and a tenth of young adults had had an unwanted sexual experience as a result of alcohol use.

Just over half of respondents have had sex under the influence of illegal drugs and four-fifths under the influence of alcohol. A quarter of respondents said they were less likely to use a condom when under the influence of illicit drugs, and a third said the same for alcohol. These results are key for campaign planning to raise awareness about the increased risk of infection transmission due to the reduced likelihood of condom use during sex under the influence of alcohol and drugs.

Just over 40% of respondents had been verbally or non-verbally sexually harassed in their nightlife at a party or bar, and 17% had unwanted sexual intercourse. More than half of those who had experienced unwanted intercourse were under the influence of alcohol or drugs. Both harassment and unwanted sexual intercourse were more likely to happen to women. Among the general population in Slovenia, alcohol-related unwanted sexual intercourse was reported by one-tenth of secondary school final year pupils in three different surveys.[6,19] Nightlife is thus an environment where drug and alcohol use and other factors can increase the risk of sexual harassment and unwanted intercourse. In designing interventions that can be targeted specifically at women or all genders, we have to provide information about such risks and how they can be reduced.

Sexually Transmitted Infections, Information, and Prevention

Just under a third of respondents acknowledge the possibility of infections with most STIs. Of those who indicated that they consider infection likely, half think it is more likely in nightlife.

Given that two-thirds did not think infection was likely, the reasons for this are interesting. The main reasons are having a steady sexual partner, not having risky sex, trusting the partner, and using a condom. Relatively few respondents reported having been infected. Most of those infected had had genital warts, chlamydia, or genital herpes, but all percentages were below 5%.

From the point of view of planning an awareness-raising campaign, it is vital to know how much information the target group already has, what information it still needs, and how new information would be received. Respondents were most informed about HIV and hepatitis and least about other STIs, which may be related to the many awareness campaigns about HIV and hepatitis in Slovenia. Two-thirds of respondents knew where they could get tested for HIV and hepatitis, while less than one-fifth had been tested. STI testing was seen as accessible to about half of the sample. Given the relatively low knowledge of testing and the low percentage of those who have already been tested, it is worthwhile to include additional information on testing in the campaign. Half of the respondents think they would need more information on STIs, and almost a third of the respondents do not have sufficient information on testing. These pieces of data can provide a sound basis for campaign planning.

The campaign was designed to ask how we could make condoms free or as cheap as possible in clubs and bars, so data on condom use and condoms were key. Only a tenth of nightlife respondents carried a condom with them when they went out. Half would get a condom from a club or bar if available. Forty percent of respondents would not refuse to have sex without a condom, of whom a quarter would opt for less risky sexual practices. The main reasons for not using a condom in clubs were not liking condoms and having a steady partner. Others indicated that they did not think infections were likely or thought they would be too intoxicated to decide to use a condom at the party.

We also wanted to know what type of STI prevention in clubs or pubs would suit young adults planning the campaign. They would most prefer to have free or discounted condoms available from a condom dispenser, information on a website, information materials on STI testing options, information materials on STIs, and outreach workers in clubs.

The "HIV Is Not Picky" Social Marketing Campaign

Based on the results described earlier, we planned the "HIV is not picky" campaign, followed by outreach work in the nightlife. Before the research, only the "advertising" part of the campaign was carried out, with roadside posters and posters in bathrooms of clubs and bars. Forty percent of the respondents have already noticed the campaign, which indicates a very good reach. DrogArt launched the two-year "HIV is not picky" campaign on December 1, 2017, which is World AIDS Day. In 2020, we continued the campaign and expanded it to the broader area of STIs in nightlife, based on the survey findings, as we found that knowledge of other STIs is relatively low in the target group and nightlife is an environment with an increased risk of transmission. The campaign aims to remind everyone, especially young adults, about safe sex and encourage them to use condoms (correctly) every time they have sex to protect themselves from HIV and other STIs. The slogan of the "HIV is not picky" campaign conveys the message that the virus does not discriminate in terms of gender, race, sexual orientation, or social status.

The "HIV is not picky" campaign had a striking graphic design, which we used to appeal to the general public in an animated television spot and posters. We addressed specific nightlife audiences directly at various nightlife venues in bars, clubs, and discos. Posters in bathrooms and leaflets highlighted responsible behavior and condom use. An important part of this was the presence of a specialized outreach team, which ensured better contact with users and a more in-depth delivery of the message. The outreach team of trained youth workers was present at more than 500 nightlife events during the project's lifetime from 2017 to 2019. More than 15,000 condoms and 30,000 awareness-raising materials were distributed to young adults during the program. We conducted 10 additional training sessions for 89 youth workers who joined the outreach team after the initial training. The campaign message was visible on more than 300 small roadside posters and 400 posters in pubs and high-profile online posts on two high-reach media portals. We expect that the project activities will increase awareness of condom use, consolidate the message about less risky sexual behavior and increase the number of STI tests performed.

Based on the survey results, we found that free or reduced-price condoms in clubs would be a good way to prevent condom use, as many people do not carry condoms. After meetings with condom providers and clubs, we realized that implementing free condoms in clubs would be too much of a technical challenge, so we decided to distribute them through the outreach team. In the light of the survey results, which clearly show the need for such a project, we continued the campaign in 2020 with a specialized nightlife campaign. Due to the COVID-19 epidemic and the complete shutdown of nightlife, the project was partially suspended, and a relaunch is planned for 2022 when the easing of measures will enable limited outreach work in clubs and bars. Despite the initial difficulties, we plan to implement special boxes for free condoms in bars and clubs when they reopen.

Conclusion

Social marketing campaigns can bring about social change and alter the habits of the target group. So far, they have been effective in health promotion, such as motivating people to eat healthily, lose weight or avoid risky behaviors.[9]

In the field of HIV/AIDS, a meta-analysis of mass media interventions for condom use and HIV-related information showed that mass media interventions impacted people from lower socioeconomic areas most in need of HIV prevention. At the same time, there was less effectiveness in relatively developed countries. Condom campaigns that ran for longer periods had a better impact than those that ran for shorter periods. The longer the campaigns lasted, the more knowledge about prevention increased, which may argue in favor of more integrated social marketing approaches and longer-lasting campaigns.

The effectiveness of a nearly two-year-long social marketing campaign to control the spread of HIV has also been demonstrated in California among people who inject drugs.[20] Exposure to prevention messages through small posters and a newsletter reduced the prevalence of HIV-related injection risk behavior, and the campaign reached most of the 7,000 heroin users in Sacramento. The campaign also proved cost-effective, as the total cost was only a fraction of the cost required for a lifetime of treatment for one HIV infection.

Campaigns can also be effective in reaching more specific target groups. We started with a description of the Chemsex campaign, which, in terms of reach and engagement with the target group, delivered good results in a group that is more difficult to reach with a traditional mass media campaign. We distributed 3,000 Chemsex leaflets and 1,800 flyers, contacted more than 1,500 people from the target group, and carried out 64 interventions in clubs during the campaign. We recorded 214 calls to the Post-Exposure Prophylaxis SOS line on safer sex and more than 50 referrals to the infectious diseases clinic. A systematic review examining the effectiveness of social marketing campaigns and mass media interventions in specific target groups found increasing evidence that these are effective in increasing HIV testing among gay, bisexual and other men who have sex with men.[21]

The "HIV is not picky" social marketing campaign, which we have expanded on using the present study results, was not evaluated in more detail, so we cannot speak of its proven effectiveness in reducing STIs beyond measuring its reach. Based on our past research, we can discuss the effectiveness of parts of the social marketing campaigns implemented at DrogArt, such as less risky drug use among those who follow the harm reduction instructions on the information leaflets or a change in the behavior of young adults who continue to use taxis to get home safely from parties even after the campaign has ended. Based on the review of research and evaluations presented here and on our findings and experience, the potential and cost-effectiveness of strategically planned, longer-term social marketing campaigns in STI prevention are good. When planning a successful campaign, it is a good idea to consider appropriate communication channels, well-designed advertisements, and tailored messages and anticipate contact and communication with the target group in the field.

References

1. European Centre for Disease Prevention and Control (2015). *Sexually transmitted infections in Europe 2013*. ECDC.
2. European Centre for Disease Prevention and Control (2018). HIV and AIDS. In ECDC (Ed.), *Annual epidemiological report for 2016*. ECDC.

3. Kreisel, K.M., Spicknall, I.H., Gargano, J.W., Lewis, F.M., Lewis, R M., Markowitz, L.E., Roberts, H., Johnson, A.S., Song, R., St Cyr, S.B., Weston, E.J., Torrone, E.A., & Weinstock, H.S. (2021). Sexually transmitted infections among US women and men: Prevalence and incidence estimates, 2018. *Sexually Transmitted Diseases, 48*(4), 208–214.
4. Centers for Disease Control and Prevention. (2021). *Sexually Transmitted Disease Surveillance 2019.* U.S. Department of Health and Human Services.
5. Jeriček Klanšček, H., Roškar, M., Drev, A., Pucelj, V., Koprivnkar, H., Zupanič, T., & Korošec, A. (2019). Z zdravjem povezana vedenja v šolskem obdobju med mladostniki v Sloveniji. Izsledki mednarodne raziskave HBSC, 2018. Nacionalni inštitut za javno zdravje.
6. Sande, M. (2021) Alcohol-related risks for Slovene secondary school students on graduation trips: Ten years later. *Archives of Psychiatry Research, 57*(2), 125–138. https://doi.org/10.20471/dec.2021.57.02.01
7. Samkange-Zeeb, F.N., Spallek, L., & Zeeb, H. (2011). Awareness and knowledge of sexually transmitted diseases (STDs) among school-going adolescents in Europe: A systematic review of published literature. *BMC Public Health, 11*, 727. https://doi.org/10.1186/1471-2458-11-727
8. Kotler, P., & Zaltman, G. (1971). Social marketing: An approach to planned social change. *Journal of Marketing, 35*(3), 3–12.
9. Green, K.M., Crawford, B.A., Williamson, K.A., & DeWan, A.A. (2019). A meta-analysis of social marketing campaigns to improve global conservation outcomes. *Social Marketing Quarterly, 25*(1), 69–87.
10. After taxi was a transfer of good practice from Trieste, Italy, where Etnoblog implemented the Overnight Taxi project.
11. We implemented the project in a consortium of three organizations—DrogArt, Legebitra, and ŠKUC Association.
12. Melkote, S.R., Moore, D., & Velu, S. (2014). What makes an effective HIV/AIDS prevention communication campaign? Insights from theory and practice. *Journal of Creative Communications, 9*(1), 85–92. https://doi.org/10.1177/0973258613517441
13. Sande, M. (2007). Evalvacija preventivnega delovanja na področju sintetičnih drog v Sloveniji. In M. Sande (Ed.), Na spidu 2 - Stanje na področju sintetičnih drog in kokaina v Sloveniji. (pp. 95–99). Association DrogArt.
14. The results are presented in more detail in Sande, M. (2020). Sex and nightlife: Risky sexual behavior and young people's attitude toward STIs. *American Journal of Sexuality Education, 15*(3), 357–370.
15. Bellis, M.A., Hughes, K., Calafat, A., Juan, M., Ramon, A., Rodriguez, J.A., Mendes, F., Schnitzer, S., & Phillips-Howard, P. (2008). Sexual uses of alcohol and drugs and the associated health risks: A cross sectional study of young people in nine European cities. *BMC Public Health, 8*, 155. https://doi.org/10.1186/1471-2458-8-155
16. Sande, M., & Purkart, B. (2011). Cocaine use in nightlife in Slovenia and Italy. In M. Sande (Ed.), *Nightlife reconsidered* (pp. 73–85). The Etnoblog Intercultural Association. http://pefprints.pef.uni-lj.si/688/1/Nightlife_reconsidered.pdf
17. Palamar, J.J., Griffin-Tomas, M., & Ompad, D.C. (2015). Illicit drug use among rave attendees in a nationally representative sample of US high school seniors. *Drug and Alcohol Dependence, 152*, 24–31. https://doi.org/10.1016/j.drugalcdep.2015.05.002
18. Lomba, L., Apóstolo, J., & Mendes, F. (2009). Drugs and alcohol consumption and sexual behaviours in night recreational settings in Portugal. *Adicciones, 21*(4), 309–325. https://doi.org/10.20882/adicciones.222
19. Dekleva, B., & Sande, M. (2003). *Tri leta kasneje—uporaba drog ob koncu srednje šole.* Združenje DrogArt.

20. Gibson, D.R., Zhang, G., Cassady, D., Pappas, L., Mitchell, J., & Kegeles, S.M. (2010). Effectiveness of HIV prevention social marketing with injecting drug users. *American Journal of Public Health, 100*(10), 1828–1830.
21. McDaid, L., Riddell, J., Teal, G., Boydell, N., Coia, N., & Flowers, P. (2019). The effectiveness of social marketing interventions to improve HIV testing among gay, bisexual and other men who have sex with men: A systematic review. *AIDS and Behavior, 23*(9), 2273–2303.

18

SEXUAL HEALTH PROMOTION AMONG UNIVERSITY STUDENTS

A Psychological Perspective

Rusi Jaspal, Liam Wignall, and Claire Bloxsom

Introduction

Sexual health is defined as "a state of physical, emotional, mental and social well-being in relation to sexuality; it is not merely the absence of disease, dysfunction or infirmity."[1] University students are at increased risk of poor sexual health outcomes and are, thus, a key population in sexual health promotion. As a major life transition, going to university can bring about significant changes to one's sense of identity. Students may face many social and psychological stressors within the university context that can challenge their psychological well-being. These include academic pressure, feeling homesick, peer pressure, relationship issues, and others. Our previous research found that exposure to stressors can lead people to engage in behaviors that put them at risk of poor health outcomes.[2,3]

There is a relatively high prevalence of poor mental health among university students in England—a recent report showed that 37% of students surveyed in 2019 believed their mental health had deteriorated since starting higher education.[4] Sexual health is another dimension of health where younger adults, including university students, experience inequalities. At the end of 2017, 420,000 diagnoses of sexually transmitted infections were reported in England, 144,000 of which (34%) were among people aged 15–24.[5] Sexual risk behavior is relatively prevalent in this population, which can increase the incidence of sexually transmitted infections and unwanted pregnancy.[6]

In this chapter, we outline the Health Adversity Risk Model (HARM), and, through its lens, we review existing research into identity, psychological stress, and sexual attitudes, behaviors, and norms among university students. The implications of the HARM for sexuality and sexual health education in universities are considered and recommendations are made for enhancing sexual health outcomes

DOI: 10.4324/9781003189787-19

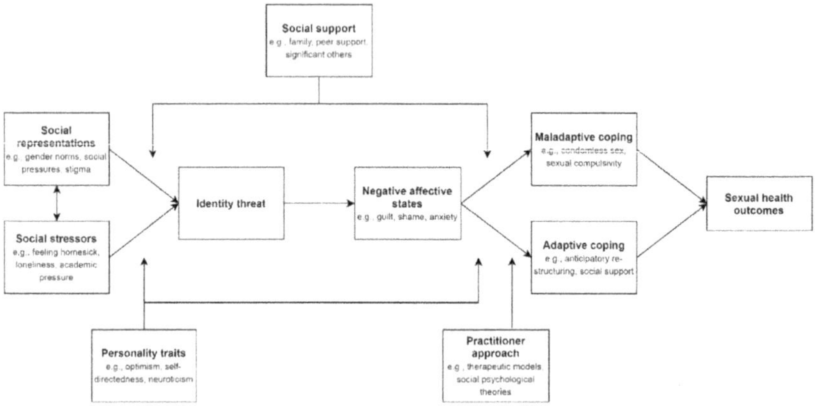

FIGURE 18.1 The health adversity risk model.

in this population. This chapter focuses on how tenets of social psychological research into sexual health promotion can benefit the practice of sexual health educators, in particular.

The HARM (Figure 18.1)[7] draws on Identity Process Theory[8] and the cognitive-behavioral model.[9] Identity Process Theory focuses on the motivational principles that guide the construction, maintenance, and protection of a positive sense of identity and predicts that people respond to "threats" to identity through the deployment of coping strategies. The cognitive-behavioral model focuses on the role of cognitive processes, such as thinking, belief formation, interpretation, and understanding, in human affect and behavior. Both models posit that emotional problems result from patterns of thought and behavior developed across the life span.

Stressors and Identity Threat

The basic premise of the HARM is that, in some contexts, such as university, individuals will be exposed to social representations (or social constructions of reality)[10] that can cause psychological stress. For instance, university students from ethnic or lower socioeconomic backgrounds may perceive a social representation that university is "not for people like me," which may lead them to question their sense of acceptance, belonging, and inclusion in this context.[11] Moreover, social representations also include social norms, that is, shared beliefs about appropriate behavior. These norms may feel coercive, and pressure to adhere to them may be psychologically stressful. For instance, in our previous research,[3] male students described a coercive social norm that young men should have multiple sexual partners, which led some less sexually active individuals to feel that they had not met dominant social expectations. In addition to negative social representations, social stressors, such as academic pressure, experiences of feeling homesick, and relationship issues, are prevalent in university contexts. Furthermore, the transition to university education entails a degree of identity change for the student—many leave home, meet new people, have to operate at a higher academic level, and think about their future career or occupational identities. All of this can cause psychological stress.

Collectively, both social representations and social stressors can result in what are deemed to be "threats" to one's sense of identity. Identity process theory posits that experiences, events, and situations with the capacity to curtail feelings of continuity, distinctiveness, self-efficacy, and self-esteem can result in identity threat. The experience of identity threat can be harmful to psychological well-being. Yet not all potentially threatening experiences, events, and situations do cause identity threat. The relationship between the two is likely to be influenced by personality traits and the availability of social support. Some personality traits may predispose an individual to threat when facing a particular experience—for instance, people who value conservation (a personality trait) may react more adversely to an event that fundamentally changes their current lifestyle (i.e., threatening their sense of continuity). Social support, which is accessible, available, and effective, can buffer the effect of the threatening stimulus, enabling the individual to act before the onset of identity threat. More generally, how one thinks about a particular event, situation, or experience will fundamentally shape its impact on identity, whether or not it results in threat. Consistent with the cognitive-behavioral approach, this pattern of thinking can be challenged if one is made aware of it.

When people face decreased levels of one or more of the four prime identity principles, they will experience negative affect, such as distress, guilt, or shame. Clearly, the specific type of affective response will partly depend on the nature of the threatening stimulus. For instance, identity threat resulting from an experience of sexual exploitation or abuse may result in feelings of shame (e.g., "I am a bad person").[12] In contrast, identity threat resulting from a social or cultural transgression that one has committed (e.g., having premarital sex despite a social or religious sanction against this) could result in feelings of guilt (e.g., "what I did was bad").[13] It is useful to distinguish between mild identity threat that does not induce any negative affect and more severe forms of threat that do. It is perhaps the intolerance of negative affect that spurs the individual to take action against the threatening stimulus, while identity threat that does not induce negative affect may not require any action on the part of the individual.

Coping With Identity Threat

Coping strategies are designed to eradicate or at least minimize the threat to identity. In the HARM, the emphasis is on two types of coping—adaptive and maladaptive. Categorizing particular coping strategies and styles as either adaptive or maladaptive will depend on context and, in particular, the health hazard that is of interest to the researcher. In the context of sexual health, coping strategies that consist of self-disclosure and the derivation of social support from others tend to be beneficial as they enable people to be communicative about their sexual behavior and thus make more informed decisions about the type of sex they have. These strategies are thus categorized as adaptive. Conversely, some individuals who face identity threat may engage in sexual risk behaviors as a form of self-validation (through validation from others),[14] and some may use drugs or alcohol as a form of escapism from the threat they are experiencing.[15] This may increase the risk of losing sexual inhibitions and engaging in risk behaviors. The HARM indicates that maladaptive coping, defined by context, may result in adverse health outcomes.

A wide range of practitioners can influence the threatened individual's pathway to coping.[16] For instance, sexual health educators may be able to support students in adopting effective coping strategies and avoiding those coping strategies that are harmful to psychological and sexual health. They may raise awareness of the mechanisms of identity threat and coping so that individuals themselves understand their own cognition, affect, and behavior and take steps to enhance their well-being. As indicated in the cognitive-behavioral model, people facing psychological adversity can work with practitioners to challenge their own patterns of thought and behavior that heighten the likelihood of maladaptive coping.

In the next section, we examine the social context (consisting of sexual attitudes, behaviors, and norms) in which university students construct and protect their identity.

Sexual Attitudes, Behaviors, and Norms

There has been a liberalization of attitudes toward sex and sexuality in Western cultures, with increasing acceptance of a range of consensual sexual activities, particularly non-marital sex and same-sex sexuality.[17] This has been part of a broader shift in the rationale for sexual behaviors,[18] moving away from a focus on procreation toward one of recreation.[19] In young adult contexts, such as university campuses,[20] this includes "hooking up" and casual sex norms. Relatedly, there is also increased visibility and adoption of queer sexual identity labels,[21] with examples of individuals eschewing sexual identity labels altogether.[22]

One key attitudinal trend is the liberalization of attitudes toward same-sex sexuality. In the United Kingdom (UK), survey data presented in the 36th British Social Attitudes report (published by the National Centre for Social Research) shows a transformation of attitudes toward gay people. In 1976, only 11% of respondents stated that same-sex sexual activity was "not wrong at all." In contrast, two-thirds of people said that in 2018[23] and shifting attitudes have seen many young men publicly support same-sex rights and condemn prejudiced attitudes and discriminatory behaviors toward sexual minorities (i.e., homonegativity).[24]

As homonegativity has decreased in university settings and more generally, men increasingly engage in tactile behaviors with each other as signs of friendship[25]—where such acts would once have called into question these men's sexualities, and there is now a carnivalesque celebration of male social bonding and friendship (which has been referred to as "homosociality" in sociology).[24] Such softening masculinities result in more progressive attitudes and behaviors among university-attending men[26] and positively impact gay men[26] and heterosexual women.[27] The liberalization of attitudes and norms may reduce exposure to stressors (e.g., discrimination). Challenging identity labels may enable individuals to construct a psychologically satisfying identity, thereby reducing the risk of identity threat.

Digital Sexualities

Alongside these changing attitudes toward sex and sexuality, there is evidence of new sexual cultures which rely on technology.[28] Technology allows sexual communication across cultural, geographical, and social boundaries,[29] provides the means to learn about sex and sexuality[30] and can help facilitate sexual encounters online and offline.[31] Moreover, these technologies have become more important to people during the era of social distancing and lockdown due to COVID-19.[32] Hook-up apps play an important role in university student culture,[33] and many single students report being on hook-up apps.[34] While these apps are often used for facilitating casual sex,[31] chatting online does not invariably lead to offline sexual encounters.[35] Furthermore, despite their name, hook-up apps perform a wide range of functions for university students, including developing relationships[36] and friendships,[37] and providing entertainment.[38]

It is noteworthy that social pressures operate on apps, which may lead to identity threat and negative affect in students. For instance, university students may be exposed to stressors on these apps, such as "catfishing" (using a fictional persona online to lure someone into a relationship or interaction), "ghosting" (sudden and unexplained ending of a relationship), rejection, and "revenge porn" (online distribution of sexually explicit material featuring a person without their consent).[39,40] Furthermore, these apps have been shown to perpetuate stigma and racial discrimination through the discourse of personal preferences.[41]

All these significant stressors could undermine each identity principle and lead to negative affect. Indeed, they are all associated with significant mental health outcomes.[39,40] Furthermore, the potential impact of these stressors on students' emotional, mental, and social well-being in relation to their sexuality is evident, and therefore their sexual health may be jeopardized. Yet the apps themselves may facilitate particular types of coping in students struggling to construct and protect their sense of identity.

Sexual Frequency

Despite the documented hook-up culture and proliferation of technology to facilitate casual sex, there have been decreases in frequency of sexual activities in certain populations, particularly university-aged individuals. For example, in the United States, one study found decreases in sexual behaviors for people aged 18–44 years between 2000 and 2018, with 31% of men and 19% of women aged between 18 and 24 years reporting no sexual activity in the past year.[42] Similar trends have been observed in the UK, with the National Survey of Sexual Attitudes and Lifestyles finding 29% of women and 29% of men reported no sex in the last month, with the highest prevalence of sexual inactivity reported in those aged 16–25 years.[43]

There are several reasons for this decline in sexual frequency. Young adults take longer to explore adulthood, reducing their sexual frequency alongside other adult activities, such as drinking, going out without parents, and paid employment when possible.[44] Furthermore, young adults are less likely to be living with a romantic/sexual partner and will instead be living with family, making it harder to have sex.[45] There is also decreased stigmatization of masturbation and other solo-sexual practices, meaning sexual satisfaction can be achieved beyond normative dyadic sexual relationship models[46]—evidenced in young adults in the UK during social lockdown.[47]

In his interview study of sixteen first-year undergraduate students in the UK, the lead author of this chapter found that interviewees viewed their entry into university as providing greater sexual freedom and thus opportunities for sexual exploration.[2] However, there were some environmental sexual risk factors specific to the university context, which could imperil sexual health outcomes, such as the social expectation to have multiple sexual partners, especially during "freshers' week" (the first week of university), widespread non-use of condoms and the trivialization of sexually transmitted infections among students. It was argued that these risk factors may lay the foundations for poor sexual health outcomes among students who are struggling to retain a positive sense of identity amid adjustment to a novel context, namely university.

In short, there is much variation in sexual attitudes, behaviors, and norms among university students in the UK. As sexual attitudes and sexual labels change, new psychological, sexual, and social opportunities emerge. Although sexual frequency may appear to be waning, a broader conceptualization of sexual health in terms of emotional, mental, physical, and social well-being will enable us to promote better outcomes.

Practical Implications for Sexual Health Promotion

Common methods of sexual health education include an "information deficit" approach to raising awareness of and providing information about sexual health so that service users can make an informed decision about sexual behavior and risk. Attempts to develop enhanced models of sexual health promotion for university students have been limited. Key factors pertinent to sexual health that apply to young people, in general, have been highlighted in the literature, such as inaccurate risk perception and knowledge about STIs,[48] social norms about sexuality,[49] reduced psychological well-being,[50] attitudes toward condoms,[51] and alcohol misuse.[52] These factors should be important foci of sexual health education programs in student populations.

Empirical Research Focusing on Students

Robust data on sexual risk in students must be collected and used to inform sexual health education. The Sexual Risk Behavior Scale explains the frequency of sexual risk in university students.[53] The scale could be used by university student services and general practitioner practices, which would enable health promoters and practitioners and students themselves to assess sexual risk behavior at particular points in time. This would enable practitioners to intervene effectively as students to develop an accurate appraisal of their own sexual risk behavior.

There is an intrinsic link between psychological health and sexual health. Thus, further research integrating measures of sexual risk and psychological health contextualized within parsimonious psychological models, such as the HARM, may provide further practical understanding on how sexual health services could be targeted dependent on additional social and psychological factors, such as coping styles, culture, identity threat, personality, race, religion, sexual identity and orientation, and situational context. These data can be used to develop and enhance student-specific sexual health education. Furthermore, a detailed collaborative research program should also delineate best practices for approaches within the student population by understanding the nuances of risk dependent on in- (and out-) group diversity.

Preventing Different Types of Risk

It would be of significant practical use to re-evaluate the "information deficit" approach to sexual health education and consider what additional components might be useful depending on the demographics of the student group in question. Of course, the provision of general sexual health education resources is vital. It is also necessary to integrate broader health assessments, challenge a "one size fits all" approach, and utilize contemporary research findings to provide a more nuanced understanding of student need. This is especially important in the context of psychological distress, volitional and non-volitional sexual risk-taking, and sexual and demographic diversity observable in our research.

We found differences between volitional sexual risk (e.g., having sex without a condom or under the influence of drugs or substances) and non-volitional sexual risk (e.g., removal of a condom during sex without consent, paying for sex, or feeling coerced into sex) among university students in the UK.[3] Drawing on the HARM, we identified two coping routes to these two types of sexual risk, both of which were predicted by psychological distress. The first route highlighted the mediating role of rethinking/planning, such as re-conceptualizing and rethinking priorities, in the relationship between psychological distress and volitional sexual risk. The second route highlighted the mediating role of social engagement, such as engaging with members of one's social group, between psychological distress and non-volitional sexual risk.

Evidence of the mediating role of rethinking/planning and social engagement could enhance sexual awareness education. For example, students who use a rethinking/planning coping style in response to psychological stress could be provided with interventions that facilitate an understanding of both their perception of the cause of their distress and how they may rethink/plan volitional actions, particularly in the context of sexual decision-making. Conversely, students who respond to psychological distress using the social engagement coping style may be at greater risk of coercion—the need to socially connect may temporarily overwhelm the motivation to keep sexually safe. The need for connection may not be inherently sexual but may reduce one's resilience and thus ability to say "no" in a sexual situation. Thus, education and interventions could be targeted to explore the causes of distress and their understanding of, and approach to, social engagement, i.e., what this means to students when in distress and how to keep themselves psychologically and sexually safe.

Educators can take some practical steps to implement effective sexual health education. First, it is important to lay the foundations for exchanging confidences and deriving social support. Students need to feel able to self-disclose and to do so in a way that promotes engagement and action. This involves fostering a social context where students feel comfortable discussing sex and sexuality. Second, it must be acknowledged that we all have complex and multi-faceted identities that sometimes include religion and minority ethnic culture. Thus, awareness of the significance of these identities to sexuality among students will be key. Third, educators will need to acknowledge and confront their own possible biases, misconceptions, and preconceptions, which may impact the nature and effectiveness of sexual health programs. Effective equality and diversity training can mitigate this risk. Consistent self-reflection will help sustain effectiveness. Fourth, it must be acknowledged that sex and sexuality are not the same for everyone. Coping behaviors, social representations, and social stressors change over time. They vary by social group. They differ in terms of socio-cultural context. Consequently, sexual health education programs must accommodate change, be dynamic, and be ready to innovate. They will need to be revised in an evidence-based manner—in collaboration with educators, researchers, and students.

Toward an Effective Sexual Health Education Program

In its original statement, the HARM focuses on introducing practical interventions once the psychological distress has already occurred. However, interventions should be both preventive (before the hazard occurs) and reactive (when it has occurred). Primary prevention ought to begin in school or college, highlighting the importance of inclusive sexual health education at this stage. Upon arrival at university, students could be offered sexual health discussions, in addition to sexual health screening, which are cognizant of the stressors, social representations, and opportunities associated with university and student life. Pre-emptive interventions must be sensitive to and inclusive of sexual and cultural diversity, and assumptions about the type of sex that students are having should be avoided. Practitioners must be cognizant of the liberalization of attitudes toward sex and same-sex sexuality and the contemporary use of online technologies, such as hook-up apps. There must also be an awareness of cultural differences in views and norms concerning sexuality. Although there has been a liberalization of attitudes toward sex and sexuality in Western cultures, this may not be the case in some cultures. It is also important to acknowledge asexuality, and practitioners must acknowledge that, although not everyone has sex, the emotional, psychological, and social dimensions of their sexual health remain relevant. More generally, as there is often a degree of stigma and embarrassment associated with sexual behavior, it is recommended that services be specific to provide a safe psychological boundary between sexual health education and other aspects of student learning.

References

1. World Health Organization (2006). *Defining sexual health: Report of a technical consultation on sexual health*. Geneva: World Health Organization.
2. Jaspal, R. (2020). Sexual health perceptions among first-year students at a British university. *American Journal of Sexuality Education, 15*(2), 158–179. https://doi.org/10.1080/15546128.2019.1701597
3. Jaspal, R., Lopes, B., Wignall, L., & Bloxsom, C. (2021). Predicting sexual risk behavior in British and European Union university students in the UK. *American Journal of Sexuality Education, 16*(1), 140–159. https://doi.org/10.1080/15546128.2020.1869129
4. Williams, M., Pollard, E., Takala, H., & Houghton, A. (2019). *Review of support for disabled students in higher education in England: Report to the office for students by the institute for employment studies and researching equity, access and participation*. Brighton: Institute for Employment Studies.
5. Public Health England. (2018). *An STI is diagnosed in a young person every 4 minutes in England*. www.gov.uk/government/news/an-sti-is-diagnosed-in-a-young-personevery-4-minutes-in-england
6. Martin-Smith, H.A., Okpo, E.A., & Bull, E.R. (2018). Exploring psychosocial predictors of STI testing in University students. *BMC Public Health, 18*, 664. https://doi.org/10.1186/s12889-018-5587-2
7. Jaspal, R., & Bayley, J. (2020). *HIV and gay men: Clinical, social & psychological aspects*. Palgrave.
8. Breakwell, G.M. (2015). *Coping with threatened identities*. Routledge.
9. Beck, A.T. (1976). *Cognitive therapy and the emotional disorders*. International Universities Press.
10. Moscovici, S. (1988). Notes towards a description of social representations. *European Journal of Social Psychology, 18*(3), 211–250. https://doi.org/10.1002/ejsp.2420180303.
11. Jaspal, R. (2015). Constructing and protecting identity in a diverse higher education context. *Perspectives: Policy and Practice in Higher Education, 19*(4), 127–134. https://doi.org/10.1080/13603108.2015.1071291

12. Feiring, C., & Taska, L.S. (2005). The persistence of shame following sexual abuse: A longitudinal look at risk and recovery. *Child Maltreatment, 10*(4), 337–349. https://doi.org/10.1177/1077559505276686
13. Hackathorn, J.M., Ashdown, B.K., & Rife, S.C. (2016). The sacred bed: Sex guilt mediates religiosity and satisfaction for unmarried people. *Sexuality & Culture: An Interdisciplinary Quarterly, 20*(1), 153–172. https://doi.org/10.1007/s12119-015-9315-0
14. Leary, M.R., Schreindorfer, L.S., & Haupt, A.L. (1995). The role of low self-esteem in emotional and behavioral problems: Why is low self-esteem dysfunctional? *Journal of Social and Clinical Psychology, 14*(3), 297–314. https://doi.org/10.1521/jscp.1995.14.3.297
15. Jaspal, R. (2021). Chemsex, identity processes and coping among gay and bisexual men. *Drugs and Alcohol Today, 21*(4) 345–355. https://doi.org/10.1108/DAT-12-2020-0083
16. Jaspal, R. (2018). *Enhancing sexual health, self-identity and wellbeing among men who have sex with men: A guide for practitioners.* Jessica Kingsley Publishers.
17. Twenge, J.M., Sherman, R.A., & Wells, B.E. (2016). Changes in American adults' reported same-sex sexual experiences and attitudes, 1973–2014. *Archives of Sexual Behavior, 45*(7), 1713–1730. https://doi.org/10.1007/s10508-016-0769-4
18. McCormack, M., Measham, F., & Wignall, L. (2021). The normalization of leisure sex and recreational drugs: Exploring associations between polydrug use and sexual practices by English festival-goers. *Contemporary Drug Problems, 48*(2), 185–200. https://doi.org/10.1177/00914509211009901
19. Treas, J., Lui, J., & Gubernskaya, Z. (2014). Attitudes on marriage and new relationships: Cross-national evidence on the deinstitutionalization of marriage. *Demographic Research, 30*, 1495–1526. https://doi.org/10.4054/DemRes.2014.30.54
20. Pham, J.M. (2017). Beyond hookup culture: Current trends in the study of college student sex and where to next. *Sociology Compass, 11*(8), e12499. https://doi.org/10.1111/soc4.12499
21. Barsigian, L.L., Hammack, P.L., Morrow, Q.J., Wilson, B.D., & Russell, S.T. (2020). Narratives of gender, sexuality, and community in three generations of genderqueer sexual minorities. *Psychology of Sexual Orientation and Gender Diversity*, 7(3), 276–292. https://doi.org/10.1037/sgd0000384
22. Wignall, L., & Driscoll, H. (2020). Women's rationales and perspectives on "mostly" as a nonexclusive sexual identity label. *Psychology of Sexual Orientation and Gender Diversity, 73*(3), 366–374. http://doi.org/10.1037/sgd0000385
23. Albakri, M., Hill, S., Kelley, N., & Rahim, N. (2019). Relationships and gender identity. In J. Curtice, E. Clery, J. Perry, M. Phillips, & N. Rahim (Eds.), *British social attitudes: The 36th report* (pp. 112–139). The National Centre for Social Research.
24. McCormack, M. (2012). *The declining significance of homophobia.* Oxford University Press.
25. Anderson, E., Ripley, M., & McCormack, M. (2019). A mixed-method study of same-sex kissing among college-attending heterosexual men in the US. *Sexuality & Culture, 23*(1), 26–44. https://doi.org/10.1007/s12119-018-9560-0
26. Anderson, E., & McCormack, M. (2018). Inclusive masculinity theory: Overview, reflection and refinement. *Journal of Gender Studies, 27*(5), 547–561. https://doi.org/10.1080/09589236.2016.1245605
27. Worthen, M.G. (2014). The cultural significance of homophobia on heterosexual women's gendered experiences in the United States: A commentary. *Sex Roles*, *71*(3–4), 141–151. https://doi.org/10.1007/s11199-014-0389-1
28. Handyside, S., & Ringrose, J. (2017) Snapchat memory and youth digital sexual cultures: mediated temporality, duration and affect. *Journal of Gender Studies*, *26*(3), 347–360. https://doi.org/10.1080/09589236.2017.1280384
29. Wignall, L. (in press). Kinky in the digital age: gay male subcultures and social identities. Oxford University Press.

30. McCormack, M., & Wignall, L. (2017). Enjoyment, exploration and education: Understanding the consumption of pornography among young men with non-exclusive sexual orientations. *Sociology, 51*(5), 975–991. https://doi.org/10.1177/0038038516629909
31. Jaspal, R. (2017). Gay men's construction and management of identity on Grindr. *Sexuality & Culture, 21*(1), 187–204. https://doi.org/10.1007/s12119-016-9389-3
32. Cascalheira, C.J., McCormack, M., Portch, E., & Wignall, L. (2021). Changes in sexual fantasy and solitary sexual practice during social lockdown among young adults in the UK. *Sexual Medicine, 9*(3), 100342. https://doi.org/10.1016/j.esxm.2021.100342
33. Weiser, D.A., Niehuis, S., Flora, J., Punyanunt-Carter, N.M., Arias, V.S., & Baird, R.H. (2018). Swiping right: Sociosexuality, intentions to engage in infidelity, and infidelity experiences on Tinder. *Personality and Individual Differences, 133*, 29–33. https://doi.org/10.1016/j.paid.2017.10.025
34. Wignall, L., Stirling, J., & Scoats, R. (2020). UK university students' perceptions and negotiations of sexual consent. *Psychology & Sexuality*. https://doi.org/10.1080/19419899.2020.1859601
35. Timmermans, E., & Courtois, C. (2018). From swiping to casual sex and/or committed relationships: Exploring the experiences of Tinder users. *The Information Society, 34*(2), 59–70. https://doi.org/10.1080/01972243.2017.1414093
36. Lundquist, J.H., & Curington, C.V. (2019). Love me Tinder, love me sweet. *Contexts, 18*(4), 22–27. https://doi.org/10.1177/1536504219883848
37. Stoian, M.S. (2019). 'Friends, dates and everything in between': Tinder as a mediating technology. *Journal of Comparative Research in Anthropology and Sociology, 10*(1), 49–57.
38. Berkowitz, D., Tinkler, J., Peck, A., & Coto, L. (2021). Tinder: A game with gendered rules and consequences. *Social Currents*. https://doi.org/10.1177/23294965211019486
39. Bates, S. (2017). Revenge porn and mental health: A qualitative analysis of the mental health effects of revenge porn on female survivors. *Feminist Criminology, 12*(1), 22–42. https://doi.org/10.1177/1557085116654565
40. Thomas, J.O. & Dubar, R.T. (2021). Disappearing in the age of hypervisibility: Definition, context, and perceived psychological consequences of social media ghosting. *Psychology of Popular Media*. https://doi.org/10.1037/ppm0000343
41. Peck, A., Berkowitz, D., & Tinkler, J. (2021). Left, right, Black, and White: how White college students talk about their inter-and intra-racial swiping preferences on Tinder. *Sociological Spectrum, 41*(4), 304–321. https://doi.org/10.1080/02732173.2021.1916663
42. Ueda, P., Mercer, C., Ghaznavi, C., & Herbenick, D. (2020). Trends in frequency of sexual activity and number of sexual partners among adults aged 18 to 44 years in the US, 2000–2018. *JAMA Network Open, 3*(6), e203833. https://doi.org/10.1001/jamanetworkopen.2020.3833. See also Twenge, J., Sherman, R., & Wells, B. (2017). Sexual inactivity during young adulthood is more common among U.S. millennials and iGen: Age, period, and cohort effects on having no sexual partners after age 18. *Archives of Sexual Behavior, 46*(2), 433–440. https://doi.org/10.1007/s10508-016-0798-z
43. Wellings, K., Palmer, M., Machiyama, K., & Slaymaker, E. (2019). Changes in, and factors associated with, frequency of sex in Britain: Evidence from three national surveys of sexual attitudes and lifestyles (Natsal). *BMJ, 365*, l1525. https://doi.org/10.1136/bmj.l1525
44. Twenge, J., & Park, H. (2019). The decline in adult activities among U.S. adolescents, 1976–2016. *Child Development, 90*(2), 638–654. https://doi.org/10.1111/cdev.12930
45. Curran, M.A., Parrott, E., Ahn, S.Y., Serido, J., & Shim, S. (2018). Young adults' life outcomes and well-being: Perceived financial socialization from parents, the romantic partner, and young adults' own financial behaviors. *Journal of Family and Economic Issues, 39*(3), 445–456. https://doi.org/10.1007/s10834-018-9572-9
46. Anderson, E. (2012). *The monogamy gap: Men, love, and the reality of cheating*. Oxford University Press.

47. Wignall, L., Portch, E., McCormack, M., Owens, R., Cascalheira, C.J., Attard-Johnson, J., & Cole, T. (2021). Changes in sexual desire and behaviors among UK young adults during social lockdown due to COVID-19. *The Journal of Sex Research*. https://doi.org/10.1080/00224499.2021.1897067
48. Collado, A., Johnson, P.S., Loya, J.M., Johnson, M.W. & Yi, R. (2017). Discounting of condom-protected sex as a measure of high risk for sexually transmitted infection among college students. *Archives of Sexual Behavior, 46*(7), 2187–2195. https://doi.org/10.1007/s10508-016-0836-x
49. Gardner, M., & Steinberg, L. (2005). Peer influence on risk taking, risk preference, and risky decision making in adolescence and adulthood: An experimental study. *Developmental Psychology, 41*(4), 625–635. https://doi.org/10.1037/0012-1649.41.4.625
50. Binfet, J., & Passmore, H. (2016). Hounds and homesickness: The effects of an animalassisted therapeutic intervention for first-year university students. *Anthrozoos, 29*, 441–454. https://doi.org/10.1080/08927936.2016.1181364
51. MacDonald, T.K., & Hynie, M. (2008). Ambivalence and unprotected sex: Failure to predict sexual activity and decreased condom use. *Journal of Applied Social Psychology, 38*(4), 1092–1107. https://doi.org/10.1111/j.1559-1816.2008.00340.x
52. Chanakira, E., O'Cathain, A., Goyder, E.C. & Freeman, J.V. (2014). Factors perceived to influence risky sexual behaviors among university students in the United Kingdom: A qualitative telephone interview study. *BMC Public Health, 14*(1055). https://doi.org/10.1186/1471-2458-14-1055
53. Fino, E., Jaspal, R., Lopes, B., Wignall, L., & Bloxsom, C. (2021) The Sexual Risk Behaviors Scale (SRBS): Development and validation in a university student sample in the UK. *Evaluation and the Health Professions, 4*(2), 152–160. https://doi.org/10.1177/01632787211003950

19

WHERE IS THE STUDENT HEALTH SERVICES BUILDING?

Sexual Health Needs of First-Generation College Students

Robert J. Zeglin, Julie Williams Merten, and Danyelle Spohn

Who Are They?

First-generation college students (FGCS) are students whose parents did not attend or graduate from college.[1,2] That is, they are the first generation in their families to attend and complete higher education. FGCS represent 30–43% of four-year universities' freshman population[3,4] and are more likely to be female, of a racial or ethnic minority identity, and socioeconomically disadvantaged.[5,6] Consequently, FGCS have a unique college experience as they, sans the support and wisdom of a previous generation to guide them, navigate the academic expectations, campus politics, financial hurdles, intrapersonal demands, social pressures, and scheduling complications of college.[7]

Research has consistently found that FGCS reported greater academic distress, family obligation, financial distress, and work demands than their non-first-generation peers.[1,7,8] Many FGCS see academic success as a form of resiliency and strive to achieve that success despite limited access to the traditional systemic supports experienced by their peers.[5] In the aggregate, the inability for FGCS to leverage their parents' college experiences teamed with the increased life demands experienced by FGCS causes a disconnect between the student and the campus services designed to support them.[9,10] FGCS may not be aware of the myriad campus services available to them and, if they are, may not have the resources or time to access those services.

One such group of services is student health services. FGCS sit squarely at the confluence of several social determinants of health, particularly poor health (e.g., gender inequity, lack of health insurance, low income, poor educational opportunities, unemployment or underemployment, and unsafe or inconsistent housing.[1,8,4,11] Compared to their non-first-generation peers, FGCS experience poorer health and health beliefs.[4,12–14] In general, about 14% of FGCS access

DOI: 10.4324/9781003189787-20

campus health services; this is half the rate of their non-first-generation classmates.[9] A heretofore understudied domain of health related to FGCS is sexual health. Emerging research has begun to call attention to prioritizing FGCS in sexual health and wellness programming and education.[11,15–20]

Research by the authors of this chapter specifically investigated the prevalence of sexually transmitted infections (STI), comparing FGCS to their non-first-generation peers.[11] The sample consisted of 642 college students, 45% of which were FGCS. That study found that FGCS were over twice as likely to report an STI history. This was true regardless of age, gender, grade point average, number of sexual partners, race, and sexual orientation. This is a remarkable difference. The authors sought to call attention to this disparity in that study and called for a dedicated prioritization of FGCS for sexual health and wellness education. What follows in this chapter is a continuation of that call, with detailed opportunities for and examples of possible intervention.

Impact of College on Health

One's health follows a trajectory over the course of their life. That trajectory is influenced by ever-shifting and -evolving personal and environmental factors. Some bend that trajectory toward good health (e.g., exercise, obtaining health insurance), while others bend that trajectory toward poor health (e.g., getting a concussion, lack of access to health providers). The Life Course Health Development Model (LCHD)[21,22] calls attention to the importance of turning points, or major life transitions, along one's health trajectory because "trajectories can be altered more readily during sensitive periods of rapid developmental change than during other periods."[21] The transition to college is one such turning point. A complementary theory, the Input-Environment-Output Model (IEO),[23] highlights the important intersection of pre-college factors (e.g., college prep, demographics) with college environments factors (e.g., campus climate, new student orientation) to facilitate the notable developmental change that happens during college years, including health outcomes. Together, these two theories point to exactly the period of transition into college as a critical turning point in the lives of FGCS, whose pre-college factors put them at risk for a poor health trajectory. The educational interventions provided to FGCS during their preparation for, transition to, and completion of college can have a profound positive influence on their health trajectory, including their sexual health trajectory.

Opportunities and Recommendations

High School Programming

Congruent with the LCHD and IEO models mentioned earlier, pre-college factors are integral in determining FGCS's health trajectory. Because college represents a period when young adults make many decisions more independently and in increasingly novel situations than ever in their lives, they must rely on the education, training, and support gained in the years preceding college.[24,25] As it relates to sexual health and wellness, K-12 students in the United States receive woefully little education, training, and support. Only 18 states in the United States require that sex education taught in school be medically accurate, and only nine states require that consent be covered.[26] Furthermore, sex education, when taught, continues to be poorly delivered by undertrained school personnel.[27,28] For high school students who will later become FGCS, the pre-college factors discussed earlier are their daily lived experience during high school. The greater family, life, and work demands can impact the consistency of the high school educational experience.[29–31] This inconsistency, teamed with the objectively poor sex education offerings in high school in general, suggests that FGCS receive only passing exposure to sex education before entering college. This, congruent with LCHD, bends their sexual health trajectory toward poor health before they even attend a campus tour.

The clearest solution to this is, of course, consistent and comprehensive sex education in K-12 schools. Providing developmentally appropriate, medically accurate, and non-stigmatizing sex education to all K-12 students can have profound lifelong health benefits.[32] There is clear evidence that pre-college sex education can influence health outcomes for college students. For instance, one study[33] found that college students that received pre-college sex education that included boundary-setting were half as likely to experience sexual assault during college.

A new study found that comprehensive sex education in a K-12 setting also aids in expanding students' understanding of diversity issues, social and emotional learning, and healthy relationships.[34] Comprehensive sex education also reduces STI risk and unintended pregnancies,[27] the latter being one of the identified barriers to FGCS completing college.[18,35] Making comprehensive sex education an educational right for all students in all grades significantly increases the number of contact points between FGCS and sexual health information. In other words, before they even step foot on a college campus, it is possible to equip FGCS with the sexual health knowledge and skills necessary to successfully, enjoyably, and independently navigate the myriad sexual decisions that college will pose to them.

New Student Orientation

New student orientation is one of the most consistently discussed college factors within the LCHD and IEO models, as they were developed to ease the transition from high school to college. They allow students to explore the campus, get acquainted with campus services, meet other students, and register for courses.[36] And more recently, colleges have added a parent and family orientation as families have become increasingly involved in their adult children's lives,[37,38] particularly among communities and cultures that are more communal and collectivist rather than individualistic, like many FGCS families.[29,39] Because new student orientation can last for up to a week,[36] there is ample time to introduce all relevant campus resources to students, including sexual health resources. These often include condom distribution programs, LGBT student resources, sexual assault prevention and intervention resources, and STI testing and education.[40,41] These resources aim to reduce poor sexual health outcomes like depression and anxiety among gender and sexual minority students, sexual assault, STIs, and unintended pregnancies. Including sexual health resource information in new student orientation is a simple way to familiarize FGCS with the sexual health resources on campus.[42,43]

As with every aspect of the college experience, Covid-19 has changed the new student orientation experience. Namely, colleges were forced to host mostly or completely online orientations during the peak Covid-19 infection period.[44] Future orientations may include more hybrid components with in-person and online modules for students and their families. A recent article titled "Sex Ed Lessons from COVID-19" provides a number of concrete recommendations for addressing sex education in a COVID era.[45] Notably, the authors of that article highlight similarities in the decision-making processes related to sexual health and COVID precautions (e.g., vaccines, social distancing). In any format, student health is an integral part of the in-person orientation process, with students being responsible for providing their immunization records and other required health documents. That process could be expanded to include tabling events during orientation to showcase sexual health services, demonstrations of telehealth capabilities, workshops on STI testing, and contraceptive options and costs. Importantly, this should include a tour of the student health building and other locations offering sexual health resources (e.g., LGBT student center). The vital role of families in gathering information about available resources should be considered, as FGCS can often rely on families to help navigate critical college decisions.[29,39,46] In summary, a new student orientation that intentionally includes sexual health resource information can positively influence the sexual health trajectory of FGCS right at the start of this crucial developmental milestone and LCHD turning point.

Freshman Seminar

Like the new student orientation, freshman seminar courses also offer a unique opportunity to provide FGCS with important sexual health information. Nearly 90% of colleges and universities offer a seminar course specifically designed for freshmen students.[47,48] Traditionally, this seminar is an intimate discussion-based course to introduce the student to the tools necessary to succeed in college.[47,48] Some colleges have already begun to design some sections of their freshman seminars for FGCS and their unique needs.[49]

Congruent with the IEO model, information presented in an academic course may be particularly impactful for FGCS, as this population of students consistently take their studies quite seriously.[5,7,50,51] Because of this commitment to coursework, FGCS may be more likely to consume the sexual health and wellness material more earnestly if presented as part of course content and assignments. The proposal to include sexual health and wellness information is not novel. *Sex Ed on Campus* succinctly noted that "by aiming this program at college students who are exploring who they are and what they want, both academically and personally, there is an opportunity to change the way these students perceive sex and what sexual health encompasses."[52] The formality of the course gives the information and resources covered therein credibility, helping FGCS trust the material and its usefulness. In fact, completion of freshman seminars has been linked to greater engagement with campus resources.[47,53] The assignments in freshman seminar can be targeted directly to familiarize FGCS with the campus sexual health resources. For example, using constructivist pedagogy,[54] one assignment might be to have students locate, contact, and interview one campus-based and one community-based sexual health organization. The possible ways to invite FGCS to get their hands on sexual health and wellness material in a freshman seminar course are limited only by the instructor's imagination.

Introductory Health Course

Understanding that new student orientation and freshman seminars may already be packed with content, thus making the inclusion of sexual health and wellness information less likely, it is also possible to include that information in an introductory health course. Much like the freshman seminar course is designed to aid freshman students in navigating the demands of college, an introductory health course is often offered to support students in making decisions related to their overall health, including exercise, mental health, nutrition, and sexual health. Such classes are easily taught by public health and health education professors.[55,56] This is especially true considering that college students are encountering many of these decisions for the first time, more independently, and with the potential for longer-term consequences,[57] congruent with IEO. College students consider sexual wellness information highly relevant to their sexual health decision-making.[57] For FGCS who, as discussed earlier and congruent with LCHD, may have had even more inconsistent sex education in their pre-college years, that relevancy is even more pronounced. Additionally, there is some indication that health-related fields and courses may be a popular option among FGCS,[58] meaning that intentionally including sexual health and wellness content in an introductory health course may successfully reach the intended audience.

Campus Offices

Returning to less formal opportunities to provide FGCS with sexual health information but trading that formality for constancy, campus resource offices can serve as an unyielding fountain of sexual health and wellness information.

There are two applicable categories of offices worth discussing here: 1) Sexual health offices and 2) Student group resource offices. First, sexual health offices on college campuses can include LGBT resource centers, sexual health clinics, and women's health centers.[40,41] It is important that staff in these offices identify the priority populations on their campus. This should include a student population, like FGCS, that may not have the time or familiarity to access the resources offered by these sexual health offices.[1,7,59] As such, and congruent with IEO, it is incumbent on these offices to reach these priority students where they are. For FGCS, this may mean in their courses (e.g., presentations/workshops in introductory courses), tabling near high-traffic areas for non-residential students (e.g., near parking garages, public transportation stops), and in the community (e.g., local malls, nearby restaurants). It also means collaborating with the second category of offices: student group resource offices.

Many colleges and universities have campus offices dedicated to serving specific student populations. This can include students with disabilities, food-insecure students, international students, military and veteran students, religious students, and students who have children.[40,59,60–62] The most obvious opportunity to provide sexual health information to FGCS is for campuses to create and maintain a campus office specific for FGCS, especially if the size of their FGCS student body is significant. However, if this is financially or pragmatically untenable, the myriad other student group resource offices can feed two proverbial birds with one scone. FGCS are not monolithic; each FGCS has numerous sociodemographic identities that converge into a unique student with equally unique needs. Being an FGCS is just one of many such identities these students hold. As the prioritization of diversity initiatives on colleges campuses has finally begun to be a part of significant conversations in higher education,[63–65] there is a growing opportunity, congruent with IEO, to capture FGCS in programming offered by various student group resource offices that speak to any one of FGCS' other intersectional sociodemographic identities (e.g., age, disability status, ethnic identity, racial identity). Each student group resource office must first recognize and build programming around the sexual health needs of their priority student population (e.g., military students, students with disabilities) and then infuse into that programming information specific to traditionally hard-to-access student populations like FGCS.

Related to all of this, college and university resource offices must, congruent with IEO and LCHD, learn to be flexible in their program delivery strategies. As already mentioned, FGCS may not be able to access programming during traditional hours or at traditional locations (e.g., a hard-to-reach area of campus). Therefore, universities should consider making resources and programming available outside traditional business hours, including evenings and weekends. College resource offices can table at community events that FGCS may frequent due to their intersecting identities (e.g., arts markets, concerts, cultural celebration days, food markets). Secondly, college resource offices may consider offering their programming virtually, either live or pre-recorded. The latter may be a particularly attractive option for student groups, like FGCS, whose schedules may be demanding and unpredictable. Research supports that virtual sexual health programming can effectively deliver important sexual health information.[66,67] In general, colleges and universities, if they wish to capture as many of their students as possible in their student resources programming, must learn to be flexible and adaptable.

Advisors

This chapter concludes by presenting the simplest opportunity to support the sexual health and wellness of FGCS. Students move through their college experience under the watchful eye of an academic advisor. College academic advisors are traditionally thought of as the singular point of contact that helps students with academic planning, such as selecting courses for their major and minors. However, the advisor role has evolved to a much more intensive position considering their sustained relationship with the student.[68] They can often be the first "college official" to know of any changes in the student's personal life. Congruent with IEO and LCHD, academic advisors can play a crucial role in promoting student health, serving as a central and personal referral source to campus resources.[69] When working with FGCS, academic advisors can commit to understanding and appreciating the students' needs, goals, and life demands. Research has shown that the strength of the advisor-student relationship is an important factor in the success of FGCS in college.[70,71] Given the greater life demands experienced by FGCS, academic advisors represent one of the first, one of the most consistent, one of the most personal, and one of the most knowledgeable relationships an FGCS will have with the institution. There are many touchpoints between the advisor and the student during which the advisor can assess the student's needs, answer questions, and provide referrals, including with respect to sexual health. However, this does mean that colleges and universities must equip their academic advisors with the knowledge of sexual health and wellness resources and empower them to support their advisees as comprehensively as possible.

References

1. Cataldi, E.F., Bennett, C.T., & Chen, X. (2018). *First-generation students: College access, persistence, and postbachelor's outcomes (Stats in Brief. NCES 2018–421)*. National Center for Education Statistics.
2. Shelton, C. (2011). Helping first-generation college students succeed. *Journal of Psychological Issues in Organizational Culture*, *1*(4), 63–75. https://doi.org/10.1002/jpoc.20041
3. Redford, J., & Mulvaney Hoyer, K. (2017). *First generation and continuing-generation college students: A comparison of high school and postsecondary experiences*. International Center for Education Statistics. https://nces.ed.gov/pubs2018/2018009.pdf.
4. Stebleton, M.J., Soria, K.M., & Huesman, R.L. (2014). First-generation students' sense of belonging, mental health, and use of counseling services at public research universities. *Journal of College Counseling*, *17*(1), 6–20.

5. Dover, T.L., Major, B., & Glace, A.M. (2020). Discrimination, health, and the costs and benefits of believing in system fairness. *Health Psychology*, *39*(3), 230.
6. National Center for Education Statistics (2019). Profile of undergraduate students: Attendance, distance and remedial education, degree program and field of study, demographics, financial aid, financial literacy, employment, and military status: 2015–16. Retrieved from https://nces.ed.gov/pubsearch/pubsinfo.asp?pubid=2019467
7. House, L.A., Neal, C., & Kolb, J. (2020). Supporting the mental health needs of first generation college students. *Journal of College Student Psychotherapy*, *34*(2), 157–167.
8. Ma, J., & Baum, S. (2016). Trends in community colleges: Enrollment, prices, student debt, and completion. *College Board Research Brief*, *4*, 1–23.
9. National Association of Student Personnel Administrators. (2020). *Use of student services among freshman first-generation college students.* https://firstgen.naspa.org/files/dmfile/NASPA_FactSheet-03_FIN.pdf
10. Ramos-Sánchez, L., & Nichols, L. (2007). Self-efficacy of first-generation and non-first-generation college students: The relationship with academic performance and college adjustment. *Journal of College Counseling*, *10*(1), 6–18.
11. Zeglin, R.J., Merten, J.W., & Niemela, D.R.M. (2020). Sexually transmitted infections among first-generation college students. *American Journal of Sexuality Education*, *15*(4), 491–501.
12. Bassett, B.S. (2021). Big enough to bother them? When low-income, first-generation students seek help from support programs. *Journal of College Student Development*, *62*(1), 19–36.
13. Gallagher, K.M. (2019). What do we know about the health of first-generation college students? A first look at compensatory health beliefs and behavior. *Perspectives In Learning*, *18*(1), 3.
14. Zuo, C., Mulfinger, E., Oswald, F.L., & Casillas, A. (2018). First-generation college student success. In R.S. Feldman (Ed.), *The first year of college: Research, theory, and practice on improving the student experience and increasing retention* (pp. 55–89). Cambridge University Press.
15. Avina, R.M., Mullen, M., Mshigeni, S., & Becerra, M.B. (2020). "I actually don't know what HIV is": A mixed methods analysis of college students' HIV literacy. *Diseases*, *8*(1), 1.
16. Eisenberg, M.E., Lust, K.A., & Garcia, C.M. (2014). Differences in sexual behaviors among unmarried sexually active students at 2-and 4-year colleges. *Research in Nursing & Health*, *37*(2), 128–134.
17. Joseph, K. (2020). *What strategies do college academic advisors use to help first-generation minority students succeed in college?* Capella University.
18. Nelson, B., Froehner, M., & Gault, B. (2013). *College students with children are common and face many challenges in completing higher education*. Briefing Paper# C404. Institute for Women's Policy Research.
19. Velazquez, E.A. (2012). Generational status, sexual behavior, and alcohol use among college students. *McNair Scholars Research Journal*, *8*(1), 13.
20. Wilson, J.D. (2020). They're crying in the all-gender bathroom: Navigating belonging in higher education while first generation and nonbinary. *The Vermont Connection*, *41*(1), 17.
21. Halfon, N, & Hochstein, M. (2002). Life course health development: An integrated framework for developing health, policy, and research. *Milbank Q.*, *80*(3), 433–479, iii. https://doi.org/10.1111/1468-0009.00019
22. Halfon, N., Larson, K., Lu, M., Tullis, E., & Russ, S. (2014). Lifecourse health development: past, present and future. *Maternal and Child Health Journal*, *18*(2), 344–365.
23. Fink, J.E. (2014). Flourishing: Exploring predictors of mental health within the college environment. *Journal of American College Health*, *62*(6), 380–388.
24. Patton, L.D., Renn, K.A., Guido, F.M., & Quaye, S.J. (2016). *Student development in college: Theory, research, and practice*. John Wiley & Sons.

25. Tyler, A. (2012). *"It takes a village to raise a child—It takes a campus to graduate a student": Exploring the Cultural Relevance of Student Development Models for African Americans in Higher Education*. Temple University.
26. Guttmacher Institute. (2021). *Sex and HIV education*. www.guttmacher.org/state-policy/explore/sex-and-hiv-education
27. Lemon, K.D. (2019). Sex education in America: Abstaining from comprehensive facts. *Journal of Midwifery & Women's Health, 64*(2), 149–153.
28. Woo, G.W., Soon, R., Thomas, J.M., & Kaneshiro, B. (2011). Factors affecting sex education in the school system. *Journal of Pediatric and Adolescent Gynecology, 24*(3), 142–146.
29. Lightweis, S. (2014). The challenges, persistence, and success of white, working-class, first-generation college students. *College Student Journal, 48*(3), 461–467.
30. Tym, C., McMillion, R., Barone, S., & Webster, J. (2004). *First-generation college students: A literature review*. TG (Texas Guaranteed Student Loan Corporation).
31. Wind, G. (2013). *Addressing precollege program needs of first generation, low income, and multicultural students*. Walden University.
32. World Health Organization (2010). *Social determinants of sexual and reproductive health*. www.who.int/social_determinants/tools/WHO_SocialDeterminantsSexualHealth_2010.pdf
33. Santelli, J.S., Grilo, S.A., Choo, T.H., Diaz, G., Walsh, K., Wall, M., Hirsch, J.S., Wilson, P.A., Gilbert, L., & Khan, S. (2018). Does sex education before college protect students from sexual assault in college? *PLoS One, 13*(11), e0205951.
34. Goldfarb, E.S., & Lieberman, L.D. (2021). Three decades of research: The case for comprehensive sex education. *Journal of Adolescent Health, 68*(1), 13–27.
35. Alonso, G. (2002). *Latinas in higher education: Overcoming barriers of teenage pregnancy*. Master's thesis, California State University, San Bernadino. https://scholarworks.lib.csusb.edu/etd-project/2205
36. Chan, M. (2019). An analysis of new student orientation programs at US four-year colleges: How can administrators enhance the first and major milestone of a student's academic journey? *Planning for Higher Education, 47*(3), 38–52.
37. Gassiot, K. (2012). *Parental engagement at new student orientation and its influence in transition of first year college students*. Texas Tech University.
38. Harper, C.E, Kiyama, J.M., Ramos, D., & Aguayo, D. (2018). Examining the inclusivity of parent and family college orientations: A directed content analysis. *Journal of College Orientation, Transition, and Retention, 25*(1).
39. Pratt, I.S., Harwood, H.B., Cavazos, J.T., & Ditzfeld, C.P. (2019). Should I stay or should I go? Retention in first-generation college students. *Journal of College Student Retention: Research, Theory & Practice, 21*(1), 105–118.
40. Eisenberg, M.E., Lechner, K.E., Frerich, E.A., Lust, K.A., & Garcia, C.M. (2012). Characterizing sexual health resources on college campuses. *Journal of Community Health, 37*(5), 940–948.
41. Habel, M.A., Coor, A., Beltran, O., Becasen, J., Pearson, W.S., & Dittus, P. (2018). The state of sexual health services at U.S. colleges and universities. *Journal of American College Health, 66*(4), 259–268. https://doi.org/10.1080/07448481.2018.1431896
42. Edwards, S.R., Hinsz, V.B., & Whitcomb, D.H. (2016). Efficacy of a very brief personalized sexual health prevention program. *Problems of Psychology in the 21st Century, 10*(1), 6–12.
43. Miller, M.B. (2019). Comparison of community college students' sexual health dimensions. *Community College Journal of Research and Practice, 43*(6), 401–415.
44. Motycki, K., & Murphy, D. (2021). Bridging systems, building a coalition, and centering students: A collaborative multi-campus approach to orientation in the time of COVID-19. *Journal of College Orientation, Transition, and Retention, 28*(2).
45. Rolleri Insignares, L.A., Bass, T.M., & Taverner, B. (2021). Sex ed lessons from COVID-19. *American Journal of Sexuality Education, 16*(4), 435–465.

46. Harper, C.E., Zhu, H., & Marquez Kiyama, J. (2020). Parents and families of first-generation college students experience their own college transition. *The Journal of Higher Education, 91*(4), 540–564.
47. Barefoot, B.O. (1992). *Helping first-year college students climb the academic ladder: Report of a national survey of freshman seminar programming in American higher education.* The College of William and Mary.
48. National Resource Center for The First-Year Experience and Students in Transition. (2016). *2012–2013 national survey of first-year seminars.* National Resource Center for The First-Year Experience and Students in Transition.
49. Peabody, M., Hutchens, N.H., Lewis, W.D., & Deffendall, M. (2011). *First-generation college students at the University of Kentucky.* University of Kentucky.
50. Martin, G.L. (2012). *Getting out, missing out, and surviving: The social class experiences of white, low-income, first-generation college students.* The University of Iowa.
51. Peabody, M. (2013). A critical analysis of the identification and treatment of first-generation college students: A social capital approach. *Kentucky Journal of Higher Education Policy and Practice, 2*(1), 4.
52. Buzzelli, M. (2016). *Sex ed on campus: Integrating comprehensive sexual health education into first-year seminar curriculum.* University of Pittsburgh.
53. Al-Sheeb, B.A., Abdulwahed, M.S., & Hamouda, A.M. (2018). Impact of first-year seminar on student engagement, awareness, and general attitudes toward higher education. *Journal of Applied Research in Higher Education, 10*(1), 15–30.
54. Johnson, E., Prucha, C., & Roter, P.M. (2008). Using problem-based learning to teach information literacy skills in a freshman seminar. In E. Connor (Ed.), *An Introduction to Instructional Services in Academic Libraries.* Taylor & Francis.
55. Kulinna, P.H., Warfield, W.W., Jonaitis, S., Dean, M., & Corbin, C. (2009). The progression and characteristics of conceptually based fitness/wellness courses at American universities and colleges. *Journal of American College Health, 58*(2), 127–131. https://doi.org/10.1080/07448480903221327
56. Woekel, E., Ebbeck, V., Concepcion, R.Y., Readdy, T., Li, K.K., Lee, H., & Cardinal, B.J. (2013). Physical activity, nutrition, and self-perception changes related to a university "Lifetime Fitness for Health" curriculum. *Physical Educator, 70*(4), 374.
57. Brewer, K., Diehr, A., & Bliss, K. (2020). Why don't we just ask them? A qualitative study regarding college student perceptions on what topics should be included in an introductory health course. *Pedagogy in Health Promotion*, 2373379920926193. https://doi.org/10.1177/2373379920926193
58. Burnett, L.L. (2017). *Characteristics associated with persistence and retention among first-generation college students majoring in science, technology, engineering, or math.* The University of Alabama.
59. Eisenberg, M.E., Garcia, C.M., Frerich, E.A., Lechner, K.E., & Lust, K.A. (2012). Through the eyes of the student: What college students look for, find, and think about sexual health resources on campus. *Sexuality Research and Social Policy, 9*(4), 306–316.
60. Brown, V., & Nichols, T.R. (2013). Pregnant and parenting students on campus: Policy and program implications for a growing population. *Educational Policy, 27*(3), 499–530.
61. Lau, J., Garza, T., & Garcia, H. (2019). International students in community colleges: On-campus services used and its affect on sense of belonging. *Community College Journal of Research and Practice, 43*(2), 109–121.
62. Twill, S.E., Bergdahl, J., & Fensler, R. (2016). Partnering to build a pantry: A university campus responds to student food insecurity. *Journal of Poverty, 20*(3), 340–358.
63. Chang, M.J., Milem, J.F., & Antonio, A.L. (2011). Campus climate and diversity. *Student Services: A Handbook for the Profession*, 43–58.

64. Clark, C. (2011). Diversity initiatives in higher education: Just how important. *Multicultural Education, 19*(3), 57–59.
65. Wilson, J.L. (2013). Emerging trend: The chief diversity officer phenomenon within higher education. *The Journal of Negro Education, 82*(4), 433–445.
66. Peskin, M.F., Shegog, R., Markham, C.M., Thiel, M., Baumler, E.R., Addy, R.C., Gabay, E.K., & Emery, S.T. (2015). Efficacy of It's your game-tech: A computer-based sexual health education program for middle school youth. *Journal of Adolescent Health, 56*(5), 515–521.
67. Scull, T.M., Kupersmidt, J.B., Malik, C.V., & Keefe, E.M. (2018). Examining the efficacy of an mhealth media literacy education program for sexual health promotion in older adolescents attending community college. *Journal of American College Health, 66*(3), 165–177.
68. Vianden, J. (2016). Ties that bind: Academic advisors as agents of student relationship management. *NACADA Journal, 36*(1), 19–29.
69. Jones Jr, L. (2011). *An evaluation of academic advisors' roles in effective retention*. Capella University.
70. Frazier, A.M. (2021). *First-generation college students: Making sense of academic advising and advisor leadership for student success*. University of New England.
71. Swecker, H.K., Fifolt, M., & Searby, L. (2013). Academic advising and first-generation college students: A quantitative study on student retention. *NACADA Journal, 33*(1), 46–53.

20

EMERGING ADULTS' SEXUAL MOTIVES AND BEHAVIORS

Implications for Youth Sexual Health Education

Kayley Davis McMahan and Spencer B. Olmstead

Introduction

Being a contemporary young adult means development in a period with unique experiences and opportunities for exploration and experimentation, referred to as "emerging adulthood."[1] Many emerging adults have numerous opportunities to explore and experiment with various identities and behaviors, deciding what they want for work, relationships, and sex.[1] Often, young adults, particularly college students, explore and experiment with sex during this period. Still, our understanding of their motivations against having sex is limited. The purpose of this chapter is to summarize our empirical article, "Motivations against Sex and Number of Sexual Partners: A Two-Study Replication and Extension," published in the *American Journal of Sexuality Education*, providing an overview of the research on sexual motivations and its application to sexual health education for young adults. After summarizing our studies, we discuss implications for sexual health education for instructors and parents, attending to the college environment, and parent-child sexual communication (PCSC).

Young Adult Sexual Activity and Health

The research on young adult sexuality is often contradictory. On the one hand, it has shown that contemporary young adults (i.e., millennials) have higher sexual partner numbers (approximately 11) compared to the number of partners older cohorts reported during their young adult years, such as GenX'ers (around seven to eight).[2] Research suggests that engaging in casual sex or hookups is normative among young adults,[3] as is having sex regularly in committed romantic relationships.[1,4] Further, adolescents and young adults ages 15–24 account for half of the

DOI: 10.4324/9781003189787-21

20 million new sexually transmitted infections (STIs) diagnosed each year.[5] These statistics suggest that emerging adults have sex often, with several partners, and are at increased risk of STI contraction.

In contrast, other research has shown that young adults are more likely to have no sexual partners as adults compared to GenX'ers,[6] have fewer sexual partners than prior cohorts,[1,4] and have sex less frequently during their young adult years than prior generations.[7] Decreases in teen and young adult pregnancy suggest that abstinence may be increasingly common.[8] These statistics indicate that emerging adults are not engaging in sex or having sex less often and with fewer people. Identifying and understanding these discrepancies is important, and studying young adults' motivations for and against sex can provide further insight into their sexual behaviors, which has implications for sexual health education.

Sexual Health Education and Sexual Motives

Comprehensive sexual health education for young adults is necessary to increase knowledge and decrease engagement in risky behaviors.[9] Evidence-based comprehensive sexual health education yields a variety of desirable outcomes, including appreciation for sexual diversity, dating and intimate partner violence prevention, the development of healthy relationships, and improved contraceptive and perceived STI knowledge.[10,11] The Centers for Disease Control and Prevention (CDC) recommends that sexual health education programs include content discussing how culture, family, media, peers, technology, and "other factors" influence sexual behavior.[12] These CDC recommendations do not explicitly mention sexual motives, but research indicates that college students benefit from sexual health education programs tailored to their sexual motivations.[13] It is unclear whether comprehensive programs consistently include information on sexual motives in curricula.

What Are Sexual Motives?

Motivations for and against sex have been defined and studied in various ways. In the 1980s and 1990s, scholars began to examine the "reasons" for having or avoiding sex[14] or "reasons" for virginity.[15] Others examined "motives" or "motivations" for having or not having sex.[13,16] More recent studies have followed these approaches, examining "reasons" for abstinence or sexual activity,[17–20] and "motivations" for or against sex.[21–26]

What exactly is a sexual motivation? There are two types of motives: approach and avoidance.[27,28] Approach motives drive us to pursue certain behaviors or outcomes, whereas avoidance motives direct us away from undesirable behaviors or outcomes.[27–29] In other words, we are motivated to either pursue things that are desirable, positive, or wanted (approach) or avoid things that are undesirable, negative, or unwanted (avoidance). Motives are also self-focused or other-focused. We can be motivated to enact certain behaviors or pursue certain outcomes out of self-interest or in relation to others.[13,29]

In the present studies, we focused on motivations against sex, which are avoidance-oriented motives. Specifically, we examined these using the Motivations Against Sex Questionnaire (MASQ),[26] which measures value, health, and not feeling ready as motives against sex. Value motives are moral or ethical oppositions to sexual activity. Health motives include the desire to avoid pregnancy and STIs. Not feeling ready motives are the feelings that one is not emotionally ready to have sex or not ready because they have not found the right person with whom to have sex.[26]

Replication and Extension of Prior Research

Prior research has examined various factors related to sexual motivations, including gender, race, and sexual experience. Specifically, studies have shown that women tend to have more motives against sex than men.[18,20,26] Black[20] and Asian American[26] youth tend to endorse more motives against sex than White youth. Youth with less sexual experience tend to have more value and not ready motives against sex, but youth with more sexual experience have more health motives against sex.[26] In our first study, we examined how these factors were related to young adults' motivations against sex.

We also sought to extend prior research and examine how relationship type, religiosity, and casual sex attitudes were related to motivations against sex. Being more religious may be associated with value motives against sex. Studies have examined how reasons for abstinence or virginity are informed by and associated with religious beliefs,[17,18,20] but studies have not examined specifically how motivations against sex are related to religiosity. It is important to distinguish motivations for abstinence or virginity and motivations against sex, as sexually active individuals can still endorse motives against sex, and abstinent individuals can still have motives for sex.

Prior research on motivations for sex and relationship type shows that those in committed relationships endorse intimacy-focused motives for sex, and those in non-committed relationships (e.g., casual sex) endorse more pleasure-focused motives.[13,21] Findings from our research on young adults' motives for sex showed that those in committed relationships had more pleasure-focused *and* intimacy-focused motives for sex, and those in non-committed relationships had more coping-focused motives.[24] These findings indicate that the context of young adults' relationships may be related to their motivations against sex, in addition to their motives for sex.

We also examined how attitudes toward casual sex were associated with motivations against sex. Emerging adults that were more permissive or accepting of casual sex reported more pleasure and coping motives and fewer intimacy motives.[24] We expected that young adults with less permissive or accepting casual sex attitudes would have more motivations against sex.

We also sought to extend prior research by examining the relationship between motivations against sex and the number of lifetime sexual partners. Contemporary emerging adults tend to have a greater number of sexual partners compared to prior cohorts.[2,30] Having more sexual partners increases the potential for unplanned pregnancy and exposure to STIs.[4,31] Although young adults today tend to have a greater number of lifetime sexual partners, some report fewer.[1,4] We expected that young adults with more motivations against sex would report fewer lifetime sexual partners.

Current Study

To continue to improve sexual health education, we must examine young adult sexual motives and consider what factors (e.g., gender, sexual attitudes) are related to motivations for and against sex and how these motivations are related to actual sexual behavior. Doing so will help us understand emerging adults' sexual motives and how these motives are related to risky and healthy sexual behaviors and practices. The purposes of our studies were to examine how various characteristics, attitudes, and experiences were related to young adults' motivations against sex and how these motivations against sex were related to young adults' number of sexual partners.

We conducted two distinct studies. Data were collected in the fall 2014 (Study 1) and spring 2015 (Study 2) semesters. There were 573 subjects in Study 1 and 859 subjects in Study 2, and the studies were similar in demographic characteristics (see Table 20.1). For a detailed overview of our study procedures, measures, and analyses, see our article.[23]

Brief Overview of Findings

As noted earlier, Study 1 examined how various demographic characteristics and known correlates were related to young adults' motivations against sex. On average, participants held less permissive attitudes toward casual sex and were moderately religious. Most (58%) had engaged in vaginal and/or anal intercourse, followed by no sexual experience (29%) and experience with oral sex only (13%). Participants reported more health motivations against sex than value motivations and not feeling ready motivations against sex.

We found that participants who were women, heterosexual, more religious, sexually inexperienced, and those with less permissive casual sex attitudes reported more value motivations against sex. Racial/ethnic minorities and those with less permissive casual sex attitudes reported more health motivations against sex. Finally, participants who were women, sexually inexperienced, and those with less permissive casual sex attitudes reported more not ready motivations against sex.

TABLE 20.1 Study 1 and 2 Demographic Information

Demographic variables (M (SD)/%)	*Study 1 (N = 573)*	*Study 2 (N = 859)*
Age	19.1 (1.17, range = 18 – 25)	19.1 (1.04, range = 18 – 24)
Gender (% female)	68.4	53.1
Race/Ethnicity		
White/Caucasian	85.9	84.2
Black/African American	5.6	6.9
Asian American/Pacific Islander	3.8	4.0
Latino/a or Hispanic	2.1	2.2
Native American/ American Indian	–	0.5
Other	2.6	2.2
Sexual Orientation		
Heterosexual	93.5	96.0
Bisexual	3.1	1.7
Gay/lesbian	1.4	1.3
Unsure	1.2	0.7
Other	0.7	0.3
Year in College		
First	49.9	72.3
Second	34.9	17.3
Third	9.4	7.0
Fourth	5.4	2.9
Other	0.3	0.5
Relationship Status		
No relationship	47.1	41.8
Casual relationship	14.1	16.6
Committed relationship	38.7	41.6

In Study 2, which examined how motivations against sex were related to lifetime sexual partner number, participants reported more health motivations against sex than value motivations and not ready motivations against sex. The average number of sexual partners was 3.4. We found that having more value motivations and not ready motivations against sex were related to having fewer lifetime sexual partners, whereas having more health motivations against sex was associated with greater lifetime sexual partner numbers. A typical participant in the sample (with the average level of all three motivations against sex) would have an average of 3.2 sexual partners. Participants with the highest level of all three motivations would have 1.9 sexual partners, and participants with the lowest level of all three motivations would have 4.5 sexual partners. Our findings suggest that health motivations against sex may be motivations for safer sex rather than motives against sex.

Implications for Sexual Health Education

We recommend that sexual health interventions emphasize the unique effects of casual sex attitudes, religiosity, sexual experience, gender, sexual orientation, and race/ethnicity on motivations and the relationship between each motive and sexual partner numbers.[12] Research has shown that it may be beneficial for people to identify their motivations for and against sex as part of sexual health education programs.[13] Sexual health educators should resist assigning personal moral preference to abstaining from or engaging in sexual activity; they should highlight the relationship between these characteristics (e.g., gender, sexual orientation, religiosity) and motivations for and against sex.

Future research should examine how various characteristics, motivations, and partner number are causally related. Specifically, we recommend that studies pursue identifying how motivations against (and for) sex are developed and whether these motives are causally related to sexual partner number or vice versa. Doing so will help educators identify key points for education and intervention in the life course.

College Sexual Health Programming

Our research has implications for sexual health education. College students benefit from programs that are tailored to their sexual motives.[13] Our motivations for or against sex are not always rational.[30] Thus, young adults may not even be aware of their sexual motives or how these characteristics are influencing them. Being knowledgeable about these relationships may promote intentional decision-making for engaging in sexual activity.

We do not maintain the position that sexual activity is inherently risky. Rather, we emphasize how important positive sexuality perspectives are and recommend that programs include this perspective. It is important to note that there are risks associated with sexual activity, particularly as sexual partner numbers increase (e.g., unplanned pregnancy, STI).[4,31] Many contemporary young adults have more sexual partners than prior cohorts during their young adult years.[2,30] Thus, educators and parents should know how some demographic characteristics (e.g., gender) and cultural norms and scripts (e.g., religiosity, attitudes toward casual sex) are associated with young adults' sexual motives, and in turn, how these motives are related to sexual behaviors.

For example, parents and educators should be aware that some motivations against sex, specifically health motivations, are actually related to having more sexual partners and be prepared to discuss these relationships with young adults. Young adults should be aware of the risks associated with having more sexual partners. Still, educators and parents should also emphasize positive, healthy sexuality and teach youth to minimize sexual risks. In classroom settings, instructors can incorporate discussions of sexual motivations in units on sexual behaviors and sexual development during the corresponding developmental stage. For example, in a college setting, instructors could ask the following discussion question:

> During young adulthood, many college students have various motivations for and against sex. Research has shown that some college students are motivated not to have sex to avoid pregnancy and STIs actually have more sexual partners. Why would health-focused motivations against sex be related to having more sexual partners?

Next, instructors could facilitate a discussion about how young adults who have sex may be more aware of and focused on health risks and discuss how to minimize these risks. The discussion could then shift focus to methods of contraception and STI prevention.

Our research has provided insight into how young adults' motivations against sex are related to various characteristics and behaviors. Still, the field would benefit from collecting samples in other developmental periods, particularly during adolescence. According to the CDC,[32] 38% of US high school students surveyed in 2019 had engaged in sexual intercourse, and of those, 9% had at least four sexual partners. Thus, understanding these relationships during early and later adolescence will inform how we approach these discussions with teenagers.

Parent-Child Sexual Communication

Emerging adults identify parents and family members as prominent sources of influence on their sexual expectations, including the sexual selves they hope for and wish to avoid becoming in the future.[33] Parent-child sexual communication (PCSC) can play a critical role in helping to shape adolescents' and young adults' motivations for and against engaging in sexual activity. A variety of factors influence engagement in PCSC, including parents' attitudes about sexual communication, their perceptions of others' expectations for them to talk with their kids about sex, and how confident they are in their knowledge on sexual topics.[34] These factors have been shown to influence parents' intentions to engage in PCSC on a variety of topics, including basic components of sex (anatomy, contraception, STIs), pleasurable aspects of sex, sex within the context of relationships, sexual orientation and gender identities, and the possible religious meanings of sex.[34]

Many of these topics overlap with motivations against engaging in sexual activity. For example, value motives against sex are consistent with discussions regarding religious meanings for sex. Research has shown that these topics are more likely to be discussed when parents are religious[35] and are typically more conservative in their values about sex.[36] Young adults reported that parents' values about sex are communicated during PCSC, but that they diverge in that some are more open or accepting regarding sexual activity, whereas others are more restrictive.[37]

Teens who perceived their parents' values as more conservative reported messages from parents focused more on abstaining from sexual activity. Also, health motives to avoid sexual activity are consistent with messages around some of the "basics" in PCSC, including anatomy, contraception, pregnancy, sexual violence, and STIs.[37] Parents of young children often report intending to engage in PCSC on this topic, which was positively related to parents' feelings of competence to communicate on these basics aspects.[34] Last, not feeling ready motives against sex may overlap PCSC on matters of sexual activity within the context of romantic relationships. A recent research team's measure of this topic included items that focused on expectations for meeting sexual partners' needs and having discussions with sexual partners about sex.[34] These topics may be influential in helping adolescents and young adults determine whether they are ready to take steps toward becoming sexually active. Thus, it seems important to promote PCSC and reduce barriers to these discussions, as motives for engaging in sex appear likely to be influenced by parent-child discussions about sex.

PCSC can be enhanced in a number of ways. For example, another research study[37] reported that many emerging adults perceived their sexual discussions with parents as awkward. They included scare tactics, were closed in communication (one direction, from parent to child), included an emphasis on abstinence, or were absent altogether. They recommended (and we concur) that PCSC should be characterized by parental support and engaging in open dialogue around a variety of topics about sex, that such discussions should begin before adolescent involvement in sexual activity, and that the use of scare tactics by parents is less effective. Parents have the potential to influence their children's motivations for avoiding sex, which may reduce the number of sexual partners they report later in emerging adulthood. Communications about sex and the conveying of values, discussion about basic aspects of sex, and feelings around readiness for sex all can and should be interwoven into discussions parents have with their children about sex.

Conclusion

This chapter provided a brief overview of our research on motivations against sex with a discussion of implications for sexual health education and PCSC. We recommend this chapter as a resource for sexual health educators and parents who want to incorporate information on sexual motives and behaviors in their discussions with children, adolescents, and young adults.

References

1. Arnett, J.J. (2015). *Emerging adulthood: The winding road from the late teens through the early twenties*, 2nd ed. Oxford University Press.
2. Twenge, J.M., Sherman, R.A., & Wells, B.E. (2015). Changes in American adults' sexual behavior and attitudes, 1972–2012. *Archives of Sexual Behavior, 44*(8), 2273–2285. https://doi.org/10.1007/s10508-015-0540-2

3. Garcia, J.R., Reiber, C., Massey, S.G., & Merriwether, A.M. (2012). Sexual hookup culture: A review. *Review of General Psychology, 16*(2), 161–176. https://doi.org/10.1037/a0027911
4. Regnerus, M., & Uecker, J. (2011). *Premarital sex in America: How young Americans meet, mate, and think about marrying*. Oxford University Press.
5. Centers for Disease Control and Prevention. (2019a). *Sexually transmitted disease surveillance 2018*. U.S. Department of Health and Human Services. https://doi.org/10.15620/cdc.79370
6. Twenge, J.M., Sherman, R.A., & Wells, B.E. (2017a). Sexual inactivity during young adulthood is more common among U.S. Millennials and iGen: Age, period, and cohort effects on having no sexual partners after age 18. *Archives of Sexual Behavior, 46*(2), 433–440. https://doi.org/10.1007/s10508-016-0798-z
7. Twenge, J.M., Sherman, R.A., & Wells, B.E. (2017b). Declines in sexual frequency among American adults, 1989–2014. *Archives of Sexual Behavior, 46*, 2389–2401. https://doi.org/10.1007/s10508-017-0953-1
8. Centers for Disease Control and Prevention. (2019b). *About teen pregnancy*. www.cdc.gov/teenpregnancy/about/index.htm
9. Fields, J., Gilbert, J., & Miller, M. (2015). Sexuality and education: Toward the promise of ambiguity. In. J. DeLamater, & R.F. Plante (Eds.), *Handbook of the Sociology of Sexualities* (pp. 371–388). Springer.
10. Goldfarb, E.S., & Lieberman, L.D. (2021). Three decades of research: The case for comprehensive sex education. *Journal of Adolescent Health, 68*, 13–27. https://doi.org/10.1016/j.jadohealth.2020.07.036
11. McMahan, K.D., Olmstead, S.B., Conrad, K.A., & Bluhm, J.E. (2021). Effectiveness of a brief sexual health seminar at improving contraception and sexually transmitted infection knowledge among first-semester college students. *Sexuality Research and Social Policy*. https://doi.org/10.1007/s13178-021-00649-9
12. Brener, N.D., Demissie, Z., McManus, T., Shanklin, S.L., Queen, B., & Kann, L. (2017). *School health profiles 2016: Characteristics of health programs among secondary schools*. CDC. www.cdc.gov/healthyyouth/data/profiles/pdf/2016/2016_Profiles_Report.pdf
13. Cooper, M.L., Shapiro, C.M., & Powers, A.M. (1998). Motivations for sex and risky sexual behavior among adolescents and young adults: A functional perspective. *Journal of Personality and Social Psychology, 75*(6), 1528–1558. https://doi.org/10.1037/00223514.75.6.1528
14. Leigh, B.C. (1989). Reasons for having and avoiding sex: Gender, sexual orientation, and relationship to sexual behavior. *Journal of Sex Research, 26*(2), 199–209. https://doi.org/10.1080/00224498909551506
15. Sprecher, S. & Regan, P.C. (1996). College virgins: How men and women perceive their sexual status. *Journal of Sex Research, 33*(1), 3–15. https://doi.org/10.1080/00224499609551810
16. Hill, C.A., & Preston, L.K. (1996). Individual differences in the experience of sexual motivation: Theory, and measurement of dispositional sexual motives. *Journal of Sex Research, 33*(1), 27–45. https://doi.org/10.1080/00224499609551812
17. Abbott, D.A., & Dalla, R.L. (2008). "It's a choice, simple as that": Youth reasoning for sexual abstinence or activity. *Journal of Youth Studies, 11*(6), 629–649. https://doi.org/10.1080/13676260802225751
18. Byers, E.S., O'Sullivan, L.F., & Brotto, L.A. (2016). Time out from sex or romance: Sexually experienced adolescents' decisions to purposefully avoid sexual activity or romantic relationships. *Journal of Youth and Adolescence, 45*(5), 831–845. https://doi.org/10.1007/s10964-016-0447-9

19. Meston, C.M. & Buss, D.M. (2007). Why humans have sex. *Archives of Sexual Behavior, 36*, 477–507. https://doi.org/10.1007/s10508-007-9175-2
20. Sprecher, S., & Treger, S. (2015). Virgin college students' reasons for and reactions to their abstinence from sex: Results from a 23-year study at a Midwestern U.S. university. *The Journal of Sex Research, 52*(8), 936–948. https://doi.org/10.1080/00224499.2014.983633
21. Armstrong, H.L. & Reissing, E.D. (2015). Women's motivations to have sex in casual and committed relationships with male and female partners. *Archives of Sexual Behavior, 44*(4), 921–934. https://doi.org/10.1007/s10508-014-0462-4
22. Jardin, C., Garey, L., & Zvolensky, M.J. (2017). Measuring sexual motives: A test of the psychometric properties of the sexual motivations scale. *The Journal of Sex Research, 54*(9), 1209–1219. https://doi.org/10.1080/00224499.2016.1238031
23. McMahan, K.D., & Olmstead, S.B. (2020). Motivations against sex and number of sexual partners: A two-study replication and extension. *American Journal of Sexuality Education, 15*, 287–309. https://doi.org/10.1080/15546128.2020.1763881
24. McMahan, K.D., & Olmstead, S.B. (2021). Are college students' perceptions of the developmental features of emerging adulthood associated with motivations for sex? Implications for research and policy. *Sexuality Research and Social Policy, 18*(2), 450–464. https://doi.org/10.1007/s13178-020-00457-7
25. Patrick, M.E. & Maggs, J.E. (2010). Profiles of motivations for alcohol use and sexual behavior among first-year university students. *Journal of Adolescence, 33*(5), 755–765. https://doi.org/10.1016/j.adolescence.2009.10.003
26. Patrick, M.E., Maggs, J.L., Cooper, M.L., & Lee, C.M. (2011). Measurement of motivations for and against sexual behavior. *Assessment, 18*(4), 502–516. https://doi.org/10.1177/107319111037229
27. Gray, J.A. (1970). The psychophysiological basis of introversion-extroversion. *Behavior Research and Therapy, 8*, 249–266. https://doi.org/10.1016/0005-7967(70)90069-0
28. Gray, J.A. (1987). Perspectives on anxiety and impulsivity: A commentary. *Journal of Research in Personality, 21*, 493–509. https://doi. org/10.1016/0092–6566(87)90036–5
29. Cooper, M.L., Barber, L.L., Zhaoyang, R., & Talley, A.E. (2011). Motivational pursuits in the context of human sexual relationships. *Journal of Personality, 79*(6), 1333–1368. https://doi.org/10.1111/j. 1467–6494.2010.00713.x
30. Lefkowitz, E.S., & Gillen, M.M. (2006). "Sex is just a normal part of life": Sexuality in emerging adulthood. In J.J. Arnett, & J.L. Tanner (Eds.), *Emerging adults in America: Coming of age in the 21st century* (pp. 235–255). American Psychological Association.
31. Snyder, A.R. (2006). Risky and casual sexual relationships among teens. In A.C. Crouter, & A. Booth (Eds.), *Romance and sex in adolescence and emerging adulthood: Risks and opportunities* (pp. 161–169). Routledge.
32. Centers for Disease Control and Prevention. (2021). *Sexual risk behaviors can lead to HIV, STDs, & teen pregnancy*. www.cdc.gov/healthyyouth/sexualbehaviors/index.htm
33. Anders, K.M., & Olmstead, S.B. (2019). A qualitative examination of the sexual possible selves and strategies of first-semester college students: How sexual possible selves are developed during the transition to college. *Archives of Sexual Behavior, 48*(6), 1859–1876. https://doi.org/10.1007/s10508-018-1332-2
34. Astle, S., Toews, M., Topham, G., & Vennum, A. (2021a). To talk or not to talk: An analysis of parents' intentions to talk with children about different sexual topics using the theory of planned behavior. *Sexuality Research and Social Policy*. Advanced online publication. https://doi.org/10.1007/s13178-021-00587-6
35. Regnerus, M.D. (2005). Talking about sex: Religion and patterns of parent-child communication about sex and contraception. *The Sociological Quarterly, 46*(1), 79–105. https://doi.org/10.1111/j.1533-8525.2005.00005.x

36. Lefkowitz, E.S., Gillen, M.M., Shearer, C.L., & Boone, T.L. (2004). Religiosity, sexual behaviors, and sexual attitudes during emerging adulthood. *Journal of Sex Research, 41*(2), 150–159. https://doi.org/10.1080/00224490409552223
37. Astle, S., McAllister, P., Emanuels, S., Rogers, J., Toews, M., & Yazedjian, A. (2021b). Just be open about it or turn up the radio: A qualitative analysis of parent-child sexual communication experiences in adolescence. *Sexuality Research and Social Policy*. Advanced online publication. https://doi.org/10.1007/s13178-020-00530-1

21

WHY LATINO BISEXUAL MEN HAVE SEX

Implications for Sexuality Education and Practice

Jonathan Garcia and Miguel Muñoz-Laboy

Scientific and popular literature has indirectly portrayed bisexual men as vectors of disease, many times implying blame for the HIV/AIDS epidemic crossing into heterosexual populations.[1–3] This sole focus on HIV, rather than on sexuality more generally, has limited the knowledge generated about the motivations for bisexual Latino men to have sex with their partners.[4]

Knowing what drives people to have sex can shed light on sex's functions and benefits.[5] One model describes four basic sexual motivations that frame our understanding of bisexual Latino men's sexual motives.[6]

1. **Acceptance.** Although approval and acceptance are central aspects of the sexual experience, the drive to seek them can have unintended consequences, including anxiety, condomless sex, dissatisfaction with sex, and intimate partner violence.[7–9]
2. **Comfort and relief from distress.** Those prone to use sex to gain approval may also use sex for comfort and relief from distress. Stress reduction is an important, unexamined dimension of the bisexual Latino men's experience. Bisexual Latino men experience enhanced stressors in their social environments because of systemic racial-ethnic discrimination, homonegativity, biphobia, and discrimination against non-heterosexual forms of sexual expression.[10]
3. **Power.** Sex is a way to control or exert power over one's partner. Regaining control and power, thus, may be critical for groups that experience systems of oppression, such as hypermasculine ideologies of masculinity or machismo. Machismo reinforces expectations of what it means to be a man, including virility, dominance over partners, and immediate gratification.[11,12]

DOI: 10.4324/9781003189787-22

4. **Nurturance and procreation.** The desire to procreate and nurture may drive sex. This need can be satisfied by having someone to love, having someone to take care of, and being needed and loved by a child.[8] Culturally, the drive to procreate and nurture can reinforce unequal heterosexual partnerships, gender norms, family arrangements, and religious values. The Roman Catholic Church, the dominant Latinx religious tradition in the United States, promotes sex for procreation and explicitly prohibits contraceptives.[13] Having children can be a way to preserve traditional family values in the transnational context of where Latino gay and bisexual men live in the United States.[14] Maintaining close emotional and physical ties and connectedness to one's families, that is, familismo,[15] is central to the cultural values of many Latinx communities.[16]

The combination of heterosexism, familismo, and religiosity promotes an orientation toward supporting the community's welfare over that of the individual, also referred to as collectivism. Collectivism may lead to distress for those not conforming to expressions not deemed acceptable by their communities.[17,18]

Our study advanced sexual education by exploring these four dimensions among bisexual Latino men. We used the AMORE scale[5] dimensions (i.e., pleasure, nurturance, power enhancement, experiencing sexual partner's power/dominance, stress relief, and procreation) to measure the concepts used in the sexual motivations framework. Our research objectives were to (1) describe bisexual men's hierarchy of motivations to have sex through their scoring of AMORE scale dimensions; (2) examine the associations between bisexual Latino men's sexual motivations and three distress indicators: perceived stress, symptoms of severe anxiety, and depression in the past seven days; and (3) examine the influences of cultural constructs in Latino social environments (i.e., machismo, familismo, and religiosity) on the types of motivations to have sex for bisexual Latino men. This chapter provides implications for sexuality education and therapeutic services for bisexual Latino men.

Bisexual Latino Men in Our Study

This chapter is based on survey results from 148 interviews and surveys with bisexual Latino men (18–49 years old) in New York and New Jersey. Behaviorally, they needed to report having had sex with a least one man and one woman within the last six months. In terms of identity, 34% self-identified as bisexual, 24% identified as bisexual and straight depending on the context, 31% identified as bisexually active with no labels, and 11% as gay and bisexual depending on the context. In our sample, 61% had impregnated a woman, 41% had children under 18, and the average number of children per individual was two (see Table 21.1).

In the prior six months, the men in the study had (oral, anal, and/or vaginal) sex with a total of 374 cis-women; 560 cis-men; 107 male-to-female, and 39 female-to-male transgender partners. The average proportion of condom use for all penetrative

TABLE 21.1 Sample Background Characteristics of Bisexual Latino Men (148 Subjects, New York-New Jersey Metropolitan Areas, 2009–2014)

Characteristic	%[19]
Age (years)	
Below 29	41
30–49	60
Marital status	
Married to cis woman	11
Married to cis man, trans man or trans woman	0
Education (Highest attainment)	
Elementary, middle school, or incomplete high school (HS)	31
HS or Graduate Equivalency Degree (GED) with/without Vocational education (e.g., plumbing)	27
1–2 years college or completed college/university degree	40
Employment (Current Status/Type)	
Unemployed	11
Administrative/managerial, sale and/or retail	39
Protective, household, or other services; Technicians	46
Daily workers, mechanics, repairers, construction workers, farmers, or groundskeepers	15
Annual individual income (salaries, wages, official and unofficial sources)	
< USD $14,999	53
USD $15,000—$49,000	30
> USD $50,000	17
Birthplace/Ethnic-national ancestry	
United States (mainland, Hawaii, or Alaska)	35
Born in US territory or foreign-born	65
Sexual partner general configurations (past two months)	
Only casual partners (cis man, cis woman, trans woman, and/or trans man)	11
Two primary partners (cis woman + cis man)	24
Only one primary partner (cis man/woman, and/or trans woman/man) plus casual partner/s	65
Reproductive characteristics	
Impregnated a cis woman at least once during lifetime	61
Average number of children (mean)	2
Currently have children (below 18 years of age)	41
Are you trying to get a woman pregnant now (% answered "Yes")	4
I'm very committed to not getting a woman pregnant at this time in my life (% answered "Yes")	83
My current female partner and I are trying to get pregnant (% answered "Yes")	2

intercourse sexual encounters in the past two months was 74%. The entire sample was HIV negative and not taking Pre-exposure prophylaxis (PrEP) medication at the time of the study. In terms of the use of contraceptives methods: 88% used condoms to prevent pregnancy; 40% of the female partners were on oral hormonal contraceptives; 29% were using rhythm method or withdrawal; 19% of the female partners were using an intrauterine device (IUD);17% used spermicide; 9% of the female partners were using Norplant or Depo Provera shot; and, none reported having a vasectomy. Close to a third of the sample (30%) reported ejaculating inside a female partner with no contraceptive method used by themselves or their partners. Box 1 shows the ranked reasons for sex reported by the men in our study.

BOX 1 RANKED MOTIVATIONS FOR SEX (AMORE SCALE)

1. Pleasure
2. Nurturance
3. Power enhancement and control
4. Stress relief
5. Experiencing a woman's power during sex
6. Experiencing a man's power during sex
7. Procreation

Depressive Symptoms and Sex for Stress Relief

In this study, the prevalence of severe depression for bisexual Latino men (26%) more than tripled the US general population (8%).[20] Considering their discriminatory social context, we expected that sex for stress-relief motives would be associated with high levels of depressive symptoms in the previous seven days.

Experiencing severe depressive symptoms was associated with higher agreement with the motivation of having sex to relieve stress. Sex may serve as a form of psychosocial relief for men dealing with depressive symptoms.[21] The chronic accumulation of depressive symptoms may lead to sexual impairments over time.[22] Thus, therapists working with bisexual Latino men who viewed sex as a form of stress relief and are experiencing severe symptoms of depression may consider discussing the notion of sex as a stress relief when addressing depression symptoms with clients. This is particularly important if there is depression-related sexual impairment where the notion of sex as a stress relief can cause further distress in the individual.

Searching for Power

Machismo is an indicator of a hypermasculinity focused on power, dominance, and control over others, but by no means is this is the only expression of masculinity in Latin America. In itself, masculinity is not a static, monolithic cultural construct across Latin American societies or Latinx communities in the United States.[23] As anticipated, motivations to feel powerful, for pleasure, and to nurture were related to higher levels of machismo.

Machismo values may explain why bisexual Latino men in our sample viewed sex as a power-enhancement tool. Viewing sex as a form of enhancing power, feeling dominant or in control during sexual encounters might not be problematic if egalitarian values, respect, and consent are central to the sexual dynamic. However, the machismo-power enhancement motive association could potentially increase inter-partner conflict and violence, an area that remains largely unexamined in bisexuality studies among racial-ethnic minorities. What we do know is that high levels of machismo among Latino men have been associated with inter-personal violence, gender-based violence, self-harming behaviors, including binge substance use, and driving while intoxicated.[24]

The association between machismo and nurturance as a motive for sex may indicate an attempt to control the sexual partnership dynamic. It may also reflect cultural values such as "caballerismo" (chivalry) that intersect with dimensions of machismo.[16] Neither chivalry nor sexual partnership dynamics were measured in this study. Future research should examine bisexual Latino men's masculinity to provide insights into nurturing motives for bisexual sex. It may question whether the desire to nurture is determined by the gender of the partner. Research may also explore if gender equity characterizes masculinity among younger generations.

Pleasure is often overlooked in sex education and sexual health programming for populations at high risk for HIV acquisition.[25,26] Pleasure-driven (i.e., sex-positive) interventions for bisexual Latinx men, women, and transgender individuals are invisible in the public health landscape. That said, the pleasure-machismo association that we found in our study is potentially problematic to the sexual health of bisexual Latino men. This association might suggest that those who score high in the machismo scale might value immediate gratification more than others who score lower in the machismo scale.[27] Decision-making that only accounts for short-term health risks has been associated with the desire for instant gratification, increasing the likelihood of sexual risk-taking practices.[28]

If machismo is an expression of patriarchy,[29] homosexual comfortability suggests a transgression of machismo ideals. Thus, the association between homosexual comfortability and experiencing a man's power during sex suggests the continuing importance of homosexual comfortability among bisexual Latino men who frequently experience homophobic and biphobic messages.[30,31]

Experiencing a woman's power during sex seems to be associated with higher levels of familismo. The benefits of the emotional support derived from familismo[32,33] might provide the tools for bisexual Latino men to transgress machismo norms. In the same vein, the emotional connectedness to familial networks that characterizes familismo might serve as an opportunity to adhere to oppositional machismo-related motives for sex, such as experiencing a woman's power during sex. Familismo is a variable construct in its effect on the sexual health of people who do not conform to heterosexuality.[34] Further research is needed to examine under which circumstances familismo can facilitate anti-patriarchal expressions of bisexuality.

Procreation Motives

Bisexual Latino men, women, and transgender individuals' reproductive attitudes and practices are largely unexamined. Our findings provide initial insights into the role of procreation in bisexual Latino men's motives for sex. Latinx cultural constructs, such as machismo, familismo, and religiosity,[35,36] have been traditionally associated with reproductive behaviors. However, these were not associated with procreation motives for sex in our sample.

However, we found a direct positive association between procreation motives for sex and both levels of perceived stress and having severe symptoms of anxiety. Given the nature of available data, reverse causation is possible. Bisexual Latino men experiencing high levels of stress or anxiety may seek to satisfy their emotional needs by having children, an association that others have found based on potential psychosocial gains of parenthood.[8] Another possibility is that those individuals with high levels of stress or anxiety might be more likely to internalize cultural-social norms of procreation motives for sex than those experiencing lower levels of perceived stress and anxiety symptoms.

We had expected that those without a history of children or impregnations would report more agreement with sex as procreative, but the opposite seems to be occurring for bisexual Latino men in our sample. We found that the experience of impregnating a woman might increase procreation motives for sex. This suggests several lines of further research, for example, exploring how impregnation, having a child, and involvement in the child's life (broken down into different types of involvement including emotional, financial, protection support) affect the role of procreation as a motive for sex through the adult sex life.

From a sexuality education and therapy perspective, discussing the stressors that lead to the motivation of sex as a stress relief method might be important to support the psychologically healthy sexual lives of bisexual Latinx communities. Similarly, discussing procreation motives for sex can be an opportunity to discuss general anxieties related to bisexual Latino men's sexual experiences. Our findings also suggest that sexual motivations are influenced by Latino bisexual men's masculinity and perceived stress, anxiety, and depression symptoms.

Limitations

This study has several limitations. As stated earlier, sexual motivations are complex. This analysis used the AMORE questionnaire to indicate sexual motives, demonstrating construct and internal validity. Another limitation is that we did not randomly select individuals; thus, self-selection bias is a potential sampling limitation. We minimized self-selection bias by not sharing the eligibility criteria for the study. Our evidence is limited in determining how exclusively self-identified bisexual men reconcile their motives for sex, experience distress indicators, and adhere to Latinx cultural constructs. The cross-sectional study design limits our ability to make causal arguments.

Conclusion

Despite the decades of educational efforts, much invisibility exists regarding the sexual organization of desires of double minority groups such as bisexual Latino men.[37–39] Depression and anxiety are major health-threatening issues affecting bisexual Latino men. Experiencing symptoms of severe depression was associated with the likelihood of viewing sex as stress relief. Experiencing symptoms of severe anxiety and reporting high levels of everyday stress was associated with viewing sex for procreative purposes. Both are concerning given the limited reproductive health education geared toward bisexual individuals and the invisibility of addressing bisexuality in mental health services, the stigmatization of mental health services, and low depression literacy in Latinx communities.[40–42]

Furthermore, because of the immediacy of dealing with men's proximal health factors, such as unprotected sexual behavior and substance use, core determinants of men's health, such as untreated symptoms of severe depression and anxiety, have remained secondary the scope of bisexual men's health programming. These analyses outline the key motives for sex for bisexual Latino men. Latinx cultural constructs did not significantly predict most of the motives for sex examined in this study, except machismo. Together with depression, machismo is a potential core determinant of Latino bisexual men's health.

In the most recent HIV surveillance report of the New York City, new diagnoses among men declined in 2017 by 4% from 2016. However, while new diagnoses and the HIV diagnosis rate among Black men decreased during this period, new diagnoses and the HIV diagnosis rate increased among Latino men.[43] This motivated recent campaigns, such as *¡Listos!* in New York City.[44] *¡Listos!* uses sex-positive education to promote the uptake of PrEP use among Latino men who have sex with men. Although a sex-positive approach that accounts for Latino culture is an important step forward, the specificity of this campaign on HIV prevention reduces the social experiences of bisexual Latino men, who would benefit from sexuality education that more broadly incorporates masculinity, procreation, and sexual desire for men and women.[30] Sexuality education programs and sexual health-promoting interventions targeting Latino bisexual men's machismo are needed to focus on questioning and reconfiguring traditional notions of hyper-masculinity. For bisexual men who experience structural stigma related to cultural and political context, online sexuality education may be particularly accessible.[45] Online telenovela web series may be a useful way to deliver effective education for bisexual Latino men.[46] For example, Sin Vergüenza focuses on HIV prevention but contextualizes the Latinx experience, accounting for family dynamics, notions of masculinity, and sexuality.[47] Sexuality education that focuses on the social experiences of bisexual men will provide much-needed visibility and address stigma associated with bisexuality.

References

1. Chu, S.Y., Peterman, T.A., Doll, L.S., Buehler, J.W., & Curran, J.W. (1992). AIDS in bisexual men in the United States: Epidemiology and transmission to women. *American Journal of Public Health*, *82*(2), 220–224.
2. Jones, R. (2010). Troubles with bisexuality in health and social care. In R.L. Jones, & R. Ward (Eds.), *LGBT issues: Looking beyond categories. Policy and Practice in Health and Social Care* (vol. 10., pp. 42–55). Dunedin Academic Press.
3. Muñoz-Laboy, M.A. (2004). Beyond 'MSM': Sexual desire among bisexually-active Latino men in New York City. *Sexualities*, 7(1), 55–80.
4. Because the Spanish word Latino implies male as default identity, in this chapter, we will use Latino when referring to bisexual cis-men, and, we will use Latinx when referring to the larger community to be inclusive of cis-women, cis-men, and transgender individuals.
5. Hill, C.A., & Preston, L.K. (1996). Individual differences in the experience of sexual motivation: Theory and measurement of dispositional sexual motives. *Journal of Sex Research*, *33*(1), 27–45.
6. Davis, D., Shaver, P.R., & Vernon, M.L. (2004). Attachment style and subjective motivations for sex. *Personality and Social Psychology Bulletin*, *30*(8), 1076–1090.
7. Davis, D., Shaver, P.R., & Vernon, M.L. (2003). Physical, emotional, and behavioral reactions to breaking up: The roles of gender, age, emotional involvement, and attachment style. *Personality and Social Psychology Bulletin*, *29*(7), 871–884.
8. Feeney, J.A., Kelly, L., Gallois, C., Peterson, C., & Terry, D.J. (1999). Attachment style, assertive communication, and safer-sex behavior. *Journal of Applied Social Psychology*, *29*(9), 1964–1983.
9. Sprecher, S., Cate, R.M., Harvey, J.H., & Wenzel, A. (2004). Sexual satisfaction and sexual expression as predictors of relationship satisfaction and stability. *The Handbook of Sexuality in Close Relationships*, 235–256.
10. Frost, D.M., Lehavot, K., & Meyer, I.H. (2015). Minority stress and physical health among sexual minority individuals. *Journal of Behavioral Medicine*, *38*(1), 1–8.
11. Cuellar, I., Arnold, B., & Gonzalez, G. (1995). Cognitive referents of acculturation: Assessment of cultural constructs in Mexican Americans. *Journal of Community Psychology*, *23*(4), 339–356.
12. Falicov, C.J. (2010). Changing constructions of machismo for Latino men in therapy: "The devil never sleeps." *Family Process*, *49*(3), 309–329.
13. LeMaire, W.J. (2017). The Roman Catholic Church and contraception. *International Journal of Reproduction, Contraception, Obstetrics and Gynecology*, *5*(6), 2065–2068.
14. Vasquez del Aguila, E. (2014). *Being a man in a transnational world: The masculinity and sexuality of migration*. Routledge.
15. Familismo is used in public health to describe how the family influences Latinx people's definition of responsibility and social support, as well as the decision-making process. Research on COVID-19 vaccine hesitancy indicates familismo can be leveraged to promote health seeking as a way to protect the family. In sexual health, familismo can create barriers to coming out due to the desire to protect the family's respectability. For further reading on familismo, see Garcia, J., Vargas, N., De La Torre, C., Magana, M.,& Clark, J. (2021) *Engaging Latino families about COVID-19 vaccines: A qualitative study conducted*. Health Education and Behavior, https://doi.org/10.1177/10901981211045937; Muñoz-Laboy, M., Ripkin, A., Garcia, J., &

Severson, N. (2015). Family and work influences on stress, anxiety and depression among bisexual Latino men in the New York City Metropolitan Area. *Journal of Immigrant and Minority Health, 17*(6), 1615–1626; and Sabogal, F., Marín, G., Otero-Sabogal, R., Marín, B.V., & Perez-Stable, E. J. (1987). Hispanic familism and acculturation: What changes and what doesn't? *Hispanic Journal of Behavioral Sciences, 9*(4), 397–412.

16. Sabogal, F., Marín, G., Otero-Sabogal, R., Marín, B.V., & Perez-Stable, E.J. (1987). Hispanic familism and acculturation: What changes and what doesn't? *Hispanic Journal of Behavioral Sciences, 9*(4), 397–412.
17. Campos, B., Ullman, J.B., Aguilera, A., & Dunkel Schetter, C. (2014). Familism and psychological health: The intervening role of closeness and social support. *Cultural Diversity and Ethnic Minority Psychology, 20*(2), 191.
18. Realo, A., Allik, J., & Greenfield, B. (2008). Radius of trust: Social capital in relation to familism and institutional collectivism. *Journal of Cross-Cultural Psychology, 39*(4), 447–462.
19. All percentages have been rounded to the nearest whole number.
20. Brody, D.J., Pratt, L.A., Hughes, J. (2018). *Prevalence of depression among adults aged 20 and over: United States, 2013–2016 (NCHS Data Brief, no 303)*. National Center for Health Statistics.
21. Brody, S. (2006). Blood pressure reactivity to stress is better for people who recently had penile—vaginal intercourse than for people who had other or no sexual activity. *Biological Psychology, 71*(2), 214–222.
22. Mills, T.C., Paul, J., Stall, R., Pollack, L., Canchola, J., Chang, Y.J., Moskowitz, J.T, & Catania, J.A. (2004). Distress and depression in men who have sex with men: The Urban Men's Health Study. *American Journal of Psychiatry, 161*(2), 278–285.
23. Arciniega, G.M., Anderson, T.C., Tovar-Blank, Z.G., & Tracey, T.J.G. (2008). Toward a fuller conception of Machismo: Development of a traditional Machismo and Caballerismo Scale. *Journal of Counseling Psychology, 55*(1), 19.
24. Aguirre-Molina, M., Borrell, L.N., & Vega, W. (2010). *Health Issues in Latino Males: A Social and Structural Approach*. Rutgers University Press.
25. Giami, A. (2002). Sexual health: the emergence, development, and diversity of a concept. *Annual Review of Sex Research, 13*(1), 1–35.
26. Robinson, B., Bockting, W.O., Simon Rosser, B.R., Miner, M., & Coleman, E. (2002). The sexual health model: Application of a sexological approach to HIV prevention. *Health Education Research, 17*(1), 43–57.
27. Wood, M.L., & Price, P. (1997). Machismo and marianismo: Implications for HIV/AIDS risk reduction and education. *American Journal of Health Studies, 13*(1), 44.
28. MacDonald, T.K., MacDonald, G., Zanna, M.P., & Fong, G. (2000). Alcohol, sexual arousal, and intentions to use condoms in young men: Applying alcohol myopia theory to risky sexual behavior. *Health Psychology, 19*(3), 290.
29. Mirandé, A. (2018). *Hombres y machos: Masculinity and Latino culture*. Routledge.
30. Diaz, R.M., Ayala, G., Bein, E., Henne, J., & Marin, B.V. (2001). The impact of homophobia, poverty, and racism on the mental health of gay and bisexual Latino men: Findings from 3 US cities. *American Journal of Public Health, 91*(6), 927.
31. Poteat, V.P., DiGiovanni, C.D., & Scheer, J.R. (2013). Predicting homophobic behavior among heterosexual youth: Domain general and sexual orientation-specific factors at the individual and contextual level. *Journal of Youth and Adolescence, 42*(3), 351–362.
32. Calderón-Tena, C.O., Knight, G.P., & Carlo, G. (2011). The socialization of prosocial behavioral tendencies among Mexican American adolescents: The role of familism values. *Cultural Diversity and Ethnic Minority Psychology, 17*(1), 98.
33. Germán, M., Gonzales, N.A., & Dumka, L. (2009). Familism values as a protective factor for Mexican-origin adolescents exposed to deviant peers. *The Journal of Early Adolescence, 29*(1), 16–42.

34. Diaz, R.M. (2013). *Latino gay men and HIV: Culture, sexuality, and risk behavior*. Routledge.
35. Edwards, L.M., Haglund, K., Fehring, R.J., & Pruszynski, J. (2011). Religiosity and sexual risk behaviors among Latina adolescents: trends from 1995 to 2008. *Journal of Women's Health, 20*(6), 871–877.
36. Jimenez, J., Potts, M.K., & Jimenez, D.R. (2002). Reproductive attitudes and behavior among Latina adolescents. *Journal of Ethnic and Cultural Diversity in Social Work, 11*(3–4), 221–249.
37. Barker, M., Richards, C., Jones, R., Bowes-Catton, H., Plowman, T., Yockney, J., & Morgan, M. (2012). *The bisexuality report: Bisexual inclusion in LGBT equality and diversity*.
38. Bostwick, W.B., Boyd, C.J., Hughes, T.L., & McCabe, S.E. (2010). Dimensions of sexual orientation and the prevalence of mood and anxiety disorders in the United States. *American Journal of Public Health, 100*(3), 468–475.
39. Clark, T. (2013). "What's your BiQ?" *American Journal of Sexuality Education, 8*(3), 172–184. https://doi.org/10.1080/15546128.2013.828341.
40. Cabassa, L.J., Hansen, M.C., Palinkas, L.A., & Ell, K. (2008). Azucar y nervios: explanatory models and treatment experiences of Hispanics with diabetes and depression. *Social Science & Medicine, 66*(12), 2413–2424
41. Cabassa, L.J., Molina, G.B., & Baron, M. (2012). Depression fotonovela: Development of a depression literacy tool for Latinos with limited English proficiency. *Health Promotion Practice, 13*(6), 747–754.
42. Hamann, J., Bühner, M., & Rüsch, N. (2017). Self-stigma and consumer participation in shared decision making in mental health services. *Psychiatric Services, 68*(8), 783–788. https://doi.org/10.1176/appi.ps.201600282.
43. New York City Department of Health and Mental Hygiene—NYC DOHMH (2018a). HIV epidemiology and field services program. In *HIV surveillance annual report, 2017*. New York City Department of Health and Mental Hygiene.
44. New York City Department of Health and Mental Hygiene—NYC DOHMH (2018b). *Health department launches "¡Listos!", first-ever campaign promoting HIV prevention medication to Latinos*. https://www1.nyc.gov/site/doh/about/press/pr2018/pr038-18.
45. Currin, J.M., Hubach, R.D., Durham, A.R., Kavanaugh, K.E., Vineyard, Z., & Croff, J.M. (2017). How gay and bisexual men compensate for the lack of meaningful sex education in a socially conservative state. *Sex Education, 17*(6), 667–681
46. Garcia, J., Perez-Brumer, A.G., Cabello, R., & Clark, J.L. (2018). "And then break the cliché": Understanding and addressing HIV vulnerability through development of an HIV prevention telenovela with men who have sex with men and transwomen in Lima, Peru. *Archives of Sexual Behavior, 47*(7), 1995–2005.
47. Sanchez, N., Sandoval, H., Seigmeth, T., Galvez, G., & Rios-Ellis, B. (2013). Telenovelas impact on the public health arena and implications for public health messaging and sustainability: 'Sin verguenza', a four-part telenovela miniseries tackles shame and stigma in the Latino community as part of a routine HIV testing campaign. In *141st APHA annual meeting (November 2—November 6, 2013). APHA*. https://apha.confex.com/apha/141am/webprogramadapt/Paper284192.html.

22

MILLENNIAL PERCEPTIONS OF SEXUALITY

Making the Case for Better Sexuality Education

Sara Hanafi, Julie Lucero, and Karla I. Rodriguez

Introduction

The World Health Organization defines sexual health as "a state of physical, mental and social well-being in relation to sexuality," with sexual choices made in the absence of coercion, discrimination, or violence.[1] This definition highlights the importance of a "positive and respectful approach to sexuality and sexual relationships, as well as the possibility of pleasurable and safe sexual experiences."[1] The ability to make informed choices is based on whether an individual has accurate knowledge of sexual health, including access to quality sexuality education, access to sexual healthcare, exposure to an environment that promotes good sexual health, and knowledge of risk vulnerability. This reasoning is a primary argument for the importance of comprehensive sexual education that begins early in life and carries on well into young adult years. With the ability to make informed choices regarding sexual health, there is a higher likelihood of encouraging young adults to engage in healthy and positive sexual health behaviors that positively influence other areas of their lives.

In the United States, sexuality education programs vary in accuracy, content, and effectiveness. According to the American College of Obstetricians and Gynecologists, comprehensive sexuality education should begin in early childhood. It should be medically accurate, age-appropriate, and emphasize communication, consent, decision-making, healthy relationships, and sexual expression.[2] However, in contrast to other similarly developed countries, the United States has continued to support and promote abstinence-only programs despite consistent evidence of its ineffectiveness.[3] With research demonstrating that young people consistently experience disproportionate consequences of unsafe sex while simultaneously facing the societal controversy of openly discussing positive sexual

DOI: 10.4324/9781003189787-23

health,[4] the need for comprehensive education that highlights positive sexuality cannot be understated.

The recent upsurge of consequences demonstrates the need for new and appropriate strategies. According to the National Conference on State Legislatures, young people currently occupying the 15–24 age range represent 25% of the sexually active population; however, of the approximately 26 million new sexually transmitted infection (STI) cases in 2018, nearly half occurred within the 15–24 age range.[5] Additionally, reported cases of chlamydia and gonorrhea are highest among this group.[4] The generation currently occupying this age range is known as "Generation Z" (aka iGen or Zoomers).[6] In this particular life stage, mental and emotional development is happening at the same time that sexual health behaviors and practices are being explored. This is especially important, as attitudes and behaviors normalized in young adulthood are likely to carry well into adulthood; the cohort just before Generation Z, known as "millennials," refers to those born between 1981 and 1996[5] and are now aged between 26 and 41 years. Given this trend, what we currently know about the sexual health perceptions and behaviors of the millennial generation may provide valuable information about the needs of future generations, including Generation Z.

Concerning the American College Health Association's (ACHA) *Best Practices for Sexual Health Promotion and Clinical Care in College Health Settings*, this chapter builds on the content from an original research project that sought to explore attitudes and perceptions of the millennial population's health, well-being, and related skills.[7] It was important to engage the millennial population in this study, as this generation faces health challenges earlier in life compared to previous generations.[8] Due to an anticipated trickle-down effect, similar concerns and challenges may be found in Generation Z, which currently includes a large number of the college-aged population. Specific to sexual health, our research sought to the following:

1. Provide insight into young adults' perception of sexual health
2. Provide insight into young adults' perception of sexuality education
3. Explore the sexual health concerns of young adults within the millennial population cohort.

This qualitative research identified four overarching themes: 1) define sexual health in terms of prevention; 2) desire for comprehensive and normalized sexuality education; 3) lack of emphasis on consent as a sexual health concern; and 4) perceived sexual communication barriers, Table 22.1 provides definitions for each theme. This chapter will build on these themes; it is hoped that by understanding the sexual health perceptions of millennial generation members, education, clinical services, and sexual health programming can be improved to benefit future generations, such as Generation Z.

TABLE 22.1 Overarching Definitions of Each Major Theme

Theme	*Definition*
1. Define sexual health in terms of prevention	Millennials perceived sexual health defined exclusively as pregnancy and prevention of (STIs). Their responses did not include emotional, mental, and social aspects of sexual health.
2. Desire for comprehensive and normalized sexuality education	Millennials expressed a need for sexual health education to be improved and communication around sex and sexual health normalized.
3. Lack of emphasis on consent as a sexual health concern	Millennials expressed concern that consent campaigns and programs to reduce sexual harassment are not changing young people's views on the importance of consent.
4. Perceived sexual communication barriers	Millennials perceived barriers to sexual communication such as difficulty in negotiating with one's sexual partner in terms of desires, and preferences, inquiring about STIs, non-disclosure of STIs, receiving incorrect or incomplete information, and shame in purchasing condoms.

Theme 1: Define Sexual Health in Terms of Prevention

A goal of our research was to establish an understanding of millennials' perceptions of sexual health. Most study participants defined sexual health in terms of prevention, specifically unplanned pregnancy and STIs. In comparison to the definition of sexual health offered by the World Health Organization, this explanation does not touch on the emotional and social parts of sexual health. The ACHA highlights that sexual health should not only be discussed concerning STIs and unintended pregnancy, but also how it can promote good emotional sexual health and intimacy.[9] This is especially important, given that a primary reason for having sex among young people is to experience pleasure and intimacy. Previous research found that historically, school-based sexuality education is largely fear-based and saturated with sexual stereotypes, highlighting the dangers of sex rather than its potential to promote healthy relationships and mental and emotional health.[10] This theme highlighted a shared value of "protecting yourself," suggesting that the idea of basing sexual decisions and actions relative to a partner's desires, body, and boundaries may not be as important. This implication is supported by literature that discusses the loss of opportunity to talk to young people about pleasure related to healthy relationships.[7] Professionals who work to promote good sexual health have also noted that such a heavy emphasis on prevention "takes away from the time and reach that they have to focus on promotion."[10] This may limit the relationship-building opportunities educators and practitioners have with young people that create space for conversations about equality, pleasure, and sexual rights within a relationship. Our research found that young people desire sexuality education that feels more relevant and applicable to their own lives, further stressing the need to keep the values and characteristics of the audience at the forefront of sexuality education.

Theme 2: Desire for Comprehensive and Normalized Sexuality Education

It is safe to assume that most perceptions of sexual health, especially for young adults, are due at least in part to the sexuality education they have (or have not) received. In this research, participants noted a universal desire for comprehensive and normalized sexuality education to encourage regular conversation about sex and decrease the stigma attached to sexuality. Many of the participants recalled having different experiences compared with the sexuality education they received, by whom it was taught, and whether these educational conversations were shared among members of the same gender. A concern attached to the common practice of gender separation in school-based sexuality education was the possibility of different knowledge levels among genders, creating potential challenges in sexual communication and relationships later in life.

Sexuality education across the United States is incredibly varied regarding what is and is not allowed to be taught. As an example, while 39 states currently (as of 2021) mandate sexuality education and/or HIV education and 31 require information on healthy relationships to be provided, only 17 states require educational content to be medically accurate, 11 states require inclusivity, nine require the importance of consent to sex to be covered, and six states require *only* negative information to be provided on homosexuality with an emphasis on heterosexuality.[11] In many parts of the United States, "abstinence-only" or "sexual risk avoidance" programs are used. This approach has been shown to be undesirable by students and does not adequately prepare students to engage in healthy adult relationships. Further, it is less effective at preventing pregnancy and STIs than comprehensive sexuality education.[12] Students who participated in abstinence-only programs reported that education held heterosexuality as the norm rather than embracing diverse sexual identities. With the insufficient information and resources provided, students generally did not feel safe in classes due to the fear and shame relied upon by educators.[10] Similarly, respondents in our study also reported thinking that the information provided was androcentric, heteronormative, and inadequate and promoted stereotypes and stigma. The variety in sexual education experiences shared by participants may be, in part, to blame for the lack of emphasis on the partners' experience as noted within the *define sexual health in terms of prevention* theme and has likely led to higher discomfort with talking about sex, especially with partners. In contrast to abstinence-only programs, comprehensive sexuality education has been found to result in an appreciation of improved increased media literacy, social/emotional learning, sexual diversity, and prevention of child abuse.[13]

For many, exposure to sexual health information may not come until college or later, which is also the same point in which many have already had experience with sex and/or relationships. There was also expressed concern for those who do not attend college—where might they receive their sexuality education if they have not already received it? As digital natives, members of this generation (and those following) will likely gravitate toward electronic platforms, such as the Internet, to gain answers to their curiosities. This practice may present issues of its own due to the large amount of inaccurate and biased information that is available online.

Theme 3: Lack of Emphasis on Consent as a Sexual Health Concern

In school, receiving education about consent has been highly associated with a significantly reduced risk of sexual assault among undergraduate college students.[14] However, participants in our study expressed concern that consent campaigns and programs to reduce sexual harassment or sexual violence are not changing young adults' attitudes about consent. This is problematic for two reasons. First, a recent review of sexuality education in the United States reported the lack of consent lessons within the K-12 sexual health curriculum, resulting in many young adults not receiving messages about consent until college.[15] However, though consent education has been mandated at some state universities, this conversation starts too late. Many young adults have already become sexually active by the time they reach college.[16] As mentioned earlier, only nine states currently require information on consent to be explicitly included in their sexuality education curriculum.

The second problem is that consent education also acts as a prevention strategy for perpetrators of sexual violence in addition to potential victims; thus, without education, sexual violence, in part, is increasing.[11,17] According to the Centers for Disease Control and Prevention, nearly one in five women and one in 38 men will experience rape in their lifetime, including attempted rape.[18] Furthermore, one in two transgender people has been sexually assaulted at some point in their lives.[19]

Theme 4: Perceived Sexual Communication Barriers

The theme of *perceived sexual communication barriers* was expressed by participants as difficulty negotiating with one's sexual partner in terms of desires and preferences, inquiring about current STI status, non-disclosure of STIs, and receiving incorrect or incomplete information. Previous research has identified three such barriers to sexual communication: (1) threat to self or protecting one's identity from embarrassment, judgment, and shame;[20] (2) threat to partner or protecting partners identity from embarrassment, judgment, and shame;[21,22] and (3) threat to the relationship and avoiding topics that might reveal incompatibilities or cause conflict or anger.[10] In short, when the perceived threat outweighs the risk of a given situation, the topics are avoided completely. Condom negotiation is one such topic. Some literature suggests that adolescent women found it easier to refuse sex completely than to initiate or discuss condom use.[23] In terms of peer influence and risk behaviors, some people may fear bringing up the idea of using a condom, as it implies unfaithfulness or uncleanliness, and both threaten self and the relationship.[24] Another topic ripe for avoidance is STI status. Youth might make assumptions regarding STI risk and not discuss sexual health with their partners.[25] In other cases, having a conversation regarding sexual health allowed most participants to feel good because they acknowledged it helps protect them against unintended pregnancy and STIs, even though topics were perceived as "awkward" or "the relationship felt too new."[26] Adolescents and young adults will benefit from sexual communication skills in their sexuality education.

Parents and trusted parent figures help normalize sexual communication. Multiple studies examining family and other adult influences on risk behaviors found that supportive parent-youth and adult-youth relationships are associated with fewer occurrences of sexual intercourse, partners,[27] and delayed initiation of sex.[28,29] For the benefit of young people, parents need to become comfortable engaging with youth in conversations about sexuality. Alternatively, parents need to become comfortable with other trusted adults (i.e., church members, coaches, teachers, etc.) talking with their children about sexuality. Other literature suggests that adolescents and young adults want sexuality education appropriate for their life stage.[30] Through comprehensive sexuality education, the focus shifts to positive education in a variety of settings while reducing risky behaviors.

Most health behavior interventionists rely on the foundation of social learning theories that posit behavior change is facilitated and modeled by influential people. For example, children learn health behaviors such as nutritional eating or physical activity habits from parents or other family members. Sexual health communicative behaviors, such as negotiating condom use or disclosing one's STI status, are health behaviors that are not modeled like other health behaviors. As the first cohort of digital natives, millennials readily had access to sexual health information from the Internet. Scholars have reported the Internet is a more common resource than medical providers, relatives, or friends on topics such as drug-assisted rape, exploring common sexual behavior, preventing pregnancy, sexual assault, or STIs.[31,32] Unfortunately, our study also confirmed that information seekers rarely confirmed digital information with reliable sources.

Implications for Practice and Additional Research Needed

Generation Z, born 1997–2015,[6] is now the dominant demographic occupying young adulthood. The overwhelming presence of these students in high school and college should serve as a call to action for educators and clinicians to de-implement ineffective programs and create or adapt programs and curricula that align with the characteristics, desires, and values of this generation.[33] Before discussing how sexuality education might be modified to suit this population, it's important to consider some of the overarching reasons they may be having sex. General knowledge of young people's relationship goals may enable clinicians, educators, parents, and programs to better meet their needs by addressing alternative ways to express sexuality and achieve their relationship goals, whatever they may be. This may be more likely to create programming with information that young people are likely to absorb and engage.[34] With this in mind, and building off research findings, the authors propose a new approach, transitioning from "comprehensive sexuality education" to "positive sexuality education." Comprehensive sexuality education teaches that sex is healthy, natural, and normal. It highlights that abstinence is the most effective tool for preventing STIs and unplanned pregnancy; however, it is not the only method covered.

Contrary to what many may believe, comprehensive sexuality education can include a wide variety of topics, including accurate information on abortion, gender identity, and masturbation, and provides values-based education that is age-appropriate and sensitive. All are important aspects of sexuality education; however, the perceptions tell us that something is still missing and could still use improvement. There is a tendency to consider sexuality education as a vehicle for risk prevention, but it can be made even more effective when it incorporates why young people are having sex in the first place; meeting young people where they are. Positive sexuality education highlights the same ideas that comprehensive sexuality education does, with a few additional points. It emphasizes that sexuality is a fundamental part of who we are as humans. It should be enjoyed, fun, and pleasurable, and open, healthy communication supports emotional pleasure and intimacy, which can only be achieved when sex is completely consensual.

The National Sexuality Education Standards (NSES) exist, in part, to address inconsistencies in sexuality education in the United States. While one of the key components of NSES is to emphasize the emotional, intellectual, physical, and social dimensions of sexual health,[35] our subjects confirmed that many of the default approaches to teaching sexuality education capture only negative consequences of sexual activity, ignoring potentially positive aspects such as achieving social skills and goals, developing a sense of intimacy, and experiencing sexual pleasure. This is especially important for college students (most of whom are now members of the Generation Z age group) and other young people. The ACHA, now primarily governing sexuality education standards for the life stage that is currently occupied by Generation Z, supports positive sexuality education, emphasizing that ignoring pleasure as the primary reason for engaging in sexual activity prevents acknowledging the realities of college students' experiences and reinforces stigma and shame around their bodies and sexuality.[9] For educators who may have little ability to modify sexuality education programming, it is recommended to keep a tight, controlled focus on talking to students about what makes them feel good and how this can support non-physical intimacy. Communication regarding abstinence and sexual behaviors is likely to be enhanced with improved trust from young people on the receiving end of the education if sexuality education recognizes the competing positive and negative motivations for sex.

The ACHA also recommends leveraging social media in sexuality education programming. Both millennial and Generation Z cohorts are considered "digital natives," that is, a person born or brought up during the age of digital technology.[6] Media and technology are often used to form relationships, including those that are intimate, research sexual health information that is accurate and inclusive, and view pornographic material. These habits implicate the need to leverage digital media and use it as a health-promotional tool—ensuring that content and messaging is engaging, has a positive tone, is not too clinical, and is focused on building upon social norms is important to connecting with digital natives.[9]

Conclusively, this research highlights the general desire for more open communication and education about sexual health. A shift toward comprehensive sexuality education that emphasizes positive sexuality is needed to better support a variety of different types of people, provide information to young people that is medically accurate and responsive to their needs and underlying motivations behind having sex. It simultaneously promotes the prevention of risky sexual behaviors highlighted by the aforementioned millennial perceptions.

References

1. World Health Organization (2006). *Sexual and reproductive health: Sexual health*. who.int. www.who.int/reproductivehealth/topics/sexual_health/sh_definitions/en/
2. American College of Obstetricians and Gynecologists. (2020). *Comprehensive sexuality education*. www.acog.org/clinical/clinical-guidance/committee-opinion/articles/2016/11/comprehensive-sexuality-education
3. Ott, M.A., & Santelli, J.S. (2018). Abstinence and abstinence only education. *Journal of Adolescent Health, 61*(3), 273–280.
4. Centers for Disease Control and Prevention. (2017). *Sexually transmitted diseases*. cdc.gov. www.cdc.gov/std/life-stages-populations/adolescents-youngadults.htm.
5. National Conference on State Legislatures. (2020). *State policies on sex education in schools*. www.ncsl.org/research/health/state-policies-on-sex-education-in-schools.aspx
6. Dimock, M. (2019, January 17). *Defining generations: Where millennials end and Generation Z begins*. Pew Research Center. https://pewrsr.ch/2szqtJz
7. Lucero, J.E., Hanafi, S.L., Emerson, A.D., Rodriguez, K.I., Davalos, L., & Grinnell, L. (2020). Sexual health and sexual health education: Contemporary perceptions and

concerns of young adults within the millennial population cohort. *American Journal of Sexuality Education, 15*(4), 476–490.
8. Blue Cross, Blue Shield Association (2019, April 24). *The health of America report: The health of millennials*. www.bcbs.com/sites/default/files/file-attachments/health-of-america-report/HOA-Millennial_Health_0.pdf
9. American College Health Association. (2020). *Best practices for sexual health promotion and clinical care in college health settings*. www.acha.org/documents/resources/guidelines/ACHA_Best_Practices_for_Sexual_Health_Promotion_and_Clinical_Care_in_College_Health_Settings_Jan2020.pdf
10. Wood, R., Hirst, J., Wilson, L., & Burns-O'Connell, G. (2019). The pleasure imperative? Reflecting on sexual pleasure's inclusion in sexuality education and sexual health. *Sexuality Education, 19*(1), 1–14.
11. Guttmacher Institute. (2021). *Sex and HIV education, general requirements for sex education and HIV education*. www.guttmacher.org/state-policy/explore/sex-and-hiv-education
12. Hoefer, S., & Hoefer, R. Worth the wait? The consequences of abstinence-only sex education for marginalized students. *American Journal of Sexuality Education, 12*(3), 257–276. https://doi.org/10.1080/15546128.2017.1359802
13. Goldfarb, E.S., & Lieberman, L.D. (2021). Three decades of research: The case for comprehensive sex education. *Journal of Adolescent Health, 68*(1), 13–27. doi: 10.1016/j.jadohealth.2020.07.036.
14. Santelli, J.S., Grilo S.A., Choo, T.H., Diaz, G., Walsh, K., Wall, M., Hirsch, J.S., Wilson, P.A., Gilbert, L., Khan, S., & Mellins, C.A. (2018) Does sex education before college protect students from sexual assault in college?. *PLos One, 13*(11), e0205951. https://doi.org/10.1371/journal.pone.0205951
15. Willis, M., Jozkowski, K.N., & Read, J. (2019). Sexual consent in k-12 sex education: An analysis of current health education standards in the United States. *Sex Education, 19*(2), 226–236. https://doi.org/10.1080/14681811.2018.1510769
16. Muehlenhard, C.L., Humphreys, T.P., Jozkowski, K.N., & Peterson, Z.D. (2016). The complexities of sexual consent among college students: A conceptual and empirical review. *Journal of Sex Research, 53*(4–5), 457–487.
17. Schneider, M., & Hirsch, J.S. (2020). Comprehensive sexuality education as a primary prevention strategy for sexual violence perpetration. *Trauma Violence Abuse, 21*(3), 439–455.
18. Centers for Disease Control and Prevention. (2021). *What is sexual violence?* www.cdc.gov/violenceprevention/sexualviolence/fastfact.html
19. James, S.E., Herman, J.L., Rankin, S., Keisling, M., Mottet, L., & Anafi, M. (2016). *The report of the 2015 U.S. transgender survey*. www.transequality.org/sites/default/files/doc s/USTS-Full-Report-FINAL.PDF
20. Guerrero, L.K., & Afifi, W.A. (1995). Some things are better left unsaid: Topic avoidance in family relationships. *Communication Quarterly, 43*(3), 276–296.
21. Redlick, M. The perceived threat of sexual communication, number of previous sexual partners and topic avoidance in romantic relationships. *Psychology & Sexuality, 8*(1–2), 148–157.
22. Rehman, U.S., Balan, D., Sutherland, S., & McNeil, J. (2019). Understanding barriers to sexual communication. *Journal of Social and Personal Relationships, 36*(9), 2605–2626. doi:10.1177/0265407518794900
23. East, L., Jackson, D., O'Brien, L., & Peters, K. (2007). Use of the male condom by heterosexual adolescents and young people: Literature review. *Journal of Advanced Nursing, 59*(2), 103–110.
24. Broaddus, M.R., & Dickson-Gomez, J. (2013). Text messaging for sexual communication and safety among African American young adults. *Qualitative Health Research, 23*(10), 1344–1353.

25. Bolton, M., McKay, A., & Schneider, M. (2010). Relational influences on condom use discontinuation: A qualitative study of young adult women in dating relationships. *Canadian Journal of Human Sexuality, 19*(3), 91–104.
26. Faulkner, S.L., & Lannutti, P.J. (2009). Examining the content and outcomes of young adults' satisfying and unsatisfying conversations about sex. *Qualitative Health Research, 20*(3), 375–385.
27. Jaccard, J., Dittus, P., & Gordon, V. (1996). Maternal correlates of adolescent sexual behavior. *Family Planning Perspectives, 28*, 159–165.
28. Danziger, S.K. (1995). Family life and teenage pregnancy in the inner-city: Experiences of African- American youth. *Children and Youth Services Review, 17*(1–2), 183–202.
29. Upchurch, D.M., Aneshensel, C.S., Sucoff, C.A., & Levy-Storms, L. (1999). Neighborhood and family contexts of adolescent sexual activity. *Journal of Marriage and Family, 61*(4), 920–933. doi:10.2307/354013
30. Leston, D., Jessen, M.C., Simon, C.B. (2012). Alaska Native and rural youth views of sexual health: A focus group project on sexually transmitted diseases, HIV/AIDS, and unplanned pregnancy. *American Indian and Alsaska Native Mental Health Research, 19*(1), 1–14.
31. Buhi, E.R., Daley, E.M., Fuhrmann, H.J., & Smith, S.A. (2009). An observational study of how young people search for online sexual health information. *Journal of American College Health, 58*(2), 101–111.
32. Patterson, S.P., Hilton, S., Flowers, P., & McDaid, L.M. (2019). What are the barriers and challenges faced by adolescents when searching for sexual health information on the Internet? Implications for policy and practice from a qualitative study. *Sexually Transmitted Infections, 95*(6), 462–467.
33. Seemiller, C., & Clayton, J. (2019). Developing the strengths of Generation Z college students. *Journal of College and Character, 20*(3), 268–275.
34. Edwards, N. (2016). Women's reflections on formal sex education and the advantage of gaining informal sexual knowledge through a feminist lens. *Sex Education: Sexuality, Society and Learning, 16*(3), 266–278.
35. Future of Sex Education. (2011). *National sexuality education standards: Core content and skills, k-12.* https://siecus.org/resources/national-sexuality-education-standards/

23

DIGITAL SEXUAL HEALTH INTERVENTIONS FOR YOUNG PEOPLE

Chiao Wen Lan, Alexandra F. Lightfoot, David Gere, Arianna Taboada, and Norweeta G. Milburn

Introduction

Theatre has a long history of being implemented globally as an educational and behavioral change strategy. Previous studies have suggested that theatre-based techniques, such as role-play and storytelling, allow for the acquisition of knowledge and skills as well as opportunities to apply, enhance, and practice learned information.[3,4] Studies consistently show that well-designed and executed live theatre performances can engage audiences, influence the knowledge, attitudes, and behaviors of audience members, and positively impact cultural, peer, and social norms.[5–8] For instance, theatre-based programs have been used to disseminate HIV/AIDS prevention information,[9] to promote healthy relationships among adolescents,[10] to reduce substance abuse among adolescents,[11] and to reduce weight-related teasing among children.[12] The purpose of this chapter is to examine and compare the efficacy of two delivery modes (live and digital)of a theatre-based sexual health intervention developed for high school-aged adolescents.[1,2]

Theatre-Based Interventions

Drama theory and research suggest that live and film performances can structure the social environment through their persuasive functions.[13] Theatrical approaches offer the opportunity to observe human behavior, peel back layers of fear and defensiveness about engaging in a new behavior and create a space in which new behavior can be imagined.[14] The work of Augusto Boal, a Brazilian director and writer, is at the core of many theatre-based interventions. Boal focused on using theatre to increase people's freedom to act and make social changes.[15] In his seminal work, *Theatre of the Oppressed*,[16] inspired by the visions of Paulo Freire, Boal

DOI: 10.4324/9781003189787-24

offers tools for liberation by using theatre methods to examine social injustice and oppression and experiment with problem-solving on various levels—individual, group, and societal. Theatre-based peer-education strategies have been engaging adolescents in HIV prevention for over two decades.[17–21] As an approach to sexual health education, theatre-based interventions[22–24] have been found effective as a strategy for engaging adolescents and facilitating the attitudinal change that precedes behavior change.[22,25]

Digital Interventions for Public Health

Film and video media have a long tradition in health promotion and education.[26–28] A recent systematic review reported that film-based interventions are useful in enhancing attitudes toward help-seeking and reducing mental health stigma in adolescents.[29] The importance of film and video as delivery strategies has grown dramatically, as has the rapid development of technology.[30] The use of digital interventions is especially critical during public health crises. Video has been adopted for public health interventions and shows promising results in changing attitudes toward people living with a disease.[31,32] Additionally, digital media have been effective in creating an emotional response and enhancing empathy in children and adolescents while providing information to viewers.[33] Engaging adolescents through technology and media, including accessing sexual health information online, building a computer or web-based sexual health education, and creating entertainment education for adolescents, can lead to overall improved results in adolescent health promotion efforts.[34] Further, peer education prevention strategies for health approaches for adolescents are culturally and developmentally appropriate for young people.[22]

Intervention Description

Arts-based, Multiple component, Peer education (AMP!) is a sexual health promotion and HIV prevention intervention that uses a theatrical approach to deliver sexual health education messages to high school students in school settings. AMP!'s interactive theatre approach uses scenarios created by college students in a university credit-bearing course. Students acquire the skills of interactive theatre and receive sexual health training from HIV prevention specialists to inform their creative, medically accurate interactive theatre scenarios. The college students (the Sex Squad) then deliver the performance live to ninth-grade student participants to supplement the standard sexual health curriculum. They also conduct workshops using strategies from Theatre of the Oppressed to enable youth to "rehearse for real-life," providing opportunities to direct the dialog and actions of stage characters, discuss their motivations, and model alternative behaviors. The performances adapt popular songs, social media, and television shows well-known to adolescents to convey messages about sexual health. They include facts about communication with peers or partners, condom negotiation skills, contraception, proper use of condoms, sexually transmitted infections (STI) and HIV testing, and substance use during sexual activity. The live mode of AMP! was delivered in the Los Angeles United School District schools in 2010, and the approach was brought to North Carolina in 2013. An analysis of the live program's efficacy at both sites showed significant effects on participant outcomes.[35] Thus, a digital mode of the intervention was piloted and evaluated to assess a potential means of scaling up its efficacy. This chapter reports on those results and compares outcomes between the live and digital modes of the intervention.[36]

Study Design

The four schools were randomly assigned to either the live intervention or digital intervention conditions. Two schools in the intervention condition received the live theatre-based program, and the two other schools in the digital condition received the digital program. A pre-test and post-test design was employed. All students enrolled in the ninth-grade health class at participating schools were invited to enroll in the study. The research project staff visited all ninth-grade health classes at participating schools, described the program to potential participants, and distributed an information packet about the program with parental consent forms. Participants had to meet the following criteria: (a) currently attending one of the four participating Los Angeles Unified School District high schools, (b) able to provide child assent, and (c) able to provide parental or legal guardians' consent forms. The study was approved by the University of California, Los Angeles institutional review board (IRB). Participants completed paper and pencil self-administered pre- and post-intervention questionnaires in the classroom. The post-test was administered to participants three weeks after the intervention sessions.

Live Condition

The live theatre program consisted of three components: (a) Sex Squad live performance delivered by undergraduate students; (b) Interactive Workshop facilitated by undergraduate student performers that included demonstrating condom negotiation with a potential partner; and (c) Positively Speaking, in which HIV-positive speakers came into the classroom and described their experiences living with HIV. Participants in the live condition received three 60-minute sessions delivered over eight weeks.

Digital Condition

Similar to the live mode, the digital sexual health intervention contained three components: (a) Sex Squad viewing of a compilation of monologues and skits created by the Sex Squad to educate students about condom use and HIV; (b)

Interactive Workshop, which included a discussion led by teachers using a facilitator guide; and (c) Positively Speaking, which involved viewing of short biographical videos, portraying men and women living with HIV. The digital program included filmed segments of the undergraduate student-created scenarios delivered during live performances, and a manual was made available for the teachers to facilitate discussion afterward. The manual's content was developed in collaboration with local artists, high school students, school district officials, and teachers. The videos and discussion guide were pilot-tested before implementation. Participants in the digital mode condition received three 60-minute sessions delivered over eight weeks. The three-episode video of vignettes and information from the manual covered the specific sexual health topics also covered in the live mode.

Measures

The survey included items from the Centers for Disease Control and Prevention's Youth Risk Behavior Surveillance survey,[37] the World Health Organization's knowledge, attitudes, and practice survey instrument for adolescents,[38] and the Towards a Healthy Tomorrow survey.[39] The survey was used in the previous pilots.[38,40]

HIV-related knowledge was assessed, including HIV awareness and HIV attitudes among the participants. The respondents were asked to rate their confidence that they can implement HIV-preventive behavior. In addition, the participants were asked whether they had ever had sexual intercourse and whether they or their partner had used a condom at their last sexual intercourse. Demographic and background information from the participants were collected, including gender and race. The participants were asked whether they had ever been taught about HIV/AIDS at school. Data on whether the participant received a free or reduced-price lunch at school was collected as a proxy for socioeconomic status.

Results

A total of 300 ninth-grade students participated in the study. Table 23.1 lists participant characteristics. Females accounted for about half of the participants. Most of the participants in the study had received HIV/AIDS education at school. About 71% of the participants self-identified as Hispanic, 10% as Asian or Pacific Islander, 7% as African American, and 5% as White. Approximately four out of five of the participants received free lunch at school. About a quarter of the participants (25%) reported ever having sexual intercourse at baseline. Of those who were sexually active, 63% reported using a condom during their last sexual encounter. More than half (61%) of the participants reported ever drinking alcohol. Except for race and receiving comprehensive sexual health education at school, there were no significant differences in sociodemographic characteristics, HIV-related knowledge, and self-efficacy for safe sex across the live and digital sexual health program at baseline.

TABLE 23.1 Demographic Characteristics of 9th Grade Students in Live and Digital Sexual Health Intervention

	Total N = *300* N *(%)*	*Live* n = *136* N *(%)*	*Digital* n = *164* N *(%)*
Gender			
Male	130 (43)	60 (44)	70 (43)
Female	170 (57)	76 (56)	94 (57)
Received free lunch			
Yes	172 (78)	78 (78)	94 (78)
No	48 (22)	22 (22)	26 (22)
Taught HIV at school			
Yes	273 (93)	117 (89)	156 (97)
No	20 (7)	15 (11)	5 (3)

Participants showed a significant increase in HIV-related knowledge for both the live and digital modes. Compared to pre-test, post-intervention questionnaire results showed that participants were more informed about HIV/AIDS, felt more comfortable discussing the impacts of HIV with peers, and were more informed about HIV testing in the community. In addition, sub-analysis among those who reported being sexually active showed a significant increase in HIV-related knowledge in both modes.

Results indicated that the mean increase for safe sex self-efficacy from pre to post-test was statistically significant in the two delivery modes. Participants felt more confident about discussing safer sex with their partners and were more likely to use a condom following both modes of the sexual health intervention conditions. Sub-analysis among participants who reported being sexually active showed no significant change in safe sex self-efficacy for either version of the intervention. Among the participants who reported being sexually active, there was no significant increase in condom use at last sexual encounter in either mode.

Implications for Practice

The digital sexual health intervention was as effective as the live theatre-based intervention in increasing HIV knowledge and self-efficacy for safe sex practices for participants. These results suggest that the adaptation of this theatre-based sexual health intervention for digital implementation could be a promising method for engaging adolescent audiences and delivering essential sexual health and HIV prevention information on a larger scale.

Theatre-based interventions are effective in creating emotional experiences for viewers that can affect attitudes at a deeper level than traditional didactic teaching methods.[22,41] A digital sexual health intervention mode that uses video content created through the live theatre approach is an easy-to-use, effective, and low-cost tool that can provide educational benefits.[42] The results support increasing the use of digital sexual health interventions to reach a broader audience in school settings. While the facilitator discussion guide tested here highlights alignment with California public school health education standards, the content can be adapted to align with other state standards or education curricula. The strength of a digital mode, supported with this study as efficacious as the live mode, is that it is scalable, offering the potential for wider reach and impact across diverse school settings.

Implications for Research

Future research should examine the efficacy of digital theatre-based interventions on a large scale. Previous research has suggested that several aspects—especially targeted, local, credible, continuous contact [43]—should be considered when developing interventions for a broad audience. Future study should also assess the adaptability of this program to school systems in other geographically and culturally diverse regions, including suburban and rural school systems. Additionally, marked racial and sexual orientation disparities in the prevalence of STI/HIV need to be addressed.[44] Findings from this study also suggest that sexual health education should be tailored to the risk level of adolescents. For those sexually active participants, both the live and digital sexual health intervention conditions were efficacious in increasing their HIV-related knowledge, yet not for safe sex self-efficacy or condom use at last sexual intercourse.

Limitations

There are limitations to the results presented. First, given privacy concerns expressed by the IRB that approved the study, questionnaires were anonymous and individual participants could not be tracked for longitudinal analyses. There was no measure to assess how each component of the digital mode (i.e., viewing the digital mode videos, discussion led by teachers, and viewing of short biographical videos portraying men and women living with HIV) influences the participants' knowledge and self-efficacy. Therefore, it was not possible to tease out which component was more effective. Finally, the study collected self-report data, which can be susceptible to social desirability bias.

Conclusions

Rates of STI/HIV among adolescents in the United States remain alarmingly high. Increased HIV knowledge and greater self-efficacy for safe sex are attainable for adolescents through a digitalized theatre-based sexual health intervention delivery approach in school settings. There is an urgent need to implement effective sexual health education programs that are developmentally and culturally appropriate to reduce risky behaviors and increase protective behaviors for adolescents. Further, programs are needed for targeted sexual risk reduction intervention for sexually experienced youth that can increase knowledge and promote safer sex practices such as consistent condom use. A digital theatre-based mode is an innovative and appealing way of communicating messages about sexual health information. Given the low cost and resource demands of a digital theatre-based sexual health intervention, it has the potential as a viable mode for sexual health education for adolescents that could be tested and disseminated more broadly.

References

1. Heartfelt thanks to the participating Los Angeles Unified School District high schools, the members of the University of California, Los Angeles (UCLA) Sex Squad, and the entire UCLA Art & Global Health Center team for their insight, creativity, and generous assistance.
2. This work was supported by a seed grant from the UCLA AIDS Institute, UCLA Center for AIDS Research, the National Center for Advancing Translational Sciences (NCATS) at UCLA, and the National Center for Research Resources (NCRR). Additional program support was provided by the Clarence and Anne Dillon Dunwalke Charitable Trust, Elizabeth Taylor AIDS Foundation, Ford Foundation, David and Linda Shaheen Foundation, and the AIDS Healthcare Foundation.
3. Helmeke, K.B., & Prouty, A.M. (2001). Do we really understand? An experiential exercise for training family therapists. *Journal of Marital and Family Therapy, 27*(4), 535–544.
4. Keveligham, E.H., Duffy, S., & Walker, J.J. (1998). Innovations in teaching obstetrics and gynaecology—the theme afternoon. *Medical Education, 32*(5), 517–521.
5. Conquergood, D. (1988). Health theatre in a Hmong refugee camp: Performance, communication, and culture. *The Drama Review, 32*(3), 174–208. doi:10.2307/1145914
6. Kincaid, D.L., Yun, S.H., Piotrow, P.T., & Yaser, Y. (1993). Turkey's mass media family planning campaign. In B. Thomas, E. Rogers, & N. Park (Eds.), *Organizational aspects of health communication campaigns: What works?* Sage Publications.
7. Piotrow, P.T., Kincaid, D.L., Rimon, J.G., Rinehart, W., & Samson, K. (1997). *Health communication: Lessons from family planning and reproductive health*. Praeger.
8. Singhal, A., & Rogers, E. (2012). *Entertainment-education: A communication strategy for social change*. Routledge.
9. Valente, T.W., Poppe, P.R., Alva, M.E., de Briceno, R.V., & Cases, D. (1994). Street theater as a tool to reduce family planning misinformation. *International Quarterly of Community Health Education, 15*(3), 279–289.
10. Fredland, N.M. (2010). Nurturing healthy relationships through a community-based interactive theatre program. *Journal of Community Health Nursing, 27*(2), 107–118. doi: 10.1080/07370011003705013
11. Guttman, N., Gesser-Edelsburg, A., & Israelashvili, M. (2008). The paradox of realism and "authenticity" in entertainment-education: A study of adolescents' views about anti-drug abuse dramas. *Health Communication, 23*(2), 128–141.
12. Haines, J., Neumark-Sztainer, D., Perry, C.L., Hannan, P.J., & Levine, M.P. (2006). VIK (Very Important Kids): A school-based program designed to reduce teasing and unhealthy weight-control behaviors. *Health Education Research, 21*(6), 884–895.
13. Capo, K.E. (1983). Performance of literature as social dialectic. *Literature in Performance, 4*(1), 31–36.

14. Dill-Shackleford, K.E., Green, M.C., Scharrer, E., Wetterer, C., & Shackleford, L.E. (2015). Setting the stage for social change: Using live theatre to dispel myths about intimate partner violence. *Journal of Health Communication, 20*(8), 969–976.
15. Österlind, E. (2008). Acting out of habits—can theatre of the oppressed promote change? Boal's theatre methods in relation to Bourdieu's concept of habitus. *Research in Drama Education, 13*(1), 71–82.
16. Boal, A. (2000). *Theatre of the oppressed*. Pluto Press.
17. Daykin, N., Orme, J., Evans, D., Salmon, D., McEachran, M., & Brain, S. (2008). The impact of participation in performing arts on adolescent and health behavior: A systematic review of the literature. *Journal of Health Psychology, 13*(2), 251–264.
18. Jackson, A. (Ed.). (2002). *Learning through theatre: New perspectives on theatre in education*. Routledge.
19. Lieberman, L.D., Berlin, C., Palen, L.A., & Ashley, O.S. (2012). A theatre-based approach to primary prevention of sexual behavior for early adolescents. *The Journal of Early Adolescence, 32*(5), 730–753.
20. McEwan, R., Bhopal, R., & Patton, W. (1991). Drama on HIV and AIDS: An evaluation of a theatre-in-education programme. *Health Education Journal, 50*(4), 155–160.
21. Valente, T.W., & Bharath, U. (1999). An evaluation of the use of drama to communicate HIV/AIDS information. *AIDS. AIDS Education and Prevention, 11*(3), 203–211.
22. Glik, D., Nowak, G., Valente, T., Sapsis, K., & Martin, C. (2002). Youth performing arts entertainment-education for HIV/AIDS prevention and health promotion: Practice and research. *Journal of Health Communication,* 7(1), 39–57.
23. Simons, S.M. (2011). Process drama and sex education: Advocating for drama-based components of adolescent health initiatives. *Journal of Applied Arts & Health, 2*(2), 113–123.
24. Taboada, A., Taggart, T., Holloway, I., Houpt, A., Gordon, R., Gere, D., Milburn, N., & Lightfoot, A.F. (2016). A critical review of the characteristics of theatre-based HIV prevention interventions for adolescents in school settings. *Health Promotion Practice, 17*(4), 537–547.
25. Lauby, J.L., LaPollo, A.B., Herbst, J.H., Painter, T.M., Batson, H., Pierre, A., & Milnamow, M. (2010). Preventing AIDS through live movement and sound: Efficacy of a theatre-based HIV prevention intervention delivered to high-risk male adolescents in juvenile justice settings. *AIDS Education and Prevention, 22*(5), 402–416.
26. Bhugra, D. (2003). Teaching psychiatry through cinema. *Psychiatric Bulletin, 27*(11), 429–430. doi:10.1192/pb.27.11.429
27. Gabbard, G.O., & Gabbard, K. (1999). *Psychiatry and the cinema*. American Psychiatric Press.
28. Jones, E. (2014). Neuro psychiatry 1943: The role of documentary film in the dissemination of medical knowledge and promotion of the UK psychiatric profession. *Journal of the History of Medicine and Allied Sciences, 69*(2), 294–324.
29. Goodwin, J., Saab, M.M., Dillon, C.B., Kilty, C., McCarthy, A., O'Brien, M., & Philpott, L.F. (2021). The use of film-based interventions in adolescent mental health education: A systematic review. *Journal of Psychiatric Research, 137,* 158–172.
30. Strasburger, V.C., Jordan, A.B., & Donnerstein, E. (2012). Children, adolescents, and the media: Health effects. *Pediatric Clinics of North America, 59*(3), 533–587.
31. Penn, D.L., Chamberlin, C., & Mueser, K.T. (2003). The effects of a documentary film about schizophrenia on psychiatric stigma. *Schizophrenia Bulletin, 29*(2), 383–391.
32. Woods, D.W., & Marcks, B.A. (2005). Controlled evaluation of an educational intervention used to modify peer attitudes and behavior toward persons with Tourette's Syndrome. *Behavior Modification, 29*(6), 900–912.
33. Strasburger, V.C. & Hogan, M.J. (2013). Children, adolescents, and the media. *Pediatrics, 132*(5), 958–961.

34. Decker, M.J., Berglas, N.F., & Brindis, C.D. (2015). A call to action: Developing and strengthening new strategies to promote adolescent sexual health. *Societies, 5*(4), 686–712.
35. Taggart, T., Taboada, A., Stein, J.A., Milburn, N.G., Gere, D., & Lightfoot, A.F. (2016). AMP!: A cross-site analysis of the effects of a theatre-based intervention on adolescent awareness, attitudes, and knowledge about HIV. *Prevention Science, 17*(5), 544–553.
36. Lan, C., Lightfoot, A., Gere, D., Taboada, A., Meyer, K., Harwood, J., Milburn, N. (2019). Live or virtual? Comparing two versions of AMP!, A theater-based sexual health intervention for adolescents. *American Journal of Sexuality Education, 14*(3), 292–314.
37. Brener, N.D., Eaton, D.K., Kann, L., Grunbaum, J.A., Gross, L.A., Kyle, T.M., & Ross, J.G. (2006). The association of survey setting and mode with self-reported health risk behaviors among high school students. *Public Opinion Quarterly, 70*(3), 354–374.
38. World Health Organization. (1989). *Interview schedule for knowledge, attitudes, beliefs and practices on AIDS of young people*. World Health Organization.
39. Stanton, B.F., Li, X., Kahihuata, J., Fitzgerald, A.M., Neumbo, S., Kanduuombe, G., Ricardo, B., Galbraith, J.S., Terrei, N., Guevara, I., Shipena, H., Strijdom, J., Clemens, R. & Zimba, R.F. (1998). Increased protected sex and abstinence among Namibian youth following a HIV risk-reduction intervention: A randomized, longitudinal study. *AIDS, 12*(18), 2473–2480.
40. Lightfoot, A.F., Taboada, A., Taggart, T., Tran, T., & Burtaine, A. (2015). "I learned to be okay with talking about sex and safety": Assessing the efficacy of a theatre-based HIV prevention approach for adolescents in North Carolina. *Sex Education, 15*(4), 348–363.
41. Joronen, K., Rankin, S.H., & Stedt-Kurki, P. (2008). School-based drama intervention in health promotion for children and adolescents: Systematic review. *Journal of Advanced Nursing, 63*(2), 116–131.
42. Clement, S., van Nieuwenhuizen, A., Kassam, A., Flach, C., Lazarus, A., De Castro, M., McCrone, P., Norman, I., & Thornicroft, G. (2012) Filmed v. Live Social Contact Interventions to Reduce Stigma: Randomised Controlled Trial. *The British Journal of Psychiatry, 201*, 57–64.
43. Corrigan, P.W. (2012). Research and the elimination of the stigma of mental illness. *The British Journal of Psychiatry: The Journal of Mental Science, 201*(1), 7–8.
44. Elster, A., Jarosik, J., VanGeest, J., & Fleming, M. (2003). Racial and ethnic disparities in health care for adolescents. *Archives of Pediatrics & Adolescent Medicine, 157*(9), 867–874.

24

VIDEO-BASED MICROSKILLS TRAINING FOR EDUCATORS

The Future of Training

Regina Firpo-Triplett, Tamara Kuhn, Lane Edwards, and Diana Dull Akers

Introduction

Consider the many challenges involved in effectively teaching sexual and reproductive health (SRH) education today. Teachers are not only required to have *instructional* skills (e.g., leading large and small groups, engaging students, teaching through distance learning)[1] and *content-specific* skills (e.g., managing role-plays, leading condom demonstrations); they also need *universal* skills. For example, how do you best answer sensitive questions? How do you integrate trauma-informed strategies? How do you teach sex ed that is LGBTQ inclusive and promotes racial justice? Ensuring that SRH educators develop both the knowledge and communication skills they need is critical since variability in educator preparedness, self-efficacy, and comfort levels can significantly impact curriculum implementation and outcomes.[2–4]

As of 2021, no states regulate the professional training of SRH educators, and only 13 states require such instruction to be "medically accurate."[5] In many US schools, health or physical education teachers are assigned to teach sexual health with little or no training, a deficit evident to both educators and students.[6] When teaching sexual health, educators report discomfort around the subject matter and a lack of skill, confidence, and certainty answering student questions and implementing unfamiliar activities (e.g., role-plays and group discussions on sensitive topics).[7] They also describe lacking needed skills to create an inclusive environment for all students, a point echoed by the fact that less than 5% of students report that LGBTQ topics are represented positively in their health courses. While students occasionally praise their SRH teachers,[8] they question their credibility for teaching sexual health, citing lack of training, reliance on

DOI: 10.4324/9781003189787-25

passive teaching methods (e.g., showing outdated films), and teacher inability to discuss sex frankly or respond to questions satisfactorily.[9,10] As a result, student perceptions about the quality of their sexual health education are negatively affected.[9–11]

Teacher Training Options

Traditional teacher training and development options often fall short for multiple reasons: (1) Sexual health training, if offered at all, commonly occurs later in an educator's career when resource and time constraints are at issue. (2) Face-to-face training is expensive and requires participants to take time away from work. (3) Trainings usually focus on a specific curriculum rather than universal skills needed to teach sexual health topics. (4) Even highly rated, face-to-face training rarely provides continuous implementation support.

Online training resources have the potential to address cost and scheduling challenges and provide ongoing support, yet they, too, are often curriculum specific and typically present information in lengthy blocks totaling several hours. The synchronous training formats can be challenging for SRH educators' time constraints, while the asynchronous trainings can result in low completion rates. Lastly, while sex educators' knowledge can be strengthened by information from credible online resources, *skill acquisition* is more difficult to produce.[12]

Until now, skills have been thought to be most effectively taught through in-person training. However, research has shown the potentially greater efficacy and utility of streaming video training, with the usefulness of video documented in numerous online training studies.[13] In addition to employing constructive learning processes, videos offer an excellent tool for skills modeling—a key construct in numerous behavior-change theories.[14] Research shows that video-based e-learning is superior to illustrated, text-based e-learning for teaching practical skills to health practitioners. Video trainings have outperformed in-person trainings for increasing teachers' knowledge of HIV risks, and for classroom management strategies, and can be used for implementation support.[15] This type of visual learning decreases learning time by 40% and is more attractive to learners.[16]

The SkillFlix® Training Technology

SkillFlix is a streaming video library designed to develop teacher skills in delivering sexual health education to youth aged 14–18. Its central innovation focuses on developing teacher "Microskills®," sub-skills of larger skills taught using ultra-short (30–120 seconds) videos. For instance, the larger skill of *answering sensitive*

TABLE 24.1 SkillFlix Terms

	Skill	*Microskill*	*Microskill steps*	*Topic*
Term	*A large or key skill (made up of Microskills)*	*Smaller sub-skills that make up a skill. Ideal for quick learning via observation.*	*Specific steps that comprise a Microskill, modeled in video with synchronized supporting text.*	*The content addressed in the Microskill video (not inherent in Microskill but a way to frame skills).*
Example	Answering Sensitive Questions	Answering a "Am I Normal?" Question Example: *"Is it normal for my penis to be hard in the morning?"*	1. Provide definition of terms in question. 2. Address facts/values embedded in question. 3. Acknowledge range of experiences, etc.	Anatomy Pornography Condom use

questions can be understood as a set of 15+ Microskills that include "introducing students to the anonymous question box" and answering shock questions, permission-seeking questions, and so on. (See Table 24.1.)

Written Microskill steps are also overlayed on the video, allowing the learner to see the steps as they are modeled. For example, if the educator is shown pausing to think about an appropriate response to a student, the screen text would read "pause to consider your response." Because many steps are repeated, learning is reinforced; this is true regardless of the path or order the learner takes as they work through the material. By first learning the carefully sequenced Microskills, the learner gains the building blocks to implement the larger skill. These short, sequenced videos also meet the time constraints reported by educators, offering their preferred fast-paced learning method.

Additionally, SkillFlix offers a customization feature to support educators with a range of experience and skills. After answering a series of questions, SkillFlix identifies the user's skill areas that need improvement and provides customized learning recommendations (video pathways). For further reflection and support, learners are encouraged to rate and comment on the video and access relevant resources for that Microskill. The latter include topical links to credible and current related content, printable summaries of Microskills steps, and tip sheets on the larger skill. When complete, the collection will offer at least 22 skillsets and approximately 300 Microskills videos, with multiple strategies for locating videos of interest (see Table 24.2).

TABLE 24.2 Methods for Locating Videos

Skill Type (Pull down options)	*Topic (Pull down options)*	*Key Word Search (Write in)*	*Customization Options*
Sent to first video in chosen skill type	Sent to search results page listing all videos addressing that topic	Sent to a results page that lists all videos addressing that keyword	Take self-assessment, receive recommended video pathways
User watches first video	User chooses a video	User chooses a video	Create a "Favorites" list
Next video in skill type sequence is recommended	User watches next video in recommended skill type sequence OR chooses video from topical search results page	User watches next video in recommended skill type sequence OR chooses video from keyword search results page	
After watching the last video in skill-type sequence, the first video in next skill-type sequence is recommended.			

The Conceptualization and Development of SkillFlix

Supporting Theories

Several learning theories guided the design and development of SkillFlix. The classic, "gold-standard" in-person training approach to skill instruction—described by Joyce and colleagues and consistent with Bandura's social learning theory[12,17]—posits that observational learning and skill modeling are central to skill acquisition. This assumption underlies SkillFlix's strategy of having learners repeat observation of videos modeling Microskills in realistic scenarios (i.e., within the context of content presentation). Bandura led training participants through a multi-step process:

- Define/name the skill
- Explain the context for/benefits of skill
- Delineate specific steps to implement skill
- Model the skill
- Lead participants through skill practice with observation feedback (often in role-plays)
- Debrief skill practice, plan for skill implementation

This process—applied to skills such as answering sensitive questions and leading role plays—led participants through an intentional cognitive and behavioral process of memorizing skill steps and practicing them. However, translating this approach to online skill instruction, especially with asynchronous training models, is extremely challenging, awkward for users, and only somewhat effective.

In contrast, the video models of the skills were extremely valuable to participants, for both *skill acquisition* and *skill support* once back in the classroom. As sexual reproductive health instruction takes teachers in many directions, they need a varied, layered set of skills to respond to class needs. SkillFlix teaches educators by (a) breaking down skills to small enough Microskills to simplify; and (b) repeated observations of videos modeling Microskills in realistic scenarios (i.e., within the context of content presentation).

The SkillFlix model is also grounded in the unifying neuroscience framework of *mirror neurons*.[18–20] In brief, the visual information received when someone watches another person perform a skill or other action, including on video, gets mapped onto the equivalent motor representation in their brain. This permits us to directly participate in another's actions without having to imitate or practice them. Experimental research with mirror neurons has shown this method has been successfully used to learn a variety of skills; it is even more effective when we see the person performing like ourselves.[21] Watching a single video can develop skill acquisition, but as users look for content, they see the same skill steps repeatedly demonstrated across Microskills. Skill acquisition takes place at an unconscious level, without the need for role-play or extended learning periods.

Finally, the SkillFlix platform and user interface were developed using tenets of Adult Learning Theory, which holds that adults want to determine their own learning path instead of being led through a linear process.[22,23] SkillFlix facilitates this self-determination by giving users multiple methods of *accessing* the material (e.g., tailored recommendations, selection of skills/Microskills) and *engaging* with the material (e.g., ability to select content of interest).

Developing the SkillFlix Resource

The conceptualization and training direction of SkillFlix was guided during multiple meetings project staff convened with four national SRH expert advisors.[24] Staff also held four 90-minute virtual focus groups with local SRH educators and national trainers, recruited through sexual and reproductive health networks, social media outlets, and listservs. The goal was to understand the training needs and interests of SRH educators working with youth, including what skills they felt were universally needed. Their input was also solicited on product features, the look and feel of the videos, and the overall site.

The Prototype Content Plan

Working closely with all advisors, the project team identified high-priority skillsets needed to teach basic sexual education topics found in comprehensive, evidence-based SRH interventions. Specifically, we: (1) analyzed numerous evidence-based teen SRH interventions for needed instructional skills; (2) culled skills from the new Professional Learning Standards for Sex Education developed as part of the Sex Education Collaborative;[25] and (3) reviewed SRH educator skill needs informed by other standards and requirements (e.g., the National Sexuality Education Standards[26] and the California Healthy Youth Act[27]). The expert advisors and focus group educators identified two skill sets—*Answering Sensitive Questions* and *LGBTQ Sensitivity*—as the highest priority and universally needed; they were chosen as the skills for the prototype.

The Microskills Videos

Next, the project team developed 48 video clips to model Microskills in the two chosen prototype skill sets. All expert advisors reviewed the conceptualized Microskills steps and characteristics. Scripts were then drafted, each focused on effective modeling of a Microskill and covering common sexual health content to facilitate demonstration of that skill in realistic contexts. Sexual health experts from dfusion,[28] ETR,[29] the expert advisory group, and the training advisory group conducted a final script review.

Video production efforts included talent recruitment (four adult educator actors and 24 student actors ages 14–18 from diverse ethnic backgrounds), location/prop preparation, and a two-camera, two-day video shoot. Microskill titles and steps (i.e., explanatory bullet-point text summarizing the Microskills) were edited into video clips, with the bottom of the screen left blank for the addition of closed captioning.

Pilot Study of SkillFlix

Pilot Study Methods

For the SkillFlix pilot study, we assessed the impact of the Microskills video training library on the instructional communication skills of eleven SRH educators teaching youth 14–18 years old. Our staff recruited local SRH educators within a 60-mile radius of dfusion's Scotts Valley, California, offices by connecting with professional contacts, school educators, and youth-serving organizations. Educator study participants had to have (1) experience educating youth; (2) three or fewer years' experience teaching teens sexual health topics; and (3) received minimal training on teaching sexual health topics. Participating educators received $400 for completing all study activities over an eight-day period.

Most SRH educators must have their sex education curricula approved by their school or district's administration to use standardized lessons expeditiously. As such, we opted not to have study educators instruct their own students. Instead, dfusion staff recruited 24 diverse youth ages 14–18 to play students in a classroom setting (school and a community center). While youth were instructed to participate in the classes as they normally would, seven were instructed to make specific comments or pose specific questions at key points in each lesson. This ensured that the educators could use the Microskills in question. Based on past online training research, project staff found that unless opportunities are provided for certain skills to be used, it can take hours of testing for such opportunities to occur naturally.

We asked the SRH educators to teach the first 30-minute lesson (pre-test) one weekend and a different lesson the second session (post-test) the following weekend. Lessons were conducted in conference rooms staged to look like classrooms, with ten students per class. During the pre-test session, half of the educators led Lesson A (*HIV Risk Continuum Activity* from the *Making Proud Choices* intervention) and half led Lesson B (*Protection Myths and Truths Activity* from the *Reducing the Risk* intervention).[30,31] Each participant then taught the other lesson during the post-test session; these measures were employed to reduce the practice effect. The lessons were self-contained, did not require additional preparation, and allowed youth to learn a variety of information related to pregnancy and sexually transmitted infection prevention. Educators were provided with teaching materials two days before each lesson.

After teaching the pre-test lesson, we provided educators access to and instructions for the SkillFlix site and asked them to view all 48 prototype videos; this task took approximately one hour viewing time). The total time between initial access to the SkillFlix site and the post-test was one week.

In running the pilot study, we used four data collection instruments:

- *Observation/Coding Form*: For inter-rater reliability (i.e., the degree of agreement among independent observers who rate, code, or assess the same phenomenon), two trained dfusion staff members twice observed and rated each educator's use of seven Microskills and applicable skill steps. This was done once during the pre-test and once during post-test classroom sessions. Educators agreed to be observed and video recorded during the lesson via a discrete GoPro video camera.
- *Interview Protocol Guide:* Immediately following both classroom sessions, we conducted 30–40 minutes in-person interviews with the educators to assess their experience using SkillFlix. Two experienced sexual and reproductive health trainers conducted the interviews, consisting of open-ended questions. We wanted to hear what they felt went right during the lesson, what could be improved, how they prepared, and what additional resources, if any, they thought they could have used. After the second lesson, educators were asked about SkillFlix's usefulness in preparing them to teach, how they applied the training in their sessions, and whether there were other resources they would have found useful. Additionally, educators were asked usability questions for improving SkillFlix videos and site features (e.g., utility of ratings questions, ease of search, and navigation functions).

- *Outcome Survey:* Immediately before leading the pre-test lesson and after leading the post-test lesson, participant educators completed a 13-item online survey to self-assess their comfort, confidence, and knowledge related to teaching sex education. The questionnaire, which took 10–20 minutes to complete, used a variety of question formats, including multiple-choice, true/false, fill-in, and seven-point Likert scale questions.
- *Tracking Data*: The SkillFlix website provided us with user data documenting the number of user logins, the duration of sessions, the number of videos viewed, and the time spent viewing videos on the site.

Next, two trained dfusion staff members viewed and scored the participant educators' teaching videos for skills demonstration. Differences in both *critical skills scores* (the top 50% of Microskill steps deemed most essential for implementing the Microskills) and *all skills scores* (all Microskill steps) shown during Lessons 1 and 2 were analyzed. The total critical skills score was calculated as the number of critical skill steps educators demonstrated in each session. For all skills, a scaled total score was created by awarding a point for each time participants demonstrated any skill steps in the session. To determine changes in both critical and total skill scores between the pre-and post-test, *t*-tests (i.e., a statistical test used to compare the means or averages of two samples) were used.

Pilot Study Results

So, what did we learn from our pilot study efforts? The short answer is that we saw significant improvements in the study educators' critical and total skills, including their integration of the two prototype skills (i.e., answering sensitive questions, LGBTQ inclusivity). The rate at which participants were able to implement LGBTQ inclusivity skills correctly more than doubled. There was a threefold increase in their ability to answer questions sensitively. Notably, the significant improvement in educators' skills documented by our rating team mirrored the educators' self-perceived improvement in their own skills.

While one might expect that the educators' skill scores would be higher the more time they spent on the site, or the more videos they watched, we were intrigued to learn this was not the case. It was promising to discover that educators' skills could be significantly impacted even if they viewed each video only once.

- *(SkillFlix) helped me think about the importance of inclusive language, correcting slang, like the "boner questions" (and) correcting derogatory language.*
- *I felt bad last week, like I'd failed the kids. Today I feel great. SkillFlix really did help. It made me feel more confident—because I knew I was doing it right. SkillFlix helped me feel more confident in what I know and in what I'm learning.*

Nearly all participants thought they did a better job implementing the second lesson than the first (i.e., after using SkillFlix). The majority believed they answered the challenging questions better and more skillfully, including the integration of an LGBTQ youth focus in their responses. For example:

- *I did a better job framing the responses. Before I just answered the questions, but today I did the whole process of affirming the question, looking for the underlying question/issue, creating a safe space, and following-up to make sure the students were clear.*
- *(The) videos are a nice reminder to be intentional about language, particularly inclusive language regarding gender, family, etc.*

Overall, the site was very well received by participants. On average, they used the site 88 minutes during the study, with all viewing each video at least once. On a seven-point Likert Scale where seven was the highest score, the mean scores for participant satisfaction with SkillFlix were 6.9; ease of use, 6.27; and liking of videos, 6.09. All participants considered the length of the videos "about right," and the consensus was near-universal that the MicroSkills videos held appeal and utility for teachers.

Through usability testing, we were intrigued to learn that some participants did not fully understand the distinctions between the content and skills portrayed in the videos. In subsequent versions of SkillFlix, we have added more information to the orientation video to clarify this distinction. Finally, as many users had a "content-seeking" approach to the site, they requested more content-related materials and links.

In sum, the pilot data provided strong preliminary evidence of the effectiveness of the SkillFlix model to improve SRH educator instructional skills. We were heartened that a) the intervention dosage was small, with most educators watching each video once; b) educators improved their Microskills regardless of whether they focused on content or skills; and c) the effect size in changes in demonstrable Microskills was large.

Reflecting on What We Learned (and How It Could Change Training)

The pilot study shed important light on asynchronous online skills instruction strategies, helping us identify factors that likely contributed to SkillFlix's success. Three interesting themes emerged:

- *Video Length "Sweet Spot".* The 30–120 seconds video length seemed short enough to keep the attention of learners, yet long enough to capture both the important context of the Microskill and the modeling of the Microskill with on-screen text, contributing to the success of the training.
- *Repetition and Reinforcement of Microskill Steps.* From the project beginning, we believed overlaying the text-based Microskill steps on the video was critical to delineate what was being done right in the videos. What we had

not initially realized was that many steps would be repeated throughout the different Microskills videos—steps such as "pause and breathe," "check for understanding," "generalize the question," and so on. The learning process was achieved, in part, through this element of repetition and reinforcement.

- *Came for the Content, Got the Skills.* Educators articulated their content focus early on, emphasizing that training on sexual health information is what they desired. Yet while they focused on the videos' topical information, they also learned Microskills for effectively teaching this content. Given that asynchronous skill instruction is challenging with motivated learners, it felt significant to accomplish it with these participants. Having each video searchable in both skill-focused and topic-focused ways kept these educators engaged in the learning and recognized the importance of skill-building to their work.

One compelling takeaway from our study was the finding that no practice was needed in learning these skills. As previously discussed, classic forms of skill instruction commonly include practicing a skill and providing corrective feedback. While the SkillFlix pilot did *not* provide practice or corrective feedback opportunities, the educators showed significant skill improvement without it. We theorize that they were receptive to how Microskills were modeled: videos were the "just right" length, Microskills groups were a manageable size, and the integrated text supported skill modeling goals. These factors allowed for easy—and possibly subconscious—learning, echoing themes from neuroscience about how we learn.

How might this Microskills model change the style and format of SRH educator trainings today? The classic "gold standard" in-person strategy of skill instruction has served the field well for many years. Yet while effective, it remains expensive to provide and attend and does not provide the ongoing implementation support educators need to effectively translate new skills into their practice. With the advancements of digital technologies and internet access, much of professional development training has shifted to online and blended delivery modes, reducing participation costs for educators and their sponsoring organizations. The SkillFlix training technology—online, searchable collections of short, sequenced videos of Microskills—is well suited to this learning landscape, providing convenient, affordable, and scalable skills-based training and implementation support. It blends the best of face-to-face methods with learning insights from neuroscience. As our pilot study shows, it significantly increased the communication skills of educators teaching sexual health lessons.

Looking Ahead

Our work with the SkillFlix model is dynamic and ongoing. We have applied the SkillFlix training technology to virtual instruction by creating 33 Microskills videos for sex educators doing remote instruction (these will be piloted soon).

Currently, we are also (a) seeking to evaluate the impact of SkillFlix's effectiveness in providing program implementation support to users applying the skills in real-time, real-life settings; (b) developing a mobile app for SkillFlix, giving users a choice in training delivery modes that best fits their needs; and (c) creating and developing two robust collections of SkillFlix:

- *SkillFlix Sex Ed* for SRH educators and parents of high school youth (English and Spanish for parent version): This project includes a two-part evaluation focusing on objective measures of educator skill acquisition and self-report measures of student impact on knowledge, comfort, and behavioral intentions.
- *SkillFlix for Pharmacies* for US pharmacy staff who participate in non-prescription syringe sales: The trainings focus on learning respectful and compliant syringe services. The evaluation will pilot the SkillFlix resource with 12 pharmacies across the nation.

We are encouraged and excited by the findings from these pilot study efforts, which lead us to believe that Microskills-based training can consistently improve skills

- remotely and asynchronously;
- with low intervention doses of learners watching each video only once;
- with no skill practice, truncating the classic process for skill acquisition and its' traditional demand on resources and participants' time.

The results also demonstrate SkillFlix's training applicability across a variety of skills, content areas, and target audiences spanning a range of ages, neurotypes, and professions/roles. We believe SkillFlix has the potential to change the way remote skill instruction is done effectively. As such, we will continue to apply the model to new populations and skills, exploring more deeply the skill acquisition process, its role in implementation support, and the sustainability of newly acquired or improved skills.

References

1. As the COVID-19 pandemic has shown, skills for teaching through distance learning have become critical skills to have. See Rolleri Insignares, L., Bass T.M. & Taverner, B. (2006). Sex ed lessons from COVID-19. *American Journal of Sexuality Education, 16*(4), 435–465.
2. Kam C., Greenberg M., & Walls C. (2003). Examining the role of implementation quality in school-based prevention using the PATHS curriculum. *Prevention Science, 4*(1), 55–63.
3. Wandersman A., & Florin P. (2003). Community interventions and effective prevention. *American Psychologist, 58*(6–7), 441.
4. Barr E.M., Goldfarb E.S., Russell S., Siebert, D., Wallen, M., & Wilson, K.L. (2014). Improving sexuality education: The development of teacher-preparation standards. *Journal of School Health, 84*(6), 396–415.

5. Guttmacher Institute (2017). Sex and HIV education. *State Policies in Brief.* www.guttmacher.org/state-policy/explore/sex-and-hiv-education.
6. Wang B., Stanton B., Deveaux L., Poitier M., Lunn, S., Koci, V., Adderley, R., Kaljee, L., Marshall, S., Li, X., & Rolle, G. (2015). Factors influencing implementation dose and fidelity thereof and related student outcomes of an evidence-based national HIV prevention program. *Implementation Science, 10*(1), 44.
7. Kosciw, J.G., Greytak, E.A., Palmer, N.A. & Boesen, M.J. (2014). *The 2013 national school climate survey: The experiences of LGBT youth in our nation's schools.* GLSEN.
8. MacDonald, J.A., Gagnon, A.J., Mitchell C., Di Meglio, G., Rennick, J.E., & Cox, J. (2011). Asking to listen: Towards a youth perspective on sexual health education and needs. *Sexuality Education, 11*, 443–457.
9. Lester, C., & Allan, A. (2006). Teenage sexual health needs: Asking the consumers. *Health Education Journal, 106*, 315–328.
10. Lindberg, L.D., Maddow, Z.I., & Boonstra H. (2016). Changes in adolescents' receipt of sex education, 2006–2013, *Journal of Adolescent Health, 58*(6), 621–627.
11. Kimmel, A., Williams, T.T., Veinot, T.C., Campbell, B., Campbell, T.R., Valacak, M., & Kruger, D.J. (2013). "I make sure I am safe, and I make sure I have myself in every way possible": African-American youth perspectives on sexuality education. *Sex Education, 13*, 172–185.
12. Joyce, B., Weil, M., & Calhoun E. (2004). *Models of teaching.* Allyn and Bacon.
13. Bayram, L. (2012). Use of online video cases in teacher training. *Procedia—Social and Behavioral Sciences, 47*, 1007–1011.
14. Buch S., Treschow, F., Svendsen, J. & Worm, B. (2014). Video-or text-based e-learning when teaching clinical procedures? A randomized controlled trial. *Advances in Medical Education and Practice, 5*, 257.
15. Hylton I. (2000). *Classroom management skills: Can video-modeling make a difference?* Doctoral Dissertation. NY University. ProQuest Dissertations & Theses UMI #9968429.
16. Clark, R., & Feldon, D. (2005). Five common but questionable principles of multimedia learning. In R. Mayer (Ed.), *Cambridge handbook of multimedia learning.* Cambridge University Press.
17. Bandura, A. (1977). Self-efficacy: Toward a unifying theory of behavioral change. *Psychological Review, 84*(2), 191–215.
18. Rizzolatti, G. (2005). The mirror neuron system and its function in humans. *Anatomy* and *Embryology, 210*, 419–421.
19. Cook R., Bird G., Catmur C., Press C., & Heyes C. (2014). Mirror neurons: From origin to function. *Behavioral and Brain Sciences, 37*(2), 177–192.
20. Del Guidice M., Manera V., & Keysers, C. (2009). Programmed to learn? The ontogeny of mirror neurons. *Developmental Science, 12*(2), 350–363.
21. Oberman, L. & Ramachandran, V.S. (2007). The simulating social mind: The role of the mirror neuron system and simulation in the social and communication deficits of ASD. *Psychological Bulletin, 133*(2), 310–327.
22. Knowles, M. (1984). *The adult learner: A neglected species*, 3rd ed. Gulf Publishing.
23. Kearsley, G. (2010). *The theory into practice database.* http://instructionaldesign.org
24. Expert advisors: Jutta Dotterweich, Director of Training and Teaching Assistant, Cornell University ACT Center for Youth Excellence; Deborah Christopher, Director of Professional and Organizational Development, ETR; Lori Rolleri, Principle of Rolleri Consulting; and Karin Coyle, Chief Science Officer, ETR.
25. *Professional learning standards for sex education*, November 2018. https://sexeducation-collaborative.org/resources/PLSSE
26. Future of Sex Education Initiative. (2012). *National sexuality education standards: Core content and skills, K-12 [a special publication of the Journal of School Health].* www.future-ofsexeducation. org/documents/josh-fose-standards-web.pdf

27. California Healthy Youth Act. *California Department of Education. 2020. [Online].* www.cde.ca.gov/Is/he/se/
28. Based in Scotts Valley, CA, diffusion creates science-driven products and solutions to advance health and wellness. All authors of this chapter are employed by diffusion.
29. ETR (Education, Training, and Research) is also a Scotts Valley, CA non-profit organization committed to improving health outcomes and advancing health equity for youth, families, and communities.
30. Jemmott, J. III, Jemmott L., & Fong G. (2016). Making proud choices intervention/curriculum. *ETR*. www.etr.org/ebi/programs/making-proud-choices/
31. Barth, R.P. (2015). *Reducing the risk: Building skills to prevent pregnancy, STD and HIV intervention/curriculum*, 4th ed. ETR Associates.

CONTRIBUTING AUTHORS

Sarah Abboud, PhD, is an assistant professor of nursing at the University of Illinois Chicago. Her research focuses on the intersections of sexuality, health, and immigration.

Nicole Achey CRC, PhD, is an assistant professor at the University of Maine at Farmington. Dr. Achey's research interests include sexual education and advocacy for individuals with intellectual disabilities.

Frances Anjelique Agudo, BSN, RN, is a University of Pennsylvania School of Nursing alum (Nu'21) who worked as a research assistant on research pertaining to family communication about sex.

Kathleen P. Allen, PhD, is the training and evaluation specialist at the Alberti Center for Bullying Abuse Prevention at the University at Buffalo, The State University of New York.

Katherine R. Allen, PhD, is a professor emerita of human development and family science at Virginia Tech and the incoming editor of the *Journal of Family Theory & Review*.

Aryn A. Benoit, MA, is a PhD student in clinical psychology at the University of New Brunswick.

Claire Bloxsom, MSc, PhD, CPsychol, is a United Kingdom Council for Psychotherapy registered integrative psychotherapist, British Psychological Society chartered psychologist, and assistant professor in psychotherapy and counseling at the University of Warwick.

Angela Cooke-Jackson, PhD, MPH, is a professor of health communication and behavioral science at California State University, Los Angeles, and co-director of the Intimate Communication Lab.

Kayley Davis McMahan, PhD, is the interpersonal wellness and sexual health coordinator and an adjunct faculty lecturer at the University of Tennessee, Knoxville.

Megan E. Dougherty OTD, OTR/L, is an occupational therapist.

Cindy Draws, RN, BSN, is a public health nurse at the Winnebago County Health Department, Wisconsin, working to improve the health of the community and its residents through practice, promotion, partnership, and research.

Diana Dull Akers, PhD, is a senior research associate with dfusion, Inc., a social and behavioral science research and development firm in Scotts Valley, California.

Lane Edwards, MPH, is a project director at dfusion. Lane has contributed to online learning projects targeting parents, young adults with autism spectrum disorder, and pharmacy staff.

Regina Firpo-Triplett, MPH, MCHES, specializes in skills-based training for sexuality educators and other professionals. She is the CEO of dfusion.

Dalmacio D. Flores, PhD, ACRN, is an assistant professor at the University of Pennsylvania School of Nursing. His research is focused on family-based LGBTQ health promotion.

Jonathan Garcia, PhD, is an associate professor and the director of global health at Oregon State University. He studies social isolation and sexual health among LGBTQAI2S+ people of color.

David Gere, PhD, is a professor of arts activism at the Department of World Arts and Cultures/Dance at the University of California, Los Angeles.

Eva S. Goldfarb, PhD, is a professor of public health at Montclair State University. She conducts research, writes curricula, and trains current and future educators on comprehensive sex education.

Katherine L. Grasso, PhD, is an associate professor of communication at DeSales University in Center Valley, Pennsylvania.

Jacqueline N. Gunning, MA, is a doctoral student at the University of Connecticut's Department of Communication and a research associate for the Intimate Communication Lab.

Scott S. Hall, PhD, CFLE, is a professor of family studies at Ball State University.

Sara Hanafi, MPH, is a faculty member of the School of Public Health at the University of Nevada, Reno.

Kate Hennessy, BSN, is a registered nurse at Philadelphia FIGHT.

Taylor E. Hilliard, MA, conducts research on pleasure alongside her primary work in business development in the Washington, DC, area.

Steven Hobaica, PhD, is a Honolulu based clinical psychologist who specializes in LGBTQ+ health and works as a research scientist for the Trevor Project.

Genevieve Hunter, MSEd, works as a program director at Duke University overseeing sexual health programs for teens while also focusing on sexual pleasure research.

Rusi Jaspal, PhD, CPsychol, is the pro vice-chancellor for the research and knowledge exchange and a professor of psychology at the University of Brighton in the United Kingdom.

Gregory H. Keiser, PhD, is a clinical psychologist specializing in queer health, conducting clinical care and research with Two-Spirit and LGBTQIA+ populations at the Carewest Operational Stress Injury Clinic in Calgary, Alberta.

Tamara Kuhn, MA, is the vice president and a research scientist at dfusion. Her work is focused on developing technology-based solutions for promoting health.

Paul Kwon, PhD, is a professor and the director of clinical training of the clinical PhD program at the University of Nevada, Reno.

Chiao Wen Lan, PhD, received a doctorate from the University of California, Los Angeles. She is passionate about improving health equities and bridging arts and health in promoting well-being.

Mark A. Levand, PhD, CSE-S, is the education practicum coordinator and an adjunct faculty member for the Center for Human Sexuality Studies at Widener University.

Gina M. Lepore, MEd, is associate faculty at Cabrillo College in California and sexual and reproductive health specialist and trainer at ETR.

Lisa D. Lieberman, PhD, is Professor and Chair, Department of Public Health, Montclair State University. Her research includes evaluation of both school and community-based sexuality education.

Alexandra F. Lightfoot, EdD, is an associate professor at the Gillings School of Global Public Health at the University of North Carolina at Chapel Hill and an AMP! partner.

Jennifer A. Livingston, PhD, is an associate professor in the School of Nursing at the University at Buffalo, The State University of New York. Her research focuses on the prevention of sexual abuse among youth and adults.

Julie Lucero is the associate dean for equity, diversity, and inclusion and associate professor in the Department of Health and Kinesiology, College of Health, University of Utah.

Eliza C. Magland, MSN, CRNP, PMHNP-BC, IBCLC, is a psychiatric mental health nurse practitioner at Lenape Valley Foundation in Doylestown, Pennsylvania.

Isabel Martinez is a student at the University of Pennsylvania School of Nursing.

Alexandra McAuliffe is a current program manager at Playworks New England, and former Global Health Corps fellow and program manager at Grassroots Health.

Norweeta G. Milburn is a research professor-in-residence at the University of California, Los Angeles Department of Psychiatry and Biobehavioral Sciences Division of Population Behavioral Health.

Dan J. Miller, PhD, is a lecturer in psychology at James Cook University, Australia. He has a research interest in pornography use and its effects.

Susan Milstein, PhD, MCHES, is the founder and lead consultant for Milstein Health Consulting. She is a Master Certified Health Education Specialist and certified sexologist.

Miguel Muñoz-Laboy, DrPH, is a professor at Stony Brook University's School of Social Welfare. His research examines social determinants of health for Latinx and migrant communities in the United States.

Anna E. Murray, OTD, OTR/L, is an occupational therapist.

Michelle M. Murray, MA, is a doctoral candidate at Virginia Tech.

Amanda B. Nickerson, PhD, NCSP, is a school psychology professor and director of the Alberti Center for Bullying Abuse Prevention at the University at Buffalo, The State University of New York.

Spencer B. Olmstead, PhD, is a professor in the department of child and family studies at the University of Tennessee. He studies young adults' romantic and sexual relationships.

Zoë D. Peterson, PhD, is a professor of counseling and educational psychology and director of the Kinsey Institute Sexual Assault Research Initiative at Indiana University.

Kaylee P. Richmond, PhD, is a psychology fellow at the Durham Veterans Administration Medical Center.

Karla I. Rodriguez, MPH, is currently the preventative health program coordinator at a federally qualified health center. Her passions lie in sexual health and working with underserved communities.

Natalie Robek, OTD, OTR/L, is an occupational therapist.

Scott T. Ronis, PhD, LPsyc, is a professor at the University of New Brunswick whose research focuses primarily on the development of typical and problem sexual behavior.

Deborah L. Rooks-Ellis, PhD, is an associate professor of early childhood and special education at the Coastal Carolina University.

Valerie Rubinsky, PhD, is an assistant professor of communication in the social science department at the University of Maine at Augusta and co-director of the Intimate Communication Lab.

Matej Sande, PhD, is an associate professor of social pedagogy at the Faculty of Education at the University of Ljubljana, Slovenia.

Elizabeth Koss Schmidt, PhD, OTR/L, is the director of research and an assistant professor of occupational therapy at Lincoln Memorial University in Knoxville, Tennessee.

Kyle A. Schofield, MS, is currently a doctoral candidate in clinical psychology at Washington State University.

Dahanah Josias Sejour is a lead data scientist at Booz Allen Hamilton with expertise in optimizing data processes and improving data quality through automation and standardization.

Juyeon Son, PhD, is an associate professor of sociology at the University of Wisconsin Oshkosh. Her expertise is in medical sociology.

Tyler Spencer, DPhil, MSc, is the founder and executive director of Grassroots Health.

Danyelle Spohn, MS, is a student at the University of North Florida working toward a career as a clinical mental health counselor.

Arianna Taboada, MSW, MSPH, is a public health social worker who has worked in reproductive health since 2002.

William J. Taverner, MA, CSE, is the founder and president of the Sex Ed Lecture Series and the chief editor of the *American Journal of Sexuality Education.*

Lauren A. Trumbull, MPH, conducted research in this book while studying at DeSales University. She is currently a pharmaceutical market researcher.

Jane Wallis is the director of programs, experienced sexual health facilitator, and curriculums developer for Grassroots Health.

Liam Wignall, PhD, is a senior lecturer of psychology at the University of Brighton and the author of *Kinky in the Digital Age.*

Julie Williams Merten, PhD, MCHES, is an associate professor of public health and director of the Office of Faculty Excellence at the University of North Florida.

Robert J. Zeglin, PhD, NCC, CST, LMHC, is the program director for the clinical mental health counseling program at the University of North Florida.

Jessica D. Zurcher, PhD, is an assistant professor in the School of Communications at Brigham Young University in Provo, Utah.

INDEX

Note: Page numbers in *italics* refer to a figure and page numbers in **bold** refer to a table on the corresponding page.

For Product Safety Concerns and Information please contact our EU representative GPSR@taylorandfrancis.com
Taylor & Francis Verlag GmbH, Kaufingerstraße 24, 80331 München, Germany

www.ingramcontent.com/pod-product-compliance
Ingram Content Group UK Ltd.
Pitfield, Milton Keynes, MK11 3LW, UK
UKHW020133200926
475702UK00005B/726
9781032012056